2016 | THE LITTLE DATA BOOK ON GENDER

WORLD BANK GROUP

Contents

Acknowledgments

The Little Data Book on Gender 2016 is a collaborative effort between the Development Data Group of the Development Economics Vice Presidency and the Gender Cross-Cutting Solution Area.

The Little Data Book on Gender 2016 was prepared by Juan Feng, Masako Hiraga, Haruna Kashiwase, Hiroko Maeda, William Prince, Umar Serajuddin, Emi Suzuki, Dereje Wolde, and Junhe Yang of the Development Data Group and Eliana Rubiano Matulevich of the Gender Cross-Cutting Solution Area. The introduction was written by Masako Hiraga and Eliana Carolina Rubiano Matulevich. Production of the book was coordinated by Azita Amjadi. The work was carried out under the management of Haishan Fu and Caren Grown. Staff from the World Bank's Publishing and Knowledge Division oversaw publication and dissemination of the book.

Introduction

The Little Data Book on Gender 2016 is a quick reference for users interested in gender statistics. It presents sex-disaggregated data for more than 200 countries in a straightforward, country-by-country reference on education, health, access to economic opportunities, and public life and decision making. Summary pages that cover regional and income group aggregates are also included.

This fourth issue of The Little Data Book on Gender reflects the structure of the World Development Report 2012 on Gender Equality and Development. The report examined the driving forces behind differences in key aspects of welfare between men and women—education and health, access to economic opportunities and productive resources, and the ability to make effective choices and take action. Gender equality is increasingly recognized as not only a core development objective, but smart economics. Over the past decades, countries have seen significant progress to raise living standards and close gaps between males and females, including visible improvements in health and education. At the same time, critical gaps persist in economic opportunity as well as agency of women and girls. Addressing gender inequalities requires continued efforts to overcome a complex set of interrelated challenges linking gaps in human capital and technology, women's disproportionate responsibility for unpaid work, legal discrimination, and gender-based violence.

At the United Nations Sustainable Development Summit on September 25, 2015, world leaders adopted the 2030 Agenda for Sustainable Development. The new agenda is based on 17 Sustainable Development Goals (SDGs) and 169 targets, including a stand-alone goal on gender equality and the empowerment of women and girls, as well as gender targets in other goals. With a new set of goals and targets, a long list of indicators will need to be monitored at different levels; both governments and development partners still need to address key data gaps by strengthening national capacities to systematically collect gender data.

As part of its strategy to provide content conveniently, the World Bank now offers an electronic product on gender. The Gender Data Portal (http://datatopics.worldbank.org/gender/) is a resource center for the latest gender-relevant data, with statistics from various sources, tools, training materials, and reference documents covering employment, education, health, public life and decision making, human rights, and demographic outcomes for women and men, and girls and boys.

Data notes

The data in this book are for 2000 and 2013 or the most recent year unless otherwise noted in the table or the glossary.

- Growth rates are proportional changes from the previous year unless otherwise noted.

- Regional aggregates include data for low- and middle-income economies only.

- Figures in italics indicate data for years or periods other than those specified.

Symbols used:

..	indicates that data are not available or that aggregates cannot be calculated because of missing data.
0 or 0.0	indicates zero or small enough that the number would round to zero at the displayed number of decimal places.
$	indicates current U.S. dollars.

Lettered notes on some country tables can be found in the notes on page 232.

Data are shown for economies with populations greater than 30,000 or for smaller economies if they are members of the World Bank. The term *country* (used interchangeably with *economy*) does not imply political independence or official recognition by the World Bank but refers to any economy for which the authorities report separate social or economic statistics.

These pages include the Millennium Development Goals indicators and some of the proposed indicators to track the Sustainable Development Goals. For more information about the eight goals—halving poverty and increasing well-being by 2015—please see the other books in the *World Development Indicators 2015* family of products.

The cutoff date for data is October 15, 2015.

Regional tables

The country composition of regions is based on the World Bank's analytical regions for FY 16 and may differ from common geographic usage. The regions exclude high-income economies.

East Asia and Pacific
American Samoa, Cambodia, China, Fiji, Indonesia, Kiribati, Democratic People's Republic of Korea, Lao People's Democratic Republic, Malaysia, Marshall Islands, Federated States of Micronesia, Mongolia, Myanmar, Palau, Papua New Guinea, Philippines, Samoa, Solomon Islands, Thailand, Timor-Leste, Tonga, Tuvalu, Vanuatu, Vietnam

Europe and Central Asia
Albania, Armenia, Azerbaijan, Belarus, Bosnia and Herzegovina, Bulgaria, Georgia, Kazakhstan, Kosovo, Kyrgyz Republic, Former Yugoslav Republic of Macedonia, Moldova, Montenegro, Romania, Serbia, Tajikistan, Turkey, Turkmenistan, Ukraine, Uzbekistan

Latin America and the Caribbean
Belize, Bolivia, Brazil, Colombia, Costa Rica, Cuba, Dominica, Dominican Republic, Ecuador, El Salvador, Grenada, Guatemala, Guyana, Haiti, Honduras, Jamaica, Mexico, Nicaragua, Panama, Paraguay, Peru, St. Lucia, St. Vincent and the Grenadines, Suriname

Middle East and North Africa
Algeria, Djibouti, Arab Republic of Egypt, Islamic Republic of Iran, Iraq, Jordan, Lebanon, Libya, Morocco, Syrian Arab Republic, Tunisia, West Bank and Gaza, Republic of Yemen

South Asia
Afghanistan, Bangladesh, Bhutan, India, Maldives, Nepal, Pakistan, Sri Lanka

Sub-Saharan Africa
Angola, Benin, Botswana, Burkina Faso, Burundi, Cabo Verde, Cameroon, Central African Republic, Chad, Comoros, Democratic Republic of Congo, Republic of Congo, Côte d'Ivoire, Eritrea, Ethiopia, Gabon, The Gambia, Ghana, Guinea, Guinea-Bissau, Kenya, Lesotho, Liberia, Madagascar, Malawi, Mali, Mauritania, Mauritius, Mozambique, Namibia, Niger, Nigeria, Rwanda, São Tomé and Príncipe, Senegal, Sierra Leone, Somalia, South Africa, South Sudan, Sudan, Swaziland, Tanzania, Togo, Uganda, Zambia, Zimbabwe

World

Population (millions)		7,261
GNI, Atlas ($ billions)		78,260
GNI per capita, Atlas ($)		10,779
Population living below $1.90 a day (%)		*13*

	2000		2013	
	Female	**Male**	**Female**	**Male**
Education				
Net primary enrollment rate (%)	81	86	88	90
Net secondary enrollment rate (%)	50	55	65	67
Gross tertiary enrollment ratio (% of relevant age group)	19	19	35	31
Primary completion rate (% of relevant age group)	78	84	91	93
Progression to secondary school (%)	87	89	90	91
Lower secondary completion rate (% of relevant age group)	60	64	74	74
Gross tertiary graduation ratio (%)	..	..	..	..
Female share of graduates in eng., manf. and constr. (%, tertiary)	..		..	
Youth literacy rate (% of population ages 15-24)	84	91	*89*	*93*
Health and related services				
Sex ratio at birth (male births per female births)	*1.08*		*1.07*	
Under-five mortality rate (per 1,000 live births)	74	78	41	44
Life expectancy at birth (years)	70	66	73	69
Pregnant women receiving prenatal care (%)	69		*82*	
Births attended by skilled health staff (% of total)	60		68	
Maternal mortality ratio (per 100,000 live births)	330		210	
Women's share of population ages 15+ living with HIV (%)	49		51	
Prevalence of HIV (% ages 15-24)	0.6	0.3	0.4	0.3
Economic structure, participation, and access to resources				
Labor force participation rate (% of population ages 15+)	52	79	50	77
Labor force participation rate (% of ages 15-24)	44	62	39	55
Wage and salaried workers (% of employed ages 15+)	..	..	..	..
Self-employed workers (% of employed ages 15+)	..	..	..	..
Unpaid family workers (% of employed ages 15+)	..	..	..	..
Employment in agriculture (% of employed ages 15+)	..	..	..	..
Employment in industry (% of employed ages 15+)	..	..	..	..
Employment in services (% of employed ages 15+)	..	..	..	..
Women in wage employment in the nonagricultural sector (%)	*37*		..	
Women's share of part-time employment (% of total)	..		..	
Maternity leave (days paid)	..		..	
Maternity leave benefits (% of wages paid)	..		..	
Employment to population ratio (% ages 15+)	49	74	47	72
Employment to population ratio (% ages 15-24)	38	54	34	48
Firms with female participation in ownership (%)	..		..	
Firms with a female top manager (%)	..		..	
Children in employment (% of children ages 7-14)	..	..	..	..
Unemployment rate (% of labor force ages 15+)	7	6	6	6
Unemployment rate (% of labor force ages 15-24)	15	13	16	13
Internet users (%)	..	..	..	..
Account at a financial institution (% age 15+)	..	..	57	64
Mobile account (% age 15+)	..	..	1.6	2.5
Saved any money last year (% age 15+)	..	..	54	59
Public life and decision making				
Seats held by women in national parliament (%)	..		23	
Female legislators, senior officials and managers (% of total)	..		..	
Proportion of women in ministerial level positions (%)	..		18	
Agency				
Total fertility rate (births per woman)	2.6		2.5	
Adolescent fertility rate (births per 1,000 women ages 15-19)	56		45	
Women first married by age 18 (% of women ages 20-24)	..		..	

East Asia & Pacific

Population (millions)	2,021
GNI, Atlas ($ billions)	12,368
GNI per capita, Atlas ($)	6,121
Population living below $1.90 a day (%)	7

	2000		2013	
	Female	Male	Female	Male
Education				
Net primary enrollment rate (%)	94	94	94	94
Net secondary enrollment rate (%)	53	55	78	76
Gross tertiary enrollment ratio (% of relevant age group)	11	12	32	28
Primary completion rate (% of relevant age group)	90	91	*105*	*104*
Progression to secondary school (%)	86	88	..	..
Lower secondary completion rate (% of relevant age group)	71	74	93	89
Gross tertiary graduation ratio (%)	..	..	..	..
Female share of graduates in eng., manf. and constr. (%, tertiary)		..		..
Youth literacy rate (% of population ages 15–24)	98	98	99	99
Health and related services				
Sex ratio at birth (male births per female births)	*1.12*		1.12	
Under-five mortality rate (per 1,000 live births)	39	45	16	20
Life expectancy at birth (years)	73	69	76	72
Pregnant women receiving prenatal care (%)	86		95	
Births attended by skilled health staff (% of total)	85		92	
Maternal mortality ratio (per 100,000 live births)	130		75	
Women's share of population ages 15+ living with HIV (%)	..		..	
Prevalence of HIV (% ages 15–24)	..	..	..	..
Economic structure, participation, and access to resources				
Labor force participation rate (% of population ages 15+)	67	83	63	79
Labor force participation rate (% of ages 15–24)	61	67	51	59
Wage and salaried workers (% of employed ages 15+)	..	..	..	..
Self-employed workers (% of employed ages 15+)	..	..	..	..
Unpaid family workers (% of employed ages 15+)	..	..	..	..
Employment in agriculture (% of employed ages 15+)	..	..	..	..
Employment in industry (% of employed ages 15+)	..	..	..	..
Employment in services (% of employed ages 15+)	..	..	..	..
Women in wage employment in the nonagricultural sector (%)	39		..	
Women's share of part-time employment (% of total)	..		..	
Maternity leave (days paid)	..		..	
Maternity leave benefits (% of wages paid)	..		..	
Employment to population ratio (% ages 15+)	65	79	60	75
Employment to population ratio (% ages 15–24)	56	59	46	52
Firms with female participation in ownership (%)	..		..	
Firms with a female top manager (%)	..		..	
Children in employment (% of children ages 7–14)	..	..	..	..
Unemployment rate (% of labor force ages 15+)	4	5	4	5
Unemployment rate (% of labor force ages 15–24)	10	12	10	12
Internet users (%)	..	..	..	..
Account at a financial institution (% age 15+)	..	..	67	71
Mobile account (% age 15+)	..	..	0.5	0.3
Saved any money last year (% age 15+)	..	..	69	72
Public life and decision making				
Seats held by women in national parliament (%)	..		19	
Female legislators, senior officials and managers (% of total)	..		..	
Proportion of women in ministerial level positions (%)	..		10	
Agency				
Total fertility rate (births per woman)	1.8		1.9	
Adolescent fertility rate (births per 1,000 women ages 15–19)	21		23	
Women first married by age 18 (% of women ages 20–24)	..		..	

Europe & Central Asia

Population (millions)	264
GNI, Atlas ($ billions)	1,815
GNI per capita, Atlas ($)	6,865
Population living below $1.90 a day (%)	2

	2000		2013	
	Female	Male	Female	Male
Education				
Net primary enrollment rate (%)	90	94	92	93
Net secondary enrollment rate (%)	77	79	88	89
Gross tertiary enrollment ratio (% of relevant age group)	29	30	56	54
Primary completion rate (% of relevant age group)	93	96	99	100
Progression to secondary school (%)	93	96	95	97
Lower secondary completion rate (% of relevant age group)	69	73	94	96
Gross tertiary graduation ratio (%)	..	..	..	..
Female share of graduates in eng., manf. and constr. (%, tertiary)	..		..	
Youth literacy rate (% of population ages 15–24)	98	99	99	100
Health and related services				
Sex ratio at birth (male births per female births)	1.06		1.06	
Under-five mortality rate (per 1,000 live births)	38	46	18	23
Life expectancy at birth (years)	73	65	76	69
Pregnant women receiving prenatal care (%)	..		95	
Births attended by skilled health staff (% of total)	90		97	
Maternal mortality ratio (per 100,000 live births)	45		28	
Women's share of population ages 15+ living with HIV (%)	..		..	
Prevalence of HIV (% ages 15–24)	..	..	..	..
Economic structure, participation, and access to resources				
Labor force participation rate (% of population ages 15+)	47	69	46	69
Labor force participation rate (% of ages 15–24)	35	51	32	49
Wage and salaried workers (% of employed ages 15+)	64	65	68	70
Self-employed workers (% of employed ages 15+)	36	35	32	30
Unpaid family workers (% of employed ages 15+)	19.4	7.0	13.3	4.6
Employment in agriculture (% of employed ages 15+)	..	..	..	..
Employment in industry (% of employed ages 15+)	..	..	..	..
Employment in services (% of employed ages 15+)	..	..	..	..
Women in wage employment in the nonagricultural sector (%)	42		43	
Women's share of part-time employment (% of total)	..		..	
Maternity leave (days paid)	..		..	
Maternity leave benefits (% of wages paid)	..		..	
Employment to population ratio (% ages 15+)	42	62	42	63
Employment to population ratio (% ages 15–24)	28	41	25	39
Firms with female participation in ownership (%)	..		..	
Firms with a female top manager (%)	..		..	
Children in employment (% of children ages 7–14)	..	..	..	..
Unemployment rate (% of labor force ages 15+)	10	10	10	10
Unemployment rate (% of labor force ages 15–24)	19	20	21	20
Internet users (%)	..	..	..	..
Account at a financial institution (% age 15+)	..	..	47	56
Mobile account (% age 15+)	..	..	0.2	0.3
Saved any money last year (% age 15+)	..	..	37	41
Public life and decision making				
Seats held by women in national parliament (%)	..		19	
Female legislators, senior officials and managers (% of total)	..		..	
Proportion of women in ministerial level positions (%)	..		13	
Agency				
Total fertility rate (births per woman)	1.9		2.0	
Adolescent fertility rate (births per 1,000 women ages 15–19)	38		28	
Women first married by age 18 (% of women ages 20–24)	..		..	

Latin America & Caribbean

Population (millions)	525
GNI, Atlas ($ billions)	4,724
GNI per capita, Atlas ($)	8,995
Population living below $1.90 a day (%)	6

	2000		2013	
	Female	Male	Female	Male
Education				
Net primary enrollment rate (%)	91	94	92	92
Net secondary enrollment rate (%)	61	58	77	72
Gross tertiary enrollment ratio (% of relevant age group)	20	18	41	34
Primary completion rate (% of relevant age group)	96	97	102	100
Progression to secondary school (%)	92	95	93	97
Lower secondary completion rate (% of relevant age group)	71	67	78	72
Gross tertiary graduation ratio (%)	..	..	..	..
Female share of graduates in eng., manf. and constr. (%, tertiary)	..		..	
Youth literacy rate (% of population ages 15-24)	96	96	98	97
Health and related services				
Sex ratio at birth (male births per female births)	1.05		1.05	
Under-five mortality rate (per 1,000 live births)	31	37	17	21
Life expectancy at birth (years)	74	68	78	72
Pregnant women receiving prenatal care (%)	..		97	
Births attended by skilled health staff (% of total)	83		92	
Maternal mortality ratio (per 100,000 live births)	110		87	
Women's share of population ages 15+ living with HIV (%)	..		..	
Prevalence of HIV (% ages 15-24)	..	..	..	..
Economic structure, participation, and access to resources				
Labor force participation rate (% of population ages 15+)	49	82	55	80
Labor force participation rate (% of ages 15-24)	44	69	45	64
Wage and salaried workers (% of employed ages 15+)	64	60	..	..
Self-employed workers (% of employed ages 15+)	33	38	..	..
Unpaid family workers (% of employed ages 15+)	8.7	4.8	..	..
Employment in agriculture (% of employed ages 15+)	12	25	10	22
Employment in industry (% of employed ages 15+)	14	26	13	27
Employment in services (% of employed ages 15+)	74	49	76	50
Women in wage employment in the nonagricultural sector (%)	43		44	
Women's share of part-time employment (% of total)	64		..	
Maternity leave (days paid)	..			
Maternity leave benefits (% of wages paid)	..		..	
Employment to population ratio (% ages 15+)	44	76	51	76
Employment to population ratio (% ages 15-24)	35	61	38	58
Firms with female participation in ownership (%)	..		..	
Firms with a female top manager (%)	..		..	
Children in employment (% of children ages 7-14)	..	..	..	..
Unemployment rate (% of labor force ages 15+)	10	6	8	5
Unemployment rate (% of labor force ages 15-24)	18	12	16	10
Internet users (%)	..	..	47	47
Account at a financial institution (% age 15+)	..	..	48	54
Mobile account (% age 15+)	..	..	1.3	2.2
Saved any money last year (% age 15+)	..	..	37	44
Public life and decision making				
Seats held by women in national parliament (%)	..		29	
Female legislators, senior officials and managers (% of total)	..		..	
Proportion of women in ministerial level positions (%)	..		23	
Agency				
Total fertility rate (births per woman)	2.7		2.2	
Adolescent fertility rate (births per 1,000 women ages 15-19)	82		65	
Women first married by age 18 (% of women ages 20-24)	..		..	

Middle East & North Africa

Population (millions)	357
GNI, Atlas ($ billions)	..
GNI per capita, Atlas ($)	..
Population living below $1.90 a day (%)	..

	2000		2013	
	Female	Male	Female	Male
Education				
Net primary enrollment rate (%)	82	90	92	96
Net secondary enrollment rate (%)	57	65	67	72
Gross tertiary enrollment ratio (% of relevant age group)	18	22	35	35
Primary completion rate (% of relevant age group)	79	87	91	95
Progression to secondary school (%)	90	90	88	89
Lower secondary completion rate (% of relevant age group)	61	65	73	73
Gross tertiary graduation ratio (%)	..	..	..	..
Female share of graduates in eng., manf. and constr. (%, tertiary)	..		..	
Youth literacy rate (% of population ages 15–24)	81	91	89	94
Health and related services				
Sex ratio at birth (male births per female births)	1.05		1.05	
Under-five mortality rate (per 1,000 live births)	43	48	23	26
Life expectancy at birth (years)	71	67	74	69
Pregnant women receiving prenatal care (%)	..		84	
Births attended by skilled health staff (% of total)	78		89	
Maternal mortality ratio (per 100,000 live births)	110		78	
Women's share of population ages 15+ living with HIV (%)	55		41	
Prevalence of HIV (% ages 15–24)	0.1	0.1	0.1	0.1
Economic structure, participation, and access to resources				
Labor force participation rate (% of population ages 15+)	18	74	20	73
Labor force participation rate (% of ages 15–24)	17	52	15	48
Wage and salaried workers (% of employed ages 15+)	..	..	..	..
Self-employed workers (% of employed ages 15+)	..	..	..	..
Unpaid family workers (% of employed ages 15+)	..	..	..	..
Employment in agriculture (% of employed ages 15+)	..	..	..	..
Employment in industry (% of employed ages 15+)	..	..	..	..
Employment in services (% of employed ages 15+)	..	..	..	..
Women in wage employment in the nonagricultural sector (%)	16		17	
Women's share of part-time employment (% of total)	..		..	
Maternity leave (days paid)	..		..	
Maternity leave benefits (% of wages paid)	..		..	
Employment to population ratio (% ages 15+)	14	65	15	66
Employment to population ratio (% ages 15–24)	10	39	7	36
Firms with female participation in ownership (%)	..		..	
Firms with a female top manager (%)	..		..	
Children in employment (% of children ages 7–14)	..		..	
Unemployment rate (% of labor force ages 15+)	24	12	23	10
Unemployment rate (% of labor force ages 15–24)	45	25	51	25
Internet users (%)	..	..	..	..
Account at a financial institution (% age 15+)	..	..	..	..
Mobile account (% age 15+)	..	..	..	..
Saved any money last year (% age 15+)	..	..	..	..
Public life and decision making				
Seats held by women in national parliament (%)	..		17	
Female legislators, senior officials and managers (% of total)	..		..	
Proportion of women in ministerial level positions (%)	..		10	
Agency				
Total fertility rate (births per woman)	3.2		2.7	
Adolescent fertility rate (births per 1,000 women ages 15–19)	44		42	
Women first married by age 18 (% of women ages 20–24)	..		..	

South Asia

Population (millions)		1,721
GNI, Atlas ($ billions)		2,584
GNI per capita, Atlas ($)		1,502
Population living below $1.90 a day (%)		*19*

	2000		2013	
	Female	Male	Female	Male
Education				
Net primary enrollment rate (%)	69	83	90	89
Net secondary enrollment rate (%)	34	45	..	..
Gross tertiary enrollment ratio (% of relevant age group)	6	10	20	22
Primary completion rate (% of relevant age group)	62	77	*90*	*92*
Progression to secondary school (%)	87	89	*91*	*90*
Lower secondary completion rate (% of relevant age group)	43	56	*70*	*72*
Gross tertiary graduation ratio (%)	..	..	..	..
Female share of graduates in eng., manf. and constr. (%, tertiary)	..		..	
Youth literacy rate (% of population ages 15-24)	64	80	*79*	*87*
Health and related services				
Sex ratio at birth (male births per female births)	*1.10*		1.10	
Under-five mortality rate (per 1,000 live births)	96	91	53	52
Life expectancy at birth (years)	64	62	69	65
Pregnant women receiving prenatal care (%)	56		72	
Births attended by skilled health staff (% of total)	36		50	
Maternal mortality ratio (per 100,000 live births)	370		190	
Women's share of population ages 15+ living with HIV (%)	..		..	
Prevalence of HIV (% ages 15-24)	..	..	..	..
Economic structure, participation, and access to resources				
Labor force participation rate (% of population ages 15+)	35	83	31	81
Labor force participation rate (% of ages 15-24)	28	66	22	55
Wage and salaried workers (% of employed ages 15+)	40	9	15	20
Self-employed workers (% of employed ages 15+)	88	77	85	80
Unpaid family workers (% of employed ages 15+)	43.5	12.8	*33.7*	*10.9*
Employment in agriculture (% of employed ages 15+)	75	53	*59*	*43*
Employment in industry (% of employed ages 15+)	11	17	*21*	*26*
Employment in services (% of employed ages 15+)	14	29	*20*	*31*
Women in wage employment in the nonagricultural sector (%)	18		*19*	
Women's share of part-time employment (% of total)	..		..	
Maternity leave (days paid)	..			
Maternity leave benefits (% of wages paid)	..		..	
Employment to population ratio (% ages 15+)	33	80	29	78
Employment to population ratio (% ages 15-24)	25	59	20	50
Firms with female participation in ownership (%)	..		..	
Firms with a female top manager (%)	..		..	
Children in employment (% of children ages 7-14)	..	..	..	..
Unemployment rate (% of labor force ages 15+)	5	4	5	4
Unemployment rate (% of labor force ages 15-24)	12	10	11	10
Internet users (%)	..	..	..	..
Account at a financial institution (% age 15+)	..	..	37	54
Mobile account (% age 15+)	..	..	1.3	3.9
Saved any money last year (% age 15+)	..	..	32	40
Public life and decision making				
Seats held by women in national parliament (%)	..		19	
Female legislators, senior officials and managers (% of total)	..		..	
Proportion of women in ministerial level positions (%)	..		10	
Agency				
Total fertility rate (births per woman)	3.3		2.6	
Adolescent fertility rate (births per 1,000 women ages 15-19)	72		35	
Women first married by age 18 (% of women ages 20-24)	..		..	

Sub-Saharan Africa

Population (millions)	973
GNI, Atlas ($ billions)	1,654
GNI per capita, Atlas ($)	1,699
Population living below $1.90 a day (%)	*43*

	2000		2013	
	Female	**Male**	**Female**	**Male**
Education				
Net primary enrollment rate (%)	57	64	75	80
Net secondary enrollment rate (%)	19	23	32	36
Gross tertiary enrollment ratio (% of relevant age group)	4	5	7	10
Primary completion rate (% of relevant age group)	50	60	66	72
Progression to secondary school (%)	70	71	77	79
Lower secondary completion rate (% of relevant age group)	22	29	34	42
Gross tertiary graduation ratio (%)	..	..	..	..
Female share of graduates in eng., manf. and constr. (%, tertiary)	..		..	
Youth literacy rate (% of population ages 15–24)	62	75	66	*76*
Health and related services				
Sex ratio at birth (male births per female births)	*1.04*		1.04	
Under-five mortality rate (per 1,000 live births)	146	162	77	89
Life expectancy at birth (years)	51	49	58	56
Pregnant women receiving prenatal care (%)	66		77	
Births attended by skilled health staff (% of total)	42		49	
Maternal mortality ratio (per 100,000 live births)	830		510	
Women's share of population ages 15+ living with HIV (%)	57		57	
Prevalence of HIV (% ages 15–24)	3.4	1.5	1.8	1.1
Economic structure, participation, and access to resources				
Labor force participation rate (% of population ages 15+)	62	77	64	77
Labor force participation rate (% of ages 15–24)	50	57	51	56
Wage and salaried workers (% of employed ages 15+)	..	..	..	..
Self-employed workers (% of employed ages 15+)	..	..	..	..
Unpaid family workers (% of employed ages 15+)	..	..	..	..
Employment in agriculture (% of employed ages 15+)	..	..	..	..
Employment in industry (% of employed ages 15+)	..	..	..	..
Employment in services (% of employed ages 15+)	..	..	..	..
Women in wage employment in the nonagricultural sector (%)	..		..	
Women's share of part-time employment (% of total)	..		..	
Maternity leave (days paid)	..		..	
Maternity leave benefits (% of wages paid)	..		..	
Employment to population ratio (% ages 15+)	56	71	58	71
Employment to population ratio (% ages 15–24)	43	50	44	50
Firms with female participation in ownership (%)	..		..	
Firms with a female top manager (%)	..		..	
Children in employment (% of children ages 7–14)	..	8	9	..
Unemployment rate (% of labor force ages 15+)	10	8	9	7
Unemployment rate (% of labor force ages 15–24)	16	14	15	13
Internet users (%)	..	..	..	..
Account at a financial institution (% age 15+)	..	..	25	33
Mobile account (% age 15+)	..	..	10.3	12.8
Saved any money last year (% age 15+)	..	..	58	62
Public life and decision making				
Seats held by women in national parliament (%)	..		23	
Female legislators, senior officials and managers (% of total)	..		..	
Proportion of women in ministerial level positions (%)	..		20	
Agency				
Total fertility rate (births per woman)	5.8		5.1	
Adolescent fertility rate (births per 1,000 women ages 15–19)	129		103	
Women first married by age 18 (% of women ages 20–24)	..		..	

Income group tables

For operational and analytical purposes the World Bank's main criterion for classifying economies is gross national income (GNI) per capita. Each economy in *The Little Data Book on Gender* is classified as low income, middle income, or high income. Low- and middle-income economies are sometimes referred to as developing economies. The use of the term is convenient; it is not intended to imply that all economies in the group are experiencing similar development or that other economies have reached a preferred or final stage of development. Classification by income does not necessarily reflect development status. Note: Classifications are fixed during the World Bank's fiscal year (ending on June 30), thus countries remain in the categories in which they are classified irrespective of any revisions to their per capita income data.

Low-income economies are those with a GNI per capita of $1,045 or less in 2014.

Middle-income economies are those with a GNI per capita of more than $1,045 but less than $12,736. Lower-middle-income and upper-middle-income economies are separated at a GNI per capita of $4,125.

High-income economies are those with a GNI per capita of $12,736 or more.

Euro area includes the member states of the Economic and Monetary Union of the European Union that have adopted the euro as their currency: Austria, Belgium, Cyprus, Estonia, Finland, France, Germany, Greece, Ireland, Italy, Latvia, Lithuania, Luxembourg, Malta, Netherlands, Portugal, Slovak Republic, Slovenia, and Spain.

Low income

	622
Population (millions)	622
GNI, Atlas ($ billions)	389
GNI per capita, Atlas ($)	626
Population living below $1.90 a day (%)	47

	2000		2013	
	Female	Male	Female	Male
Education				
Net primary enrollment rate (%)	51	60	78	82
Net secondary enrollment rate (%)	15	21	29	34
Gross tertiary enrollment ratio (% of relevant age group)	2	4	6	10
Primary completion rate (% of relevant age group)	37	49	63	70
Progression to secondary school (%)	66	67	75	77
Lower secondary completion rate (% of relevant age group)	16	24	31	40
Gross tertiary graduation ratio (%)	..	..	..	..
Female share of graduates in eng., manf. and constr. (%, tertiary)	..		..	
Youth literacy rate (% of population ages 15–24)	56	71	63	74
Health and related services				
Sex ratio at birth (male births per female births)	*1.04*		1.04	
Under-five mortality rate (per 1,000 live births)	142	157	71	81
Life expectancy at birth (years)	53	51	61	58
Pregnant women receiving prenatal care (%)	58		77	
Births attended by skilled health staff (% of total)	34		52	
Maternal mortality ratio (per 100,000 live births)	870		510	
Women's share of population ages 15+ living with HIV (%)	56		57	
Prevalence of HIV (% ages 15–24)	2.2	1.1	1.2	0.8
Economic structure, participation, and access to resources				
Labor force participation rate (% of population ages 15+)	71	84	72	83
Labor force participation rate (% of ages 15–24)	63	67	62	66
Wage and salaried workers (% of employed ages 15+)	..	..	..	..
Self-employed workers (% of employed ages 15+)	..	..	..	..
Unpaid family workers (% of employed ages 15+)	..	..	..	..
Employment in agriculture (% of employed ages 15+)	..	..	..	..
Employment in industry (% of employed ages 15+)	..	..	..	..
Employment in services (% of employed ages 15+)	..	..	..	..
Women in wage employment in the nonagricultural sector (%)	..		..	
Women's share of part-time employment (% of total)	..		..	
Maternity leave (days paid)	..		..	
Maternity leave benefits (% of wages paid)	..		..	
Employment to population ratio (% ages 15+)	66	80	68	80
Employment to population ratio (% ages 15–24)	56	62	56	61
Firms with female participation in ownership (%)	..		..	
Firms with a female top manager (%)	..		..	
Children in employment (% of children ages 7–14)	..	..	..	..
Unemployment rate (% of labor force ages 15+)	7	5	6	4
Unemployment rate (% of labor force ages 15–24)	11	8	10	8
Internet users (%)	..	..	..	..
Account at a financial institution (% age 15+)	..	..	19	25
Mobile account (% age 15+)	..	..	8.8	11.3
Saved any money last year (% age 15+)	..	..	45	48
Public life and decision making				
Seats held by women in national parliament (%)	..		22	
Female legislators, senior officials and managers (% of total)	..		..	
Proportion of women in ministerial level positions (%)	..		18	
Agency				
Total fertility rate (births per woman)	5.9		4.8	
Adolescent fertility rate (births per 1,000 women ages 15–19)	126		98	
Women first married by age 18 (% of women ages 20–24)	..		..	

Middle income

Population (millions)		5,240
GNI, Atlas ($ billions)		24,382
GNI per capita, Atlas ($)		4,653
Population living below $1.90 a day (%)		*13*

	2000		2013	
	Female	**Male**	**Female**	**Male**
Education				
Net primary enrollment rate (%)	82	88	89	90
Net secondary enrollment rate (%)	47	52	65	68
Gross tertiary enrollment ratio (% of relevant age group)	12	13	29	27
Primary completion rate (% of relevant age group)	80	86	95	96
Progression to secondary school (%)	87	89	92	92
Lower secondary completion rate (% of relevant age group)	59	65	77	77
Gross tertiary graduation ratio (%)	..	..	..	..
Female share of graduates in eng., manf. and constr. (%, tertiary)	..		..	
Youth literacy rate (% of population ages 15–24)	84	91	*90*	*93*
Health and related services				
Sex ratio at birth (male births per female births)	*1.09*		1.09	
Under-five mortality rate (per 1,000 live births)	72	75	39	42
Life expectancy at birth (years)	69	65	72	68
Pregnant women receiving prenatal care (%)	71		83	
Births attended by skilled health staff (% of total)	62		71	
Maternal mortality ratio (per 100,000 live births)	280		170	
Women's share of population ages 15+ living with HIV (%)	..		..	
Prevalence of HIV (% ages 15–24)	..	..	..	..
Economic structure, participation, and access to resources				
Labor force participation rate (% of population ages 15+)	51	81	48	78
Labor force participation rate (% of ages 15–24)	42	63	35	55
Wage and salaried workers (% of employed ages 15+)	..	..	..	..
Self-employed workers (% of employed ages 15+)	..	..	..	..
Unpaid family workers (% of employed ages 15+)	..	..	..	..
Employment in agriculture (% of employed ages 15+)	..	..	..	..
Employment in industry (% of employed ages 15+)	..	..	..	..
Employment in services (% of employed ages 15+)	..	..	..	..
Women in wage employment in the nonagricultural sector (%)	*34*		..	
Women's share of part-time employment (% of total)	..		..	
Maternity leave (days paid)	..		..	
Maternity leave benefits (% of wages paid)	..		..	
Employment to population ratio (% ages 15+)	48	76	45	74
Employment to population ratio (% ages 15–24)	37	55	31	48
Firms with female participation in ownership (%)	..		..	
Firms with a female top manager (%)	..		..	
Children in employment (% of children ages 7–14)	..	..	..	..
Unemployment rate (% of labor force ages 15+)	6	6	6	5
Unemployment rate (% of labor force ages 15–24)	16	13	16	13
Internet users (%)	..	..	..	..
Account at a financial institution (% age 15+)	..	..	53	62
Mobile account (% age 15+)	..	..	1.1	2.0
Saved any money last year (% age 15+)	..	..	52	57
Public life and decision making				
Seats held by women in national parliament (%)	..		21	
Female legislators, senior officials and managers (% of total)	..		..	
Proportion of women in ministerial level positions (%)	..		16	
Agency				
Total fertility rate (births per woman)	2.6		2.4	
Adolescent fertility rate (births per 1,000 women ages 15–19)	54		41	
Women first married by age 18 (% of women ages 20–24)	..		..	

Lower middle income

Population (millions)	2,879
GNI, Atlas ($ billions)	5,793
GNI per capita, Atlas ($)	2,012
Population living below $1.90 a day (%)	*19*

	2000		2013	
	Female	**Male**	**Female**	**Male**
Education				
Net primary enrollment rate (%)	74	83	87	88
Net secondary enrollment rate (%)	38	46	56	61
Gross tertiary enrollment ratio (% of relevant age group)	10	13	22	23
Primary completion rate (% of relevant age group)	70	81	90	91
Progression to secondary school (%)	85	87	89	90
Lower secondary completion rate (% of relevant age group)	46	56	68	70
Gross tertiary graduation ratio (%)	..	..	..	..
Female share of graduates in eng., manf. and constr. (%, tertiary)	..		..	
Youth literacy rate (% of population ages 15–24)	73	85	*83*	*89*
Health and related services				
Sex ratio at birth (male births per female births)	*1.08*		*1.08*	
Under-five mortality rate (per 1,000 live births)	92	93	51	55
Life expectancy at birth (years)	64	61	69	65
Pregnant women receiving prenatal care (%)	64		77	
Births attended by skilled health staff (% of total)	46		57	
Maternal mortality ratio (per 100,000 live births)	380		240	
Women's share of population ages 15+ living with HIV (%)	..		..	
Prevalence of HIV (% ages 15–24)	..	..	..	..
Economic structure, participation, and access to resources				
Labor force participation rate (% of population ages 15+)	41	81	39	79
Labor force participation rate (% of ages 15–24)	33	62	29	54
Wage and salaried workers (% of employed ages 15+)	40	16	..	..
Self-employed workers (% of employed ages 15+)	79	73	..	..
Unpaid family workers (% of employed ages 15+)	39.9	12.7	..	..
Employment in agriculture (% of employed ages 15+)	65	50	..	..
Employment in industry (% of employed ages 15+)	12	18	..	..
Employment in services (% of employed ages 15+)	23	31	..	..
Women in wage employment in the nonagricultural sector (%)	25		25	
Women's share of part-time employment (% of total)	..		..	
Maternity leave (days paid)	..		..	
Maternity leave benefits (% of wages paid)	..		..	
Employment to population ratio (% ages 15+)	38	76	36	75
Employment to population ratio (% ages 15–24)	28	55	24	48
Firms with female participation in ownership (%)	..		..	
Firms with a female top manager (%)	..		..	
Children in employment (% of children ages 7–14)	..	..	6	..
Unemployment rate (% of labor force ages 15+)	6	6	6	5
Unemployment rate (% of labor force ages 15–24)	15	12	16	12
Internet users (%)	..	..	..	..
Account at a financial institution (% age 15+)	..	..	35	48
Mobile account (% age 15+)	..	..	1.5	3.4
Saved any money last year (% age 15+)	..	..	43	48
Public life and decision making				
Seats held by women in national parliament (%)	..		17	
Female legislators, senior officials and managers (% of total)	..		..	
Proportion of women in ministerial level positions (%)	..		16	
Agency				
Total fertility rate (births per woman)	3.4		2.8	
Adolescent fertility rate (births per 1,000 women ages 15–19)	70		47	
Women first married by age 18 (% of women ages 20–24)	..		..	

Upper middle income

Population (millions)	2,361
GNI, Atlas ($ billions)	18,586
GNI per capita, Atlas ($)	7,873
Population living below $1.90 a day (%)	5

	2000		2013	
	Female	Male	Female	Male
Education				
Net primary enrollment rate (%)	93	95	93	95
Net secondary enrollment rate (%)	58	60	81	80
Gross tertiary enrollment ratio (% of relevant age group)	14	14	38	33
Primary completion rate (% of relevant age group)	90	92	_103_	_104_
Progression to secondary school (%)	88	91	..	..
Lower secondary completion rate (% of relevant age group)	73	75	91	88
Gross tertiary graduation ratio (%)	..	..	..	..
Female share of graduates in eng., manf. and constr. (%, tertiary)	..		..	
Youth literacy rate (% of population ages 15–24)	97	98	98	99
Health and related services				
Sex ratio at birth (male births per female births)	_1.10_		1.10	
Under-five mortality rate (per 1,000 live births)	37	42	18	20
Life expectancy at birth (years)	73	69	76	72
Pregnant women receiving prenatal care (%)	87		95	
Births attended by skilled health staff (% of total)	92		98	
Maternal mortality ratio (per 100,000 live births)	93		57	
Women's share of population ages 15+ living with HIV (%)	..		..	
Prevalence of HIV (% ages 15–24)	..	..	..	..
Economic structure, participation, and access to resources				
Labor force participation rate (% of population ages 15+)	60	81	57	77
Labor force participation rate (% of ages 15–24)	53	65	45	57
Wage and salaried workers (% of employed ages 15+)	..	..	..	..
Self-employed workers (% of employed ages 15+)	..	..	..	..
Unpaid family workers (% of employed ages 15+)	..	..	..	..
Employment in agriculture (% of employed ages 15+)	..	..	..	..
Employment in industry (% of employed ages 15+)	..	..	..	..
Employment in services (% of employed ages 15+)	..	..	..	..
Women in wage employment in the nonagricultural sector (%)	_39_		..	
Women's share of part-time employment (% of total)	..		..	
Maternity leave (days paid)	..		..	
Maternity leave benefits (% of wages paid)	..		..	
Employment to population ratio (% ages 15+)	57	76	54	73
Employment to population ratio (% ages 15–24)	47	56	40	49
Firms with female participation in ownership (%)	..		..	
Firms with a female top manager (%)	..		..	
Children in employment (% of children ages 7–14)	..	..	..	..
Unemployment rate (% of labor force ages 15+)	6	6	6	6
Unemployment rate (% of labor force ages 15–24)	16	14	16	14
Internet users (%)	..	..	..	..
Account at a financial institution (% age 15+)	..	..	67	74
Mobile account (% age 15+)	..	..	0.6	0.8
Saved any money last year (% age 15+)	..	..	60	65
Public life and decision making				
Seats held by women in national parliament (%)	..		24	
Female legislators, senior officials and managers (% of total)	..		..	
Proportion of women in ministerial level positions (%)	..		16	
Agency				
Total fertility rate (births per woman)	1.9		1.9	
Adolescent fertility rate (births per 1,000 women ages 15–19)	34		31	
Women first married by age 18 (% of women ages 20–24)	..		..	

Low and middle income

Population (millions)	5,862
GNI, Atlas ($ billions)	24,773
GNI per capita, Atlas ($)	4,226
Population living below $1.90 a day (%)	*15*

	2000		2013	
	Female	**Male**	**Female**	**Male**
Education				
Net primary enrollment rate (%)	79	85	87	89
Net secondary enrollment rate (%)	44	49	60	64
Gross tertiary enrollment ratio (% of relevant age group)	11	13	26	25
Primary completion rate (% of relevant age group)	75	83	90	92
Progression to secondary school (%)	86	88	89	90
Lower secondary completion rate (% of relevant age group)	54	61	70	72
Gross tertiary graduation ratio (%)	..	..	..	..
Female share of graduates in eng., manf. and constr. (%, tertiary)	..		..	
Youth literacy rate (% of population ages 15–24)	81	89	87	*91*
Health and related services				
Sex ratio at birth (male births per female births)	*1.08*		*1.08*	
Under-five mortality rate (per 1,000 live births)	83	87	45	49
Life expectancy at birth (years)	67	64	71	67
Pregnant women receiving prenatal care (%)	69		82	
Births attended by skilled health staff (% of total)	58		67	
Maternal mortality ratio (per 100,000 live births)	370		230	
Women's share of population ages 15+ living with HIV (%)	..		..	
Prevalence of HIV (% ages 15–24)	..	..	..	..
Economic structure, participation, and access to resources				
Labor force participation rate (% of population ages 15+)	52	81	50	79
Labor force participation rate (% of ages 15–24)	44	64	38	57
Wage and salaried workers (% of employed ages 15+)	..	..	..	..
Self-employed workers (% of employed ages 15+)	..	..	..	..
Unpaid family workers (% of employed ages 15+)	..	..	..	..
Employment in agriculture (% of employed ages 15+)	..	..	..	..
Employment in industry (% of employed ages 15+)	..	..	..	..
Employment in services (% of employed ages 15+)	..		..	
Women in wage employment in the nonagricultural sector (%)	*34*		..	
Women's share of part-time employment (% of total)	..		..	
Maternity leave (days paid)	..		..	
Maternity leave benefits (% of wages paid)	..		..	
Employment to population ratio (% ages 15+)	49	76	47	75
Employment to population ratio (% ages 15–24)	38	56	34	50
Firms with female participation in ownership (%)	..		..	
Firms with a female top manager (%)	..		..	
Children in employment (% of children ages 7–14)	..	..	..	..
Unemployment rate (% of labor force ages 15+)	6	6	6	5
Unemployment rate (% of labor force ages 15–24)	15	13	15	13
Internet users (%)	..	..	..	..
Account at a financial institution (% age 15+)	..	..	49	58
Mobile account (% age 15+)	..	..	2.0	3.1
Saved any money last year (% age 15+)	..	..	51	56
Public life and decision making				
Seats held by women in national parliament (%)	..		21	
Female legislators, senior officials and managers (% of total)	..		..	
Proportion of women in ministerial level positions (%)	..		16	
Agency				
Total fertility rate (births per woman)	2.9		2.6	
Adolescent fertility rate (births per 1,000 women ages 15–19)	61		49	
Women first married by age 18 (% of women ages 20–24)	..		..	

High income

Population (millions)			1,399
GNI, Atlas ($ billions)			53,597
GNI per capita, Atlas ($)			38,317
Population living below $1.90 a day (%)			..

	2000		2013	
	Female	Male	Female	Male
Education				
Net primary enrollment rate (%)	96	96	96	96
Net secondary enrollment rate (%)	86	85	91	89
Gross tertiary enrollment ratio (% of relevant age group)	59	51	83	66
Primary completion rate (% of relevant age group)	96	95	99	99
Progression to secondary school (%)	97	96	97	97
Lower secondary completion rate (% of relevant age group)	89	84	93	89
Gross tertiary graduation ratio (%)	..	..	..	..
Female share of graduates in eng., manf. and constr. (%, tertiary)	..		..	
Youth literacy rate (% of population ages 15-24)	99	99	*100*	*100*
Health and related services				
Sex ratio at birth (male births per female births)	*1.05*		1.05	
Under-five mortality rate (per 1,000 live births)	10	12	6	8
Life expectancy at birth (years)	79	73	82	76
Pregnant women receiving prenatal care (%)	..		..	
Births attended by skilled health staff (% of total)	..		..	
Maternal mortality ratio (per 100,000 live births)	22		22	
Women's share of population ages 15+ living with HIV (%)	..		..	
Prevalence of HIV (% ages 15-24)	..	..	..	..
Economic structure, participation, and access to resources				
Labor force participation rate (% of population ages 15+)	51	71	53	69
Labor force participation rate (% of ages 15-24)	46	53	41	48
Wage and salaried workers (% of employed ages 15+)	87	83	89	85
Self-employed workers (% of employed ages 15+)	13	17	*11*	17
Unpaid family workers (% of employed ages 15+)	3.1	0.8	*1.9*	*0.6*
Employment in agriculture (% of employed ages 15+)	5	7	*3*	*4*
Employment in industry (% of employed ages 15+)	16	35	*11*	*31*
Employment in services (% of employed ages 15+)	79	58	*86*	*64*
Women in wage employment in the nonagricultural sector (%)	46		47	
Women's share of part-time employment (% of total)	71		69	
Maternity leave (days paid)	..		..	
Maternity leave benefits (% of wages paid)	..		..	
Employment to population ratio (% ages 15+)	47	66	48	64
Employment to population ratio (% ages 15-24)	39	45	35	39
Firms with female participation in ownership (%)	..		..	
Firms with a female top manager (%)	..		..	
Children in employment (% of children ages 7-14)	..	..	..	..
Unemployment rate (% of labor force ages 15+)	8	7	8	8
Unemployment rate (% of labor force ages 15-24)	17	16	19	18
Internet users (%)	..	..	..	..
Account at a financial institution (% age 15+)	..	..	90	91
Mobile account (% age 15+)	..	..	..	..
Saved any money last year (% age 15+)	..	..	65	69
Public life and decision making				
Seats held by women in national parliament (%)	..		26	
Female legislators, senior officials and managers (% of total)	..		..	
Proportion of women in ministerial level positions (%)	..		21	
Agency				
Total fertility rate (births per woman)	1.7		1.7	
Adolescent fertility rate (births per 1,000 women ages 15-19)	28		20	
Women first married by age 18 (% of women ages 20-24)	..		..	

Euro area

Population (millions)			339
GNI, Atlas ($ billions)			13,269
GNI per capita, Atlas ($)			39,173
Population living below $1.90 a day (%)			..

	2000 Female	2000 Male	2013 Female	2013 Male
Education				
Net primary enrollment rate (%)	98	98	98	97
Net secondary enrollment rate (%)	86	85	91	90
Gross tertiary enrollment ratio (% of relevant age group)	56	49	74	63
Primary completion rate (% of relevant age group)	99	98	98	97
Progression to secondary school (%)	98	98	98	98
Lower secondary completion rate (% of relevant age group)	89	83	84	83
Gross tertiary graduation ratio (%)	..	..	..	..
Female share of graduates in eng., manf. and constr. (%, tertiary)	..		..	
Youth literacy rate (% of population ages 15–24)	100	100	*100*	*100*
Health and related services				
Sex ratio at birth (male births per female births)	*1.06*		*1.06*	
Under-five mortality rate (per 1,000 live births)	5	7	4	4
Life expectancy at birth (years)	82	75	84	79
Pregnant women receiving prenatal care (%)	..		..	
Births attended by skilled health staff (% of total)	..		..	
Maternal mortality ratio (per 100,000 live births)	8		7	
Women's share of population ages 15+ living with HIV (%)	..		..	
Prevalence of HIV (% ages 15–24)	..	..	..	..
Economic structure, participation, and access to resources				
Labor force participation rate (% of population ages 15+)	45	65	50	64
Labor force participation rate (% of ages 15–24)	41	49	38	44
Wage and salaried workers (% of employed ages 15+)	87	80	89	80
Self-employed workers (% of employed ages 15+)	13	20	11	20
Unpaid family workers (% of employed ages 15+)	3.2	1.2	1.2	0.6
Employment in agriculture (% of employed ages 15+)	4	6	*3*	*4*
Employment in industry (% of employed ages 15+)	17	40	12	36
Employment in services (% of employed ages 15+)	79	54	85	60
Women in wage employment in the nonagricultural sector (%)	44		48	
Women's share of part-time employment (% of total)	78		76	
Maternity leave (days paid)	..		..	
Maternity leave benefits (% of wages paid)	..		..	
Employment to population ratio (% ages 15+)	40	60	44	56
Employment to population ratio (% ages 15–24)	33	41	29	33
Firms with female participation in ownership (%)	..		..	
Firms with a female top manager (%)	..		..	
Children in employment (% of children ages 7–14)	..	..	..	..
Unemployment rate (% of labor force ages 15+)	11	8	12	12
Unemployment rate (% of labor force ages 15–24)	22	17	27	27
Internet users (%)	..	..	73	79
Account at a financial institution (% age 15+)	..	..	94	96
Mobile account (% age 15+)	..	..	..	..
Saved any money last year (% age 15+)	..	..	64	71
Public life and decision making				
Seats held by women in national parliament (%)	..		30	
Female legislators, senior officials and managers (% of total)	..		..	
Proportion of women in ministerial level positions (%)	..		30	
Agency				
Total fertility rate (births per woman)	1.5		1.5	
Adolescent fertility rate (births per 1,000 women ages 15–19)	11		8	
Women first married by age 18 (% of women ages 20–24)	..		..	

Country tables

China

Unless otherwise noted, data for China do not include data for Hong Kong SAR, China; Macao SAR, China; or Taiwan, China.

Cyprus

GNI and data calculated using GNI refer to the area controlled by the government of Cyprus.

France

Data for Mayotte, to which a reference appeared in previous editions, are included in data for France.

Georgia

GNI and population data and data calculated using GNI and population exclude Abkhazia and South Ossetia.

Kosovo, Montenegro, and Serbia

Data for each country are shown separately where available. However, some indicators for Serbia prior to 2006 include data for Montenegro; these data are noted in the tables. Moreover, data for most indicators for Serbia from 1999 onward exclude data for Kosovo, which in 1999 became a territory under international administration pursuant to UN Security Council Resolution 1244 (1999). Kosovo became a member of the World Bank on June 29, 2009, and its data are shown where available.

Moldova

GNI and population data and data calculated using GNI and population exclude Transnistria.

Morocco

GNI and data calculated using GNI include Former Spanish Sahara.

South Sudan and Sudan

South Sudan declared its independence on July 9, 2011. Data are shown separately for South Sudan where available. However, data reported for Sudan to 2011 include South Sudan unless otherwise noted.

Tanzania

GNI data and data calculated using GNI refer to mainland Tanzania only.

For more information, see *World Development Indicators 2015* or data.worldbank.org.

Afghanistan

South Asia	Low income

Population (millions)	32
GNI, Atlas ($ billions)	21
GNI per capita, Atlas ($)	670
Population living below $1.90 a day (%)	

	2000 Female	Male	2013 Female	Male
Education				
Net primary enrollment rate (%)	..	..	..	..
Net secondary enrollment rate (%)	..	..	33	60
Gross tertiary enrollment ratio (% of relevant age group)	..	..	2	6
Primary completion rate (% of relevant age group)	..	..	..	..
Progression to secondary school (%)	..	..	..	..
Lower secondary completion rate (% of relevant age group)	..	..	..	..
Gross tertiary graduation ratio (%)	..	..	..	..
Female share of graduates in eng., manf. and constr. (%, tertiary)	..		..	
Youth literacy rate (% of population ages 15–24)	..	..	32	62
Health and related services				
Sex ratio at birth (male births per female births)	*1.06*		1.06	
Under-five mortality rate (per 1,000 live births)	133	141	87	95
Life expectancy at birth (years)	56	54	62	60
Pregnant women receiving prenatal care (%)	37		*48*	
Births attended by skilled health staff (% of total)	12		39	
Maternal mortality ratio (per 100,000 live births)	1,100		400	
Women's share of population ages 15+ living with HIV (%)	40		42	
Prevalence of HIV (% ages 15–24)	0.1	0.1	0.1	0.1
Economic structure, participation, and access to resources				
Labor force participation rate (% of population ages 15+)	13	81	16	80
Labor force participation rate (% of ages 15–24)	11	62	13	61
Wage and salaried workers (% of employed ages 15+)	..	..	..	..
Self-employed workers (% of employed ages 15+)	..	..	..	..
Unpaid family workers (% of employed ages 15+)	..	..	..	..
Employment in agriculture (% of employed ages 15+)	..	..	..	..
Employment in industry (% of employed ages 15+)	..	..	..	..
Employment in services (% of employed ages 15+)	..		..	
Women in wage employment in the nonagricultural sector (%)	*19*		..	
Women's share of part-time employment (% of total)	..			
Maternity leave (days paid)			90	
Maternity leave benefits (% of wages paid)	..		100	
Employment to population ratio (% ages 15+)	12	78	14	74
Employment to population ratio (% ages 15–24)	10	58	10	51
Firms with female participation in ownership (%)	..		2[a]	
Firms with a female top manager (%)			5[a]	
Children in employment (% of children ages 7–14)	..	..	5	*13*
Unemployment rate (% of labor force ages 15+)	11	4	12	7
Unemployment rate (% of labor force ages 15–24)	13	7	23	16
Internet users (%)	..	..	..	..
Account at a financial institution (% age 15+)	..	..	4	16
Mobile account (% age 15+)	..	..	0.2	0.4
Saved any money last year (% age 15+)	..	..	19	32
Public life and decision making				
Seats held by women in national parliament (%)	..		28	
Female legislators, senior officials and managers (% of total)	..		..	
Proportion of women in ministerial level positions (%)	..		10	
Agency				
Total fertility rate (births per woman)	7.7		4.9	
Adolescent fertility rate (births per 1,000 women ages 15–19)	154		77	
Women first married by age 18 (% of women ages 20–24)	..		*40*	

Albania

Europe & Central Asia	Upper middle income
Population (millions)	3
GNI, Atlas ($ billions)	13
GNI per capita, Atlas ($)	4,460
Population living below $1.90 a day (%)	<2

	2000		2013	
	Female	Male	Female	Male
Education				
Net primary enrollment rate (%)	93	94	..	..
Net secondary enrollment rate (%)	61	64	..	..
Gross tertiary enrollment ratio (% of relevant age group)	16	11	66	51
Primary completion rate (% of relevant age group)	95	94	..	..
Progression to secondary school (%)	98	97	99	100
Lower secondary completion rate (% of relevant age group)	77	77	..	..
Gross tertiary graduation ratio (%)	11	6	52	27
Female share of graduates in eng., manf. and constr. (%, tertiary)	21		39	
Youth literacy rate (% of population ages 15-24)	99	99	99	99
Health and related services				
Sex ratio at birth (male births per female births)	1.07		1.08	
Under-five mortality rate (per 1,000 live births)	23	29	13	15
Life expectancy at birth (years)	77	71	81	75
Pregnant women receiving prenatal care (%)	95		..	
Births attended by skilled health staff (% of total)	99		..	
Maternal mortality ratio (per 100,000 live births)	28		21	
Women's share of population ages 15+ living with HIV (%)	..		..	
Prevalence of HIV (% ages 15-24)	..	..	..	..
Economic structure, participation, and access to resources				
Labor force participation rate (% of population ages 15+)	51	73	45	66
Labor force participation rate (% of ages 15-24)	48	59	30	42
Wage and salaried workers (% of employed ages 15+)	..	..	37	43
Self-employed workers (% of employed ages 15+)	..	..	63	57
Unpaid family workers (% of employed ages 15+)	..	..	45.2	24.7
Employment in agriculture (% of employed ages 15+)	..	..	53	33
Employment in industry (% of employed ages 15+)	..	..	11	28
Employment in services (% of employed ages 15+)	..	..	37	39
Women in wage employment in the nonagricultural sector (%)	29		41	
Women's share of part-time employment (% of total)	40		..	
Maternity leave (days paid)	..		365	
Maternity leave benefits (% of wages paid)	..		65	
Employment to population ratio (% ages 15+)	44	64	39	54
Employment to population ratio (% ages 15-24)	37	44	23	28
Firms with female participation in ownership (%)	..		13	
Firms with a female top manager (%)	..		12	
Children in employment (% of children ages 7-14)	32	41	5	6
Unemployment rate (% of labor force ages 15+)	14	13	14	18
Unemployment rate (% of labor force ages 15-24)	23	26	24	32
Internet users (%)	..	..	..	..
Account at a financial institution (% age 15+)	..	..	34	43
Mobile account (% age 15+)	..	..	..	..
Saved any money last year (% age 15+)	..	..	35	42
Public life and decision making				
Seats held by women in national parliament (%)	..		21	
Female legislators, senior officials and managers (% of total)	..		..	
Proportion of women in ministerial level positions (%)	..		35	
Agency				
Total fertility rate (births per woman)	2.4		1.8	
Adolescent fertility rate (births per 1,000 women ages 15-19)	19		21	
Women first married by age 18 (% of women ages 20-24)	..		..	

Algeria

Middle East & North Africa	Upper middle income
Population (millions)	39
GNI, Atlas ($ billions)	213
GNI per capita, Atlas ($)	5,480
Population living below $1.90 a day (%)	..

	2000		2013	
	Female	Male	Female	Male
Education				
Net primary enrollment rate (%)	86	89	..	..
Net secondary enrollment rate (%)	..	..	..	..
Gross tertiary enrollment ratio (% of relevant age group)	..	..	40	27
Primary completion rate (% of relevant age group)	77	78	105	106
Progression to secondary school (%)	94	92	97	100
Lower secondary completion rate (% of relevant age group)	54	45	90	74
Gross tertiary graduation ratio (%)	..	..	..	..
Female share of graduates in eng., manf. and constr. (%, tertiary)	..		32	
Youth literacy rate (% of population ages 15-24)	86	94	..	..
Health and related services				
Sex ratio at birth (male births per female births)	1.05		1.05	
Under-five mortality rate (per 1,000 live births)	37	43	24	27
Life expectancy at birth (years)	71	67	73	69
Pregnant women receiving prenatal care (%)	79		93	
Births attended by skilled health staff (% of total)	93		97	
Maternal mortality ratio (per 100,000 live births)	120		89	
Women's share of population ages 15+ living with HIV (%)	36		46	
Prevalence of HIV (% ages 15-24)	0.1	0.1	0.1	0.1
Economic structure, participation, and access to resources				
Labor force participation rate (% of population ages 15+)	12	75	15	72
Labor force participation rate (% of ages 15-24)	12	59	10	47
Wage and salaried workers (% of employed ages 15+)	58	61	74	68
Self-employed workers (% of employed ages 15+)	38	38	26	32
Unpaid family workers (% of employed ages 15+)	6.1	8.8	2.9	2.0
Employment in agriculture (% of employed ages 15+)	13	23	3	12
Employment in industry (% of employed ages 15+)	28	24	24	32
Employment in services (% of employed ages 15+)	59	54	73	56
Women in wage employment in the nonagricultural sector (%)	13		18	
Women's share of part-time employment (% of total)	..		..	
Maternity leave (days paid)	..		98	
Maternity leave benefits (% of wages paid)	..		100	
Employment to population ratio (% ages 15+)	5	56	13	66
Employment to population ratio (% ages 15-24)	3	32	6	37
Firms with female participation in ownership (%)	..		..	
Firms with a female top manager (%)	..		..	
Children in employment (% of children ages 7-14)	..	..	..	..
Unemployment rate (% of labor force ages 15+)	56	26	17	8
Unemployment rate (% of labor force ages 15-24)	77	46	39	21
Internet users (%)	..		..	
Account at a financial institution (% age 15+)	..	..	40	61
Mobile account (% age 15+)	..	..	..	..
Saved any money last year (% age 15+)	..	..	37	53
Public life and decision making				
Seats held by women in national parliament (%)			32	
Female legislators, senior officials and managers (% of total)	5		11	
Proportion of women in ministerial level positions (%)	..		20	
Agency				
Total fertility rate (births per woman)	2.5		2.8	
Adolescent fertility rate (births per 1,000 women ages 15-19)	12		11	
Women first married by age 18 (% of women ages 20-24)	..		..	

American Somoa

East Asia & Pacific	Upper middle income
Population (thousands)	55
GNI, Atlas ($ millions)	..
GNI per capita, Atlas ($)	..
Population living below $1.90 a day (%)	..

	2000 Female	2000 Male	2013 Female	2013 Male
Education				
Net primary enrollment rate (%)	..	..	..	..
Net secondary enrollment rate (%)	..	..	..	..
Gross tertiary enrollment ratio (% of relevant age group)	..	..	..	..
Primary completion rate (% of relevant age group)	..	..	..	..
Progression to secondary school (%)	..	..	..	..
Lower secondary completion rate (% of relevant age group)	..	..	..	..
Gross tertiary graduation ratio (%)	..	..	..	..
Female share of graduates in eng., manf. and constr. (%, tertiary)	..		..	
Youth literacy rate (% of population ages 15–24)	..	..	..	..
Health and related services				
Sex ratio at birth (male births per female births)	..		..	
Under-five mortality rate (per 1,000 live births)	..	..	..	..
Life expectancy at birth (years)	..	..	..	..
Pregnant women receiving prenatal care (%)	..		..	
Births attended by skilled health staff (% of total)	100		..	
Maternal mortality ratio (per 100,000 live births)	..		..	
Women's share of population ages 15+ living with HIV (%)	..		..	
Prevalence of HIV (% ages 15–24)	..	..	..	..
Economic structure, participation, and access to resources				
Labor force participation rate (% of population ages 15+)	..	..	..	..
Labor force participation rate (% of ages 15–24)	..	..	..	..
Wage and salaried workers (% of employed ages 15+)	..	..	..	..
Self-employed workers (% of employed ages 15+)	..	..	..	..
Unpaid family workers (% of employed ages 15+)	..	..	..	..
Employment in agriculture (% of employed ages 15+)	..	..	..	..
Employment in industry (% of employed ages 15+)	..	..	..	..
Employment in services (% of employed ages 15+)	..	..	..	..
Women in wage employment in the nonagricultural sector (%)	..		..	
Women's share of part-time employment (% of total)	..		..	
Maternity leave (days paid)	..		..	
Maternity leave benefits (% of wages paid)	..		..	
Employment to population ratio (% ages 15+)	..	..	..	..
Employment to population ratio (% ages 15–24)	..	..	..	..
Firms with female participation in ownership (%)	..		..	
Firms with a female top manager (%)	..		..	
Children in employment (% of children ages 7–14)	..		..	
Unemployment rate (% of labor force ages 15+)	..	..	..	..
Unemployment rate (% of labor force ages 15–24)	..	..	..	..
Internet users (%)	..	..	..	..
Account at a financial institution (% age 15+)	..	..	..	..
Mobile account (% age 15+)	..	..	..	..
Saved any money last year (% age 15+)	..	..	..	..
Public life and decision making				
Seats held by women in national parliament (%)	..		..	
Female legislators, senior officials and managers (% of total)	..		..	
Proportion of women in ministerial level positions (%)	..		..	
Agency				
Total fertility rate (births per woman)	..		..	
Adolescent fertility rate (births per 1,000 women ages 15–19)	..		..	
Women first married by age 18 (% of women ages 20–24)	..		..	

Andorra

			High income
Population (thousands)			73
GNI, Atlas ($ billions)			3
GNI per capita, Atlas ($)			43,270
Population living below $1.90 a day (%)			..

	2000		2013	
	Female	Male	Female	Male
Education				
Net primary enrollment rate (%)	..	..	..	..
Net secondary enrollment rate (%)	..	..	..	..
Gross tertiary enrollment ratio (% of relevant age group)	..	..	..	..
Primary completion rate (% of relevant age group)	..	..	..	..
Progression to secondary school (%)	..	..	..	..
Lower secondary completion rate (% of relevant age group)	..	..	..	..
Gross tertiary graduation ratio (%)	..	..	..	..
Female share of graduates in eng., manf. and constr. (%, tertiary)	..		33	
Youth literacy rate (% of population ages 15–24)	..	..	..	..
Health and related services				
Sex ratio at birth (male births per female births)	..		..	
Under-five mortality rate (per 1,000 live births)	4	5	3	3
Life expectancy at birth (years)	..		..	
Pregnant women receiving prenatal care (%)	..		..	
Births attended by skilled health staff (% of total)	..		..	
Maternal mortality ratio (per 100,000 live births)	..		..	
Women's share of population ages 15+ living with HIV (%)	..		..	
Prevalence of HIV (% ages 15–24)	..	..	..	..
Economic structure, participation, and access to resources				
Labor force participation rate (% of population ages 15+)	..	..	..	..
Labor force participation rate (% of ages 15–24)	..	..	..	..
Wage and salaried workers (% of employed ages 15+)	..	..	..	..
Self-employed workers (% of employed ages 15+)	..	..	..	..
Unpaid family workers (% of employed ages 15+)	..	..	..	..
Employment in agriculture (% of employed ages 15+)	..	..	..	..
Employment in industry (% of employed ages 15+)	..	..	..	..
Employment in services (% of employed ages 15+)	..	..	..	..
Women in wage employment in the nonagricultural sector (%)	..		..	
Women's share of part-time employment (% of total)	..		..	
Maternity leave (days paid)	..		..	
Maternity leave benefits (% of wages paid)	..		..	
Employment to population ratio (% ages 15+)	..	..	..	..
Employment to population ratio (% ages 15–24)	..	..	..	..
Firms with female participation in ownership (%)	..		..	
Firms with a female top manager (%)	..		..	
Children in employment (% of children ages 7–14)	..		..	
Unemployment rate (% of labor force ages 15+)	..	..	..	..
Unemployment rate (% of labor force ages 15–24)	..	..	..	..
Internet users (%)	..	..	..	..
Account at a financial institution (% age 15+)	..	..	..	..
Mobile account (% age 15+)	..	..	..	..
Saved any money last year (% age 15+)	..	..	..	..
Public life and decision making				
Seats held by women in national parliament (%)	..		39	
Female legislators, senior officials and managers (% of total)	..		..	
Proportion of women in ministerial level positions (%)	..		25	
Agency				
Total fertility rate (births per woman)	..		1.2	
Adolescent fertility rate (births per 1,000 women ages 15–19)	..		..	
Women first married by age 18 (% of women ages 20–24)	..		..	

Angola

Sub-Saharan Africa	**Upper middle income**
Population (millions)	24
GNI, Atlas ($ billions)	117
GNI per capita, Atlas ($)	4,850
Population living below $1.90 a day (%)	..

	2000		2013	
	Female	Male	Female	Male
Education				
Net primary enrollment rate (%)	49	58	74	97
Net secondary enrollment rate (%)	..	..	12	15
Gross tertiary enrollment ratio (% of relevant age group)	0	1	4	11
Primary completion rate (% of relevant age group)	..	..	40	69
Progression to secondary school (%)	..	..		
Lower secondary completion rate (% of relevant age group)	..	..	20	29
Gross tertiary graduation ratio (%)	0	0	..	..
Female share of graduates in eng., manf. and constr. (%, tertiary)	25		19	
Youth literacy rate (% of population ages 15-24)	63	84	67	79
Health and related services				
Sex ratio at birth (male births per female births)	1.03		1.03	
Under-five mortality rate (per 1,000 live births)	206	227	149	165
Life expectancy at birth (years)	47	44	53	50
Pregnant women receiving prenatal care (%)	66		..	
Births attended by skilled health staff (% of total)	45		..	
Maternal mortality ratio (per 100,000 live births)	1,100		460	
Women's share of population ages 15+ living with HIV (%)	58		59	
Prevalence of HIV (% ages 15-24)	1.0	0.5	1.1	0.6
Economic structure, participation, and access to resources				
Labor force participation rate (% of population ages 15+)	68	75	63	77
Labor force participation rate (% of ages 15-24)	53	55	50	56
Wage and salaried workers (% of employed ages 15+)	..	..	..	..
Self-employed workers (% of employed ages 15+)	..	..	..	..
Unpaid family workers (% of employed ages 15+)	..	..	..	..
Employment in agriculture (% of employed ages 15+)	..	..	..	..
Employment in industry (% of employed ages 15+)	..	..	..	..
Employment in services (% of employed ages 15+)	..	..	..	..
Women in wage employment in the nonagricultural sector (%)	..		..	
Women's share of part-time employment (% of total)	..		..	
Maternity leave (days paid)	..		90	
Maternity leave benefits (% of wages paid)	..		100	
Employment to population ratio (% ages 15+)	63	70	59	72
Employment to population ratio (% ages 15-24)	47	49	44	50
Firms with female participation in ownership (%)	..		57	
Firms with a female top manager (%)	..		14	
Children in employment (% of children ages 7-14)	30	30	..	..
Unemployment rate (% of labor force ages 15+)	7	7	7	7
Unemployment rate (% of labor force ages 15-24)	11	10	11	10
Internet users (%)	..	..	..	..
Account at a financial institution (% age 15+)	..	..	22	36
Mobile account (% age 15+)	..	..	..	..
Saved any money last year (% age 15+)	..	..	49	57
Public life and decision making				
Seats held by women in national parliament (%)	..		37	
Female legislators, senior officials and managers (% of total)	..		..	
Proportion of women in ministerial level positions (%)	..		22	
Agency				
Total fertility rate (births per woman)	6.8		5.9	
Adolescent fertility rate (births per 1,000 women ages 15-19)	211		167	
Women first married by age 18 (% of women ages 20-24)	..		..	

Antigua and Barbuda

	High income
Population (thousands)	91
GNI, Atlas ($ billions)	1.2
GNI per capita, Atlas ($)	13,360
Population living below $1.90 a day (%)	..

	2000		2013	
	Female	Male	Female	Male
Education				
Net primary enrollment rate (%)	..	..	84	87
Net secondary enrollment rate (%)	67	72	94	88
Gross tertiary enrollment ratio (% of relevant age group)	..	..	31	15
Primary completion rate (% of relevant age group)	..	..	96	104
Progression to secondary school (%)	..	..	..	..
Lower secondary completion rate (% of relevant age group)	..	..	104	96
Gross tertiary graduation ratio (%)	..	..	3	1
Female share of graduates in eng., manf. and constr. (%, tertiary)	..		..	
Youth literacy rate (% of population ages 15-24)	..	..	..	..
Health and related services				
Sex ratio at birth (male births per female births)	1.03		1.03	
Under-five mortality rate (per 1,000 live births)	14	17	7	9
Life expectancy at birth (years)	76	71	78	73
Pregnant women receiving prenatal care (%)	100		..	
Births attended by skilled health staff (% of total)	100		100	
Maternal mortality ratio (per 100,000 live births)	..		..	
Women's share of population ages 15+ living with HIV (%)	..		..	
Prevalence of HIV (% ages 15-24)	..	..	..	..
Economic structure, participation, and access to resources				
Labor force participation rate (% of population ages 15+)	..	..	..	..
Labor force participation rate (% of ages 15-24)	..	..	..	..
Wage and salaried workers (% of employed ages 15+)	82	77	..	..
Self-employed workers (% of employed ages 15+)	10	14	..	..
Unpaid family workers (% of employed ages 15+)	0.5	0.5	..	..
Employment in agriculture (% of employed ages 15+)	1	4	..	..
Employment in industry (% of employed ages 15+)	5	24	..	..
Employment in services (% of employed ages 15+)	87	65	..	..
Women in wage employment in the nonagricultural sector (%)	51		..	
Women's share of part-time employment (% of total)	..		..	
Maternity leave (days paid)			91	
Maternity leave benefits (% of wages paid)	..		78	
Employment to population ratio (% ages 15+)	..	..	..	..
Employment to population ratio (% ages 15-24)	..	..	..	..
Firms with female participation in ownership (%)	..		21	
Firms with a female top manager (%)	..		18	
Children in employment (% of children ages 7-14)	..	..	..	..
Unemployment rate (% of labor force ages 15+)	..	..	..	..
Unemployment rate (% of labor force ages 15-24)	..	..	..	..
Internet users (%)	..	..	..	..
Account at a financial institution (% age 15+)	..	..	..	..
Mobile account (% age 15+)	..	..	..	..
Saved any money last year (% age 15+)	..	..	..	..
Public life and decision making				
Seats held by women in national parliament (%)	..		11	
Female legislators, senior officials and managers (% of total)	45		..	
Proportion of women in ministerial level positions (%)	..		8	
Agency				
Total fertility rate (births per woman)	2.3		2.1	
Adolescent fertility rate (births per 1,000 women ages 15-19)	65		46	
Women first married by age 18 (% of women ages 20-24)	..		..	

Argentina

High income

Population (millions)	43
GNI, Atlas ($ billions)	609
GNI per capita, Atlas ($)	14,160
Population living below $1.90 a day (%)	<2

	2000		2013	
	Female	Male	Female	Male
Education				
Net primary enrollment rate (%)	99	100	..	..
Net secondary enrollment rate (%)	77	72	92	86
Gross tertiary enrollment ratio (% of relevant age group)	65	42	98	63
Primary completion rate (% of relevant age group)	101	97	111	109
Progression to secondary school (%)	..	..	94	88
Lower secondary completion rate (% of relevant age group)	..	..	85	64
Gross tertiary graduation ratio (%)	10	8	16	10
Female share of graduates in eng., manf. and constr. (%, tertiary)	..		31	
Youth literacy rate (% of population ages 15-24)	99	99	99	99
Health and related services				
Sex ratio at birth (male births per female births)	1.04		1.04	
Under-five mortality rate (per 1,000 live births)	18	22	11	14
Life expectancy at birth (years)	78	70	80	73
Pregnant women receiving prenatal care (%)	98		98	
Births attended by skilled health staff (% of total)	98		98	
Maternal mortality ratio (per 100,000 live births)	63		69	
Women's share of population ages 15+ living with HIV (%)	30		30	
Prevalence of HIV (% ages 15-24)	0.1	0.2	0.1	0.2
Economic structure, participation, and access to resources				
Labor force participation rate (% of population ages 15+)	43	74	48	75
Labor force participation rate (% of ages 15-24)	34	54	31	51
Wage and salaried workers (% of employed ages 15+)	76	70	81	74
Self-employed workers (% of employed ages 15+)	24	30	19	26
Unpaid family workers (% of employed ages 15+)	1.8	0.7	0.8	0.3
Employment in agriculture (% of employed ages 15+)	0	1	0	1
Employment in industry (% of employed ages 15+)	10	31	10	33
Employment in services (% of employed ages 15+)	89	68	90	65
Women in wage employment in the nonagricultural sector (%)	43		42	
Women's share of part-time employment (% of total)	62		63	
Maternity leave (days paid)	..		90	
Maternity leave benefits (% of wages paid)	..		100	
Employment to population ratio (% ages 15+)	35	64	43	70
Employment to population ratio (% ages 15-24)	23	42	24	42
Firms with female participation in ownership (%)	..		38	
Firms with a female top manager (%)	..		9	
Children in employment (% of children ages 7-14)	..	..	6	8
Unemployment rate (% of labor force ages 15+)	17	14	9	7
Unemployment rate (% of labor force ages 15-24)	32	23	24	17
Internet users (%)	..	..	..	..
Account at a financial institution (% age 15+)	..	..	51	49
Mobile account (% age 15+)	..	..	0.2	0.7
Saved any money last year (% age 15+)	..	..	21	25
Public life and decision making				
Seats held by women in national parliament (%)	..		36	
Female legislators, senior officials and managers (% of total)	27		..	
Proportion of women in ministerial level positions (%)	..		22	
Agency				
Total fertility rate (births per woman)	2.5		2.2	
Adolescent fertility rate (births per 1,000 women ages 15-19)	67		64	
Women first married by age 18 (% of women ages 20-24)	..		..	

Armenia

Europe & Central Asia				Lower middle income

Population (millions)	3
GNI, Atlas ($ billions)	11
GNI per capita, Atlas ($)	3,780
Population living below $1.90 a day (%)	2

	2000		2013	
	Female	Male	Female	Male
Education				
Net primary enrollment rate (%)	86	84	..	..
Net secondary enrollment rate (%)	..	..	..	..
Gross tertiary enrollment ratio (% of relevant age group)	39	31	57	38
Primary completion rate (% of relevant age group)	95	93	..	..
Progression to secondary school (%)	98	98	99	99
Lower secondary completion rate (% of relevant age group)	87	83	..	..
Gross tertiary graduation ratio (%)	20	17	58	39
Female share of graduates in eng., manf. and constr. (%, tertiary)	..		29	
Youth literacy rate (% of population ages 15–24)	100	100	100	100
Health and related services				
Sex ratio at birth (male births per female births)	1.17		1.14	
Under-five mortality rate (per 1,000 live births)	27	33	13	16
Life expectancy at birth (years)	75	68	78	71
Pregnant women receiving prenatal care (%)	92		99	
Births attended by skilled health staff (% of total)	97		100	
Maternal mortality ratio (per 100,000 live births)	43		29	
Women's share of population ages 15+ living with HIV (%)	20		18	
Prevalence of HIV (% ages 15–24)	0.1	0.1	0.1	0.2
Economic structure, participation, and access to resources				
Labor force participation rate (% of population ages 15+)	58	73	54	73
Labor force participation rate (% of ages 15–24)	48	63	30	42
Wage and salaried workers (% of employed ages 15+)	..	..	52	59
Self-employed workers (% of employed ages 15+)	..	..	30	31
Unpaid family workers (% of employed ages 15+)	..	..	..	..
Employment in agriculture (% of employed ages 15+)	43	48	46	33
Employment in industry (% of employed ages 15+)	11	22	7	26
Employment in services (% of employed ages 15+)	46	30	48	41
Women in wage employment in the nonagricultural sector (%)	45		44	
Women's share of part-time employment (% of total)	..			
Maternity leave (days paid)			140	
Maternity leave benefits (% of wages paid)	..		100	
Employment to population ratio (% ages 15+)	46	60	45	62
Employment to population ratio (% ages 15–24)	28	43	19	30
Firms with female participation in ownership (%)	..		25	
Firms with a female top manager (%)	..		19	
Children in employment (% of children ages 7–14)	..	..	8	12
Unemployment rate (% of labor force ages 15+)	20	18	18	15
Unemployment rate (% of labor force ages 15–24)	41	31	39	30
Internet users (%)	..	..	..	..
Account at a financial institution (% age 15+)	..	..	14	21
Mobile account (% age 15+)	..	..	0.4	1.0
Saved any money last year (% age 15+)	..	..	19	24
Public life and decision making				
Seats held by women in national parliament (%)	..		11	
Female legislators, senior officials and managers (% of total)	24		..	
Proportion of women in ministerial level positions (%)	..		11	
Agency				
Total fertility rate (births per woman)	1.7		1.7	
Adolescent fertility rate (births per 1,000 women ages 15–19)	40		24	
Women first married by age 18 (% of women ages 20–24)	19		7	

Aruba

Population (thousands)	103
GNI, Atlas ($ millions)	..
GNI per capita, Atlas ($)	..
Population living below $1.90 a day (%)	..

	2000		2013	
	Female	Male	Female	Male
Education				
Net primary enrollment rate (%)	98	98	..	..
Net secondary enrollment rate (%)	79	75	81	73
Gross tertiary enrollment ratio (% of relevant age group)	36	24	46	30
Primary completion rate (% of relevant age group)	97	97	98	92
Progression to secondary school (%)	99	100	..	..
Lower secondary completion rate (% of relevant age group)	96	93	..	..
Gross tertiary graduation ratio (%)	11	3	17	6
Female share of graduates in eng., manf. and constr. (%, tertiary)	15		20	
Youth literacy rate (% of population ages 15-24)	99	99	99	99
Health and related services				
Sex ratio at birth (male births per female births)	1.05		1.05	
Under-five mortality rate (per 1,000 live births)	..	..	..	..
Life expectancy at birth (years)	76	71	78	73
Pregnant women receiving prenatal care (%)	..			
Births attended by skilled health staff (% of total)	96		..	
Maternal mortality ratio (per 100,000 live births)	..		..	
Women's share of population ages 15+ living with HIV (%)	..		..	
Prevalence of HIV (% ages 15-24)	..	..	..	..
Economic structure, participation, and access to resources				
Labor force participation rate (% of population ages 15+)	..	..	..	..
Labor force participation rate (% of ages 15-24)	..	..	..	..
Wage and salaried workers (% of employed ages 15+)	93	87	..	..
Self-employed workers (% of employed ages 15+)	6	13	..	..
Unpaid family workers (% of employed ages 15+)	0.4	0.2	..	..
Employment in agriculture (% of employed ages 15+)	0	1	..	..
Employment in industry (% of employed ages 15+)	5	27	..	..
Employment in services (% of employed ages 15+)	95	72	..	..
Women in wage employment in the nonagricultural sector (%)	48		52	
Women's share of part-time employment (% of total)	..		..	
Maternity leave (days paid)	..		..	
Maternity leave benefits (% of wages paid)	..		..	
Employment to population ratio (% ages 15+)	..	..	..	..
Employment to population ratio (% ages 15-24)	..	..	..	..
Firms with female participation in ownership (%)	..		..	
Firms with a female top manager (%)	..		..	
Children in employment (% of children ages 7-14)	..	..	..	..
Unemployment rate (% of labor force ages 15+)	..	..	..	..
Unemployment rate (% of labor force ages 15-24)	..	..	..	..
Internet users (%)	..	..	..	..
Account at a financial institution (% age 15+)	..	..	..	..
Mobile account (% age 15+)	..	..	..	..
Saved any money last year (% age 15+)	..	..	..	..
Public life and decision making				
Seats held by women in national parliament (%)	..		..	
Female legislators, senior officials and managers (% of total)	36		43	
Proportion of women in ministerial level positions (%)	..		..	
Agency				
Total fertility rate (births per woman)	1.9		1.7	
Adolescent fertility rate (births per 1,000 women ages 15-19)	44		23	
Women first married by age 18 (% of women ages 20-24)	..		..	

Australia

	High income
Population (millions)	23
GNI, Atlas ($ billions)	1,519
GNI per capita, Atlas ($)	64,680
Population living below $1.90 a day (%)	..

	2000		2013	
	Female	Male	Female	Male
Education				
Net primary enrollment rate (%)	94	94	98	97
Net secondary enrollment rate (%)	88	87	86	85
Gross tertiary enrollment ratio (% of relevant age group)	72	58	103	75
Primary completion rate (% of relevant age group)	..	..	..	..
Progression to secondary school (%)	..	..	..	..
Lower secondary completion rate (% of relevant age group)	..	..	..	..
Gross tertiary graduation ratio (%)	59	42	79	51
Female share of graduates in eng., manf. and constr. (%, tertiary)	22		22	
Youth literacy rate (% of population ages 15–24)	..	..	..	..
Health and related services				
Sex ratio at birth (male births per female births)	1.06		1.06	
Under-five mortality rate (per 1,000 live births)	6	7	3	4
Life expectancy at birth (years)	82	77	84	80
Pregnant women receiving prenatal care (%)	..		..	
Births attended by skilled health staff (% of total)	100		..	
Maternal mortality ratio (per 100,000 live births)	9		6	
Women's share of population ages 15+ living with HIV (%)	..		..	
Prevalence of HIV (% ages 15–24)	..	..	..	..
Economic structure, participation, and access to resources				
Labor force participation rate (% of population ages 15+)	55	72	59	72
Labor force participation rate (% of ages 15–24)	69	72	67	69
Wage and salaried workers (% of employed ages 15+)	89	83	91	87
Self-employed workers (% of employed ages 15+)	11	17	9	13
Unpaid family workers (% of employed ages 15+)	1.1	0.6	0.3	0.2
Employment in agriculture (% of employed ages 15+)	4	6	..	..
Employment in industry (% of employed ages 15+)	11	31	..	..
Employment in services (% of employed ages 15+)	86	63	..	..
Women in wage employment in the nonagricultural sector (%)	46		47	
Women's share of part-time employment (% of total)	73		71	
Maternity leave (days paid)[c]	..		..	
Maternity leave benefits (% of wages paid)	..		..	
Employment to population ratio (% ages 15+)	51	68	56	68
Employment to population ratio (% ages 15–24)	61	63	59	60
Firms with female participation in ownership (%)	..		..	
Firms with a female top manager (%)	..		..	
Children in employment (% of children ages 7–14)	..	..	..	..
Unemployment rate (% of labor force ages 15+)	6	7	6	6
Unemployment rate (% of labor force ages 15–24)	11	13	11	13
Internet users (%)	..	..	83	84
Account at a financial institution (% age 15+)	..	..	99	99
Mobile account (% age 15+)	..	..	..	..
Saved any money last year (% age 15+)	..	..	80	83
Public life and decision making				
Seats held by women in national parliament (%)	..		27	
Female legislators, senior officials and managers (% of total)	33		..	
Proportion of women in ministerial level positions (%)	..		17	
Agency				
Total fertility rate (births per woman)	1.8		1.9	
Adolescent fertility rate (births per 1,000 women ages 15–19)	18		14	
Women first married by age 18 (% of women ages 20–24)	..		..	

Austria

Population (millions)	9
GNI, Atlas ($ billions)	427
GNI per capita, Atlas ($)	50,390
Population living below $1.90 a day (%)	..

	2000 Female	2000 Male	2013 Female	2013 Male
Education				
Net primary enrollment rate (%)	..	..	..	..
Net secondary enrollment rate (%)	..	..	..	..
Gross tertiary enrollment ratio (% of relevant age group)	59	55	88	73
Primary completion rate (% of relevant age group)	102	101	98	98
Progression to secondary school (%)	99	100	100	100
Lower secondary completion rate (% of relevant age group)	104	104	97	96
Gross tertiary graduation ratio (%)	16	17	47	29
Female share of graduates in eng., manf. and constr. (%, tertiary)	15		21	
Youth literacy rate (% of population ages 15-24)	..	..	..	..
Health and related services				
Sex ratio at birth (male births per female births)	1.06		1.06	
Under-five mortality rate (per 1,000 live births)	5	6	3	4
Life expectancy at birth (years)	81	75	83	79
Pregnant women receiving prenatal care (%)	..		..	
Births attended by skilled health staff (% of total)	..		..	
Maternal mortality ratio (per 100,000 live births)	5		4	
Women's share of population ages 15+ living with HIV (%)	..		..	
Prevalence of HIV (% ages 15-24)	..	..	..	..
Economic structure, participation, and access to resources				
Labor force participation rate (% of population ages 15+)	48	69	55	68
Labor force participation rate (% of ages 15-24)	51	60	55	65
Wage and salaried workers (% of employed ages 15+)	88	86	89	84
Self-employed workers (% of employed ages 15+)	13	14	11	16
Unpaid family workers (% of employed ages 15+)	4.1	1.6	2.0	1.8
Employment in agriculture (% of employed ages 15+)	6	6	5	5
Employment in industry (% of employed ages 15+)	14	43	13	38
Employment in services (% of employed ages 15+)	80	52	83	57
Women in wage employment in the nonagricultural sector (%)	44		48	
Women's share of part-time employment (% of total)	88		81	
Maternity leave (days paid)	..		112	
Maternity leave benefits (% of wages paid)	..		100	
Employment to population ratio (% ages 15+)	47	67	52	64
Employment to population ratio (% ages 15-24)	48	57	50	59
Firms with female participation in ownership (%)	..		..	
Firms with a female top manager (%)	..		..	
Children in employment (% of children ages 7-14)	..	..	..	..
Unemployment rate (% of labor force ages 15+)	4	3	5	5
Unemployment rate (% of labor force ages 15-24)	5	5	10	9
Internet users (%)	..	..	77	84
Account at a financial institution (% age 15+)	..	..	97	96
Mobile account (% age 15+)	..	..	..	..
Saved any money last year (% age 15+)	..	..	84	75
Public life and decision making				
Seats held by women in national parliament (%)			31	
Female legislators, senior officials and managers (% of total)	30		27	
Proportion of women in ministerial level positions (%)	..		31	
Agency				
Total fertility rate (births per woman)	1.4		1.4	
Adolescent fertility rate (births per 1,000 women ages 15-19)	14		7	
Women first married by age 18 (% of women ages 20-24)	..		..	

Azerbaijan

Europe & Central Asia   **Upper middle income**

Population (millions)	10
GNI, Atlas ($ billions)	72
GNI per capita, Atlas ($)	7,590
Population living below $1.90 a day (%)	..

	2000		2013	
	Female	Male	Female	Male
Education				
Net primary enrollment rate (%)	88	88	88	90
Net secondary enrollment rate (%)	..		86	88
Gross tertiary enrollment ratio (% of relevant age group)	..	..	21	20
Primary completion rate (% of relevant age group)	85	94	92	92
Progression to secondary school (%)	97	99	100	98
Lower secondary completion rate (% of relevant age group)	37	40	93	95
Gross tertiary graduation ratio (%)	11	15	14	17
Female share of graduates in eng., manf. and constr. (%, tertiary)	..		24	
Youth literacy rate (% of population ages 15–24)	100	100	100[a]	100[a]
Health and related services				
Sex ratio at birth (male births per female births)	1.17		1.14	
Under-five mortality rate (per 1,000 live births)	68	80	29	34
Life expectancy at birth (years)	70	64	74	68
Pregnant women receiving prenatal care (%)	66		..	
Births attended by skilled health staff (% of total)	84		99	
Maternal mortality ratio (per 100,000 live births)	57		26	
Women's share of population ages 15+ living with HIV (%)	29		30	
Prevalence of HIV (% ages 15–24)	0.1	0.1	0.1	0.1
Economic structure, participation, and access to resources				
Labor force participation rate (% of population ages 15+)	57	72	63	70
Labor force participation rate (% of ages 15–24)	46	48	42	28
Wage and salaried workers (% of employed ages 15+)	..	..	29	38
Self-employed workers (% of employed ages 15+)	..	..	71	63
Unpaid family workers (% of employed ages 15+)	..	..	33.7	26.3
Employment in agriculture (% of employed ages 15+)	46	36	44	32
Employment in industry (% of employed ages 15+)	8	14	6	22
Employment in services (% of employed ages 15+)	46	50	50	46
Women in wage employment in the nonagricultural sector (%)	48		43	
Women's share of part-time employment (% of total)	..		..	
Maternity leave (days paid)			126	
Maternity leave benefits (% of wages paid)	..		100	
Employment to population ratio (% ages 15+)	50	64	59	67
Employment to population ratio (% ages 15–24)	34	34	35	24
Firms with female participation in ownership (%)	..		4	
Firms with a female top manager (%)	..		2	
Children in employment (% of children ages 7–14)	7	12	..	..
Unemployment rate (% of labor force ages 15+)	13	11	7	4
Unemployment rate (% of labor force ages 15–24)	27	29	16	13
Internet users (%)	..	..	..	..
Account at a financial institution (% age 15+)	..	..	26	33
Mobile account (% age 15+)	..	..	..	..
Saved any money last year (% age 15+)	..	..	38	41
Public life and decision making				
Seats held by women in national parliament (%)	..		16	
Female legislators, senior officials and managers (% of total)	..		..	
Proportion of women in ministerial level positions (%)	..		3	
Agency				
Total fertility rate (births per woman)	2.0		2.0	
Adolescent fertility rate (births per 1,000 women ages 15–19)	37		59	
Women first married by age 18 (% of women ages 20–24)	..		..	

Bahamas, The

High income

Population (thousands)	383
GNI, Atlas ($ billions)	8
GNI per capita, Atlas ($)	20,980
Population living below $1.90 a day (%)	..

	2000		2013	
	Female	**Male**	**Female**	**Male**
Education				
Net primary enrollment rate (%)	90	92	..	..
Net secondary enrollment rate (%)	70	71	86	80
Gross tertiary enrollment ratio (% of relevant age group)	..	..	..	..
Primary completion rate (% of relevant age group)	84	80	95	92
Progression to secondary school (%)	..	..	..	..
Lower secondary completion rate (% of relevant age group)	81	82	97	96
Gross tertiary graduation ratio (%)	..		..	
Female share of graduates in eng., manf. and constr. (%, tertiary)	..		..	
Youth literacy rate (% of population ages 15-24)	..	..	..	..
Health and related services				
Sex ratio at birth (male births per female births)	1.06		1.06	
Under-five mortality rate (per 1,000 live births)	15	17	11	13
Life expectancy at birth (years)	75	69	78	72
Pregnant women receiving prenatal care (%)	87		..	
Births attended by skilled health staff (% of total)	99		99	
Maternal mortality ratio (per 100,000 live births)	44		37	
Women's share of population ages 15+ living with HIV (%)	..		..	
Prevalence of HIV (% ages 15-24)	..	..	..	..
Economic structure, participation, and access to resources				
Labor force participation rate (% of population ages 15+)	66	75	69	79
Labor force participation rate (% of ages 15-24)	51	57	55	61
Wage and salaried workers (% of employed ages 15+)	90	81	90	81
Self-employed workers (% of employed ages 15+)	9	18	9	19
Unpaid family workers (% of employed ages 15+)	0.2	0.0	0.4	0.2
Employment in agriculture (% of employed ages 15+)	1	7	2	6
Employment in industry (% of employed ages 15+)	6	27	4	22
Employment in services (% of employed ages 15+)	92	66	94	72
Women in wage employment in the nonagricultural sector (%)	50		52	
Women's share of part-time employment (% of total)	53		..	
Maternity leave (days paid)	..		91	
Maternity leave benefits (% of wages paid)	..		100	
Employment to population ratio (% ages 15+)	60	71	60	69
Employment to population ratio (% ages 15-24)	41	50	38	45
Firms with female participation in ownership (%)	..		58	
Firms with a female top manager (%)	..		33	
Children in employment (% of children ages 7-14)	..	..	..	..
Unemployment rate (% of labor force ages 15+)	9	6	14	13
Unemployment rate (% of labor force ages 15-24)	20	11	31	27
Internet users (%)	..	..	67	62
Account at a financial institution (% age 15+)	..	..	..	..
Mobile account (% age 15+)	..	..	..	..
Saved any money last year (% age 15+)	..	..	..	..
Public life and decision making				
Seats held by women in national parliament (%)	..		13	
Female legislators, senior officials and managers (% of total)	40		52	
Proportion of women in ministerial level positions (%)	..		20	
Agency				
Total fertility rate (births per woman)	2.1		1.9	
Adolescent fertility rate (births per 1,000 women ages 15-19)	51		31	
Women first married by age 18 (% of women ages 20-24)	..		..	

Bahrain

		High income
Population (millions)		1.4
GNI, Atlas ($ billions)		28
GNI per capita, Atlas ($)		21,050
Population living below $1.90 a day (%)		..

	2000 Female	2000 Male	2013 Female	2013 Male
Education				
Net primary enrollment rate (%)	96	97	..	..
Net secondary enrollment rate (%)	94	87	92	95
Gross tertiary enrollment ratio (% of relevant age group)	28	16	59[a]	27[a]
Primary completion rate (% of relevant age group)	99	100	..	..
Progression to secondary school (%)	100	99	100	100
Lower secondary completion rate (% of relevant age group)	99	93	99	99
Gross tertiary graduation ratio (%)	..	..		
Female share of graduates in eng., manf. and constr. (%, tertiary)	..		28[a]	
Youth literacy rate (% of population ages 15–24)	97	97	98	99
Health and related services				
Sex ratio at birth (male births per female births)	1.03		1.04	
Under-five mortality rate (per 1,000 live births)	12	13	6	6
Life expectancy at birth (years)	76	74	77	76
Pregnant women receiving prenatal care (%)	..		..	
Births attended by skilled health staff (% of total)	..		..	
Maternal mortality ratio (per 100,000 live births)	27		22	
Women's share of population ages 15+ living with HIV (%)	..		..	
Prevalence of HIV (% ages 15–24)	..	..	..	..
Economic structure, participation, and access to resources				
Labor force participation rate (% of population ages 15+)	35	86	39	87
Labor force participation rate (% of ages 15–24)	26	57	31	54
Wage and salaried workers (% of employed ages 15+)	98	95	99	96
Self-employed workers (% of employed ages 15+)	2	5	2	4
Unpaid family workers (% of employed ages 15+)	0.8	0.5	0.8	0.5
Employment in agriculture (% of employed ages 15+)	0	2	0	1
Employment in industry (% of employed ages 15+)	13	32	9	42
Employment in services (% of employed ages 15+)	86	64	90	55
Women in wage employment in the nonagricultural sector (%)	20		21	
Women's share of part-time employment (% of total)	..		..	
Maternity leave (days paid)	..		60	
Maternity leave benefits (% of wages paid)	..		100	
Employment to population ratio (% ages 15+)	31	83	32	83
Employment to population ratio (% ages 15–24)	19	46	21	40
Firms with female participation in ownership (%)	..		..	
Firms with a female top manager (%)	..			
Children in employment (% of children ages 7–14)	..	..	..	..
Unemployment rate (% of labor force ages 15+)	12	4	18	5
Unemployment rate (% of labor force ages 15–24)	28	19	33	26
Internet users (%)	..		105	82
Account at a financial institution (% age 15+)	..	..	67	90
Mobile account (% age 15+)	..	..	..	..
Saved any money last year (% age 15+)	..	..	57	70
Public life and decision making				
Seats held by women in national parliament (%)	..		8	
Female legislators, senior officials and managers (% of total)	12		..	
Proportion of women in ministerial level positions (%)	..		5	
Agency				
Total fertility rate (births per woman)	2.8		2.1	
Adolescent fertility rate (births per 1,000 women ages 15–19)	17		14	
Women first married by age 18 (% of women ages 20–24)	..		..	

Bangladesh

South Asia	Lower middle income

Population (millions)	159
GNI, Atlas ($ billions)	172
GNI per capita, Atlas ($)	1,080
Population living below $1.90 a day (%)	44

	2000		2013	
	Female	Male	Female	Male
Education				
Net primary enrollment rate (%)	..	..	93	90
Net secondary enrollment rate (%)	45	44	51	44
Gross tertiary enrollment ratio (% of relevant age group)	4	7	11	15
Primary completion rate (% of relevant age group)	..	..	80	70
Progression to secondary school (%)	..	..	..	..
Lower secondary completion rate (% of relevant age group)	56	49	65	52
Gross tertiary graduation ratio (%)	3	6	6	8
Female share of graduates in eng., manf. and constr. (%, tertiary)	10		17	
Youth literacy rate (% of population ages 15–24)	60	67	83	79
Health and related services				
Sex ratio at birth (male births per female births)	1.05		1.05	
Under-five mortality rate (per 1,000 live births)	85	91	35	40
Life expectancy at birth (years)	66	65	71	70
Pregnant women receiving prenatal care (%)	33		53	
Births attended by skilled health staff (% of total)	12		34	
Maternal mortality ratio (per 100,000 live births)	340		170	
Women's share of population ages 15+ living with HIV (%)	20		33	
Prevalence of HIV (% ages 15–24)	0.1	0.1	0.1	0.1
Economic structure, participation, and access to resources				
Labor force participation rate (% of population ages 15+)	54	86	57	84
Labor force participation rate (% of ages 15–24)	52	72	51	67
Wage and salaried workers (% of employed ages 15+)	8	15	..	..
Self-employed workers (% of employed ages 15+)	84	60	..	..
Unpaid family workers (% of employed ages 15+)	73.2	10.1	..	..
Employment in agriculture (% of employed ages 15+)	77	53	..	..
Employment in industry (% of employed ages 15+)	9	11	..	..
Employment in services (% of employed ages 15+)	12	30	..	..
Women in wage employment in the nonagricultural sector (%)	25		18	
Women's share of part-time employment (% of total)	..		..	
Maternity leave (days paid)			112	
Maternity leave benefits (% of wages paid)	..		100	
Employment to population ratio (% ages 15+)	52	83	55	81
Employment to population ratio (% ages 15–24)	47	65	46	61
Firms with female participation in ownership (%)	..		13	
Firms with a female top manager (%)	..		5	
Children in employment (% of children ages 7–14)	..	..	..	..
Unemployment rate (% of labor force ages 15+)	3	3	5	4
Unemployment rate (% of labor force ages 15–24)	9	10	10	9
Internet users (%)	..	..	5	8
Account at a financial institution (% age 15+)	..	..	25	33
Mobile account (% age 15+)	..	..	2.1	3.2
Saved any money last year (% age 15+)	..	..	25	23
Public life and decision making				
Seats held by women in national parliament (%)	..		20	
Female legislators, senior officials and managers (% of total)	..		5	
Proportion of women in ministerial level positions (%)	..		7	
Agency				
Total fertility rate (births per woman)	3.1		2.2	
Adolescent fertility rate (births per 1,000 women ages 15–19)	112		83	
Women first married by age 18 (% of women ages 20–24)	65		65	

Barbados

High income

Population (thousands)	283
GNI, Atlas ($ billions)	4
GNI per capita, Atlas ($)	14,960
Population living below $1.90 a day (%)	..

	2000		2013	
	Female	**Male**	**Female**	**Male**
Education				
Net primary enrollment rate (%)	98	92	97	97
Net secondary enrollment rate (%)	96	90	96	84
Gross tertiary enrollment ratio (% of relevant age group)	61	22	88	36
Primary completion rate (% of relevant age group)	100	98	107	101
Progression to secondary school (%)	98	100	..	..
Lower secondary completion rate (% of relevant age group)	107	98	..	..
Gross tertiary graduation ratio (%)	25	11	41	15
Female share of graduates in eng., manf. and constr. (%, tertiary)	..		9	
Youth literacy rate (% of population ages 15-24)	..	..	..	..
Health and related services				
Sex ratio at birth (male births per female births)	1.04		1.04	
Under-five mortality rate (per 1,000 live births)	15	18	12	14
Life expectancy at birth (years)	75	71	78	73
Pregnant women receiving prenatal care (%)	98		..	
Births attended by skilled health staff (% of total)	98		100	
Maternal mortality ratio (per 100,000 live births)	42		52	
Women's share of population ages 15+ living with HIV (%)	..		..	
Prevalence of HIV (% ages 15-24)	..	..	..	..
Economic structure, participation, and access to resources				
Labor force participation rate (% of population ages 15+)	64	76	66	77
Labor force participation rate (% of ages 15-24)	57	64	53	61
Wage and salaried workers (% of employed ages 15+)	92	83	88	78
Self-employed workers (% of employed ages 15+)	8	17	12	21
Unpaid family workers (% of employed ages 15+)	0.2	0.1	..	..
Employment in agriculture (% of employed ages 15+)	3	4	2	3
Employment in industry (% of employed ages 15+)	11	29	10	28
Employment in services (% of employed ages 15+)	73	57	83	63
Women in wage employment in the nonagricultural sector (%)	50		52	
Women's share of part-time employment (% of total)	..		..	
Maternity leave (days paid)	..		84	
Maternity leave benefits (% of wages paid)	..		100	
Employment to population ratio (% ages 15+)	56	71	56	69
Employment to population ratio (% ages 15-24)	45	53	37	46
Firms with female participation in ownership (%)	..		44	
Firms with a female top manager (%)	..		25	
Children in employment (% of children ages 7-14)	..	..	..	..
Unemployment rate (% of labor force ages 15+)	12	7	15	10
Unemployment rate (% of labor force ages 15-24)	22	18	30	24
Internet users (%)	..	..	..	..
Account at a financial institution (% age 15+)	..	..	..	..
Mobile account (% age 15+)	..	..	..	..
Saved any money last year (% age 15+)	..	..	..	..
Public life and decision making				
Seats held by women in national parliament (%)	..		17	
Female legislators, senior officials and managers (% of total)	35		48	
Proportion of women in ministerial level positions (%)	..		12	
Agency				
Total fertility rate (births per woman)	1.8		1.8	
Adolescent fertility rate (births per 1,000 women ages 15-19)	50		42	
Women first married by age 18 (% of women ages 20-24)	..		..	

Belarus

Europe & Central Asia   **Upper middle income**

Population (millions)	9
GNI, Atlas ($ billions)	70
GNI per capita, Atlas ($)	7,340
Population living below $1.90 a day (%)	<2

	2000 Female	2000 Male	2013 Female	2013 Male
Education				
Net primary enrollment rate (%)	..	..	94	92
Net secondary enrollment rate (%)	..	..	97	96
Gross tertiary enrollment ratio (% of relevant age group)	62	47	107	79
Primary completion rate (% of relevant age group)	100	100	100	100
Progression to secondary school (%)	100	100	99	98
Lower secondary completion rate (% of relevant age group)	95	94	99	100
Gross tertiary graduation ratio (%)	27	22	67	39
Female share of graduates in eng., manf. and constr. (%, tertiary)	..		30	
Youth literacy rate (% of population ages 15-24)	100	100	..	..
Health and related services				
Sex ratio at birth (male births per female births)	1.06		1.06	
Under-five mortality rate (per 1,000 live births)	12	16	4	5
Life expectancy at birth (years)	75	63	78	67
Pregnant women receiving prenatal care (%)	100		100	
Births attended by skilled health staff (% of total)	100		100	
Maternal mortality ratio (per 100,000 live births)	32		1	
Women's share of population ages 15+ living with HIV (%)	35		34	
Prevalence of HIV (% ages 15-24)	0.1	0.1	0.2	0.1
Economic structure, participation, and access to resources				
Labor force participation rate (% of population ages 15+)	53	65	50	63
Labor force participation rate (% of ages 15-24)	40	47	34	44
Wage and salaried workers (% of employed ages 15+)	..	..	..	..
Self-employed workers (% of employed ages 15+)	..	..	..	..
Unpaid family workers (% of employed ages 15+)	..	..	..	..
Employment in agriculture (% of employed ages 15+)	..	..	..	..
Employment in industry (% of employed ages 15+)	..	..	..	..
Employment in services (% of employed ages 15+)	..	..	..	..
Women in wage employment in the nonagricultural sector (%)	52		51	
Women's share of part-time employment (% of total)	..		..	
Maternity leave (days paid)	..		126	
Maternity leave benefits (% of wages paid)	..		100	
Employment to population ratio (% ages 15+)	50	60	48	59
Employment to population ratio (% ages 15-24)	34	41	30	39
Firms with female participation in ownership (%)			44	
Firms with a female top manager (%)	..		33	
Children in employment (% of children ages 7-14)	..	..	3	2
Unemployment rate (% of labor force ages 15+)	5	8	4	7
Unemployment rate (% of labor force ages 15-24)	13	15	13	12
Internet users (%)	..	..	52	58
Account at a financial institution (% age 15+)	..	..	72	72
Mobile account (% age 15+)	..	..	..	..
Saved any money last year (% age 15+)	..	..	52	48
Public life and decision making				
Seats held by women in national parliament (%)	..		27	
Female legislators, senior officials and managers (% of total)	..		..	
Proportion of women in ministerial level positions (%)	..		11	
Agency				
Total fertility rate (births per woman)	1.3		1.6	
Adolescent fertility rate (births per 1,000 women ages 15-19)	28		19	
Women first married by age 18 (% of women ages 20-24)	..		3	

Belgium

	High income
Population (millions)	11
GNI, Atlas ($ billions)	528
GNI per capita, Atlas ($)	47,030
Population living below $1.90 a day (%)	..

	2000		2013	
	Female	Male	Female	Male
Education				
Net primary enrollment rate (%)	99	99	98	98
Net secondary enrollment rate (%)	..	..	97	96
Gross tertiary enrollment ratio (% of relevant age group)	61	54	82	63
Primary completion rate (% of relevant age group)	..	..	92	88
Progression to secondary school (%)	..	..	..	..
Lower secondary completion rate (% of relevant age group)	..	..	99	96
Gross tertiary graduation ratio (%)	18	18	21	17
Female share of graduates in eng., manf. and constr. (%, tertiary)	22		21	
Youth literacy rate (% of population ages 15–24)	..	..	..	..
Health and related services				
Sex ratio at birth (male births per female births)	1.05		1.05	
Under-five mortality rate (per 1,000 live births)	5	7	4	5
Life expectancy at birth (years)	81	75	83	78
Pregnant women receiving prenatal care (%)	..		..	
Births attended by skilled health staff (% of total)	99		..	
Maternal mortality ratio (per 100,000 live births)	9		6	
Women's share of population ages 15+ living with HIV (%)	..		..	
Prevalence of HIV (% ages 15–24)	..	..	..	..
Economic structure, participation, and access to resources				
Labor force participation rate (% of population ages 15+)	44	61	48	59
Labor force participation rate (% of ages 15–24)	33	39	28	34
Wage and salaried workers (% of employed ages 15+)	86	82	89	81
Self-employed workers (% of employed ages 15+)	14	18	11	19
Unpaid family workers (% of employed ages 15+)	4.2	0.5	1.5	0.4
Employment in agriculture (% of employed ages 15+)	1	2	1	2
Employment in industry (% of employed ages 15+)	12	36	9	33
Employment in services (% of employed ages 15+)	87	61	91	66
Women in wage employment in the nonagricultural sector (%)	43		48	
Women's share of part-time employment (% of total)	79		80	
Maternity leave (days paid)	..		105	
Maternity leave benefits (% of wages paid)	..		77	
Employment to population ratio (% ages 15+)	40	58	44	54
Employment to population ratio (% ages 15–24)	27	34	22	25
Firms with female participation in ownership (%)	..		..	
Firms with a female top manager (%)	..			
Children in employment (% of children ages 7–14)	..	..	..	..
Unemployment rate (% of labor force ages 15+)	8	5	8	9
Unemployment rate (% of labor force ages 15–24)	18	13	22	24
Internet users (%)	..	..	80	84
Account at a financial institution (% age 15+)	..	..	100	97
Mobile account (% age 15+)	..	..	..	..
Saved any money last year (% age 15+)	..	..	71	79
Public life and decision making				
Seats held by women in national parliament (%)	..		39	
Female legislators, senior officials and managers (% of total)	32		30	
Proportion of women in ministerial level positions (%)	..		23	
Agency				
Total fertility rate (births per woman)	1.7		1.8	
Adolescent fertility rate (births per 1,000 women ages 15–19)	11		8	
Women first married by age 18 (% of women ages 20–24)	..		..	

Belize

Latin America & the Caribbean	Upper middle income
Population (thousands)	352
GNI, Atlas ($ billions)	1.5
GNI per capita, Atlas ($)	4,350
Population living below $1.90 a day (%)	..

	2000		2013	
	Female	Male	Female	Male
Education				
Net primary enrollment rate (%)	97	99	96	97
Net secondary enrollment rate (%)	60	57	77	72
Gross tertiary enrollment ratio (% of relevant age group)	19	12	33	19
Primary completion rate (% of relevant age group)	98	103	110	109
Progression to secondary school (%)	95	94	95	95
Lower secondary completion rate (% of relevant age group)	55	49	74	66
Gross tertiary graduation ratio (%)	..	..	18	9
Female share of graduates in eng., manf. and constr. (%, tertiary)	..		..	
Youth literacy rate (% of population ages 15-24)	..	..	..	..
Health and related services				
Sex ratio at birth (male births per female births)	1.03		1.03	
Under-five mortality rate (per 1,000 live births)	22	28	15	18
Life expectancy at birth (years)	74	67	77	71
Pregnant women receiving prenatal care (%)	100		96	
Births attended by skilled health staff (% of total)	100		96	
Maternal mortality ratio (per 100,000 live births)	110		45	
Women's share of population ages 15+ living with HIV (%)	44		47	
Prevalence of HIV (% ages 15-24)	1.5	1.3	0.4	0.3
Economic structure, participation, and access to resources				
Labor force participation rate (% of population ages 15+)	40	84	49	82
Labor force participation rate (% of ages 15-24)	36	71	42	65
Wage and salaried workers (% of employed ages 15+)	72	62	..	..
Self-employed workers (% of employed ages 15+)	29	38	..	..
Unpaid family workers (% of employed ages 15+)	3.5	3.3	..	..
Employment in agriculture (% of employed ages 15+)	6	37	..	..
Employment in industry (% of employed ages 15+)	12	19	..	..
Employment in services (% of employed ages 15+)	83	44	..	..
Women in wage employment in the nonagricultural sector (%)	35		..	
Women's share of part-time employment (% of total)	49		..	
Maternity leave (days paid)	..		98	
Maternity leave benefits (% of wages paid)	..		80	
Employment to population ratio (% ages 15+)	33	77	39	73
Employment to population ratio (% ages 15-24)	26	60	24	51
Firms with female participation in ownership (%)	..		30	
Firms with a female top manager (%)	..		26	
Children in employment (% of children ages 7-14)	..	..	..	..
Unemployment rate (% of labor force ages 15+)	17	8	21	11
Unemployment rate (% of labor force ages 15-24)	28	15	42	22
Internet users (%)	..	..	..	..
Account at a financial institution (% age 15+)	..	..	52	44
Mobile account (% age 15+)	..	..	..	..
Saved any money last year (% age 15+)	..	..	63	56
Public life and decision making				
Seats held by women in national parliament (%)	..		3	
Female legislators, senior officials and managers (% of total)	31		..	
Proportion of women in ministerial level positions (%)	..		13	
Agency				
Total fertility rate (births per woman)	3.6		2.7	
Adolescent fertility rate (births per 1,000 women ages 15-19)	97		67	
Women first married by age 18 (% of women ages 20-24)	..		26	

Benin

Sub-Saharan Africa	Low income
Population (millions)	11
GNI, Atlas ($ billions)	9
GNI per capita, Atlas ($)	810
Population living below $1.90 a day (%)	53

	2000 Female	Male	2013 Female	Male
Education				
Net primary enrollment rate (%)	..	..	88	100
Net secondary enrollment rate (%)	11	24	34	50
Gross tertiary enrollment ratio (% of relevant age group)	1	6	5	19
Primary completion rate (% of relevant age group)	25	49	68	83
Progression to secondary school (%)	100	98	87	90
Lower secondary completion rate (% of relevant age group)	9	21	35	55
Gross tertiary graduation ratio (%)	..	..	..	..
Female share of graduates in eng., manf. and constr. (%, tertiary)	14		17	
Youth literacy rate (% of population ages 15–24)	33	59	..	..
Health and related services				
Sex ratio at birth (male births per female births)	1.04		1.04	
Under-five mortality rate (per 1,000 live births)	139	150	95	104
Life expectancy at birth (years)	57	53	61	58
Pregnant women receiving prenatal care (%)	81		84	
Births attended by skilled health staff (% of total)	66		81	
Maternal mortality ratio (per 100,000 live births)	490		340	
Women's share of population ages 15+ living with HIV (%)	59		59	
Prevalence of HIV (% ages 15–24)	0.8	0.4	0.4	0.2
Economic structure, participation, and access to resources				
Labor force participation rate (% of population ages 15+)	64	81	68	78
Labor force participation rate (% of ages 15–24)	58	63	57	56
Wage and salaried workers (% of employed ages 15+)	..	..	..	..
Self-employed workers (% of employed ages 15+)	..	..	..	..
Unpaid family workers (% of employed ages 15+)	..	..	..	..
Employment in agriculture (% of employed ages 15+)	..	..	..	..
Employment in industry (% of employed ages 15+)	..	..	..	..
Employment in services (% of employed ages 15+)	..	..	..	..
Women in wage employment in the nonagricultural sector (%)	24		26	
Women's share of part-time employment (% of total)	..			
Maternity leave (days paid)	..		98	
Maternity leave benefits (% of wages paid)	..		100	
Employment to population ratio (% ages 15+)	64	81	67	78
Employment to population ratio (% ages 15–24)	57	62	56	55
Firms with female participation in ownership (%)	..		..	
Firms with a female top manager (%)	..		..	
Children in employment (% of children ages 7–14)	..	..	24	24
Unemployment rate (% of labor force ages 15+)	1	1	1	1
Unemployment rate (% of labor force ages 15–24)	1	1	2	2
Internet users (%)	..	..	..	..
Account at a financial institution (% age 15+)	..	..	13	19
Mobile account (% age 15+)			1.1	2.9
Saved any money last year (% age 15+)	..	..	60	62
Public life and decision making				
Seats held by women in national parliament (%)	..		7	
Female legislators, senior officials and managers (% of total)	..		..	
Proportion of women in ministerial level positions (%)	..		15	
Agency				
Total fertility rate (births per woman)	6.0		4.8	
Adolescent fertility rate (births per 1,000 women ages 15–19)	119		85	
Women first married by age 18 (% of women ages 20–24)	37		32	

Bermuda

High income

Population (thousands)	65
GNI, Atlas ($ billions)	7
GNI per capita, Atlas ($)	106,140
Population living below $1.90 a day (%)	..

	2000 Female	2000 Male	2013 Female	2013 Male
Education				
Net primary enrollment rate (%)	..	..	82	85
Net secondary enrollment rate (%)	..	..	79	68
Gross tertiary enrollment ratio (% of relevant age group)	..	..	39[a]	19[a]
Primary completion rate (% of relevant age group)	95	99	88	90
Progression to secondary school (%)	97	96	100	87
Lower secondary completion rate (% of relevant age group)	93	85	83	69
Gross tertiary graduation ratio (%)	..		..	
Female share of graduates in eng., manf. and constr. (%, tertiary)	10		9	
Youth literacy rate (% of population ages 15–24)	..	..	..	..
Health and related services				
Sex ratio at birth (male births per female births)	..		..	
Under-five mortality rate (per 1,000 live births)	..	..	..	..
Life expectancy at birth (years)	81	75	84	77
Pregnant women receiving prenatal care (%)	..		..	
Births attended by skilled health staff (% of total)	..		..	
Maternal mortality ratio (per 100,000 live births)	..		..	
Women's share of population ages 15+ living with HIV (%)	..		..	
Prevalence of HIV (% ages 15–24)	..	..	..	..
Economic structure, participation, and access to resources				
Labor force participation rate (% of population ages 15+)	..	..	..	..
Labor force participation rate (% of ages 15–24)	..	..	..	..
Wage and salaried workers (% of employed ages 15+)	..	..	..	..
Self-employed workers (% of employed ages 15+)	..	..	..	..
Unpaid family workers (% of employed ages 15+)	..	..	..	..
Employment in agriculture (% of employed ages 15+)	0	2	..	..
Employment in industry (% of employed ages 15+)	4	25	..	..
Employment in services (% of employed ages 15+)	86	65	..	..
Women in wage employment in the nonagricultural sector (%)	50		55	
Women's share of part-time employment (% of total)	..		..	
Maternity leave (days paid)	..		..	
Maternity leave benefits (% of wages paid)	..		..	
Employment to population ratio (% ages 15+)	..	..	..	..
Employment to population ratio (% ages 15–24)	..	..	..	..
Firms with female participation in ownership (%)	..		..	
Firms with a female top manager (%)	..		..	
Children in employment (% of children ages 7–14)	..	..	..	..
Unemployment rate (% of labor force ages 15+)	..	..	..	..
Unemployment rate (% of labor force ages 15–24)	..	..	..	..
Internet users (%)	..	..	..	..
Account at a financial institution (% age 15+)	..	..	..	..
Mobile account (% age 15+)	..	..	..	..
Saved any money last year (% age 15+)	..	..	..	..
Public life and decision making				
Seats held by women in national parliament (%)	..		..	
Female legislators, senior officials and managers (% of total)	55		44	
Proportion of women in ministerial level positions (%)	..		..	
Agency				
Total fertility rate (births per woman)	1.7		1.6	
Adolescent fertility rate (births per 1,000 women ages 15–19)	..		..	
Women first married by age 18 (% of women ages 20–24)	..		..	

Bhutan

South Asia			**Lower middle income**	
Population (thousands)				765
GNI, Atlas ($ billions)				1.8
GNI per capita, Atlas ($)				2,390
Population living below $1.90 a day (%)				2

	2000		2013	
	Female	Male	Female	Male
Education				
Net primary enrollment rate (%)	56	62	89	87
Net secondary enrollment rate (%)	22	23	64	56
Gross tertiary enrollment ratio (% of relevant age group)	2	3	9	13
Primary completion rate (% of relevant age group)	47	55	101	96
Progression to secondary school (%)	95	92	97	96
Lower secondary completion rate (% of relevant age group)	20	28	75	69
Gross tertiary graduation ratio (%)	..	..	..	..
Female share of graduates in eng., manf. and constr. (%, tertiary)	..		25	
Youth literacy rate (% of population ages 15–24)	..	..	..	..
Health and related services				
Sex ratio at birth (male births per female births)	1.04		1.04	
Under-five mortality rate (per 1,000 live births)	75	84	30	36
Life expectancy at birth (years)	60	60	69	68
Pregnant women receiving prenatal care (%)	51		97	
Births attended by skilled health staff (% of total)	24		65	
Maternal mortality ratio (per 100,000 live births)	390		120	
Women's share of population ages 15+ living with HIV (%)	..		..	
Prevalence of HIV (% ages 15–24)	..	..	..	..
Economic structure, participation, and access to resources				
Labor force participation rate (% of population ages 15+)	53	79	67	77
Labor force participation rate (% of ages 15–24)	43	51	51	46
Wage and salaried workers (% of employed ages 15+)	..	..	14	41
Self-employed workers (% of employed ages 15+)	..	..	86	59
Unpaid family workers (% of employed ages 15+)	..	..	3.2	3.4
Employment in agriculture (% of employed ages 15+)	..	..	75	49
Employment in industry (% of employed ages 15+)	..	..	7	10
Employment in services (% of employed ages 15+)	..	..	18	41
Women in wage employment in the nonagricultural sector (%)	24		26	
Women's share of part-time employment (% of total)	..		76	
Maternity leave (days paid)	..		56	
Maternity leave benefits (% of wages paid)	..		100	
Employment to population ratio (% ages 15+)	52	78	65	76
Employment to population ratio (% ages 15–24)	41	49	47	43
Firms with female participation in ownership (%)	..		..	
Firms with a female top manager (%)	..		..	
Children in employment (% of children ages 7–14)	..	..	..	..
Unemployment rate (% of labor force ages 15+)	2	1	3	2
Unemployment rate (% of labor force ages 15–24)	5	4	7	7
Internet users (%)	..	..	..	..
Account at a financial institution (% age 15+)	..	..	28	39
Mobile account (% age 15+)	..	..	..	..
Saved any money last year (% age 15+)	..	..	33	32
Public life and decision making				
Seats held by women in national parliament (%)			9	
Female legislators, senior officials and managers (% of total)	..		17	
Proportion of women in ministerial level positions (%)	..		10	
Agency				
Total fertility rate (births per woman)	3.6		2.2	
Adolescent fertility rate (births per 1,000 women ages 15–19)	79		23	
Women first married by age 18 (% of women ages 20–24)	..		26	

Bolivia

Latin America & the Caribbean	Lower middle income
Population (millions)	11
GNI, Atlas ($ billions)	31
GNI per capita, Atlas ($)	2,910
Population living below $1.90 a day (%)	8

	2000		2013	
	Female	Male	Female	Male
Education				
Net primary enrollment rate (%)	92	92	81	82
Net secondary enrollment rate (%)	..	..	72	71
Gross tertiary enrollment ratio (% of relevant age group)	..	..	..	..
Primary completion rate (% of relevant age group)	93	99	90	89
Progression to secondary school (%)	93	92	96	97
Lower secondary completion rate (% of relevant age group)	75	81	86	84
Gross tertiary graduation ratio (%)	..	..	..	..
Female share of graduates in eng., manf. and constr. (%, tertiary)	..		..	
Youth literacy rate (% of population ages 15–24)	96	99	99	99
Health and related services				
Sex ratio at birth (male births per female births)	1.05		1.05	
Under-five mortality rate (per 1,000 live births)	75	85	35	42
Life expectancy at birth (years)	65	61	69	65
Pregnant women receiving prenatal care (%)	83		..	
Births attended by skilled health staff (% of total)	69		84	
Maternal mortality ratio (per 100,000 live births)	330		200	
Women's share of population ages 15+ living with HIV (%)	29		31	
Prevalence of HIV (% ages 15–24)	0.1	0.2	0.1	0.2
Economic structure, participation, and access to resources				
Labor force participation rate (% of population ages 15+)	60	82	64	81
Labor force participation rate (% of ages 15–24)	46	61	50	59
Wage and salaried workers (% of employed ages 15+)	20	36	..	..
Self-employed workers (% of employed ages 15+)	74	64	..	..
Unpaid family workers (% of employed ages 15+)	36.7	14.7	..	..
Employment in agriculture (% of employed ages 15+)	35	38	..	..
Employment in industry (% of employed ages 15+)	10	27	..	..
Employment in services (% of employed ages 15+)	55	35	..	..
Women in wage employment in the nonagricultural sector (%)	39		37	
Women's share of part-time employment (% of total)	58		..	
Maternity leave (days paid)	..		90	
Maternity leave benefits (% of wages paid)	..		100	
Employment to population ratio (% ages 15+)	56	79	62	79
Employment to population ratio (% ages 15–24)	42	56	47	57
Firms with female participation in ownership (%)	..		41	
Firms with a female top manager (%)	..		22	
Children in employment (% of children ages 7–14)	23	24	..	..
Unemployment rate (% of labor force ages 15+)	6	4	3	2
Unemployment rate (% of labor force ages 15–24)	11	8	6	4
Internet users (%)	..	..	34	40
Account at a financial institution (% age 15+)	..	..	38	44
Mobile account (% age 15+)	..	..	0.9	4.8
Saved any money last year (% age 15+)	..	..	60	69
Public life and decision making				
Seats held by women in national parliament (%)	..		53	
Female legislators, senior officials and managers (% of total)	39		..	
Proportion of women in ministerial level positions (%)	..		29	
Agency				
Total fertility rate (births per woman)	4.1		3.2	
Adolescent fertility rate (births per 1,000 women ages 15–19)	90		71	
Women first married by age 18 (% of women ages 20–24)	21		..	

Bosnia and Herzegovina

Europe & Central Asia	Upper middle income
Population (millions)	4
GNI, Atlas ($ billions)	18
GNI per capita, Atlas ($)	4,780
Population living below $1.90 a day (%)	..

	2000		2013	
	Female	Male	Female	Male
Education				
Net primary enrollment rate (%)	..	..	..	..
Net secondary enrollment rate (%)	..	..	..	..
Gross tertiary enrollment ratio (% of relevant age group)	..	..	..	..
Primary completion rate (% of relevant age group)	..	..	..	..
Progression to secondary school (%)	..	..	..	..
Lower secondary completion rate (% of relevant age group)	..	..	..	..
Gross tertiary graduation ratio (%)	..	..	..	..
Female share of graduates in eng., manf. and constr. (%, tertiary)	..		37	
Youth literacy rate (% of population ages 15–24)	100	100	100	100
Health and related services				
Sex ratio at birth (male births per female births)	*1.07*		1.06	
Under-five mortality rate (per 1,000 live births)	8	10	5	6
Life expectancy at birth (years)	77	72	79	74
Pregnant women receiving prenatal care (%)	99		87	
Births attended by skilled health staff (% of total)	100		*100*	
Maternal mortality ratio (per 100,000 live births)	11		8	
Women's share of population ages 15+ living with HIV (%)	..		..	
Prevalence of HIV (% ages 15–24)	..	..	..	..
Economic structure, participation, and access to resources				
Labor force participation rate (% of population ages 15+)	33	58	34	57
Labor force participation rate (% of ages 15–24)	24	38	26	39
Wage and salaried workers (% of employed ages 15+)	..	..	76	74
Self-employed workers (% of employed ages 15+)	..	..	24	26
Unpaid family workers (% of employed ages 15+)	..	..	8.8	2.1
Employment in agriculture (% of employed ages 15+)	..	..	23	19
Employment in industry (% of employed ages 15+)	..	..	17	38
Employment in services (% of employed ages 15+)	..	..	61	42
Women in wage employment in the nonagricultural sector (%)	..		38	
Women's share of part-time employment (% of total)	..		41	
Maternity leave (days paid)			365	
Maternity leave benefits (% of wages paid)	..		60	
Employment to population ratio (% ages 15+)	24	45	24	42
Employment to population ratio (% ages 15–24)	11	20	10	16
Firms with female participation in ownership (%)	..		27	
Firms with a female top manager (%)	..		24	
Children in employment (% of children ages 7–14)	18	23	..	..
Unemployment rate (% of labor force ages 15+)	27	24	31	27
Unemployment rate (% of labor force ages 15–24)	55	49	62	60
Internet users (%)	..	..	..	..
Account at a financial institution (% age 15+)	..	..	47	59
Mobile account (% age 15+)	..	..	..	..
Saved any money last year (% age 15+)	..	..	24	27
Public life and decision making				
Seats held by women in national parliament (%)	..		21	
Female legislators, senior officials and managers (% of total)	..		..	
Proportion of women in ministerial level positions (%)	..		0	
Agency				
Total fertility rate (births per woman)	1.4		1.3	
Adolescent fertility rate (births per 1,000 women ages 15–19)	20		9	
Women first married by age 18 (% of women ages 20–24)	..		4	

Botswana

Sub-Saharan Africa			Upper middle income	
Population (millions)				2
GNI, Atlas ($ billions)				16
GNI per capita, Atlas ($)				7,240
Population living below $1.90 a day (%)				..

	2000		2013	
	Female	Male	Female	Male
Education				
Net primary enrollment rate (%)	82	79	91	90
Net secondary enrollment rate (%)	57	50	..	..
Gross tertiary enrollment ratio (% of relevant age group)	5	6	28	22
Primary completion rate (% of relevant age group)	91	87	99	96
Progression to secondary school (%)	97	95	..	..
Lower secondary completion rate (% of relevant age group)	91	81	89	87
Gross tertiary graduation ratio (%)	..	..	..	..
Female share of graduates in eng., manf. and constr. (%, tertiary)	..		..	
Youth literacy rate (% of population ages 15–24)	..	..	99	96
Health and related services				
Sex ratio at birth (male births per female births)	1.03		1.03	
Under-five mortality rate (per 1,000 live births)	79	87	40	47
Life expectancy at birth (years)	52	49	47	48
Pregnant women receiving prenatal care (%)	97		..	
Births attended by skilled health staff (% of total)	94		..	
Maternal mortality ratio (per 100,000 live births)	390		170	
Women's share of population ages 15+ living with HIV (%)	56		57	
Prevalence of HIV (% ages 15–24)	17.4	9.4	8.9	5.7
Economic structure, participation, and access to resources				
Labor force participation rate (% of population ages 15+)	70	80	72	82
Labor force participation rate (% of ages 15–24)	57	62	57	61
Wage and salaried workers (% of employed ages 15+)	..	..	65	71
Self-employed workers (% of employed ages 15+)	..	..	18	13
Unpaid family workers (% of employed ages 15+)	..	..	6.2	5.3
Employment in agriculture (% of employed ages 15+)	17	22	..	..
Employment in industry (% of employed ages 15+)	14	26	..	..
Employment in services (% of employed ages 15+)	67	51	..	..
Women in wage employment in the nonagricultural sector (%)	43		41	
Women's share of part-time employment (% of total)	..		..	
Maternity leave (days paid)			84	
Maternity leave benefits (% of wages paid)			50	
Employment to population ratio (% ages 15+)	53	64	56	69
Employment to population ratio (% ages 15–24)	31	40	34	44
Firms with female participation in ownership (%)	..		55	
Firms with a female top manager (%)	..		16	
Children in employment (% of children ages 7–14)				
Unemployment rate (% of labor force ages 15+)	24	21	22	16
Unemployment rate (% of labor force ages 15–24)	45	36	40	29
Internet users (%)	..	..	..	..
Account at a financial institution (% age 15+)	..	..	46	53
Mobile account (% age 15+)	..	..	19.5	22.1
Saved any money last year (% age 15+)	..	..	57	59
Public life and decision making				
Seats held by women in national parliament (%)	..		10	
Female legislators, senior officials and managers (% of total)	35		39	
Proportion of women in ministerial level positions (%)	..		13	
Agency				
Total fertility rate (births per woman)	3.4		2.6	
Adolescent fertility rate (births per 1,000 women ages 15–19)	65		34	
Women first married by age 18 (% of women ages 20–24)	..		..	

Brazil

Latin America & the Caribbean	Upper middle income
Population (millions)	206
GNI, Atlas ($ billions)	2,375
GNI per capita, Atlas ($)	11,530
Population living below $1.90 a day (%)	5

	2000 Female	2000 Male	2013 Female	2013 Male
Education				
Net primary enrollment rate (%)	..	..	..	..
Net secondary enrollment rate (%)	..	..	..	..
Gross tertiary enrollment ratio (% of relevant age group)	..	..	..	..
Primary completion rate (% of relevant age group)	..	..	..	..
Progression to secondary school (%)	..	..	..	..
Lower secondary completion rate (% of relevant age group)	..	..	..	..
Gross tertiary graduation ratio (%)	..	..	..	..
Female share of graduates in eng., manf. and constr. (%, tertiary)	31		30	
Youth literacy rate (% of population ages 15–24)	96	93	99	98
Health and related services				
Sex ratio at birth (male births per female births)	1.05		1.05	
Under-five mortality rate (per 1,000 live births)	29	35	15	18
Life expectancy at birth (years)	74	67	78	70
Pregnant women receiving prenatal care (%)	..		..	
Births attended by skilled health staff (% of total)	96		98	
Maternal mortality ratio (per 100,000 live births)	85		69	
Women's share of population ages 15+ living with HIV (%)	..		..	
Prevalence of HIV (% ages 15–24)	..	..	..	..
Economic structure, participation, and access to resources				
Labor force participation rate (% of population ages 15+)	55	82	59	81
Labor force participation rate (% of ages 15–24)	52	74	55	71
Wage and salaried workers (% of employed ages 15+)	74	62	..	..
Self-employed workers (% of employed ages 15+)	24	34	..	..
Unpaid family workers (% of employed ages 15+)	5.5	3.1	..	..
Employment in agriculture (% of employed ages 15+)	16	24	11	18
Employment in industry (% of employed ages 15+)	10	27	12	29
Employment in services (% of employed ages 15+)	74	50	77	52
Women in wage employment in the nonagricultural sector (%)	46		47	
Women's share of part-time employment (% of total)	69		..	
Maternity leave (days paid)	..		120	
Maternity leave benefits (% of wages paid)	..		100	
Employment to population ratio (% ages 15+)	48	76	55	77
Employment to population ratio (% ages 15-24)	40	63	45	63
Firms with female participation in ownership (%)	..		..	
Firms with a female top manager (%)	..		..	
Children in employment (% of children ages 7–14)	..	..	3	6
Unemployment rate (% of labor force ages 15+)	12	8	8	5
Unemployment rate (% of labor force ages 15–24)	23	15	18	11
Internet users (%)	..	..	53	49
Account at a financial institution (% age 15+)	..	..	65	72
Mobile account (% age 15+)	..	..	0.4	1.3
Saved any money last year (% age 15+)	..	..	25	32
Public life and decision making				
Seats held by women in national parliament (%)	..		10	
Female legislators, senior officials and managers (% of total)	31		..	
Proportion of women in ministerial level positions (%)	..		15	
Agency				
Total fertility rate (births per woman)	2.4		1.8	
Adolescent fertility rate (births per 1,000 women ages 15–19)	82		67	
Women first married by age 18 (% of women ages 20–24)	..		..	

Brunei Darussalam

Population (thousands)	417
GNI, Atlas ($ billions)	15
GNI per capita, Atlas ($)	37,320
Population living below $1.90 a day (%)	..

	2000		2013	
	Female	Male	Female	Male
Education				
Net primary enrollment rate (%)	..	..	91	91
Net secondary enrollment rate (%)	..	..	93	91
Gross tertiary enrollment ratio (% of relevant age group)	16	9	33	18
Primary completion rate (% of relevant age group)	113	119	97	99
Progression to secondary school (%)	93	87	99	100
Lower secondary completion rate (% of relevant age group)	..	..	109	109
Gross tertiary graduation ratio (%)	7	5	21	9
Female share of graduates in eng., manf. and constr. (%, tertiary)	42		42	
Youth literacy rate (% of population ages 15-24)	99	99	100	99
Health and related services				
Sex ratio at birth (male births per female births)	1.06		1.06	
Under-five mortality rate (per 1,000 live births)	9	10	9	11
Life expectancy at birth (years)	78	74	80	77
Pregnant women receiving prenatal care (%)	..			
Births attended by skilled health staff (% of total)	99		..	
Maternal mortality ratio (per 100,000 live births)	24		27	
Women's share of population ages 15+ living with HIV (%)	..		..	
Prevalence of HIV (% ages 15-24)	..	..	..	..
Economic structure, participation, and access to resources				
Labor force participation rate (% of population ages 15+)	56	80	53	75
Labor force participation rate (% of ages 15-24)	44	54	41	51
Wage and salaried workers (% of employed ages 15+)	..	..	..	..
Self-employed workers (% of employed ages 15+)	..	..	..	..
Unpaid family workers (% of employed ages 15+)	..	..	..	..
Employment in agriculture (% of employed ages 15+)	0	2	..	..
Employment in industry (% of employed ages 15+)	11	29	..	..
Employment in services (% of employed ages 15+)	88	69	..	..
Women in wage employment in the nonagricultural sector (%)	30		..	
Women's share of part-time employment (% of total)	..		..	
Maternity leave (days paid)	..		91	
Maternity leave benefits (% of wages paid)	..		100	
Employment to population ratio (% ages 15+)	53	77	50	73
Employment to population ratio (% ages 15-24)	39	48	36	45
Firms with female participation in ownership (%)	..		..	
Firms with a female top manager (%)	..		..	
Children in employment (% of children ages 7-14)	..	..	..	..
Unemployment rate (% of labor force ages 15+)	5	4	4	4
Unemployment rate (% of labor force ages 15-24)	12	11	13	11
Internet users (%)	..	..	..	..
Account at a financial institution (% age 15+)	..	..	..	..
Mobile account (% age 15+)	..	..	..	..
Saved any money last year (% age 15+)	..	..	..	..
Public life and decision making				
Seats held by women in national parliament (%)	..		..	
Female legislators, senior officials and managers (% of total)	26		..	
Proportion of women in ministerial level positions (%)	..		0	
Agency				
Total fertility rate (births per woman)	2.4		2.0	
Adolescent fertility rate (births per 1,000 women ages 15-19)	26		21	
Women first married by age 18 (% of women ages 20-24)	..		..	

Bulgaria

Europe & Central Asia | **Upper middle income**

Population (millions)	7
GNI, Atlas ($ billions)	54
GNI per capita, Atlas ($)	7,420
Population living below $1.90 a day (%)	2

	2000		2013	
	Female	**Male**	**Female**	**Male**
Education				
Net primary enrollment rate (%)	95	97	95	95
Net secondary enrollment rate (%)	85	87	86	89
Gross tertiary enrollment ratio (% of relevant age group)	52	37	75	59
Primary completion rate (% of relevant age group)	96	97	96	98
Progression to secondary school (%)	99	100	99	100
Lower secondary completion rate (% of relevant age group)	55	66	38	47
Gross tertiary graduation ratio (%)	27	11	43	27
Female share of graduates in eng., manf. and constr. (%, tertiary)	40		33	
Youth literacy rate (% of population ages 15–24)	98	98	98	98
Health and related services				
Sex ratio at birth (male births per female births)	1.06		1.06	
Under-five mortality rate (per 1,000 live births)	19	23	9	12
Life expectancy at birth (years)	75	68	78	71
Pregnant women receiving prenatal care (%)	..		..	
Births attended by skilled health staff (% of total)	100		100	
Maternal mortality ratio (per 100,000 live births)	29		5	
Women's share of population ages 15+ living with HIV (%)	..		..	
Prevalence of HIV (% ages 15–24)	..	..	..	..
Economic structure, participation, and access to resources				
Labor force participation rate (% of population ages 15+)	44	56	48	59
Labor force participation rate (% of ages 15–24)	26	35	25	35
Wage and salaried workers (% of employed ages 15+)	87	80	91	85
Self-employed workers (% of employed ages 15+)	13	19	9	15
Unpaid family workers (% of employed ages 15+)	2.4	1.1	0.9	0.4
Employment in agriculture (% of employed ages 15+)	11	15	4	8
Employment in industry (% of employed ages 15+)	27	38	25	37
Employment in services (% of employed ages 15+)	62	47	71	55
Women in wage employment in the nonagricultural sector (%)	50		50	
Women's share of part-time employment (% of total)	54		53	
Maternity leave (days paid)	..		410	
Maternity leave benefits (% of wages paid)	..		90	
Employment to population ratio (% ages 15+)	37	47	42	51
Employment to population ratio (% ages 15–24)	18	22	18	24
Firms with female participation in ownership (%)	..		39	
Firms with a female top manager (%)	..		24	
Children in employment (% of children ages 7–14)	..	..	..	..
Unemployment rate (% of labor force ages 15+)	16	17	12	14
Unemployment rate (% of labor force ages 15–24)	30	36	26	32
Internet users (%)	..	..	52	54
Account at a financial institution (% age 15+)	..	..	63	63
Mobile account (% age 15+)	..	..	..	..
Saved any money last year (% age 15+)	..	..	25	30
Public life and decision making				
Seats held by women in national parliament (%)	..		20	
Female legislators, senior officials and managers (% of total)	30		37	
Proportion of women in ministerial level positions (%)	..		35	
Agency				
Total fertility rate (births per woman)	1.3		1.5	
Adolescent fertility rate (births per 1,000 women ages 15–19)	44		39	
Women first married by age 18 (% of women ages 20–24)	..		..	

Burkina Faso

Sub-Saharan Africa				Low income

Population (millions)				18
GNI, Atlas ($ billions)				12
GNI per capita, Atlas ($)				710
Population living below $1.90 a day (%)				..

	2000		2013	
	Female	Male	Female	Male
Education				
Net primary enrollment rate (%)	30	42	66	69
Net secondary enrollment rate (%)	6	10	20	23
Gross tertiary enrollment ratio (% of relevant age group)	0	2	3	6
Primary completion rate (% of relevant age group)	21	30	63	63
Progression to secondary school (%)	62	62	67	69
Lower secondary completion rate (% of relevant age group)	5	8	20	23
Gross tertiary graduation ratio (%)	..	..	..	..
Female share of graduates in eng., manf. and constr. (%, tertiary)	..		21	
Youth literacy rate (% of population ages 15–24)	..	..	..	..
Health and related services				
Sex ratio at birth (male births per female births)	1.05		1.05	
Under-five mortality rate (per 1,000 live births)	179	192	83	94
Life expectancy at birth (years)	52	49	57	56
Pregnant women receiving prenatal care (%)	61		94	
Births attended by skilled health staff (% of total)	31		66	
Maternal mortality ratio (per 100,000 live births)	580		400	
Women's share of population ages 15+ living with HIV (%)	59		60	
Prevalence of HIV (% ages 15–24)	0.7	0.4	0.5	0.4
Economic structure, participation, and access to resources				
Labor force participation rate (% of population ages 15+)	77	90	77	90
Labor force participation rate (% of ages 15–24)	74	83	72	81
Wage and salaried workers (% of employed ages 15+)	..	..	..	..
Self-employed workers (% of employed ages 15+)	..	..	..	..
Unpaid family workers (% of employed ages 15+)	..	..	..	..
Employment in agriculture (% of employed ages 15+)	..	..	..	..
Employment in industry (% of employed ages 15+)	..	..	..	..
Employment in services (% of employed ages 15+)	..	..	..	..
Women in wage employment in the nonagricultural sector (%)	23		..	
Women's share of part-time employment (% of total)	..		..	
Maternity leave (days paid)	..		98	
Maternity leave benefits (% of wages paid)	..		100	
Employment to population ratio (% ages 15+)	75	87	75	87
Employment to population ratio (% ages 15–24)	71	78	69	76
Firms with female participation in ownership (%)	..		..	
Firms with a female top manager (%)	..		..	
Children in employment (% of children ages 7–14)	..	..	45	56
Unemployment rate (% of labor force ages 15+)	2	4	2	4
Unemployment rate (% of labor force ages 15–24)	4	6	4	6
Internet users (%)	..	..	..	..
Account at a financial institution (% age 15+)	..	..	12	15
Mobile account (% age 15+)	..	..	3.1	3.1
Saved any money last year (% age 15+)	..	..	52	49
Public life and decision making				
Seats held by women in national parliament (%)	..		13	
Female legislators, senior officials and managers (% of total)	..		..	
Proportion of women in ministerial level positions (%)	..		13	
Agency				
Total fertility rate (births per woman)	6.6		5.6	
Adolescent fertility rate (births per 1,000 women ages 15–19)	139		110	
Women first married by age 18 (% of women ages 20–24)	62		52	

Burundi

Sub-Saharan Africa				Low income
Population (millions)				11
GNI, Atlas ($ billions)				3
GNI per capita, Atlas ($)				270
Population living below $1.90 a day (%)				..

	2000		2013	
	Female	Male	Female	Male
Education				
Net primary enrollment rate (%)	37	45	90	100
Net secondary enrollment rate (%)	..	..	21	22
Gross tertiary enrollment ratio (% of relevant age group)	1	2	3	6
Primary completion rate (% of relevant age group)	22	26	72	67
Progression to secondary school (%)	..	..	73	79
Lower secondary completion rate (% of relevant age group)	..	..	21	27
Gross tertiary graduation ratio (%)	0	1	2	5
Female share of graduates in eng., manf. and constr. (%, tertiary)	0		14	
Youth literacy rate (% of population ages 15–24)	70	77	..	..
Health and related services				
Sex ratio at birth (male births per female births)	1.03		1.03	
Under-five mortality rate (per 1,000 live births)	143	161	76	88
Life expectancy at birth (years)	49	47	56	52
Pregnant women receiving prenatal care (%)	78		99	
Births attended by skilled health staff (% of total)	25		60	
Maternal mortality ratio (per 100,000 live births)	1,000		740	
Women's share of population ages 15+ living with HIV (%)	54		59	
Prevalence of HIV (% ages 15–24)	1.6	0.9	0.4	0.3
Economic structure, participation, and access to resources				
Labor force participation rate (% of population ages 15+)	85	84	83	82
Labor force participation rate (% of population ages 15–24)	73	68	68	61
Wage and salaried workers (% of employed ages 15+)	2	10	..	..
Self-employed workers (% of employed ages 15+)	98	90	..	..
Unpaid family workers (% of employed ages 15+)	9.4	3.6	..	..
Employment in agriculture (% of employed ages 15+)	97	87	..	..
Employment in industry (% of employed ages 15+)	1	4	..	..
Employment in services (% of employed ages 15+)	3	9	..	..
Women in wage employment in the nonagricultural sector (%)	..		..	
Women's share of part-time employment (% of total)	..		..	
Maternity leave (days paid)			84	
Maternity leave benefits (% of wages paid)			100	
Employment to population ratio (% ages 15+)	78	78	77	77
Employment to population ratio (% ages 15–24)	64	61	60	55
Firms with female participation in ownership (%)			44[a]	
Firms with a female top manager (%)	..		16[a]	
Children in employment (% of children ages 7–14)	36	38	32	31
Unemployment rate (% of labor force ages 15+)	8	7	7	6
Unemployment rate (% of labor force ages 15–24)	12	10	11	10
Internet users (%)	..	..	..	..
Account at a financial institution (% age 15+)	..	..	7	7
Mobile account (% age 15+)	..	..	0.7	0.8
Saved any money last year (% age 15+)	..	..	32	38
Public life and decision making				
Seats held by women in national parliament (%)	..		30	
Female legislators, senior officials and managers (% of total)	..		..	
Proportion of women in ministerial level positions (%)	..		35	
Agency				
Total fertility rate (births per woman)	7.1		6.0	
Adolescent fertility rate (births per 1,000 women ages 15–19)	41		29	
Women first married by age 18 (% of women ages 20–24)	..		20	

Cabo Verde

Sub-Saharan Africa	**Lower middle income**
Population (thousands)	514
GNI, Atlas ($ billions)	1.8
GNI per capita, Atlas ($)	3,450
Population living below $1.90 a day (%)	..

	2000		2013	
	Female	Male	Female	Male
Education				
Net primary enrollment rate (%)	98	100	97	99
Net secondary enrollment rate (%)	59	55	75	65
Gross tertiary enrollment ratio (% of relevant age group)	2	2	27	19
Primary completion rate (% of relevant age group)	107	104	94	96
Progression to secondary school (%)	90	85	98	94
Lower secondary completion rate (% of relevant age group)	..	..	88	70
Gross tertiary graduation ratio (%)	..	..	8	5
Female share of graduates in eng., manf. and constr. (%, tertiary)	..		..	
Youth literacy rate (% of population ages 15-24)	..	..	98	98
Health and related services				
Sex ratio at birth (male births per female births)	1.03		1.03	
Under-five mortality rate (per 1,000 live births)	32	39	22	27
Life expectancy at birth (years)	74	66	79	71
Pregnant women receiving prenatal care (%)	99		..	
Births attended by skilled health staff (% of total)	89		..	
Maternal mortality ratio (per 100,000 live births)	84		53	
Women's share of population ages 15+ living with HIV (%)	38		26	
Prevalence of HIV (% ages 15-24)	0.5	0.6	0.3	0.8
Economic structure, participation, and access to resources				
Labor force participation rate (% of population ages 15+)	46	84	52	84
Labor force participation rate (% of ages 15-24)	46	75	47	72
Wage and salaried workers (% of employed ages 15+)	33	44	..	..
Self-employed workers (% of employed ages 15+)	46	39	..	..
Unpaid family workers (% of employed ages 15+)	14.8	6.5	..	..
Employment in agriculture (% of employed ages 15+)	..	..	..	..
Employment in industry (% of employed ages 15+)	..	..	..	..
Employment in services (% of employed ages 15+)	..	..	..	..
Women in wage employment in the nonagricultural sector (%)	39		..	
Women's share of part-time employment (% of total)	..		..	
Maternity leave (days paid)	..			
Maternity leave benefits (% of wages paid)	..		..	
Employment to population ratio (% ages 15+)	43	78	48	78
Employment to population ratio (% ages 15-24)	41	67	42	65
Firms with female participation in ownership (%)	..		..	
Firms with a female top manager (%)	..		..	
Children in employment (% of children ages 7-14)	..	..	7	..
Unemployment rate (% of labor force ages 15+)	8	7	7	7
Unemployment rate (% of labor force ages 15-24)	11	10	11	10
Internet users (%)	..	..	..	..
Account at a financial institution (% age 15+)	..	..	..	..
Mobile account (% age 15+)	..	..	..	..
Saved any money last year (% age 15+)	..	..	..	..
Public life and decision making				
Seats held by women in national parliament (%)	..		21	
Female legislators, senior officials and managers (% of total)	..		..	
Proportion of women in ministerial level positions (%)	..		53	
Agency				
Total fertility rate (births per woman)	3.7		2.3	
Adolescent fertility rate (births per 1,000 women ages 15-19)	98		74	
Women first married by age 18 (% of women ages 20-24)	..		..	

Cambodia

East Asia & Pacific		**Low income**
Population (millions)		15
GNI, Atlas ($ billions)		16
GNI per capita, Atlas ($)		1,020
Population living below $1.90 a day (%)		6

	2000		2013	
	Female	Male	Female	Male
Education				
Net primary enrollment rate (%)	87	97	97	100
Net secondary enrollment rate (%)	11	20	..	..
Gross tertiary enrollment ratio (% of relevant age group)	1	4	12	20
Primary completion rate (% of relevant age group)	46	56	95	100
Progression to secondary school (%)	72	83	81	79
Lower secondary completion rate (% of relevant age group)	11	22	48	48
Gross tertiary graduation ratio (%)	1	3	..	..
Female share of graduates in eng., manf. and constr. (%, tertiary)	2		..	
Youth literacy rate (% of population ages 15–24)	71	82	..	..
Health and related services				
Sex ratio at birth (male births per female births)	1.03		1.05	
Under-five mortality rate (per 1,000 live births)	100	116	25	32
Life expectancy at birth (years)	65	59	75	69
Pregnant women receiving prenatal care (%)	38		89	
Births attended by skilled health staff (% of total)	32		74	
Maternal mortality ratio (per 100,000 live births)	540		170	
Women's share of population ages 15+ living with HIV (%)	40		53	
Prevalence of HIV (% ages 15–24)	1.3	1.2	0.2	0.1
Economic structure, participation, and access to resources				
Labor force participation rate (% of population ages 15+)	76	81	79	87
Labor force participation rate (% of ages 15–24)	72	63	73	72
Wage and salaried workers (% of employed ages 15+)	12	19	30	41
Self-employed workers (% of employed ages 15+)	88	81	70	59
Unpaid family workers (% of employed ages 15+)	59.0	26.6	9.3	8.8
Employment in agriculture (% of employed ages 15+)	75	72	53	49
Employment in industry (% of employed ages 15+)	10	7	18	19
Employment in services (% of employed ages 15+)	16	20	29	32
Women in wage employment in the nonagricultural sector (%)	41		41	
Women's share of part-time employment (% of total)	..		..	
Maternity leave (days paid)			90	
Maternity leave benefits (% of wages paid)	..		50	
Employment to population ratio (% ages 15+)	74	80	79	86
Employment to population ratio (% ages 15–24)	67	60	73	72
Firms with female participation in ownership (%)	..			
Firms with a female top manager (%)	..		..	
Children in employment (% of children ages 7–14)	52	52	12	11
Unemployment rate (% of labor force ages 15+)	3	2	0	0
Unemployment rate (% of labor force ages 15–24)	6	5	1	1
Internet users (%)	..	..	..	..
Account at a financial institution (% age 15+)	..	..	11	15
Mobile account (% age 15+)	..	..	12.8	13.9
Saved any money last year (% age 15+)	..	..	64	70
Public life and decision making				
Seats held by women in national parliament (%)	..		20	
Female legislators, senior officials and managers (% of total)	13		..	
Proportion of women in ministerial level positions (%)	..		7	
Agency				
Total fertility rate (births per woman)	3.8		2.9	
Adolescent fertility rate (births per 1,000 women ages 15–19)	50		51	
Women first married by age 18 (% of women ages 20–24)	25		18	

Cameroon

Sub-Saharan Africa	Lower middle income
Population (millions)	23
GNI, Atlas ($ billions)	31
GNI per capita, Atlas ($)	1,360
Population living below $1.90 a day (%)	..

	2000 Female	2000 Male	2013 Female	2013 Male
Education				
Net primary enrollment rate (%)	..	..	86	97
Net secondary enrollment rate (%)	..	..	37	43
Gross tertiary enrollment ratio (% of relevant age group)	4	6	10	14
Primary completion rate (% of relevant age group)	45	52	68[a]	76[a]
Progression to secondary school (%)	30	31	69	62
Lower secondary completion rate (% of relevant age group)	..	..	39	41
Gross tertiary graduation ratio (%)	..	..	..	..
Female share of graduates in eng., manf. and constr. (%, tertiary)	..		..	
Youth literacy rate (% of population ages 15–24)	78	88	76	85
Health and related services				
Sex ratio at birth (male births per female births)	1.03		1.03	
Under-five mortality rate (per 1,000 live births)	142	159	82	94
Life expectancy at birth (years)	53	51	56	54
Pregnant women receiving prenatal care (%)	75		85	
Births attended by skilled health staff (% of total)	60		64	
Maternal mortality ratio (per 100,000 live births)	740		590	
Women's share of population ages 15+ living with HIV (%)	57		59	
Prevalence of HIV (% ages 15–24)	2.9	1.5	2.1	1.2
Economic structure, participation, and access to resources				
Labor force participation rate (% of population ages 15+)	61	77	64	77
Labor force participation rate (% of ages 15–24)	44	51	44	51
Wage and salaried workers (% of employed ages 15+)	9	29	11	29
Self-employed workers (% of employed ages 15+)	89	67	89	71
Unpaid family workers (% of employed ages 15+)	27.2	9.5	37.2	22.3
Employment in agriculture (% of employed ages 15+)	65	58	58	49
Employment in industry (% of employed ages 15+)	7	11	12	13
Employment in services (% of employed ages 15+)	22	24	30	38
Women in wage employment in the nonagricultural sector (%)	22		26	
Women's share of part-time employment (% of total)	..		..	
Maternity leave (days paid)	..		98	
Maternity leave benefits (% of wages paid)	..		100	
Employment to population ratio (% ages 15+)	57	72	61	74
Employment to population ratio (% ages 15–24)	39	46	41	47
Firms with female participation in ownership (%)	..		..	
Firms with a female top manager (%)	..		..	
Children in employment (% of children ages 7–14)	17	14	60	64
Unemployment rate (% of labor force ages 15+)	7	5	4	4
Unemployment rate (% of labor force ages 15–24)	12	10	8	7
Internet users (%)	..	..	..	..
Account at a financial institution (% age 15+)	..	..	9	14
Mobile account (% age 15+)	..	..	2.1	1.5
Saved any money last year (% age 15+)	..	..	65	63
Public life and decision making				
Seats held by women in national parliament (%)	..		31	
Female legislators, senior officials and managers (% of total)	..		..	
Proportion of women in ministerial level positions (%)	..		14	
Agency				
Total fertility rate (births per woman)	5.6		4.8	
Adolescent fertility rate (births per 1,000 women ages 15–19)	156		107	
Women first married by age 18 (% of women ages 20–24)	43		38	

Canada

	High income
Population (millions)	36
GNI, Atlas ($ billions)	1,837
GNI per capita, Atlas ($)	51,690
Population living below $1.90 a day (%)	..

	2000 Female	2000 Male	2013 Female	2013 Male
Education				
Net primary enrollment rate (%)	*100*	*100*	*100*	*99*
Net secondary enrollment rate (%)	..	..	..	..
Gross tertiary enrollment ratio (% of relevant age group)	68	51	..	..
Primary completion rate (% of relevant age group)	97	97	..	..
Progression to secondary school (%)	..	..	..	..
Lower secondary completion rate (% of relevant age group)	..	..	..	..
Gross tertiary graduation ratio (%)	*38*	*25*	..	..
Female share of graduates in eng., manf. and constr. (%, tertiary)	*20*		..	
Youth literacy rate (% of population ages 15-24)	..	..	..	..
Health and related services				
Sex ratio at birth (male births per female births)	*1.05*		*1.06*	
Under-five mortality rate (per 1,000 live births)	6	7	5	5
Life expectancy at birth (years)	82	77	84	79
Pregnant women receiving prenatal care (%)	..		..	
Births attended by skilled health staff (% of total)	98		..	
Maternal mortality ratio (per 100,000 live births)	7		11	
Women's share of population ages 15+ living with HIV (%)	..		..	
Prevalence of HIV (% ages 15-24)	..	..	..	..
Economic structure, participation, and access to resources				
Labor force participation rate (% of population ages 15+)	59	72	62	71
Labor force participation rate (% of ages 15-24)	63	66	64	64
Wage and salaried workers (% of employed ages 15+)	88	81	92	90
Self-employed workers (% of employed ages 15+)	12	19	8	10
Unpaid family workers (% of employed ages 15+)	0.4	0.2	*0.1*	*0.1*
Employment in agriculture (% of employed ages 15+)	2	5	..	..
Employment in industry (% of employed ages 15+)	11	32	..	..
Employment in services (% of employed ages 15+)	87	63	..	..
Women in wage employment in the nonagricultural sector (%)	48		50	
Women's share of part-time employment (% of total)	69		67	
Maternity leave (days paid)	..		105	
Maternity leave benefits (% of wages paid)	..		34	
Employment to population ratio (% ages 15+)	55	67	58	66
Employment to population ratio (% ages 15-24)	56	57	56	54
Firms with female participation in ownership (%)	..		..	
Firms with a female top manager (%)	..		..	
Children in employment (% of children ages 7-14)	..	..	..	..
Unemployment rate (% of labor force ages 15+)	7	7	7	8
Unemployment rate (% of labor force ages 15-24)	11	14	12	15
Internet users (%)	..	..	79	82
Account at a financial institution (% age 15+)	..	..	99	99
Mobile account (% age 15+)	..	..	..	..
Saved any money last year (% age 15+)	..	..	80	85
Public life and decision making				
Seats held by women in national parliament (%)	..		25	
Female legislators, senior officials and managers (% of total)	35		..	
Proportion of women in ministerial level positions (%)	..		31	
Agency				
Total fertility rate (births per woman)	1.5		1.6	
Adolescent fertility rate (births per 1,000 women ages 15-19)	17		10	
Women first married by age 18 (% of women ages 20-24)	..		..	

Cayman Islands

High income

Population (thousands)	59
GNI, Atlas ($ millions)	..
GNI per capita, Atlas ($)	..
Population living below $1.90 a day (%)	..

	2000		2013	
	Female	Male	Female	Male
Education				
Net primary enrollment rate (%)	..		..	..
Net secondary enrollment rate (%)	..	..	..	..
Gross tertiary enrollment ratio (% of relevant age group)	..	..	..	..
Primary completion rate (% of relevant age group)	..		..	
Progression to secondary school (%)	91	94	100	93
Lower secondary completion rate (% of relevant age group)	..	..	..	..
Gross tertiary graduation ratio (%)	..		..	
Female share of graduates in eng., manf. and constr. (%, tertiary)	..		..	
Youth literacy rate (% of population ages 15–24)	..	..	..	..
Health and related services				
Sex ratio at birth (male births per female births)		..		..
Under-five mortality rate (per 1,000 live births)	..	..	..	..
Life expectancy at birth (years)	..	..	..	..
Pregnant women receiving prenatal care (%)		..		..
Births attended by skilled health staff (% of total)		..		..
Maternal mortality ratio (per 100,000 live births)		..		..
Women's share of population ages 15+ living with HIV (%)		..		..
Prevalence of HIV (% ages 15–24)	..	..	..	..
Economic structure, participation, and access to resources				
Labor force participation rate (% of population ages 15+)	..	..	..	..
Labor force participation rate (% of ages 15–24)	..	..	..	..
Wage and salaried workers (% of employed ages 15+)	..	..	..	..
Self-employed workers (% of employed ages 15+)	..	..	..	..
Unpaid family workers (% of employed ages 15+)	..	..	..	..
Employment in agriculture (% of employed ages 15+)	..	..	..	..
Employment in industry (% of employed ages 15+)	..	..	..	..
Employment in services (% of employed ages 15+)	..		..	
Women in wage employment in the nonagricultural sector (%)	51		52	
Women's share of part-time employment (% of total)	..		..	
Maternity leave (days paid)	..		..	
Maternity leave benefits (% of wages paid)	..		..	
Employment to population ratio (% ages 15+)	..	..	..	..
Employment to population ratio (% ages 15–24)	..	..	..	..
Firms with female participation in ownership (%)	..		..	
Firms with a female top manager (%)	..		..	
Children in employment (% of children ages 7–14)	..	..	..	..
Unemployment rate (% of labor force ages 15+)	..	..	..	..
Unemployment rate (% of labor force ages 15–24)	..	..	..	..
Internet users (%)	..	..	..	..
Account at a financial institution (% age 15+)	..	..	..	..
Mobile account (% age 15+)	..	..	..	..
Saved any money last year (% age 15+)	..	..	..	..
Public life and decision making				
Seats held by women in national parliament (%)	..		..	
Female legislators, senior officials and managers (% of total)	..		..	
Proportion of women in ministerial level positions (%)	..		..	
Agency				
Total fertility rate (births per woman)	..		..	
Adolescent fertility rate (births per 1,000 women ages 15–19)	..		..	
Women first married by age 18 (% of women ages 20–24)	..		..	

Central African Republic

Sub-Saharan Africa				**Low income**
Population (millions)				5
GNI, Atlas ($ billions)				1.6
GNI per capita, Atlas ($)				330
Population living below $1.90 a day (%)				..

	2000		2013	
	Female	**Male**	**Female**	**Male**
Education				
Net primary enrollment rate (%)	..	..	63	81
Net secondary enrollment rate (%)	..	..	10	18
Gross tertiary enrollment ratio (% of relevant age group)	1	3	2	4
Primary completion rate (% of relevant age group)	..	..	35	56
Progression to secondary school (%)	..	..	68	81
Lower secondary completion rate (% of relevant age group)	..	..	9	18
Gross tertiary graduation ratio (%)	..	..	..	..
Female share of graduates in eng., manf. and constr. (%, tertiary)	..		..	
Youth literacy rate (% of population ages 15-24)	49	73	27	49
Health and related services				
Sex ratio at birth (male births per female births)	1.03		1.03	
Under-five mortality rate (per 1,000 live births)	167	182	123	137
Life expectancy at birth (years)	45	42	52	48
Pregnant women receiving prenatal care (%)	62		68	
Births attended by skilled health staff (% of total)	44		54	
Maternal mortality ratio (per 100,000 live births)	1,200		880	
Women's share of population ages 15+ living with HIV (%)	58		58	
Prevalence of HIV (% ages 15-24)	4.5	2.3	2.0	1.4
Economic structure, participation, and access to resources				
Labor force participation rate (% of population ages 15+)	71	86	73	85
Labor force participation rate (% of ages 15-24)	57	70	57	68
Wage and salaried workers (% of employed ages 15+)	..	..	..	..
Self-employed workers (% of employed ages 15+)	..	..	..	..
Unpaid family workers (% of employed ages 15+)	..	..	..	..
Employment in agriculture (% of employed ages 15+)	..	..	..	..
Employment in industry (% of employed ages 15+)	..	..	..	..
Employment in services (% of employed ages 15+)	..	..	..	..
Women in wage employment in the nonagricultural sector (%)	..		..	
Women's share of part-time employment (% of total)	..		..	
Maternity leave (days paid)	..		..	
Maternity leave benefits (% of wages paid)	..		..	
Employment to population ratio (% ages 15+)	65	80	67	79
Employment to population ratio (% ages 15-24)	51	63	49	60
Firms with female participation in ownership (%)	..		53	
Firms with a female top manager (%)	..		12	
Children in employment (% of children ages 7-14)	68	67	38	37
Unemployment rate (% of labor force ages 15+)	7	7	8	7
Unemployment rate (% of labor force ages 15-24)	11	10	14	11
Internet users (%)	..	..	..	..
Account at a financial institution (% age 15+)	..	..	3	3
Mobile account (% age 15+)	..	..	..	..
Saved any money last year (% age 15+)	..	..	..	..
Public life and decision making				
Seats held by women in national parliament (%)	..		..	
Female legislators, senior officials and managers (% of total)	..		..	
Proportion of women in ministerial level positions (%)	..		24	
Agency				
Total fertility rate (births per woman)	5.4		4.4	
Adolescent fertility rate (births per 1,000 women ages 15-19)	127		93	
Women first married by age 18 (% of women ages 20-24)				

Chad

Sub-Saharan Africa	Low income
Population (millions)	14
GNI, Atlas ($ billions)	13
GNI per capita, Atlas ($)	980
Population living below $1.90 a day (%)	38

	2000		2013	
	Female	Male	Female	Male
Education				
Net primary enrollment rate (%)	41	62	75	96
Net secondary enrollment rate (%)	3	11	..	..
Gross tertiary enrollment ratio (% of relevant age group)	0	1	1	4
Primary completion rate (% of relevant age group)	13	32	30	47
Progression to secondary school (%)	70	78	87	100
Lower secondary completion rate (% of relevant age group)	4	14	11	25
Gross tertiary graduation ratio (%)	0	1	..	..
Female share of graduates in eng., manf. and constr. (%, tertiary)	..		..	
Youth literacy rate (% of population ages 15–24)	23	56	46	54
Health and related services				
Sex ratio at birth (male births per female births)	1.03		1.03	
Under-five mortality rate (per 1,000 live births)	181	199	131	146
Life expectancy at birth (years)	48	46	52	50
Pregnant women receiving prenatal care (%)	42		53	
Births attended by skilled health staff (% of total)	16		23	
Maternal mortality ratio (per 100,000 live births)	1,500		980	
Women's share of population ages 15+ living with HIV (%)	58		59	
Prevalence of HIV (% ages 15–24)	1.9	1.0	1.0	0.6
Economic structure, participation, and access to resources				
Labor force participation rate (% of population ages 15+)	64	80	64	79
Labor force participation rate (% of ages 15–24)	57	57	56	57
Wage and salaried workers (% of employed ages 15+)	..	..	..	..
Self-employed workers (% of employed ages 15+)	..	..	..	..
Unpaid family workers (% of employed ages 15+)	..	..	..	..
Employment in agriculture (% of employed ages 15+)	..	..	..	..
Employment in industry (% of employed ages 15+)	..	..	..	..
Employment in services (% of employed ages 15+)	..	..	..	..
Women in wage employment in the nonagricultural sector (%)	..		..	
Women's share of part-time employment (% of total)	..		..	
Maternity leave (days paid)	..		98	
Maternity leave benefits (% of wages paid)	..		50	
Employment to population ratio (% ages 15+)	59	74	59	74
Employment to population ratio (% ages 15–24)	50	51	50	51
Firms with female participation in ownership (%)	..		..	
Firms with a female top manager (%)	..		..	
Children in employment (% of children ages 7–14)	..	..	34	32
Unemployment rate (% of labor force ages 15+)	8	7	8	7
Unemployment rate (% of labor force ages 15–24)	12	10	11	10
Internet users (%)	..	..	..	..
Account at a financial institution (% age 15+)	..	..	4	12
Mobile account (% age 15+)	..	..	4.4	7.2
Saved any money last year (% age 15+)	..	..	45	52
Public life and decision making				
Seats held by women in national parliament (%)	..		15	
Female legislators, senior officials and managers (% of total)	..		..	
Proportion of women in ministerial level positions (%)	..		14	
Agency				
Total fertility rate (births per woman)	7.4		6.3	
Adolescent fertility rate (births per 1,000 women ages 15–19)	212		137	
Women first married by age 18 (% of women ages 20–24)	..		68	

Channel Islands

				163
Population (thousands)				163
GNI, Atlas ($ billions)				..
GNI per capita, Atlas ($)				..
Population living below $1.90 a day (%)				..

	2000		2013	
	Female	Male	Female	Male
Education				
Net primary enrollment rate (%)	..	..	..	..
Net secondary enrollment rate (%)	..	..	..	..
Gross tertiary enrollment ratio (% of relevant age group)	..	..	..	..
Primary completion rate (% of relevant age group)	..	..	..	..
Progression to secondary school (%)	..	..	..	..
Lower secondary completion rate (% of relevant age group)	..	..	..	..
Gross tertiary graduation ratio (%)	..		..	
Female share of graduates in eng., manf. and constr. (%, tertiary)	..		..	
Youth literacy rate (% of population ages 15–24)	..	..	..	..
Health and related services				
Sex ratio at birth (male births per female births)	*1.06*		1.06	
Under-five mortality rate (per 1,000 live births)	..	..	..	..
Life expectancy at birth (years)	80	75	82	78
Pregnant women receiving prenatal care (%)	..			
Births attended by skilled health staff (% of total)	..			
Maternal mortality ratio (per 100,000 live births)	..		..	
Women's share of population ages 15+ living with HIV (%)	..		..	
Prevalence of HIV (% ages 15–24)	..	..	..	..
Economic structure, participation, and access to resources				
Labor force participation rate (% of population ages 15+)	..	..	..	..
Labor force participation rate (% of ages 15–24)	..	..	..	..
Wage and salaried workers (% of employed ages 15+)	..	..	..	..
Self-employed workers (% of employed ages 15+)	..	..	..	..
Unpaid family workers (% of employed ages 15+)	..	..	..	..
Employment in agriculture (% of employed ages 15+)	..	..	..	..
Employment in industry (% of employed ages 15+)	..	..	..	..
Employment in services (% of employed ages 15+)	..	..	..	..
Women in wage employment in the nonagricultural sector (%)	..		..	
Women's share of part-time employment (% of total)	..		..	
Maternity leave (days paid)	..			
Maternity leave benefits (% of wages paid)	..			
Employment to population ratio (% ages 15+)	..	..	..	..
Employment to population ratio (% ages 15–24)	..	..	..	..
Firms with female participation in ownership (%)	..		..	
Firms with a female top manager (%)	..		..	
Children in employment (% of children ages 7–14)	..	..	..	..
Unemployment rate (% of labor force ages 15+)	..	..	..	..
Unemployment rate (% of labor force ages 15–24)	..	..	..	..
Internet users (%)	..	..	..	..
Account at a financial institution (% age 15+)	..	..	..	..
Mobile account (% age 15+)	..	..	..	..
Saved any money last year (% age 15+)	..	..	..	..
Public life and decision making				
Seats held by women in national parliament (%)	..		..	
Female legislators, senior officials and managers (% of total)	..		..	
Proportion of women in ministerial level positions (%)	..		..	
Agency				
Total fertility rate (births per woman)	1.4		1.5	
Adolescent fertility rate (births per 1,000 women ages 15–19)	13		7	
Women first married by age 18 (% of women ages 20–24)	..		..	

Chile

	High income
Population (millions)	18
GNI, Atlas ($ billions)	265
GNI per capita, Atlas ($)	14,910
Population living below $1.90 a day (%)	<2

	2000		**2013**	
	Female	Male	Female	Male
Education				
Net primary enrollment rate (%)	..	..	92	92
Net secondary enrollment rate (%)	..	..	89	86
Gross tertiary enrollment ratio (% of relevant age group)	36	39	83	75
Primary completion rate (% of relevant age group)	..	..	96	97
Progression to secondary school (%)	..	..	100	99
Lower secondary completion rate (% of relevant age group)	..	..	94	92
Gross tertiary graduation ratio (%)	13	13	22	16
Female share of graduates in eng., manf. and constr. (%, tertiary)	..		18	
Youth literacy rate (% of population ages 15–24)	99	99	100	99
Health and related services				
Sex ratio at birth (male births per female births)	1.04		1.04	
Under-five mortality rate (per 1,000 live births)	10	12	7	9
Life expectancy at birth (years)	80	74	83	77
Pregnant women receiving prenatal care (%)	..		..	
Births attended by skilled health staff (% of total)	100		100	
Maternal mortality ratio (per 100,000 live births)	29		22	
Women's share of population ages 15+ living with HIV (%)	10		10	
Prevalence of HIV (% ages 15–24)	0.1	0.2	0.1	0.2
Economic structure, participation, and access to resources				
Labor force participation rate (% of population ages 15+)	36	75	49	75
Labor force participation rate (% of ages 15–24)	24	42	32	44
Wage and salaried workers (% of employed ages 15+)	75	67	62	73
Self-employed workers (% of employed ages 15+)	25	33	26	27
Unpaid family workers (% of employed ages 15+)	3.8	1.6	2.2	0.9
Employment in agriculture (% of employed ages 15+)	5	19	5	14
Employment in industry (% of employed ages 15+)	12	29	11	32
Employment in services (% of employed ages 15+)	83	52	85	55
Women in wage employment in the nonagricultural sector (%)	33		39	
Women's share of part-time employment (% of total)	54		59	
Maternity leave (days paid)	..		126	
Maternity leave benefits (% of wages paid)	..		100	
Employment to population ratio (% ages 15+)	32	68	46	71
Employment to population ratio (% ages 15–24)	18	34	26	38
Firms with female participation in ownership (%)	..		30	
Firms with a female top manager (%)	..		5	
Children in employment (% of children ages 7–14)	..	..	3	6
Unemployment rate (% of labor force ages 15+)	10	9	7	5
Unemployment rate (% of labor force ages 15–24)	25	20	19	14
Internet users (%)	..	..	..	..
Account at a financial institution (% age 15+)	..	..	59	68
Mobile account (% age 15+)	..	..	2.7	5.0
Saved any money last year (% age 15+)	..	..	31	41
Public life and decision making				
Seats held by women in national parliament (%)	..		16	
Female legislators, senior officials and managers (% of total)	33		..	
Proportion of women in ministerial level positions (%)	..		35	
Agency				
Total fertility rate (births per woman)	2.1		1.8	
Adolescent fertility rate (births per 1,000 women ages 15–19)	57		48	
Women first married by age 18 (% of women ages 20–24)	..		..	

China

	East Asia & Pacific		Upper middle income	

Population (millions)			1,364
GNI, Atlas ($ billions)			10,069
GNI per capita, Atlas ($)			7,380
Population living below $1.90 a day (%)			*11*

	2000		2013	
	Female	Male	Female	Male
Education				
Net primary enrollment rate (%)	..	..	..	..
Net secondary enrollment rate (%)	..	..	..	..
Gross tertiary enrollment ratio (% of relevant age group)	..	..	32	28
Primary completion rate (% of relevant age group)	..	..	..	..
Progression to secondary school (%)	..	..	..	..
Lower secondary completion rate (% of relevant age group)	..	..	102	99
Gross tertiary graduation ratio (%)	..	..	18	16
Female share of graduates in eng., manf. and constr. (%, tertiary)	..		..	
Youth literacy rate (% of population ages 15–24)	99	99	*100*	*100*
Health and related services				
Sex ratio at birth (male births per female births)	*1.16*		*1.16*	
Under-five mortality rate (per 1,000 live births)	35	39	10	11
Life expectancy at birth (years)	74	71	77	74
Pregnant women receiving prenatal care (%)	89		95	
Births attended by skilled health staff (% of total)	97		100	
Maternal mortality ratio (per 100,000 live births)	63		32	
Women's share of population ages 15+ living with HIV (%)	..		..	
Prevalence of HIV (% ages 15–24)	..	..	..	..
Economic structure, participation, and access to resources				
Labor force participation rate (% of population ages 15+)	71	83	64	78
Labor force participation rate (% of ages 15–24)	68	69	54	59
Wage and salaried workers (% of employed ages 15+)	..	..	..	..
Self-employed workers (% of employed ages 15+)	..	..	..	..
Unpaid family workers (% of employed ages 15+)	..	..	..	..
Employment in agriculture (% of employed ages 15+)	..	..	..	..
Employment in industry (% of employed ages 15+)	..	..	..	..
Employment in services (% of employed ages 15+)	..	..	..	..
Women in wage employment in the nonagricultural sector (%)	39		..	
Women's share of part-time employment (% of total)	..		..	
Maternity leave (days paid)			128	
Maternity leave benefits (% of wages paid)	..		100	
Employment to population ratio (% ages 15+)	68	79	62	74
Employment to population ratio (% ages 15–24)	63	61	50	52
Firms with female participation in ownership (%)	..		64	
Firms with a female top manager (%)	..		18	
Children in employment (% of children ages 7–14)	..	..	..	..
Unemployment rate (% of labor force ages 15+)	4	5	4	5
Unemployment rate (% of labor force ages 15–24)	8	11	8	12
Internet users (%)	..	..	..	..
Account at a financial institution (% age 15+)	..	..	76	81
Mobile account (% age 15+)	..	..	..	..
Saved any money last year (% age 15+)	..	..	70	74
Public life and decision making				
Seats held by women in national parliament (%)	..		24	
Female legislators, senior officials and managers (% of total)	..		..	
Proportion of women in ministerial level positions (%)	..		12	
Agency				
Total fertility rate (births per woman)	1.5		1.7	
Adolescent fertility rate (births per 1,000 women ages 15–19)	9		7	
Women first married by age 18 (% of women ages 20–24)	..		..	

Colombia

Latin America & the Caribbean	Upper middle income
Population (millions)	48
GNI, Atlas ($ billions)	381
GNI per capita, Atlas ($)	7,970
Population living below $1.90 a day (%)	6

	2000		2013	
	Female	Male	Female	Male
Education				
Net primary enrollment rate (%)	93	94	87	88
Net secondary enrollment rate (%)	..	..	77	71
Gross tertiary enrollment ratio (% of relevant age group)	25	23	52	45
Primary completion rate (% of relevant age group)	97	92	115	112
Progression to secondary school (%)	92	93	95	98
Lower secondary completion rate (% of relevant age group)	63	55	77	67
Gross tertiary graduation ratio (%)	5	4	22	15
Female share of graduates in eng., manf. and constr. (%, tertiary)	35		32	
Youth literacy rate (% of population ages 15-24)	..	..	99	98
Health and related services				
Sex ratio at birth (male births per female births)	1.05		1.05	
Under-five mortality rate (per 1,000 live births)	22	28	14	18
Life expectancy at birth (years)	75	67	78	70
Pregnant women receiving prenatal care (%)	91		97	
Births attended by skilled health staff (% of total)	86		99	
Maternal mortality ratio (per 100,000 live births)	130		83	
Women's share of population ages 15+ living with HIV (%)	40		31	
Prevalence of HIV (% ages 15-24)	0.3	0.4	0.1	0.2
Economic structure, participation, and access to resources				
Labor force participation rate (% of population ages 15+)	49	82	56	80
Labor force participation rate (% of ages 15-24)	41	64	39	53
Wage and salaried workers (% of employed ages 15+)	55	50	46	47
Self-employed workers (% of employed ages 15+)	45	50	54	53
Unpaid family workers (% of employed ages 15+)	5.3	3.2	8.0	3.8
Employment in agriculture (% of employed ages 15+)	1	2	7	24
Employment in industry (% of employed ages 15+)	20	30	17	24
Employment in services (% of employed ages 15+)	80	68	76	52
Women in wage employment in the nonagricultural sector (%)	49		46	
Women's share of part-time employment (% of total)	55		61	
Maternity leave (days paid)	..		98	
Maternity leave benefits (% of wages paid)	..		100	
Employment to population ratio (% ages 15+)	38	71	48	73
Employment to population ratio (% ages 15-24)	25	48	29	44
Firms with female participation in ownership (%)	..		35	
Firms with a female top manager (%)	..		12	
Children in employment (% of children ages 7-14)	..	..	5	10
Unemployment rate (% of labor force ages 15+)	22	13	14	8
Unemployment rate (% of labor force ages 15-24)	40	25	26	16
Internet users (%)	..	..	51	52
Account at a financial institution (% age 15+)	..	..	34	43
Mobile account (% age 15+)	..	..	1.8	2.7
Saved any money last year (% age 15+)	..	..	40	48
Public life and decision making				
Seats held by women in national parliament (%)	..		20	
Female legislators, senior officials and managers (% of total)	..		53	
Proportion of women in ministerial level positions (%)	..		29	
Agency				
Total fertility rate (births per woman)	2.6		2.3	
Adolescent fertility rate (births per 1,000 women ages 15-19)	85		52	
Women first married by age 18 (% of women ages 20-24)	21		23	

Comoros

Sub-Saharan Africa				Low income
Population (thousands)				770
GNI, Atlas ($ millions)				631
GNI per capita, Atlas ($)				820
Population living below $1.90 a day (%)				..

	2000		2013	
	Female	Male	Female	Male
Education				
Net primary enrollment rate (%)	70	83	79	84
Net secondary enrollment rate (%)	..	..	49	46
Gross tertiary enrollment ratio (% of relevant age group)	1	2	9	11
Primary completion rate (% of relevant age group)	51	55	76	72
Progression to secondary school (%)	80	80	..	..
Lower secondary completion rate (% of relevant age group)	26	32	52	45
Gross tertiary graduation ratio (%)	1	2	..	..
Female share of graduates in eng., manf. and constr. (%, tertiary)	..		..	
Youth literacy rate (% of population ages 15–24)	78	84	87	87
Health and related services				
Sex ratio at birth (male births per female births)	1.05		1.05	
Under-five mortality rate (per 1,000 live births)	94	107	68	79
Life expectancy at birth (years)	59	56	62	59
Pregnant women receiving prenatal care (%)	74		92	
Births attended by skilled health staff (% of total)	62		82	
Maternal mortality ratio (per 100,000 live births)	480		350	
Women's share of population ages 15+ living with HIV (%)	..		..	
Prevalence of HIV (% ages 15–24)	..	..	..	..
Economic structure, participation, and access to resources				
Labor force participation rate (% of population ages 15+)	31	79	35	80
Labor force participation rate (% of ages 15–24)	24	55	25	53
Wage and salaried workers (% of employed ages 15+)	..	..	..	..
Self-employed workers (% of employed ages 15+)	..	..	..	..
Unpaid family workers (% of employed ages 15+)	..	..	..	..
Employment in agriculture (% of employed ages 15+)	..	..	..	..
Employment in industry (% of employed ages 15+)	..	..	..	..
Employment in services (% of employed ages 15+)	..	..	..	..
Women in wage employment in the nonagricultural sector (%)	..		..	
Women's share of part-time employment (% of total)	..		..	
Maternity leave (days paid)	..		..	
Maternity leave benefits (% of wages paid)	..		..	
Employment to population ratio (% ages 15+)	28	74	33	75
Employment to population ratio (% ages 15–24)	21	49	22	48
Firms with female participation in ownership (%)	..		..	
Firms with a female top manager (%)	..		..	
Children in employment (% of children ages 7–14)	..	..	..	..
Unemployment rate (% of labor force ages 15+)	7	7	7	6
Unemployment rate (% of labor force ages 15–24)	12	10	11	10
Internet users (%)	..	..	..	..
Account at a financial institution (% age 15+)	..	..	18	26
Mobile account (% age 15+)	..	..	..	..
Saved any money last year (% age 15+)	..	..	..	..
Public life and decision making				
Seats held by women in national parliament (%)	..		3	
Female legislators, senior officials and managers (% of total)	..		..	
Proportion of women in ministerial level positions (%)	..		20	
Agency				
Total fertility rate (births per woman)	5.3		4.7	
Adolescent fertility rate (births per 1,000 women ages 15–19)	95		70	
Women first married by age 18 (% of women ages 20–24)	..		32	

Congo, Dem. Rep.

Sub-Saharan Africa	**Low income**
Population (millions)	75
GNI, Atlas ($ billions)	29
GNI per capita, Atlas ($)	380
Population living below $1.90 a day (%)	77

	2000 Female	2000 Male	2013 Female	2013 Male
Education				
Net primary enrollment rate (%)	35	37	..	..
Net secondary enrollment rate (%)	..	..	..	..
Gross tertiary enrollment ratio (% of relevant age group)	..	..	4	9
Primary completion rate (% of relevant age group)	32	37	65	80
Progression to secondary school (%)	..	..	71	73
Lower secondary completion rate (% of relevant age group)	..	..	34	52
Gross tertiary graduation ratio (%)	..		..	
Female share of graduates in eng., manf. and constr. (%, tertiary)	..		..	
Youth literacy rate (% of population ages 15-24)	63	78	77	91
Health and related services				
Sex ratio at birth (male births per female births)	1.03		1.03	
Under-five mortality rate (per 1,000 live births)	152	170	91	105
Life expectancy at birth (years)	48	45	52	48
Pregnant women receiving prenatal care (%)	68		88[a]	
Births attended by skilled health staff (% of total)	61		80[a]	
Maternal mortality ratio (per 100,000 live births)	1,100		730	
Women's share of population ages 15+ living with HIV (%)	57		59	
Prevalence of HIV (% ages 15-24)	0.8	0.4	0.5	0.3
Economic structure, participation, and access to resources				
Labor force participation rate (% of population ages 15+)	71	74	71	73
Labor force participation rate (% of ages 15-24)	51	42	48	42
Wage and salaried workers (% of employed ages 15+)	..	..	..	..
Self-employed workers (% of employed ages 15+)	..	..	..	..
Unpaid family workers (% of employed ages 15+)	..	..	..	..
Employment in agriculture (% of employed ages 15+)	..	..	..	..
Employment in industry (% of employed ages 15+)	..	..	..	..
Employment in services (% of employed ages 15+)	..	..	..	..
Women in wage employment in the nonagricultural sector (%)	..		..	
Women's share of part-time employment (% of total)	..		..	
Maternity leave (days paid)	..		98	
Maternity leave benefits (% of wages paid)	..		67	
Employment to population ratio (% ages 15+)	65	68	64	68
Employment to population ratio (% ages 15-24)	43	36	41	36
Firms with female participation in ownership (%)	..		15	
Firms with a female top manager (%)	..		11	
Children in employment (% of children ages 7-14)	40	40	21	20
Unemployment rate (% of labor force ages 15+)	9	7	9	7
Unemployment rate (% of labor force ages 15-24)	16	15	15	14
Internet users (%)	..	..	..	..
Account at a financial institution (% age 15+)	..	..	9	13
Mobile account (% age 15+)	..	..	7.4	11.0
Saved any money last year (% age 15+)	..	..	64	67
Public life and decision making				
Seats held by women in national parliament (%)	..		9	
Female legislators, senior officials and managers (% of total)	..		..	
Proportion of women in ministerial level positions (%)	..		8	
Agency				
Total fertility rate (births per woman)	7.1		5.9	
Adolescent fertility rate (births per 1,000 women ages 15-19)	131		123	
Women first married by age 18 (% of women ages 20-24)	..		37[a]	

Congo, Rep.

Sub-Saharan Africa   **Lower middle income**

Population (millions)	5
GNI, Atlas ($ billions)	12
GNI per capita, Atlas ($)	2,710
Population living below $1.90 a day (%)	29

	2000		2013	
	Female	**Male**	**Female**	**Male**
Education				
Net primary enrollment rate (%)	..	..	94	86
Net secondary enrollment rate (%)	..	..	..	..
Gross tertiary enrollment ratio (% of relevant age group)	2	8	8	11
Primary completion rate (% of relevant age group)	57	57	77	69
Progression to secondary school (%)	58	89	75	78
Lower secondary completion rate (% of relevant age group)	22	33	50	52
Gross tertiary graduation ratio (%)	..	..	..	
Female share of graduates in eng., manf. and constr. (%, tertiary)			..	
Youth literacy rate (% of population ages 15–24)	..	..	77	86
Health and related services				
Sex ratio at birth (male births per female births)	*1.03*		1.03	
Under-five mortality rate (per 1,000 live births)	115	128	41	49
Life expectancy at birth (years)	53	51	60	57
Pregnant women receiving prenatal care (%)	..		93	
Births attended by skilled health staff (% of total)	..		93	
Maternal mortality ratio (per 100,000 live births)	610		410	
Women's share of population ages 15+ living with HIV (%)	56		61	
Prevalence of HIV (% ages 15–24)	2.4	1.3	1.4	0.9
Economic structure, participation, and access to resources				
Labor force participation rate (% of population ages 15+)	65	72	69	73
Labor force participation rate (% of ages 15–24)	45	45	44	45
Wage and salaried workers (% of employed ages 15+)	..	..	..	..
Self-employed workers (% of employed ages 15+)	..	..	..	..
Unpaid family workers (% of employed ages 15+)	..	..	..	..
Employment in agriculture (% of employed ages 15+)	..	..	..	..
Employment in industry (% of employed ages 15+)	..	..	..	..
Employment in services (% of employed ages 15+)	..	..	..	..
Women in wage employment in the nonagricultural sector (%)			..	
Women's share of part-time employment (% of total)	..		..	
Maternity leave (days paid)	..		105	
Maternity leave benefits (% of wages paid)	..		100	
Employment to population ratio (% ages 15+)	61	67	64	68
Employment to population ratio (% ages 15–24)	40	40	39	40
Firms with female participation in ownership (%)	..		..	
Firms with a female top manager (%)			..	
Children in employment (% of children ages 7–14)	..	..	32	31
Unemployment rate (% of labor force ages 15+)	7	6	7	6
Unemployment rate (% of labor force ages 15–24)	11	10	11	10
Internet users (%)	..	..	..	..
Account at a financial institution (% age 15+)	..	..	14	19
Mobile account (% age 15+)	..	..	2.5	1.4
Saved any money last year (% age 15+)	..	..	56	56
Public life and decision making				
Seats held by women in national parliament (%)	..		7	
Female legislators, senior officials and managers (% of total)	..		..	
Proportion of women in ministerial level positions (%)	..		11	
Agency				
Total fertility rate (births per woman)	5.1		5.0	
Adolescent fertility rate (births per 1,000 women ages 15–19)	136		119	
Women first married by age 18 (% of women ages 20–24)	..		*33*	

Costa Rica

Population (millions)	5
GNI, Atlas ($ billions)	48
GNI per capita, Atlas ($)	10,120
Population living below $1.90 a day (%)	<2

	2000		2013	
	Female	**Male**	**Female**	**Male**
Education				
Net primary enrollment rate (%)	..	..	90	90
Net secondary enrollment rate (%)	..	..	76	71
Gross tertiary enrollment ratio (% of relevant age group)	..	..	53	43
Primary completion rate (% of relevant age group)	89	85	91	89
Progression to secondary school (%)	82	84	90	98
Lower secondary completion rate (% of relevant age group)	46	39	57	50
Gross tertiary graduation ratio (%)	35	20	49	26
Female share of graduates in eng., manf. and constr. (%, tertiary)	28		34	
Youth literacy rate (% of population ages 15–24)	98	97	99	99
Health and related services				
Sex ratio at birth (male births per female births)	1.05		1.05	
Under-five mortality rate (per 1,000 live births)	12	14	9	11
Life expectancy at birth (years)	80	75	82	78
Pregnant women receiving prenatal care (%)	70		98	
Births attended by skilled health staff (% of total)	98		99	
Maternal mortality ratio (per 100,000 live births)	44		38	
Women's share of population ages 15+ living with HIV (%)	29		27	
Prevalence of HIV (% ages 15–24)	0.1	0.1	0.1	0.1
Economic structure, participation, and access to resources				
Labor force participation rate (% of population ages 15+)	37	82	47	79
Labor force participation rate (% of ages 15–24)	35	67	37	58
Wage and salaried workers (% of employed ages 15+)	77	68	80	74
Self-employed workers (% of employed ages 15+)	23	32	20	26
Unpaid family workers (% of employed ages 15+)	3.3	2.2	1.8	1.2
Employment in agriculture (% of employed ages 15+)	5	27	4	19
Employment in industry (% of employed ages 15+)	17	25	11	24
Employment in services (% of employed ages 15+)	77	47	85	56
Women in wage employment in the nonagricultural sector (%)	39		43	
Women's share of part-time employment (% of total)	57		55	
Maternity leave (days paid)	..		120	
Maternity leave benefits (% of wages paid)	..		100	
Employment to population ratio (% ages 15+)	35	78	42	74
Employment to population ratio (% ages 15–24)	30	61	28	49
Firms with female participation in ownership (%)	..		44	
Firms with a female top manager (%)	..		15	
Children in employment (% of children ages 7–14)	..	..	2	3
Unemployment rate (% of labor force ages 15+)	7	4	10	6
Unemployment rate (% of labor force ages 15–24)	15	9	24	15
Internet users (%)	..	..	47	49
Account at a financial institution (% age 15+)	..	..	60	69
Mobile account (% age 15+)	..	..	..	..
Saved any money last year (% age 15+)	..	..	53	66
Public life and decision making				
Seats held by women in national parliament (%)	..		33	
Female legislators, senior officials and managers (% of total)	33		35	
Proportion of women in ministerial level positions (%)	..		41	
Agency				
Total fertility rate (births per woman)	2.4		1.8	
Adolescent fertility rate (births per 1,000 women ages 15–19)	75		57	
Women first married by age 18 (% of women ages 20–24)	..		21	

Côte d'Ivoire

Sub-Saharan Africa	Lower middle income
Population (millions)	22
GNI, Atlas ($ billions)	32
GNI per capita, Atlas ($)	1,460
Population living below $1.90 a day (%)	..

	2000		2013	
	Female	Male	Female	Male
Education				
Net primary enrollment rate (%)	50	67	74	80
Net secondary enrollment rate (%)	..	..	..	..
Gross tertiary enrollment ratio (% of relevant age group)	4	10	7	11
Primary completion rate (% of relevant age group)	35	55	53	67
Progression to secondary school (%)	63	71	68	77
Lower secondary completion rate (% of relevant age group)	26	22	28	40
Gross tertiary graduation ratio (%)	..	..	..	..
Female share of graduates in eng., manf. and constr. (%, tertiary)	..		..	
Youth literacy rate (% of population ages 15–24)	52	71	39	58
Health and related services				
Sex ratio at birth (male births per female births)	1.03		1.03	
Under-five mortality rate (per 1,000 live births)	134	157	84	101
Life expectancy at birth (years)	47	46	52	50
Pregnant women receiving prenatal care (%)	88		91	
Births attended by skilled health staff (% of total)	63		59	
Maternal mortality ratio (per 100,000 live births)	670		720	
Women's share of population ages 15+ living with HIV (%)	54		59	
Prevalence of HIV (% ages 15–24)	2.8	1.4	1.4	0.9
Economic structure, participation, and access to resources				
Labor force participation rate (% of population ages 15+)	49	82	52	81
Labor force participation rate (% of ages 15–24)	41	62	41	61
Wage and salaried workers (% of employed ages 15+)	12	25	..	..
Self-employed workers (% of employed ages 15+)	84	70	..	..
Unpaid family workers (% of employed ages 15+)	44.2	15.8	..	..
Employment in agriculture (% of employed ages 15+)	..	..	..	..
Employment in industry (% of employed ages 15+)	..	..	..	..
Employment in services (% of employed ages 15+)	..	..	..	..
Women in wage employment in the nonagricultural sector (%)	21		21	
Women's share of part-time employment (% of total)	..		..	
Maternity leave (days paid)			98	
Maternity leave benefits (% of wages paid)	..		100	
Employment to population ratio (% ages 15+)	47	79	51	78
Employment to population ratio (% ages 15–24)	38	58	38	58
Firms with female participation in ownership (%)	..			
Firms with a female top manager (%)	..		..	
Children in employment (% of children ages 7–14)	41	41	36	37
Unemployment rate (% of labor force ages 15+)	4	4	4	4
Unemployment rate (% of labor force ages 15–24)	5	6	5	6
Internet users (%)	..	..	..	..
Account at a financial institution (% age 15+)	..	..	12	18
Mobile account (% age 15+)	..	..	20.0	28.3
Saved any money last year (% age 15+)	..	..	59	67
Public life and decision making				
Seats held by women in national parliament (%)	..		9	
Female legislators, senior officials and managers (% of total)	..		..	
Proportion of women in ministerial level positions (%)	..		17	
Agency				
Total fertility rate (births per woman)	5.4		4.9	
Adolescent fertility rate (births per 1,000 women ages 15–19)	138		135	
Women first married by age 18 (% of women ages 20–24)	33		33	

Croatia

Population (millions)	4
GNI, Atlas ($ billions)	55
GNI per capita, Atlas ($)	13,020
Population living below $1.90 a day (%)	<2

	2000		2013	
	Female	Male	Female	Male
Education				
Net primary enrollment rate (%)	87	88	89	90
Net secondary enrollment rate (%)	84	82	95	92
Gross tertiary enrollment ratio (% of relevant age group)	33	29	71	52
Primary completion rate (% of relevant age group)	92	94	93	93
Progression to secondary school (%)	100	99	100	100
Lower secondary completion rate (% of relevant age group)	91	90	97	96
Gross tertiary graduation ratio (%)	18	11	59	37
Female share of graduates in eng., manf. and constr. (%, tertiary)	30		30	
Youth literacy rate (% of population ages 15-24)	100	100	100	100
Health and related services				
Sex ratio at birth (male births per female births)	1.06		1.06	
Under-five mortality rate (per 1,000 live births)	8	9	4	5
Life expectancy at birth (years)	77	69	80	74
Pregnant women receiving prenatal care (%)	100		100	
Births attended by skilled health staff (% of total)	100		100	
Maternal mortality ratio (per 100,000 live births)	11		13	
Women's share of population ages 15+ living with HIV (%)	..		..	
Prevalence of HIV (% ages 15-24)	..	..	..	..
Economic structure, participation, and access to resources				
Labor force participation rate (% of population ages 15+)	45	63	45	58
Labor force participation rate (% of ages 15-24)	39	45	25	34
Wage and salaried workers (% of employed ages 15+)	78	75	85	80
Self-employed workers (% of employed ages 15+)	22	25	16	20
Unpaid family workers (% of employed ages 15+)	8.2	2.2	2.4	0.9
Employment in agriculture (% of employed ages 15+)	15	14	14	14
Employment in industry (% of employed ages 15+)	20	36	17	36
Employment in services (% of employed ages 15+)	65	50	69	50
Women in wage employment in the nonagricultural sector (%)	47		48	
Women's share of part-time employment (% of total)	56		54	
Maternity leave (days paid)	..		208	
Maternity leave benefits (% of wages paid)	..		100	
Employment to population ratio (% ages 15+)	38	53	37	48
Employment to population ratio (% ages 15-24)	25	27	12	16
Firms with female participation in ownership (%)	..		32	
Firms with a female top manager (%)	..		19	
Children in employment (% of children ages 7-14)	..	..	..	..
Unemployment rate (% of labor force ages 15+)	17	16	17	18
Unemployment rate (% of labor force ages 15-24)	37	40	52	51
Internet users (%)	..	..	60	74
Account at a financial institution (% age 15+)	..	..	88	84
Mobile account (% age 15+)	..	..	..	..
Saved any money last year (% age 15+)	..	..	55	48
Public life and decision making				
Seats held by women in national parliament (%)	..		26	
Female legislators, senior officials and managers (% of total)	25		25	
Proportion of women in ministerial level positions (%)	..		20	
Agency				
Total fertility rate (births per woman)	1.4		1.5	
Adolescent fertility rate (births per 1,000 women ages 15-19)	17		10	
Women first married by age 18 (% of women ages 20-24)	..		..	

Cuba

Latin America & the Caribbean	Upper middle income
Population (millions)	11
GNI, Atlas ($ billions)	67
GNI per capita, Atlas ($)	5,880
Population living below $1.90 a day (%)	..

	2000		2013	
	Female	Male	Female	Male
Education				
Net primary enrollment rate (%)	96	97	96	96
Net secondary enrollment rate (%)	82	79	89	88
Gross tertiary enrollment ratio (% of relevant age group)	24	20	60	36
Primary completion rate (% of relevant age group)	96	96	94	92
Progression to secondary school (%)	98	97	99	99
Lower secondary completion rate (% of relevant age group)	99	90	97	93
Gross tertiary graduation ratio (%)	14	8	72	38
Female share of graduates in eng., manf. and constr. (%, tertiary)	..		28	
Youth literacy rate (% of population ages 15–24)	100	100	100	100
Health and related services				
Sex ratio at birth (male births per female births)	1.06		1.06	
Under-five mortality rate (per 1,000 live births)	7	9	5	6
Life expectancy at birth (years)	79	75	81	77
Pregnant women receiving prenatal care (%)	100		100	
Births attended by skilled health staff (% of total)	100		100	
Maternal mortality ratio (per 100,000 live births)	63		80	
Women's share of population ages 15+ living with HIV (%)	17		21	
Prevalence of HIV (% ages 15–24)	0.1	0.1	0.1	0.2
Economic structure, participation, and access to resources				
Labor force participation rate (% of population ages 15+)	38	70	43	70
Labor force participation rate (% of ages 15–24)	26	46	37	47
Wage and salaried workers (% of employed ages 15+)	92	75	89	70
Self-employed workers (% of employed ages 15+)	9	25	11	30
Unpaid family workers (% of employed ages 15+)	..	..	..	..
Employment in agriculture (% of employed ages 15+)	14	34	9	26
Employment in industry (% of employed ages 15+)	14	22	12	20
Employment in services (% of employed ages 15+)	72	44	79	54
Women in wage employment in the nonagricultural sector (%)	43		45	
Women's share of part-time employment (% of total)	..		..	
Maternity leave (days paid)	..		..	
Maternity leave benefits (% of wages paid)	..		..	
Employment to population ratio (% ages 15+)	35	67	42	68
Employment to population ratio (% ages 15–24)	23	41	34	44
Firms with female participation in ownership (%)	..		..	
Firms with a female top manager (%)	..		..	
Children in employment (% of children ages 7–14)	..	..	..	..
Unemployment rate (% of labor force ages 15+)	6	5	4	3
Unemployment rate (% of labor force ages 15–24)	13	11	8	6
Internet users (%)	..	..	30	25
Account at a financial institution (% age 15+)	..	..	..	..
Mobile account (% age 15+)	..	..	..	..
Saved any money last year (% age 15+)	..	..	..	..
Public life and decision making				
Seats held by women in national parliament (%)	..		49	
Female legislators, senior officials and managers (% of total)	..		..	
Proportion of women in ministerial level positions (%)	..		31	
Agency				
Total fertility rate (births per woman)	1.6		1.4	
Adolescent fertility rate (births per 1,000 women ages 15–19)	58		46	
Women first married by age 18 (% of women ages 20–24)	..		40	

Curaçao

High income

Population (thousands)	156
GNI, Atlas ($ millions)	..
GNI per capita, Atlas ($)	..
Population living below $1.90 a day (%)	..

	2000		2013	
	Female	Male	Female	Male
Education				
Net primary enrollment rate (%)	..	..	..	..
Net secondary enrollment rate (%)	..	..	..	..
Gross tertiary enrollment ratio (% of relevant age group)	..	..	29	13
Primary completion rate (% of relevant age group)	..	..	..	..
Progression to secondary school (%)	..	..	..	..
Lower secondary completion rate (% of relevant age group)	..	..	..	..
Gross tertiary graduation ratio (%)	..		..	
Female share of graduates in eng., manf. and constr. (%, tertiary)	..		..	
Youth literacy rate (% of population ages 15–24)	..	..	..	..
Health and related services				
Sex ratio at birth (male births per female births)	1.05		1.05	
Under-five mortality rate (per 1,000 live births)	..	..	..	..
Life expectancy at birth (years)	..	..	81	74
Pregnant women receiving prenatal care (%)	..		..	
Births attended by skilled health staff (% of total)	..		..	
Maternal mortality ratio (per 100,000 live births)	..		..	
Women's share of population ages 15+ living with HIV (%)	..		..	
Prevalence of HIV (% ages 15–24)	..	..	..	..
Economic structure, participation, and access to resources				
Labor force participation rate (% of population ages 15+)	..	..	..	..
Labor force participation rate (% of ages 15–24)	..	..	..	..
Wage and salaried workers (% of employed ages 15+)	..	..	..	..
Self-employed workers (% of employed ages 15+)	..	..	..	..
Unpaid family workers (% of employed ages 15+)	..	..	..	..
Employment in agriculture (% of employed ages 15+)	..	..	..	..
Employment in industry (% of employed ages 15+)	..	..	..	..
Employment in services (% of employed ages 15+)	..	..	..	..
Women in wage employment in the nonagricultural sector (%)	..		..	
Women's share of part-time employment (% of total)	..		..	
Maternity leave (days paid)	..		..	
Maternity leave benefits (% of wages paid)	..		..	
Employment to population ratio (% ages 15+)	..	..	..	..
Employment to population ratio (% ages 15–24)	..	..	..	..
Firms with female participation in ownership (%)	..		..	
Firms with a female top manager (%)	..		..	
Children in employment (% of children ages 7–14)	..	..	..	..
Unemployment rate (% of labor force ages 15+)	..	..	..	..
Unemployment rate (% of labor force ages 15–24)	..	..	..	..
Internet users (%)	..	..	..	..
Account at a financial institution (% age 15+)	..	..	..	..
Mobile account (% age 15+)	..	..	..	..
Saved any money last year (% age 15+)	..	..	..	..
Public life and decision making				
Seats held by women in national parliament (%)	..		..	
Female legislators, senior officials and managers (% of total)	..		..	
Proportion of women in ministerial level positions (%)	..		..	
Agency				
Total fertility rate (births per woman)	..		2.2	
Adolescent fertility rate (births per 1,000 women ages 15–19)	39		34	
Women first married by age 18 (% of women ages 20–24)	..		..	

Cyprus

	High income
Population (millions)	1.2
GNI, Atlas ($ billions)	23
GNI per capita, Atlas ($)	26,370
Population living below $1.90 a day (%)	..

	2000		**2013**	
	Female	**Male**	**Female**	**Male**
Education				
Net primary enrollment rate (%)	96	95	98	98
Net secondary enrollment rate (%)	89	87	93	91
Gross tertiary enrollment ratio (% of relevant age group)	22	17	50	42
Primary completion rate (% of relevant age group)	97	98	100	100
Progression to secondary school (%)	99	100	100	98
Lower secondary completion rate (% of relevant age group)	93	89	96	95
Gross tertiary graduation ratio (%)	7	2	27	13
Female share of graduates in eng., manf. and constr. (%, tertiary)	22		50	
Youth literacy rate (% of population ages 15–24)	100	100	100	100
Health and related services				
Sex ratio at birth (male births per female births)	1.07		1.07	
Under-five mortality rate (per 1,000 live births)	6	7	3	3
Life expectancy at birth (years)	80	76	82	78
Pregnant women receiving prenatal care (%)	..		..	
Births attended by skilled health staff (% of total)	...		..	
Maternal mortality ratio (per 100,000 live births)	16		10	
Women's share of population ages 15+ living with HIV (%)	..		..	
Prevalence of HIV (% ages 15–24)	..	..	..	..
Economic structure, participation, and access to resources				
Labor force participation rate (% of population ages 15+)	50	72	56	71
Labor force participation rate (% of ages 15–24)	41	45	37	43
Wage and salaried workers (% of employed ages 15+)	84	70	89	77
Self-employed workers (% of employed ages 15+)	17	30	12	23
Unpaid family workers (% of employed ages 15+)	6.6	0.7	2.1	1.2
Employment in agriculture (% of employed ages 15+)	5	6	2	4
Employment in industry (% of employed ages 15+)	13	31	9	31
Employment in services (% of employed ages 15+)	82	63	90	65
Women in wage employment in the nonagricultural sector (%)	44		52	
Women's share of part-time employment (% of total)	69		62	
Maternity leave (days paid)	..		..	
Maternity leave benefits (% of wages paid)	..		..	
Employment to population ratio (% ages 15+)	46	70	48	59
Employment to population ratio (% ages 15–24)	36	43	24	26
Firms with female participation in ownership (%)	..		..	
Firms with a female top manager (%)	..		..	
Children in employment (% of children ages 7–14)	..	..	..	..
Unemployment rate (% of labor force ages 15+)	7	3	15	17
Unemployment rate (% of labor force ages 15–24)	13	6	35	39
Internet users (%)	..	..	64	67
Account at a financial institution (% age 15+)	..	..	90	90
Mobile account (% age 15+)	..	..	..	..
Saved any money last year (% age 15+)	..	..	40	43
Public life and decision making				
Seats held by women in national parliament (%)	..		13	
Female legislators, senior officials and managers (% of total)	15		14	
Proportion of women in ministerial level positions (%)	..		9	
Agency				
Total fertility rate (births per woman)	1.7		1.5	
Adolescent fertility rate (births per 1,000 women ages 15–19)	10		5	
Women first married by age 18 (% of women ages 20–24)	..		..	

Czech Republic

	High income
Population (millions)	11
GNI, Atlas ($ billions)	199
GNI per capita, Atlas ($)	18,970
Population living below $1.90 a day (%)	<2

	2000		2013	
	Female	Male	Female	Male
Education				
Net primary enrollment rate (%)	..	..	..	..
Net secondary enrollment rate (%)	..	..	..	..
Gross tertiary enrollment ratio (% of relevant age group)	29	28	75	52
Primary completion rate (% of relevant age group)	99	99	102	100
Progression to secondary school (%)	100	100	100	99
Lower secondary completion rate (% of relevant age group)	94	90	98	96
Gross tertiary graduation ratio (%)	15	14	55	30
Female share of graduates in eng., manf. and constr. (%, tertiary)	27		28	
Youth literacy rate (% of population ages 15–24)	..	..	..	..
Health and related services				
Sex ratio at birth (male births per female births)	1.06		1.06	
Under-five mortality rate (per 1,000 live births)	6	7	3	4
Life expectancy at birth (years)	78	72	81	75
Pregnant women receiving prenatal care (%)	..		..	
Births attended by skilled health staff (% of total)	100		100	
Maternal mortality ratio (per 100,000 live births)	7		5	
Women's share of population ages 15+ living with HIV (%)	..		..	
Prevalence of HIV (% ages 15–24)	..	..	..	..
Economic structure, participation, and access to resources				
Labor force participation rate (% of population ages 15+)	52	70	51	68
Labor force participation rate (% of ages 15–24)	41	52	26	37
Wage and salaried workers (% of employed ages 15+)	90	81	87	79
Self-employed workers (% of employed ages 15+)	10	19	14	21
Unpaid family workers (% of employed ages 15+)	1.0	0.2	1.6	0.5
Employment in agriculture (% of employed ages 15+)	4	6	2	4
Employment in industry (% of employed ages 15+)	28	49	23	49
Employment in services (% of employed ages 15+)	69	45	75	47
Women in wage employment in the nonagricultural sector (%)	47		46	
Women's share of part-time employment (% of total)	73		70	
Maternity leave (days paid)	..		196	
Maternity leave benefits (% of wages paid)	..		70	
Employment to population ratio (% ages 15+)	46	65	47	64
Employment to population ratio (% ages 15–24)	34	43	21	30
Firms with female participation in ownership (%)	..		31	
Firms with a female top manager (%)	..		12	
Children in employment (% of children ages 7–14)	..	..	..	..
Unemployment rate (% of labor force ages 15+)	11	7	8	6
Unemployment rate (% of labor force ages 15–24)	17	17	19	19
Internet users (%)	..	..	73	75
Account at a financial institution (% age 15+)	..	..	79	85
Mobile account (% age 15+)	..	..	..	..
Saved any money last year (% age 15+)	..	..	60	66
Public life and decision making				
Seats held by women in national parliament (%)	..		20	
Female legislators, senior officials and managers (% of total)	24		26	
Proportion of women in ministerial level positions (%)	..		19	
Agency				
Total fertility rate (births per woman)	1.2		1.5	
Adolescent fertility rate (births per 1,000 women ages 15–19)	13		10	
Women first married by age 18 (% of women ages 20–24)	..		..	

Denmark

	High income
Population (millions)	6
GNI, Atlas ($ billions)	346
GNI per capita, Atlas ($)	61,310
Population living below $1.90 a day (%)	..

	2000		2013	
	Female	Male	Female	Male
Education				
Net primary enrollment rate (%)	98	97	98	98
Net secondary enrollment rate (%)	90	88	93	90
Gross tertiary enrollment ratio (% of relevant age group)	66	49	96	70
Primary completion rate (% of relevant age group)	100	100	100	99
Progression to secondary school (%)	100	100	100	100
Lower secondary completion rate (% of relevant age group)	..	..	99	99
Gross tertiary graduation ratio (%)	47	25	64	40
Female share of graduates in eng., manf. and constr. (%, tertiary)	30		35	
Youth literacy rate (% of population ages 15–24)	..	..	..	..
Health and related services				
Sex ratio at birth (male births per female births)	1.05		1.06	
Under-five mortality rate (per 1,000 live births)	5	6	3	4
Life expectancy at birth (years)	79	74	82	78
Pregnant women receiving prenatal care (%)	..		..	
Births attended by skilled health staff (% of total)	..		..	
Maternal mortality ratio (per 100,000 live births)	9		5	
Women's share of population ages 15+ living with HIV (%)	26		27	
Prevalence of HIV (% ages 15–24)	0.1	0.1	0.1	0.1
Economic structure, participation, and access to resources				
Labor force participation rate (% of population ages 15+)	60	72	59	66
Labor force participation rate (% of ages 15–24)	69	75	62	61
Wage and salaried workers (% of employed ages 15+)	94	88	94	88
Self-employed workers (% of employed ages 15+)	6	12	6	12
Unpaid family workers (% of employed ages 15+)	1.8	0.2	0.3	0.1
Employment in agriculture (% of employed ages 15+)	2	5	1	4
Employment in industry (% of employed ages 15+)	14	35	10	29
Employment in services (% of employed ages 15+)	85	60	89	67
Women in wage employment in the nonagricultural sector (%)	49		50	
Women's share of part-time employment (% of total)	69		61	
Maternity leave (days paid)	..		126	
Maternity leave benefits (% of wages paid)	..		50	
Employment to population ratio (% ages 15+)	57	69	54	62
Employment to population ratio (% ages 15–24)	64	71	55	52
Firms with female participation in ownership (%)	..		..	
Firms with a female top manager (%)	..		..	
Children in employment (% of children ages 7–14)	..	..	..	..
Unemployment rate (% of labor force ages 15+)	5	4	7	7
Unemployment rate (% of labor force ages 15–24)	7	7	12	14
Internet users (%)	..	..	94	95
Account at a financial institution (% age 15+)	..	..	100	100
Mobile account (% age 15+)	..	..	..	..
Saved any money last year (% age 15+)	..	..	78	84
Public life and decision making				
Seats held by women in national parliament (%)	..		38	
Female legislators, senior officials and managers (% of total)	24		28	
Proportion of women in ministerial level positions (%)	..		26	
Agency				
Total fertility rate (births per woman)	1.8		1.7	
Adolescent fertility rate (births per 1,000 women ages 15–19)	7		4	
Women first married by age 18 (% of women ages 20–24)	..		..	

Djibouti

Middle East & North Africa **Lower middle income**

Population (thousands)	876
GNI, Atlas ($ billions)	..
GNI per capita, Atlas ($)	..
Population living below $1.90 a day (%)	18

	2000		2013	
	Female	Male	Female	Male
Education				
Net primary enrollment rate (%)	22	29	55[a]	63[a]
Net secondary enrollment rate (%)	11	17	..	..
Gross tertiary enrollment ratio (% of relevant age group)	0	0	4	6
Primary completion rate (% of relevant age group)	21	31	55[a]	66[a]
Progression to secondary school (%)	79	80	100	99
Lower secondary completion rate (% of relevant age group)	12	17	40[a]	49[a]
Gross tertiary graduation ratio (%)	0	0	..	
Female share of graduates in eng., manf. and constr. (%, tertiary)	..		..	
Youth literacy rate (% of population ages 15–24)	..	..	..	..
Health and related services				
Sex ratio at birth (male births per female births)	1.04		1.04	
Under-five mortality rate (per 1,000 live births)	93	108	59	71
Life expectancy at birth (years)	59	55	63	60
Pregnant women receiving prenatal care (%)	..		88	
Births attended by skilled health staff (% of total)	..		87	
Maternal mortality ratio (per 100,000 live births)	360		230	
Women's share of population ages 15+ living with HIV (%)	52		56	
Prevalence of HIV (% ages 15–24)	1.7	0.9	0.8	0.5
Economic structure, participation, and access to resources				
Labor force participation rate (% of population ages 15+)	31	66	36	68
Labor force participation rate (% of ages 15–24)	41	50	41	49
Wage and salaried workers (% of employed ages 15+)	..	..	..	..
Self-employed workers (% of employed ages 15+)	..	..	..	..
Unpaid family workers (% of employed ages 15+)	..	..	..	..
Employment in agriculture (% of employed ages 15+)	..	..	..	..
Employment in industry (% of employed ages 15+)	..	..	..	..
Employment in services (% of employed ages 15+)	..	..	..	..
Women in wage employment in the nonagricultural sector (%)	27		..	
Women's share of part-time employment (% of total)	..		..	
Maternity leave (days paid)	..		98	
Maternity leave benefits (% of wages paid)	..		100	
Employment to population ratio (% ages 15+)	..	..	..	..
Employment to population ratio (% ages 15–24)	..	..	..	..
Firms with female participation in ownership (%)	..		22	
Firms with a female top manager (%)	..		14	
Children in employment (% of children ages 7–14)	..	..	..	..
Unemployment rate (% of labor force ages 15+)	..	..	..	..
Unemployment rate (% of labor force ages 15–24)	..	..	..	..
Internet users (%)	..	..	..	..
Account at a financial institution (% age 15+)	..	..	9	17
Mobile account (% age 15+)	..	..	..	..
Saved any money last year (% age 15+)	..	..	..	..
Public life and decision making				
Seats held by women in national parliament (%)	..		13	
Female legislators, senior officials and managers (% of total)	..		..	
Proportion of women in ministerial level positions (%)	..		5	
Agency				
Total fertility rate (births per woman)	4.5		3.4	
Adolescent fertility rate (births per 1,000 women ages 15–19)	33		22	
Women first married by age 18 (% of women ages 20–24)	..		..	

Dominica

Latin America & the Caribbean	Upper middle income
Population (thousands)	72
GNI, Atlas ($ millions)	511
GNI per capita, Atlas ($)	7,070
Population living below $1.90 a day (%)	..

	2000		2013	
	Female	Male	Female	Male
Education				
Net primary enrollment rate (%)	..	..	..	..
Net secondary enrollment rate (%)	90	78	82	76
Gross tertiary enrollment ratio (% of relevant age group)	..	..	..	..
Primary completion rate (% of relevant age group)	125	114	103	103
Progression to secondary school (%)	96	86	95	95
Lower secondary completion rate (% of relevant age group)	..	..	75	83
Gross tertiary graduation ratio (%)	..	..	..	
Female share of graduates in eng., manf. and constr. (%, tertiary)	..		..	
Youth literacy rate (% of population ages 15-24)	..	..	..	..
Health and related services				
Sex ratio at birth (male births per female births)	..		..	
Under-five mortality rate (per 1,000 live births)	14	16	20	23
Life expectancy at birth (years)	79	75	..	..
Pregnant women receiving prenatal care (%)	100		..	
Births attended by skilled health staff (% of total)	100		100	
Maternal mortality ratio (per 100,000 live births)	..		..	
Women's share of population ages 15+ living with HIV (%)	..		..	
Prevalence of HIV (% ages 15-24)	..	..	..	..
Economic structure, participation, and access to resources				
Labor force participation rate (% of population ages 15+)	..	..	..	..
Labor force participation rate (% of ages 15-24)	..	..	..	..
Wage and salaried workers (% of employed ages 15+)	76	64	..	..
Self-employed workers (% of employed ages 15+)	24	36	..	..
Unpaid family workers (% of employed ages 15+)	1.9	1.2	..	..
Employment in agriculture (% of employed ages 15+)	8	29	..	..
Employment in industry (% of employed ages 15+)	10	27	..	..
Employment in services (% of employed ages 15+)	82	44	..	..
Women in wage employment in the nonagricultural sector (%)	44		..	
Women's share of part-time employment (% of total)	..		..	
Maternity leave (days paid)			84	
Maternity leave benefits (% of wages paid)			60	
Employment to population ratio (% ages 15+)	..	..	..	..
Employment to population ratio (% ages 15-24)	..	..	..	..
Firms with female participation in ownership (%)	..		41	
Firms with a female top manager (%)	..		24	
Children in employment (% of children ages 7-14)	..	..	..	..
Unemployment rate (% of labor force ages 15+)	..	..	..	..
Unemployment rate (% of labor force ages 15-24)	..	..	..	..
Internet users (%)	..	..	..	..
Account at a financial institution (% age 15+)	..	..	..	..
Mobile account (% age 15+)	..	..	..	..
Saved any money last year (% age 15+)	..	..	..	..
Public life and decision making				
Seats held by women in national parliament (%)	..		22	
Female legislators, senior officials and managers (% of total)	57		..	
Proportion of women in ministerial level positions (%)	..		25	
Agency				
Total fertility rate (births per woman)	1.9		..	
Adolescent fertility rate (births per 1,000 women ages 15-19)	..		..	
Women first married by age 18 (% of women ages 20-24)	..		..	

Dominican Republic

Latin America & the Caribbean	Upper middle income
Population (millions)	10
GNI, Atlas ($ billions)	63
GNI per capita, Atlas ($)	6,030
Population living below $1.90 a day (%)	2

	2000 Female	2000 Male	2013 Female	2013 Male
Education				
Net primary enrollment rate (%)	83	82	85	88
Net secondary enrollment rate (%)	44	36	66	58
Gross tertiary enrollment ratio (% of relevant age group)	..	..	57	36
Primary completion rate (% of relevant age group)	81	73	91	90
Progression to secondary school (%)	93	90	97	93
Lower secondary completion rate (% of relevant age group)	65	54	81	72
Gross tertiary graduation ratio (%)	..	..	25	14
Female share of graduates in eng., manf. and constr. (%, tertiary)	..		34	
Youth literacy rate (% of population ages 15–24)	95	93	98	97
Health and related services				
Sex ratio at birth (male births per female births)	1.05		1.05	
Under-five mortality rate (per 1,000 live births)	37	45	28	34
Life expectancy at birth (years)	74	68	77	70
Pregnant women receiving prenatal care (%)	98		99	
Births attended by skilled health staff (% of total)	98		99	
Maternal mortality ratio (per 100,000 live births)	120		100	
Women's share of population ages 15+ living with HIV (%)	43		48	
Prevalence of HIV (% ages 15–24)	1.3	1.4	0.4	0.4
Economic structure, participation, and access to resources				
Labor force participation rate (% of population ages 15+)	46	80	51	79
Labor force participation rate (% of ages 15–24)	38	63	42	61
Wage and salaried workers (% of employed ages 15+)	70	50	45	39
Self-employed workers (% of employed ages 15+)	30	50	24	52
Unpaid family workers (% of employed ages 15+)	2.5	2.0	2.1	1.6
Employment in agriculture (% of employed ages 15+)	3	23	3	21
Employment in industry (% of employed ages 15+)	20	26	10	22
Employment in services (% of employed ages 15+)	77	51	88	56
Women in wage employment in the nonagricultural sector (%)	37		42	
Women's share of part-time employment (% of total)	49		51	
Maternity leave (days paid)	..		84	
Maternity leave benefits (% of wages paid)	..		100	
Employment to population ratio (% ages 15+)	36	73	40	71
Employment to population ratio (% ages 15–24)	25	53	25	48
Firms with female participation in ownership (%)	..		30	
Firms with a female top manager (%)	..		11	
Children in employment (% of children ages 7–14)	1	6	..	..
Unemployment rate (% of labor force ages 15+)	24	9	23	10
Unemployment rate (% of labor force ages 15–24)	35	16	42	22
Internet users (%)	..	..	..	..
Account at a financial institution (% age 15+)	..	..	56	52
Mobile account (% age 15+)	..	..	0.8	3.8
Saved any money last year (% age 15+)	..	..	55	59
Public life and decision making				
Seats held by women in national parliament (%)	..		21	
Female legislators, senior officials and managers (% of total)	31		37	
Proportion of women in ministerial level positions (%)	..		19	
Agency				
Total fertility rate (births per woman)	2.9		2.5	
Adolescent fertility rate (births per 1,000 women ages 15–19)	110		98	
Women first married by age 18 (% of women ages 20–24)	31		37	

Ecuador

Latin America & the Caribbean	Upper middle income
Population (millions)	16
GNI, Atlas ($ billions)	97
GNI per capita, Atlas ($)	6,070
Population living below $1.90 a day (%)	4

	2000		2013	
	Female	Male	Female	Male
Education				
Net primary enrollment rate (%)	97	96	96	94
Net secondary enrollment rate (%)	49	48	85	82
Gross tertiary enrollment ratio (% of relevant age group)	..	..	46	35
Primary completion rate (% of relevant age group)	98	97	111	110
Progression to secondary school (%)	68	72	97	99
Lower secondary completion rate (% of relevant age group)	58	58	89	87
Gross tertiary graduation ratio (%)	..	..	..	..
Female share of graduates in eng., manf. and constr. (%, tertiary)	..		20	
Youth literacy rate (% of population ages 15–24)	96	96	99	99
Health and related services				
Sex ratio at birth (male births per female births)	1.05		1.05	
Under-five mortality rate (per 1,000 live births)	30	38	19	24
Life expectancy at birth (years)	76	71	79	74
Pregnant women receiving prenatal care (%)	69		..	
Births attended by skilled health staff (% of total)	99		91	
Maternal mortality ratio (per 100,000 live births)	120		87	
Women's share of population ages 15+ living with HIV (%)	28		24	
Prevalence of HIV (% ages 15–24)	0.2	0.3	0.1	0.2
Economic structure, participation, and access to resources				
Labor force participation rate (% of population ages 15+)	50	84	55	83
Labor force participation rate (% of ages 15–24)	42	66	41	61
Wage and salaried workers (% of employed ages 15+)	49	56	56	38
Self-employed workers (% of employed ages 15+)	51	44	44	62
Unpaid family workers (% of employed ages 15+)	18.6	7.4	10.5	8.0
Employment in agriculture (% of employed ages 15+)	21	34	21	32
Employment in industry (% of employed ages 15+)	14	23	11	22
Employment in services (% of employed ages 15+)	65	43	68	46
Women in wage employment in the nonagricultural sector (%)	39		38	
Women's share of part-time employment (% of total)	52		56	
Maternity leave (days paid)	..		84	
Maternity leave benefits (% of wages paid)	..		100	
Employment to population ratio (% ages 15+)	45	79	52	80
Employment to population ratio (% ages 15–24)	34	58	36	56
Firms with female participation in ownership (%)	..		24	
Firms with a female top manager (%)	..		17	
Children in employment (% of children ages 7–14)	..	..	3	4
Unemployment rate (% of labor force ages 15+)	10	6	6	3
Unemployment rate (% of labor force ages 15–24)	20	13	13	8
Internet users (%)	..	..	..	..
Account at a financial institution (% age 15+)	..	..	41	52
Mobile account (% age 15+)	..	..	..	..
Saved any money last year (% age 15+)	..	..	31	33
Public life and decision making				
Seats held by women in national parliament (%)	..		42	
Female legislators, senior officials and managers (% of total)	29		40	
Proportion of women in ministerial level positions (%)	..		24	
Agency				
Total fertility rate (births per woman)	3.1		2.6	
Adolescent fertility rate (births per 1,000 women ages 15–19)	83		76	
Women first married by age 18 (% of women ages 20–24)	..		..	

Egypt, Arab Rep.

Middle East & North Africa   **Lower middle income**

Population (millions)	90
GNI, Atlas ($ billions)	273
GNI per capita, Atlas ($)	3,050
Population living below $1.90 a day (%)	..

	2000 Female	2000 Male	2013 Female	2013 Male
Education				
Net primary enrollment rate (%)	91	96	..	..
Net secondary enrollment rate (%)	..	..	85	86
Gross tertiary enrollment ratio (% of relevant age group)	27	35	31	35
Primary completion rate (% of relevant age group)	94	101	110	111
Progression to secondary school (%)	96	91	95	89
Lower secondary completion rate (% of relevant age group)	..	..	87	85
Gross tertiary graduation ratio (%)	21	24	27	27
Female share of graduates in eng., manf. and constr. (%, tertiary)	..		25	
Youth literacy rate (% of population ages 15–24)	..	..	90	94
Health and related services				
Sex ratio at birth (male births per female births)	1.05		1.05	
Under-five mortality rate (per 1,000 live births)	45	48	23	25
Life expectancy at birth (years)	71	66	74	69
Pregnant women receiving prenatal care (%)	53		..	
Births attended by skilled health staff (% of total)	61		..	
Maternal mortality ratio (per 100,000 live births)	75		45	
Women's share of population ages 15+ living with HIV (%)	27		29	
Prevalence of HIV (% ages 15–24)	0.1	0.1	0.1	0.1
Economic structure, participation, and access to resources				
Labor force participation rate (% of population ages 15+)	19	73	24	75
Labor force participation rate (% of ages 15–24)	19	44	20	48
Wage and salaried workers (% of employed ages 15+)	57	61	52	63
Self-employed workers (% of employed ages 15+)	43	39	48	37
Unpaid family workers (% of employed ages 15+)	26.0	8.2	34.9	5.5
Employment in agriculture (% of employed ages 15+)	39	27	43	26
Employment in industry (% of employed ages 15+)	7	25	5	28
Employment in services (% of employed ages 15+)	54	48	52	46
Women in wage employment in the nonagricultural sector (%)	19		19	
Women's share of part-time employment (% of total)	..		..	
Maternity leave (days paid)	..		90	
Maternity leave benefits (% of wages paid)	..		100	
Employment to population ratio (% ages 15+)	15	69	17	69
Employment to population ratio (% ages 15–24)	10	36	6	35
Firms with female participation in ownership (%)	..		..	
Firms with a female top manager (%)	..			
Children in employment (% of children ages 7–14)	..	..	..	..
Unemployment rate (% of labor force ages 15+)	22	6	29	7
Unemployment rate (% of labor force ages 15–24)	46	17	71	26
Internet users (%)	..	..	..	..
Account at a financial institution (% age 15+)	..	..	9	18
Mobile account (% age 15+)	..	..	0.1	2.1
Saved any money last year (% age 15+)	..	..	24	28
Public life and decision making				
Seats held by women in national parliament (%)	..		..	
Female legislators, senior officials and managers (% of total)	10		7	
Proportion of women in ministerial level positions (%)	..		12	
Agency				
Total fertility rate (births per woman)	3.3		2.8	
Adolescent fertility rate (births per 1,000 women ages 15–19)	54		52	
Women first married by age 18 (% of women ages 20–24)	20		..	

El Salvador

Latin America & the Caribbean	Lower middle income
Population (millions)	6
GNI, Atlas ($ billions)	24
GNI per capita, Atlas ($)	3,950
Population living below $1.90 a day (%)	3

	2000		2013	
	Female	Male	Female	Male
Education				
Net primary enrollment rate (%)	83	83	91	91
Net secondary enrollment rate (%)	44	44	64	61
Gross tertiary enrollment ratio (% of relevant age group)	22	19	28	24
Primary completion rate (% of relevant age group)	82	84	101	100
Progression to secondary school (%)	94	93	95	96
Lower secondary completion rate (% of relevant age group)	59	57	80	77
Gross tertiary graduation ratio (%)	7	6	13	9
Female share of graduates in eng., manf. and constr. (%, tertiary)	26		27	
Youth literacy rate (% of population ages 15–24)	..	..	98	97
Health and related services				
Sex ratio at birth (male births per female births)	1.05		1.05	
Under-five mortality rate (per 1,000 live births)	29	36	15	19
Life expectancy at birth (years)	74	65	77	68
Pregnant women receiving prenatal care (%)	76		..	
Births attended by skilled health staff (% of total)	90		100	
Maternal mortality ratio (per 100,000 live births)	80		69	
Women's share of population ages 15+ living with HIV (%)	32		35	
Prevalence of HIV (% ages 15–24)	0.3	0.4	0.2	0.2
Economic structure, participation, and access to resources				
Labor force participation rate (% of population ages 15+)	45	79	48	79
Labor force participation rate (% of ages 15–24)	33	64	34	64
Wage and salaried workers (% of employed ages 15+)	41	60	41	62
Self-employed workers (% of employed ages 15+)	49	39	49	37
Unpaid family workers (% of employed ages 15+)	7.4	8.3	8.5	7.1
Employment in agriculture (% of employed ages 15+)	4	34	5	32
Employment in industry (% of employed ages 15+)	24	24	18	23
Employment in services (% of employed ages 15+)	72	42	77	45
Women in wage employment in the nonagricultural sector (%)	32		33	
Women's share of part-time employment (% of total)	53		60	
Maternity leave (days paid)	..		84	
Maternity leave benefits (% of wages paid)	..		100	
Employment to population ratio (% ages 15+)	43	72	46	73
Employment to population ratio (% ages 15–24)	29	55	31	56
Firms with female participation in ownership (%)	..		40	
Firms with a female top manager (%)	..		21	
Children in employment (% of children ages 7–14)	..	..	4	10
Unemployment rate (% of labor force ages 15+)	5	9	4	8
Unemployment rate (% of labor force ages 15–24)	10	15	11	13
Internet users (%)	..	..	21	25
Account at a financial institution (% age 15+)	..	..	29	40
Mobile account (% age 15+)	..	..	4.4	4.7
Saved any money last year (% age 15+)	..	..	54	61
Public life and decision making				
Seats held by women in national parliament (%)	..		32	
Female legislators, senior officials and managers (% of total)	26		37	
Proportion of women in ministerial level positions (%)	..		21	
Agency				
Total fertility rate (births per woman)	2.9		2.2	
Adolescent fertility rate (births per 1,000 women ages 15–19)	88		66	
Women first married by age 18 (% of women ages 20–24)	..		..	

Equatorial Guinea

High income

Population (thousands)	821
GNI, Atlas ($ billions)	10
GNI per capita, Atlas ($)	12,640
Population living below $1.90 a day (%)	..

	2000 Female	2000 Male	2013 Female	2013 Male
Education				
Net primary enrollment rate (%)	61	75	61	61
Net secondary enrollment rate (%)	12	37	..	..
Gross tertiary enrollment ratio (% of relevant age group)	2	5	..	..
Primary completion rate (% of relevant age group)	42	54	55	54
Progression to secondary school (%)	..	..	92	100
Lower secondary completion rate (% of relevant age group)	12	22	32	36
Gross tertiary graduation ratio (%)	..	..		
Female share of graduates in eng., manf. and constr. (%, tertiary)	..		..	
Youth literacy rate (% of population ages 15–24)	97	98	99	98
Health and related services				
Sex ratio at birth (male births per female births)	1.03		1.03	
Under-five mortality rate (per 1,000 live births)	143	161	88	101
Life expectancy at birth (years)	49	46	55	52
Pregnant women receiving prenatal care (%)	86		91	
Births attended by skilled health staff (% of total)	65		68	
Maternal mortality ratio (per 100,000 live births)	790		290	
Women's share of population ages 15+ living with HIV (%)	55		56	
Prevalence of HIV (% ages 15–24)	1.1	0.5	2.5	1.3
Economic structure, participation, and access to resources				
Labor force participation rate (% of population ages 15+)	80	93	81	92
Labor force participation rate (% of ages 15–24)	64	89	64	88
Wage and salaried workers (% of employed ages 15+)	..	..	..	..
Self-employed workers (% of employed ages 15+)	..	..	..	..
Unpaid family workers (% of employed ages 15+)	..	..	..	..
Employment in agriculture (% of employed ages 15+)	..	..	..	..
Employment in industry (% of employed ages 15+)	..	..	..	..
Employment in services (% of employed ages 15+)	..	..	..	..
Women in wage employment in the nonagricultural sector (%)	..		..	
Women's share of part-time employment (% of total)	..		..	
Maternity leave (days paid)	..		84	
Maternity leave benefits (% of wages paid)	..		75	
Employment to population ratio (% ages 15+)	75	87	74	85
Employment to population ratio (% ages 15–24)	58	80	55	77
Firms with female participation in ownership (%)	..		..	
Firms with a female top manager (%)	..		..	
Children in employment (% of children ages 7–14)	..	..	..	..
Unemployment rate (% of labor force ages 15+)	7	7	8	8
Unemployment rate (% of labor force ages 15–24)	10	10	13	12
Internet users (%)	..	..	..	..
Account at a financial institution (% age 15+)	..	..	..	..
Mobile account (% age 15+)	..	..	..	..
Saved any money last year (% age 15+)	..	..	..	..
Public life and decision making				
Seats held by women in national parliament (%)	..		24	
Female legislators, senior officials and managers (% of total)	..		..	
Proportion of women in ministerial level positions (%)	..		9	
Agency				
Total fertility rate (births per woman)	5.8		4.8	
Adolescent fertility rate (births per 1,000 women ages 15–19)	131		110	
Women first married by age 18 (% of women ages 20–24)	..		..	

Eritrea

Sub-Saharan Africa				Low income
Population (millions)				5
GNI, Atlas ($ billions)				3
GNI per capita, Atlas ($)				680
Population living below $1.90 a day (%)				..

	2000		2013	
	Female	Male	Female	Male
Education				
Net primary enrollment rate (%)	..	..	..	..
Net secondary enrollment rate (%)	..	..	..	..
Gross tertiary enrollment ratio (% of relevant age group)	0	2	1[a]	3[a]
Primary completion rate (% of relevant age group)	..	..	..	..
Progression to secondary school (%)	85	88	96	99
Lower secondary completion rate (% of relevant age group)	..	..	..	..
Gross tertiary graduation ratio (%)	0	1	..	..
Female share of graduates in eng., manf. and constr. (%, tertiary)	3		16[a]	
Youth literacy rate (% of population ages 15–24)	69	86	90	94
Health and related services				
Sex ratio at birth (male births per female births)	*1.05*		1.05	
Under-five mortality rate (per 1,000 live births)	82	96	41	51
Life expectancy at birth (years)	58	54	65	60
Pregnant women receiving prenatal care (%)	70		89	
Births attended by skilled health staff (% of total)	28		34	
Maternal mortality ratio (per 100,000 live births)	670		380	
Women's share of population ages 15+ living with HIV (%)	68		64	
Prevalence of HIV (% ages 15–24)	1.1	0.4	0.3	0.2
Economic structure, participation, and access to resources				
Labor force participation rate (% of population ages 15+)	75	91	80	90
Labor force participation rate (% of ages 15–24)	75	83	74	80
Wage and salaried workers (% of employed ages 15+)	..	..	..	..
Self-employed workers (% of employed ages 15+)	..	..	..	..
Unpaid family workers (% of employed ages 15+)	..	..	..	..
Employment in agriculture (% of employed ages 15+)	..	..	..	..
Employment in industry (% of employed ages 15+)	..	..	..	..
Employment in services (% of employed ages 15+)	..	..	..	..
Women in wage employment in the nonagricultural sector (%)	..		..	
Women's share of part-time employment (% of total)	..		..	
Maternity leave (days paid)	..		..	
Maternity leave benefits (% of wages paid)	..		..	
Employment to population ratio (% ages 15+)	69	84	74	84
Employment to population ratio (% ages 15–24)	65	74	66	72
Firms with female participation in ownership (%)	..		..	
Firms with a female top manager (%)	..		..	
Children in employment (% of children ages 7–14)	..	..	..	..
Unemployment rate (% of labor force ages 15+)	8	7	8	7
Unemployment rate (% of labor force ages 15–24)	12	10	11	10
Internet users (%)	..	..	..	..
Account at a financial institution (% age 15+)	..	..	..	..
Mobile account (% age 15+)	..	..	..	..
Saved any money last year (% age 15+)	..	..	..	..
Public life and decision making				
Seats held by women in national parliament (%)	..		22	
Female legislators, senior officials and managers (% of total)	..		..	
Proportion of women in ministerial level positions (%)	..		17	
Agency				
Total fertility rate (births per woman)	5.9		4.7	
Adolescent fertility rate (births per 1,000 women ages 15–19)	89		56	
Women first married by age 18 (% of women ages 20–24)	*47*		*41*	

Estonia

High income

Population (millions)	1.3
GNI, Atlas ($ billions)	24
GNI per capita, Atlas ($)	18,530
Population living below $1.90 a day (%)	<2

	2000		2013	
	Female	**Male**	**Female**	**Male**
Education				
Net primary enrollment rate (%)	96	97	95	95
Net secondary enrollment rate (%)	86	83	90	88
Gross tertiary enrollment ratio (% of relevant age group)	67	46	94	63
Primary completion rate (% of relevant age group)	94	95	98	98
Progression to secondary school (%)	100	100	99	100
Lower secondary completion rate (% of relevant age group)	92	86	97	100
Gross tertiary graduation ratio (%)	13	7	34	17
Female share of graduates in eng., manf. and constr. (%, tertiary)	32		30	
Youth literacy rate (% of population ages 15-24)	100	100	100	100
Health and related services				
Sex ratio at birth (male births per female births)	1.06		1.06	
Under-five mortality rate (per 1,000 live births)	10	12	3	3
Life expectancy at birth (years)	76	65	82	71
Pregnant women receiving prenatal care (%)	..		..	
Births attended by skilled health staff (% of total)	100		..	
Maternal mortality ratio (per 100,000 live births)	26		11	
Women's share of population ages 15+ living with HIV (%)	..		..	
Prevalence of HIV (% ages 15-24)	..	..	..	..
Economic structure, participation, and access to resources				
Labor force participation rate (% of population ages 15+)	52	67	56	69
Labor force participation rate (% of ages 15-24)	31	42	37	44
Wage and salaried workers (% of employed ages 15+)	94	90	94	88
Self-employed workers (% of employed ages 15+)	6	10	6	12
Unpaid family workers (% of employed ages 15+)	0.4	0.4	0.3	0.3
Employment in agriculture (% of employed ages 15+)	4	10	3	7
Employment in industry (% of employed ages 15+)	23	43	18	45
Employment in services (% of employed ages 15+)	72	48	80	48
Women in wage employment in the nonagricultural sector (%)	52		52	
Women's share of part-time employment (% of total)	69		72	
Maternity leave (days paid)	..		140	
Maternity leave benefits (% of wages paid)	..		100	
Employment to population ratio (% ages 15+)	46	57	52	63
Employment to population ratio (% ages 15-24)	24	32	30	37
Firms with female participation in ownership (%)	..		36	
Firms with a female top manager (%)	..		25	
Children in employment (% of children ages 7-14)	..	..	..	..
Unemployment rate (% of labor force ages 15+)	12	15	8	9
Unemployment rate (% of labor force ages 15-24)	22	25	19	17
Internet users (%)	..	..	79	81
Account at a financial institution (% age 15+)	..	..	97	98
Mobile account (% age 15+)	..	..	..	..
Saved any money last year (% age 15+)	..	..	53	50
Public life and decision making				
Seats held by women in national parliament (%)	..		24	
Female legislators, senior officials and managers (% of total)	40		36	
Proportion of women in ministerial level positions (%)	..		46	
Agency				
Total fertility rate (births per woman)	1.4		1.6	
Adolescent fertility rate (births per 1,000 women ages 15-19)	26		14	
Women first married by age 18 (% of women ages 20-24)	..		..	

Ethiopia

Sub-Saharan Africa				Low income
Population (millions)				97
GNI, Atlas ($ billions)				53
GNI per capita, Atlas ($)				550
Population living below $1.90 a day (%)				*34*

	2000		2013	
	Female	Male	Female	Male
Education				
Net primary enrollment rate (%)	34	46	..	..
Net secondary enrollment rate (%)	10	15	..	..
Gross tertiary enrollment ratio (% of relevant age group)	1	2	..	..
Primary completion rate (% of relevant age group)	16	29	..	..
Progression to secondary school (%)	99	95	97	100
Lower secondary completion rate (% of relevant age group)	6	10	..	..
Gross tertiary graduation ratio (%)	0	2	..	..
Female share of graduates in eng., manf. and constr. (%, tertiary)	4		14	
Youth literacy rate (% of population ages 15–24)	..	..	..	..
Health and related services				
Sex ratio at birth (male births per female births)	*1.04*		*1.04*	
Under-five mortality rate (per 1,000 live births)	135	155	54	65
Life expectancy at birth (years)	53	51	65	62
Pregnant women receiving prenatal care (%)	27		43	
Births attended by skilled health staff (% of total)	6		23	
Maternal mortality ratio (per 100,000 live births)	990		420	
Women's share of population ages 15+ living with HIV (%)	63		62	
Prevalence of HIV (% ages 15–24)	1.6	0.6	0.6	0.5
Economic structure, participation, and access to resources				
Labor force participation rate (% of population ages 15+)	73	90	78	89
Labor force participation rate (% of ages 15–24)	74	84	74	79
Wage and salaried workers (% of employed ages 15+)	6	10	..	..
Self-employed workers (% of employed ages 15+)	93	90	..	..
Unpaid family workers (% of employed ages 15+)	*63.6*	*34.3*	..	..
Employment in agriculture (% of employed ages 15+)	..	..	..	..
Employment in industry (% of employed ages 15+)	..	..	..	..
Employment in services (% of employed ages 15+)	..	..	..	..
Women in wage employment in the nonagricultural sector (%)	*41*		39	
Women's share of part-time employment (% of total)	..		..	
Maternity leave (days paid)			90	
Maternity leave benefits (% of wages paid)	..		100	
Employment to population ratio (% ages 15+)	64	87	71	87
Employment to population ratio (% ages 15–24)	62	78	65	76
Firms with female participation in ownership (%)	..		35	
Firms with a female top manager (%)	..		14	
Children in employment (% of children ages 7–14)	..	..	20	33
Unemployment rate (% of labor force ages 15+)	13	4	9	3
Unemployment rate (% of labor force ages 15–24)	17	6	12	4
Internet users (%)	..	..	..	..
Account at a financial institution (% age 15+)	..	..	21	23
Mobile account (% age 15+)	..	..	0.1	0.0
Saved any money last year (% age 15+)	..	..	45	51
Public life and decision making				
Seats held by women in national parliament (%)	..		28[a]	
Female legislators, senior officials and managers (% of total)	*18*		22	
Proportion of women in ministerial level positions (%)	..		13	
Agency				
Total fertility rate (births per woman)	6.5		4.5	
Adolescent fertility rate (births per 1,000 women ages 15–19)	110		60	
Women first married by age 18 (% of women ages 20–24)	49		*41*	

Faeroe Islands

High income

Population (thousands)	48
GNI, Atlas ($ millions)	..
GNI per capita, Atlas ($)	..
Population living below $1.90 a day (%)	..

	2000		2013	
	Female	Male	Female	Male
Education				
Net primary enrollment rate (%)	..	..	..	..
Net secondary enrollment rate (%)	..	..	..	..
Gross tertiary enrollment ratio (% of relevant age group)	..	..	..	..
Primary completion rate (% of relevant age group)	..	..	..	..
Progression to secondary school (%)	..	..	..	..
Lower secondary completion rate (% of relevant age group)	..	..	..	..
Gross tertiary graduation ratio (%)	..	..	..	..
Female share of graduates in eng., manf. and constr. (%, tertiary)	..		..	
Youth literacy rate (% of population ages 15–24)	..	..	..	..
Health and related services				
Sex ratio at birth (male births per female births)	..		..	
Under-five mortality rate (per 1,000 live births)	..	..	..	..
Life expectancy at birth (years)	81	76	83	79
Pregnant women receiving prenatal care (%)	..		..	
Births attended by skilled health staff (% of total)	..		..	
Maternal mortality ratio (per 100,000 live births)	..		..	
Women's share of population ages 15+ living with HIV (%)	..		..	
Prevalence of HIV (% ages 15–24)	..	..	..	..
Economic structure, participation, and access to resources				
Labor force participation rate (% of population ages 15+)	..	..	..	..
Labor force participation rate (% of ages 15–24)	..	..	..	..
Wage and salaried workers (% of employed ages 15+)	..	..	..	..
Self-employed workers (% of employed ages 15+)	..	..	..	..
Unpaid family workers (% of employed ages 15+)	..	..	..	..
Employment in agriculture (% of employed ages 15+)	..	..	..	..
Employment in industry (% of employed ages 15+)	..	..	..	..
Employment in services (% of employed ages 15+)	..	..	..	..
Women in wage employment in the nonagricultural sector (%)	..		..	
Women's share of part-time employment (% of total)	..		..	
Maternity leave (days paid)	..		..	
Maternity leave benefits (% of wages paid)	..		..	
Employment to population ratio (% ages 15+)	..	..	..	..
Employment to population ratio (% ages 15–24)	..	..	..	..
Firms with female participation in ownership (%)	..		..	
Firms with a female top manager (%)	..		..	
Children in employment (% of children ages 7–14)	..	..	..	..
Unemployment rate (% of labor force ages 15+)	..	..	..	..
Unemployment rate (% of labor force ages 15–24)	..	..	..	..
Internet users (%)	..	..	..	..
Account at a financial institution (% age 15+)	..	..	..	..
Mobile account (% age 15+)	..	..	..	..
Saved any money last year (% age 15+)	..	..	..	..
Public life and decision making				
Seats held by women in national parliament (%)	..		..	
Female legislators, senior officials and managers (% of total)	..		..	
Proportion of women in ministerial level positions (%)	..		..	
Agency				
Total fertility rate (births per woman)	..		..	
Adolescent fertility rate (births per 1,000 women ages 15–19)	..		..	
Women first married by age 18 (% of women ages 20–24)	..		..	

Fiji

East Asia & Pacific			Upper middle income	
Population (thousands)				886
GNI, Atlas ($ billions)				4
GNI per capita, Atlas ($)				4,540
Population living below $1.90 a day (%)				..

	2000		2013	
	Female	Male	Female	Male
Education				
Net primary enrollment rate (%)	92	93	97	96
Net secondary enrollment rate (%)	76	69	88	79
Gross tertiary enrollment ratio (% of relevant age group)	..	..	..	..
Primary completion rate (% of relevant age group)	94	96	105	103
Progression to secondary school (%)	97	100	97	91
Lower secondary completion rate (% of relevant age group)	..	..	99	90
Gross tertiary graduation ratio (%)	..	..	..	..
Female share of graduates in eng., manf. and constr. (%, tertiary)	..		..	
Youth literacy rate (% of population ages 15–24)	..	..	..	..
Health and related services				
Sex ratio at birth (male births per female births)	*1.06*		1.06	
Under-five mortality rate (per 1,000 live births)	22	27	20	24
Life expectancy at birth (years)	70	65	73	67
Pregnant women receiving prenatal care (%)	..		..	
Births attended by skilled health staff (% of total)	99		100	
Maternal mortality ratio (per 100,000 live births)	72		59	
Women's share of population ages 15+ living with HIV (%)	28		40	
Prevalence of HIV (% ages 15–24)	0.1	0.1	0.1	0.1
Economic structure, participation, and access to resources				
Labor force participation rate (% of population ages 15+)	39	76	38	72
Labor force participation rate (% of ages 15–24)	31	55	32	50
Wage and salaried workers (% of employed ages 15+)	55	60	..	..
Self-employed workers (% of employed ages 15+)	45	40	..	..
Unpaid family workers (% of employed ages 15+)	26.9	9.8	..	..
Employment in agriculture (% of employed ages 15+)	..	..	..	..
Employment in industry (% of employed ages 15+)	..	..	..	..
Employment in services (% of employed ages 15+)	..	..	..	..
Women in wage employment in the nonagricultural sector (%)	33		..	
Women's share of part-time employment (% of total)	..		..	
Maternity leave (days paid)			84	
Maternity leave benefits (% of wages paid)			100	
Employment to population ratio (% ages 15+)	34	71	33	67
Employment to population ratio (% ages 15–24)	24	47	24	43
Firms with female participation in ownership (%)	..		..	
Firms with a female top manager (%)	..		..	
Children in employment (% of children ages 7–14)	..	..	..	..
Unemployment rate (% of labor force ages 15+)	11	6	11	6
Unemployment rate (% of labor force ages 15–24)	22	14	25	16
Internet users (%)	..	..	..	..
Account at a financial institution (% age 15+)	..	..	..	..
Mobile account (% age 15+)	..	..	..	..
Saved any money last year (% age 15+)	..	..	..	..
Public life and decision making				
Seats held by women in national parliament (%)	..		14	
Female legislators, senior officials and managers (% of total)	..		..	
Proportion of women in ministerial level positions (%)	..		13	
Agency				
Total fertility rate (births per woman)	3.1		2.6	
Adolescent fertility rate (births per 1,000 women ages 15–19)	43		44	
Women first married by age 18 (% of women ages 20–24)	..		..	

Finland

High income

Population (millions)	5
GNI, Atlas ($ billions)	266
GNI per capita, Atlas ($)	48,910
Population living below $1.90 a day (%)	..

	2000		2013	
	Female	**Male**	**Female**	**Male**
Education				
Net primary enrollment rate (%)	100	100	99	99
Net secondary enrollment rate (%)	95	94	94	94
Gross tertiary enrollment ratio (% of relevant age group)	90	75	101	83
Primary completion rate (% of relevant age group)	97	96	98	100
Progression to secondary school (%)	100	100	100	100
Lower secondary completion rate (% of relevant age group)	..	..	98	97
Gross tertiary graduation ratio (%)	56	32	63	39
Female share of graduates in eng., manf. and constr. (%, tertiary)	20		22	
Youth literacy rate (% of population ages 15–24)	..	..	..	..
Health and related services				
Sex ratio at birth (male births per female births)	1.05		1.04	
Under-five mortality rate (per 1,000 live births)	4	5	2	3
Life expectancy at birth (years)	81	74	84	78
Pregnant women receiving prenatal care (%)	..		..	
Births attended by skilled health staff (% of total)	..		..	
Maternal mortality ratio (per 100,000 live births)	7		4	
Women's share of population ages 15+ living with HIV (%)	..		..	
Prevalence of HIV (% ages 15–24)	..	..	..	..
Economic structure, participation, and access to resources				
Labor force participation rate (% of population ages 15+)	57	67	56	64
Labor force participation rate (% of ages 15–24)	51	57	53	54
Wage and salaried workers (% of employed ages 15+)	91	82	91	82
Self-employed workers (% of employed ages 15+)	9	18	9	18
Unpaid family workers (% of employed ages 15+)	0.6	0.7	0.3	0.6
Employment in agriculture (% of employed ages 15+)	4	8	2	6
Employment in industry (% of employed ages 15+)	14	39	9	36
Employment in services (% of employed ages 15+)	82	53	88	58
Women in wage employment in the nonagricultural sector (%)	50		52	
Women's share of part-time employment (% of total)	64		62	
Maternity leave (days paid)	..		147	
Maternity leave benefits (% of wages paid)	..		58	
Employment to population ratio (% ages 15+)	51	61	52	58
Employment to population ratio (% ages 15–24)	40	46	43	43
Firms with female participation in ownership (%)	..		..	
Firms with a female top manager (%)	..		..	
Children in employment (% of children ages 7–14)	..	..	..	..
Unemployment rate (% of labor force ages 15+)	11	9	8	9
Unemployment rate (% of labor force ages 15–24)	22	19	18	22
Internet users (%)	..	..	91	92
Account at a financial institution (% age 15+)	..	..	100	100
Mobile account (% age 15+)	..	..	..	..
Saved any money last year (% age 15+)	..	..	74	68
Public life and decision making				
Seats held by women in national parliament (%)	..		42	
Female legislators, senior officials and managers (% of total)	27		32	
Proportion of women in ministerial level positions (%)	..		63	
Agency				
Total fertility rate (births per woman)	1.7		1.8	
Adolescent fertility rate (births per 1,000 women ages 15–19)	10		7	
Women first married by age 18 (% of women ages 20–24)	..		..	

France

		High income
Population (millions)		66
GNI, Atlas ($ billions)		2,852
GNI per capita, Atlas ($)		43,070
Population living below $1.90 a day (%)		..

	2000		2013	
	Female	Male	Female	Male
Education				
Net primary enrollment rate (%)	99	99	99	98
Net secondary enrollment rate (%)	92	90	98	97
Gross tertiary enrollment ratio (% of relevant age group)	63	51	66	53
Primary completion rate (% of relevant age group)	..	..	..	..
Progression to secondary school (%)	..	..	..	..
Lower secondary completion rate (% of relevant age group)	..	..	102	100
Gross tertiary graduation ratio (%)	46	34	48	35
Female share of graduates in eng., manf. and constr. (%, tertiary)	19		26	
Youth literacy rate (% of population ages 15–24)	..	..	..	..
Health and related services				
Sex ratio at birth (male births per female births)	*1.05*		1.05	
Under-five mortality rate (per 1,000 live births)	5	6	4	5
Life expectancy at birth (years)	83	75	85	79
Pregnant women receiving prenatal care (%)	..		..	
Births attended by skilled health staff (% of total)	..		..	
Maternal mortality ratio (per 100,000 live births)	10		12	
Women's share of population ages 15+ living with HIV (%)	..		..	
Prevalence of HIV (% ages 15–24)	..	..	..	..
Economic structure, participation, and access to resources				
Labor force participation rate (% of population ages 15+)	48	63	51	62
Labor force participation rate (% of ages 15–24)	32	39	34	41
Wage and salaried workers (% of employed ages 15+)	92	86	92	86
Self-employed workers (% of employed ages 15+)	8	14	8	15
Unpaid family workers (% of employed ages 15+)	2.3	0.4	0.7	0.2
Employment in agriculture (% of employed ages 15+)	3	5	2	4
Employment in industry (% of employed ages 15+)	14	36	10	32
Employment in services (% of employed ages 15+)	83	59	87	64
Women in wage employment in the nonagricultural sector (%)	47		50	
Women's share of part-time employment (% of total)	83		80	
Maternity leave (days paid)	..		112	
Maternity leave benefits (% of wages paid)	..		73	
Employment to population ratio (% ages 15+)	43	58	45	55
Employment to population ratio (% ages 15–24)	25	32	26	32
Firms with female participation in ownership (%)	..		..	
Firms with a female top manager (%)	..		..	
Children in employment (% of children ages 7–14)	..	..	..	..
Unemployment rate (% of labor force ages 15+)	12	9	10	10
Unemployment rate (% of labor force ages 15–24)	23	19	25	23
Internet users (%)	..	..	80	84
Account at a financial institution (% age 15+)	..	..	95	98
Mobile account (% age 15+)	..	..	..	..
Saved any money last year (% age 15+)	..	..	64	70
Public life and decision making				
Seats held by women in national parliament (%)	..		26	
Female legislators, senior officials and managers (% of total)	35		39	
Proportion of women in ministerial level positions (%)	..		50	
Agency				
Total fertility rate (births per woman)	1.9		2.0	
Adolescent fertility rate (births per 1,000 women ages 15–19)	10		9	
Women first married by age 18 (% of women ages 20–24)	..		..	

French Polynesia

High income

Population (thousands)	280
GNI, Atlas ($ billions)	..
GNI per capita, Atlas ($)	..
Population living below $1.90 a day (%)	..

	2000 Female	2000 Male	2013 Female	2013 Male
Education				
Net primary enrollment rate (%)	..	..	..	..
Net secondary enrollment rate (%)	..	..	..	..
Gross tertiary enrollment ratio (% of relevant age group)	..	..	..	..
Primary completion rate (% of relevant age group)	..	..	..	..
Progression to secondary school (%)	..	..	..	..
Lower secondary completion rate (% of relevant age group)	..	..	..	..
Gross tertiary graduation ratio (%)	..	..	..	..
Female share of graduates in eng., manf. and constr. (%, tertiary)	..		..	
Youth literacy rate (% of population ages 15–24)	..	..	..	..
Health and related services				
Sex ratio at birth (male births per female births)	1.05		1.05	
Under-five mortality rate (per 1,000 live births)	..	..	..	..
Life expectancy at birth (years)	75	70	79	74
Pregnant women receiving prenatal care (%)	..			
Births attended by skilled health staff (% of total)	99		..	
Maternal mortality ratio (per 100,000 live births)	..		..	
Women's share of population ages 15+ living with HIV (%)	..		..	
Prevalence of HIV (% ages 15–24)	..	..	..	..
Economic structure, participation, and access to resources				
Labor force participation rate (% of population ages 15+)	48	69	47	64
Labor force participation rate (% of ages 15–24)	32	47	32	46
Wage and salaried workers (% of employed ages 15+)	84	79	..	..
Self-employed workers (% of employed ages 15+)	16	21	..	..
Unpaid family workers (% of employed ages 15+)	3.0	2.1	..	..
Employment in agriculture (% of employed ages 15+)	5	12	..	..
Employment in industry (% of employed ages 15+)	8	24	..	..
Employment in services (% of employed ages 15+)	87	64	..	..
Women in wage employment in the nonagricultural sector (%)	42		45	
Women's share of part-time employment (% of total)	..		..	
Maternity leave (days paid)	..		..	
Maternity leave benefits (% of wages paid)	..		..	
Employment to population ratio (% ages 15+)	..	..	..	..
Employment to population ratio (% ages 15–24)	..	..	..	..
Firms with female participation in ownership (%)	..		..	
Firms with a female top manager (%)	..		..	
Children in employment (% of children ages 7–14)	..	..	..	..
Unemployment rate (% of labor force ages 15+)	..	..	..	..
Unemployment rate (% of labor force ages 15–24)	..	..	..	..
Internet users (%)	..	..	..	..
Account at a financial institution (% age 15+)	..	..	..	..
Mobile account (% age 15+)	..	..	..	..
Saved any money last year (% age 15+)	..	..	..	..
Public life and decision making				
Seats held by women in national parliament (%)	..		..	
Female legislators, senior officials and managers (% of total)	..		..	
Proportion of women in ministerial level positions (%)	..		..	
Agency				
Total fertility rate (births per woman)	2.5		2.1	
Adolescent fertility rate (births per 1,000 women ages 15–19)	47		36	
Women first married by age 18 (% of women ages 20–24)	..		..	

Gabon

Sub-Saharan Africa   **Upper middle income**

Population (millions)	1.7
GNI, Atlas ($ billions)	16
GNI per capita, Atlas ($)	9,450
Population living below $1.90 a day (%)	..

	2000		2013	
	Female	Male	Female	Male
Education				
Net primary enrollment rate (%)	..	..	..	..
Net secondary enrollment rate (%)	..	..	..	..
Gross tertiary enrollment ratio (% of relevant age group)	7	10	..	..
Primary completion rate (% of relevant age group)	76	73	..	..
Progression to secondary school (%)	..	..	..	..
Lower secondary completion rate (% of relevant age group)	..	..	..	..
Gross tertiary graduation ratio (%)	..	..	..	..
Female share of graduates in eng., manf. and constr. (%, tertiary)	..		..	
Youth literacy rate (% of population ages 15–24)	..	..	89	87
Health and related services				
Sex ratio at birth (male births per female births)	1.03		1.03	
Under-five mortality rate (per 1,000 live births)	79	92	46	55
Life expectancy at birth (years)	61	59	64	62
Pregnant women receiving prenatal care (%)	94		95	
Births attended by skilled health staff (% of total)	86		89	
Maternal mortality ratio (per 100,000 live births)	330		240	
Women's share of population ages 15+ living with HIV (%)	70		67	
Prevalence of HIV (% ages 15–24)	4.2	1.2	1.3	0.6
Economic structure, participation, and access to resources				
Labor force participation rate (% of population ages 15+)	55	66	56	65
Labor force participation rate (% of ages 15–24)	26	32	24	28
Wage and salaried workers (% of employed ages 15+)	..	..	..	..
Self-employed workers (% of employed ages 15+)	..	..	..	..
Unpaid family workers (% of employed ages 15+)	..	..	..	..
Employment in agriculture (% of employed ages 15+)	..	..	..	..
Employment in industry (% of employed ages 15+)	..	..	..	..
Employment in services (% of employed ages 15+)	..	..	..	..
Women in wage employment in the nonagricultural sector (%)	..		35	
Women's share of part-time employment (% of total)	..		..	
Maternity leave (days paid)	..		98	
Maternity leave benefits (% of wages paid)	..		100	
Employment to population ratio (% ages 15+)	40	56	42	56
Employment to population ratio (% ages 15–24)	15	21	14	19
Firms with female participation in ownership (%)	..		..	
Firms with a female top manager (%)	..		..	
Children in employment (% of children ages 7–14)	..	..	23	26
Unemployment rate (% of labor force ages 15+)	26	16	26	14
Unemployment rate (% of labor force ages 15–24)	42	33	41	31
Internet users (%)	..	..	..	..
Account at a financial institution (% age 15+)	..	..	28	32
Mobile account (% age 15+)	..	..	6.1	7.2
Saved any money last year (% age 15+)	..	..	56	56
Public life and decision making				
Seats held by women in national parliament (%)	..		14	
Female legislators, senior officials and managers (% of total)	..		..	
Proportion of women in ministerial level positions (%)	..		13	
Agency				
Total fertility rate (births per woman)	4.6		4.1	
Adolescent fertility rate (births per 1,000 women ages 15–19)	148		102	
Women first married by age 18 (% of women ages 20–24)	34		22	

Gambia, The

Sub-Saharan Africa	Low income
Population (millions)	1.9
GNI, Atlas ($ millions)	855
GNI per capita, Atlas ($)	440
Population living below $1.90 a day (%)	..

	2000		2013	
	Female	Male	Female	Male
Education				
Net primary enrollment rate (%)	68	75	71	66
Net secondary enrollment rate (%)	..	..	..	..
Gross tertiary enrollment ratio (% of relevant age group)	..	..	..	..
Primary completion rate (% of relevant age group)	64	80	72	69
Progression to secondary school (%)	69	74	94	93
Lower secondary completion rate (% of relevant age group)	30	49	64	65
Gross tertiary graduation ratio (%)	..	..	..	..
Female share of graduates in eng., manf. and constr. (%, tertiary)	..		..	
Youth literacy rate (% of population ages 15–24)	41	64	67	74
Health and related services				
Sex ratio at birth (male births per female births)	1.03		1.03	
Under-five mortality rate (per 1,000 live births)	113	125	64	74
Life expectancy at birth (years)	56	54	60	58
Pregnant women receiving prenatal care (%)	91		98	
Births attended by skilled health staff (% of total)	55		57	
Maternal mortality ratio (per 100,000 live births)	580		430	
Women's share of population ages 15+ living with HIV (%)	59		61	
Prevalence of HIV (% ages 15–24)	1.1	0.6	0.7	0.4
Economic structure, participation, and access to resources				
Labor force participation rate (% of population ages 15+)	71	84	72	83
Labor force participation rate (% of ages 15–24)	65	66	64	64
Wage and salaried workers (% of employed ages 15+)	..	..	..	..
Self-employed workers (% of employed ages 15+)	..	..	..	..
Unpaid family workers (% of employed ages 15+)	..	..	..	..
Employment in agriculture (% of employed ages 15+)	..	..	..	..
Employment in industry (% of employed ages 15+)	..	..	..	..
Employment in services (% of employed ages 15+)	..	..	..	..
Women in wage employment in the nonagricultural sector (%)	32		..	
Women's share of part-time employment (% of total)	..		..	
Maternity leave (days paid)	..		..	
Maternity leave benefits (% of wages paid)	..		..	
Employment to population ratio (% ages 15+)	66	78	67	77
Employment to population ratio (% ages 15–24)	58	60	57	58
Firms with female participation in ownership (%)	..		..	
Firms with a female top manager (%)	..		..	
Children in employment (% of children ages 7–14)	25	25	..	..
Unemployment rate (% of labor force ages 15+)	8	7	7	7
Unemployment rate (% of labor force ages 15–24)	11	10	11	10
Internet users (%)	..	..	..	..
Account at a financial institution (% age 15+)	..	..	..	..
Mobile account (% age 15+)	..	..	..	..
Saved any money last year (% age 15+)	..	..	..	..
Public life and decision making				
Seats held by women in national parliament (%)	..		9	
Female legislators, senior officials and managers (% of total)	..		..	
Proportion of women in ministerial level positions (%)	..		21	
Agency				
Total fertility rate (births per woman)	5.9		5.8	
Adolescent fertility rate (births per 1,000 women ages 15–19)	124		114	
Women first married by age 18 (% of women ages 20–24)	...		36	

Georgia

Europe & Central Asia	Lower middle income
Population (millions)	5
GNI, Atlas ($ billions)	17
GNI per capita, Atlas ($)	3,720
Population living below $1.90 a day (%)	11

	2000		2013	
	Female	**Male**	**Female**	**Male**
Education				
Net primary enrollment rate (%)	..	..	97	96
Net secondary enrollment rate (%)	77	77	92	92
Gross tertiary enrollment ratio (% of relevant age group)	37	39	37	29
Primary completion rate (% of relevant age group)	98	98	110	107
Progression to secondary school (%)	98	98	*100*	*100*
Lower secondary completion rate (% of relevant age group)	84	85	115	114
Gross tertiary graduation ratio (%)	..	..	*22*	*15*
Female share of graduates in eng., manf. and constr. (%, tertiary)	29		23	
Youth literacy rate (% of population ages 15-24)	*100*	*100*	100	100
Health and related services				
Sex ratio at birth (male births per female births)	*1.11*		*1.11*	
Under-five mortality rate (per 1,000 live births)	31	40	11	13
Life expectancy at birth (years)	75	68	78	71
Pregnant women receiving prenatal care (%)	*95*		*98*	
Births attended by skilled health staff (% of total)	96		100	
Maternal mortality ratio (per 100,000 live births)	60		41	
Women's share of population ages 15+ living with HIV (%)	35		20	
Prevalence of HIV (% ages 15-24)	0.1	0.1	0.1	0.3
Economic structure, participation, and access to resources				
Labor force participation rate (% of population ages 15+)	55	74	57	75
Labor force participation rate (% of ages 15-24)	28	44	25	42
Wage and salaried workers (% of employed ages 15+)	37	38	37	40
Self-employed workers (% of employed ages 15+)	62	62	62	60
Unpaid family workers (% of employed ages 15+)	36.7	22.7	34.2	16.1
Employment in agriculture (% of employed ages 15+)	58	47	..	..
Employment in industry (% of employed ages 15+)	4	15	..	..
Employment in services (% of employed ages 15+)	38	38	..	..
Women in wage employment in the nonagricultural sector (%)	*49*		*47*	
Women's share of part-time employment (% of total)	..		..	
Maternity leave (days paid)			183	
Maternity leave benefits (% of wages paid)	..		100	
Employment to population ratio (% ages 15+)	49	66	49	64
Employment to population ratio (% ages 15-24)	22	34	16	30
Firms with female participation in ownership (%)	..		34	
Firms with a female top manager (%)	..		32	
Children in employment (% of children ages 7-14)	..	..	..	..
Unemployment rate (% of labor force ages 15+)	10	11	13	15
Unemployment rate (% of labor force ages 15-24)	20	21	35	29
Internet users (%)	..	..	42	45
Account at a financial institution (% age 15+)	..	..	40	40
Mobile account (% age 15+)	..	..	..	..
Saved any money last year (% age 15+)	..	..	12	15
Public life and decision making				
Seats held by women in national parliament (%)	..		11	
Female legislators, senior officials and managers (% of total)	19		..	
Proportion of women in ministerial level positions (%)	..		16	
Agency				
Total fertility rate (births per woman)	1.6		1.8	
Adolescent fertility rate (births per 1,000 women ages 15-19)	53		41	
Women first married by age 18 (% of women ages 20-24)	..		*14*	

Germany

High income

Population (millions)	81
GNI, Atlas ($ billions)	3,853
GNI per capita, Atlas ($)	47,640
Population living below $1.90 a day (%)	..

	2000		2013	
	Female	Male	Female	Male
Education				
Net primary enrollment rate (%)	98	98	97	98
Net secondary enrollment rate (%)	..	..	..	..
Gross tertiary enrollment ratio (% of relevant age group)	..	..	58	62
Primary completion rate (% of relevant age group)	103	102	98	99
Progression to secondary school (%)	100	100	..	..
Lower secondary completion rate (% of relevant age group)	..	..	56	56
Gross tertiary graduation ratio (%)	17	19	34	31
Female share of graduates in eng., manf. and constr. (%, tertiary)	16		..	
Youth literacy rate (% of population ages 15–24)	..	..	..	..
Health and related services				
Sex ratio at birth (male births per female births)	1.06		1.06	
Under-five mortality rate (per 1,000 live births)	5	6	3	4
Life expectancy at birth (years)	81	75	83	79
Pregnant women receiving prenatal care (%)	..		..	
Births attended by skilled health staff (% of total)	..		..	
Maternal mortality ratio (per 100,000 live births)	7		7	
Women's share of population ages 15+ living with HIV (%)	..		..	
Prevalence of HIV (% ages 15–24)	..	..	..	..
Economic structure, participation, and access to resources				
Labor force participation rate (% of population ages 15+)	49	68	54	66
Labor force participation rate (% of ages 15–24)	48	55	48	53
Wage and salaried workers (% of employed ages 15+)	92	87	92	86
Self-employed workers (% of employed ages 15+)	8	13	8	14
Unpaid family workers (% of employed ages 15+)	1.4	0.3	0.7	0.3
Employment in agriculture (% of employed ages 15+)	2	3	1	2
Employment in industry (% of employed ages 15+)	18	45	14	40
Employment in services (% of employed ages 15+)	80	52	85	58
Women in wage employment in the nonagricultural sector (%)	45		48	
Women's share of part-time employment (% of total)	85		79	
Maternity leave (days paid)	..		98	
Maternity leave benefits (% of wages paid)	..		100	
Employment to population ratio (% ages 15+)	45	63	51	63
Employment to population ratio (% ages 15–24)	45	50	45	48
Firms with female participation in ownership (%)	..		..	
Firms with a female top manager (%)	..		..	
Children in employment (% of children ages 7–14)				
Unemployment rate (% of labor force ages 15+)	8	7	5	6
Unemployment rate (% of labor force ages 15–24)	7	9	7	9
Internet users (%)	..	..	82	87
Account at a financial institution (% age 15+)	..	..	99	98
Mobile account (% age 15+)	..	..	..	..
Saved any money last year (% age 15+)	..	..	79	80
Public life and decision making				
Seats held by women in national parliament (%)	..		36	
Female legislators, senior officials and managers (% of total)	27		30	
Proportion of women in ministerial level positions (%)	..		33	
Agency				
Total fertility rate (births per woman)	1.4		1.4	
Adolescent fertility rate (births per 1,000 women ages 15–19)	13		7	
Women first married by age 18 (% of women ages 20–24)	..		..	

Ghana

Sub-Saharan Africa	Lower middle income
Population (millions)	27
GNI, Atlas ($ billions)	43
GNI per capita, Atlas ($)	1,600
Population living below $1.90 a day (%)	..

	2000		2013	
	Female	Male	Female	Male
Education				
Net primary enrollment rate (%)	64	66	89[a]	89[a]
Net secondary enrollment rate (%)	32	37	54[a]	55[a]
Gross tertiary enrollment ratio (% of relevant age group)	..	..	11	18
Primary completion rate (% of relevant age group)	67	76	96[a]	98[a]
Progression to secondary school (%)	86	85	89	88
Lower secondary completion rate (% of relevant age group)	49	59	66[a]	72[a]
Gross tertiary graduation ratio (%)	..	..	8	10
Female share of graduates in eng., manf. and constr. (%, tertiary)	..		18	
Youth literacy rate (% of population ages 15–24)	65	76	83	88
Health and related services				
Sex ratio at birth (male births per female births)	1.05		1.05	
Under-five mortality rate (per 1,000 live births)	94	107	56	67
Life expectancy at birth (years)	58	56	62	60
Pregnant women receiving prenatal care (%)	88		96	
Births attended by skilled health staff (% of total)	44		68	
Maternal mortality ratio (per 100,000 live births)	570		380	
Women's share of population ages 15+ living with HIV (%)	58		60	
Prevalence of HIV (% ages 15–24)	1.2	0.6	0.6	0.4
Economic structure, participation, and access to resources				
Labor force participation rate (% of population ages 15+)	73	77	67	71
Labor force participation rate (% of ages 15–24)	54	53	38	39
Wage and salaried workers (% of employed ages 15+)	..	..	11	25
Self-employed workers (% of employed ages 15+)	..	..	89	75
Unpaid family workers (% of employed ages 15+)	..	..	14.2	8.7
Employment in agriculture (% of employed ages 15+)	50	60	38	46
Employment in industry (% of employed ages 15+)	15	14	14	17
Employment in services (% of employed ages 15+)	36	27	49	37
Women in wage employment in the nonagricultural sector (%)	32		32	
Women's share of part-time employment (% of total)	..		..	
Maternity leave (days paid)	..		84	
Maternity leave benefits (% of wages paid)	..		100	
Employment to population ratio (% ages 15+)	65	69	64	68
Employment to population ratio (% ages 15–24)	45	45	34	36
Firms with female participation in ownership (%)	..		32	
Firms with a female top manager (%)	..		15	
Children in employment (% of children ages 7–14)	..	..	..	..
Unemployment rate (% of labor force ages 15+)	11	10	5	4
Unemployment rate (% of labor force ages 15–24)	17	16	10	7
Internet users (%)	..	..	..	..
Account at a financial institution (% age 15+)	..	..	34	35
Mobile account (% age 15+)	..	..	11.8	14.2
Saved any money last year (% age 15+)	..		53	58
Public life and decision making				
Seats held by women in national parliament (%)	..		11	
Female legislators, senior officials and managers (% of total)	..		..	
Proportion of women in ministerial level positions (%)	..		23	
Agency				
Total fertility rate (births per woman)	4.7		3.9	
Adolescent fertility rate (births per 1,000 women ages 15–19)	81		68	
Women first married by age 18 (% of women ages 20–24)	36		21	

Greece

	High income
Population (millions)	11
GNI, Atlas ($ billions)	242
GNI per capita, Atlas ($)	22,090
Population living below $1.90 a day (%)	..

	2000		2013	
	Female	**Male**	**Female**	**Male**
Education				
Net primary enrollment rate (%)	94	94	100	99
Net secondary enrollment rate (%)	84	78	99	99
Gross tertiary enrollment ratio (% of relevant age group)	53	49	118	115
Primary completion rate (% of relevant age group)	..	..	101	101
Progression to secondary school (%)	..	..	97	100
Lower secondary completion rate (% of relevant age group)	..	..	100	99
Gross tertiary graduation ratio (%)	17	11	37	20
Female share of graduates in eng., manf. and constr. (%, tertiary)	..		32	
Youth literacy rate (% of population ages 15–24)	99	99	99	99
Health and related services				
Sex ratio at birth (male births per female births)	1.07		1.07	
Under-five mortality rate (per 1,000 live births)	7	8	4	5
Life expectancy at birth (years)	81	75	83	78
Pregnant women receiving prenatal care (%)	..		..	
Births attended by skilled health staff (% of total)	..		..	
Maternal mortality ratio (per 100,000 live births)	5		5	
Women's share of population ages 15+ living with HIV (%)	..		..	
Prevalence of HIV (% ages 15–24)	..	..	..	..
Economic structure, participation, and access to resources				
Labor force participation rate (% of population ages 15+)	40	65	44	63
Labor force participation rate (% of ages 15–24)	36	44	28	33
Wage and salaried workers (% of employed ages 15+)	61	56	68	59
Self-employed workers (% of employed ages 15+)	39	44	32	41
Unpaid family workers (% of employed ages 15+)	17.2	5.1	7.7	2.9
Employment in agriculture (% of employed ages 15+)	20	16	13	13
Employment in industry (% of employed ages 15+)	12	29	8	23
Employment in services (% of employed ages 15+)	68	55	80	64
Women in wage employment in the nonagricultural sector (%)	39		43	
Women's share of part-time employment (% of total)	65		63	
Maternity leave (days paid)	..		119	
Maternity leave benefits (% of wages paid)	..		100	
Employment to population ratio (% ages 15+)	34	60	30	47
Employment to population ratio (% ages 15–24)	23	34	10	15
Firms with female participation in ownership (%)	..		..	
Firms with a female top manager (%)	..		..	
Children in employment (% of children ages 7–14)	..	..	..	..
Unemployment rate (% of labor force ages 15+)	17	8	31	24
Unemployment rate (% of labor force ages 15–24)	37	22	64	54
Internet users (%)	..	..	56	64
Account at a financial institution (% age 15+)	..	..	87	88
Mobile account (% age 15+)	..	..	..	..
Saved any money last year (% age 15+)	..	..	22	26
Public life and decision making				
Seats held by women in national parliament (%)	..		23	
Female legislators, senior officials and managers (% of total)	25		23	
Proportion of women in ministerial level positions (%)	..		10	
Agency				
Total fertility rate (births per woman)	1.3		1.3	
Adolescent fertility rate (births per 1,000 women ages 15–19)	11		8	
Women first married by age 18 (% of women ages 20–24)	..		..	

Greenland

Population (thousands)	56
GNI, Atlas ($ billions)	..
GNI per capita, Atlas ($)	..
Population living below $1.90 a day (%)	..

	2000		2013	
	Female	Male	Female	Male
Education				
Net primary enrollment rate (%)	..	..	..	..
Net secondary enrollment rate (%)	..	..	..	..
Gross tertiary enrollment ratio (% of relevant age group)	..	..	..	..
Primary completion rate (% of relevant age group)	..	..	..	..
Progression to secondary school (%)	..	..	..	..
Lower secondary completion rate (% of relevant age group)	..	..	..	..
Gross tertiary graduation ratio (%)	..		..	
Female share of graduates in eng., manf. and constr. (%, tertiary)	..		..	
Youth literacy rate (% of population ages 15–24)	..	..	..	..
Health and related services				
Sex ratio at birth (male births per female births)	..		..	
Under-five mortality rate (per 1,000 live births)	..	..	..	..
Life expectancy at birth (years)	70	64	74	68
Pregnant women receiving prenatal care (%)	..		..	
Births attended by skilled health staff (% of total)	..		..	
Maternal mortality ratio (per 100,000 live births)	..		..	
Women's share of population ages 15+ living with HIV (%)	..		..	
Prevalence of HIV (% ages 15–24)	..	..	..	..
Economic structure, participation, and access to resources				
Labor force participation rate (% of population ages 15+)	..	..	..	..
Labor force participation rate (% of ages 15–24)	..	..	..	..
Wage and salaried workers (% of employed ages 15+)	..	..	..	..
Self-employed workers (% of employed ages 15+)	..	..	..	..
Unpaid family workers (% of employed ages 15+)	..	..	..	..
Employment in agriculture (% of employed ages 15+)	..	..	..	..
Employment in industry (% of employed ages 15+)	..	..	..	..
Employment in services (% of employed ages 15+)	..	..	..	..
Women in wage employment in the nonagricultural sector (%)	49		..	
Women's share of part-time employment (% of total)	..		..	
Maternity leave (days paid)	..		..	
Maternity leave benefits (% of wages paid)	..		..	
Employment to population ratio (% ages 15+)	..	..	..	..
Employment to population ratio (% ages 15–24)	..	..	..	..
Firms with female participation in ownership (%)	..		..	
Firms with a female top manager (%)	..		..	
Children in employment (% of children ages 7–14)	..	..	..	..
Unemployment rate (% of labor force ages 15+)	..	..	..	..
Unemployment rate (% of labor force ages 15–24)	..	..	..	..
Internet users (%)	..	..	..	..
Account at a financial institution (% age 15+)	..	..	..	..
Mobile account (% age 15+)	..	..	..	..
Saved any money last year (% age 15+)	..	..	..	..
Public life and decision making				
Seats held by women in national parliament (%)	..		..	
Female legislators, senior officials and managers (% of total)	..		..	
Proportion of women in ministerial level positions (%)	..		..	
Agency				
Total fertility rate (births per woman)	2.3		2.1	
Adolescent fertility rate (births per 1,000 women ages 15–19)	..		..	
Women first married by age 18 (% of women ages 20–24)	..		..	

Grenada

Latin America & the Caribbean	Upper middle income
Population (thousands)	106
GNI, Atlas ($ millions)	835
GNI per capita, Atlas ($)	7,850
Population living below $1.90 a day (%)	..

	2000		2013	
	Female	Male	Female	Male
Education				
Net primary enrollment rate (%)	94	95	90	91
Net secondary enrollment rate (%)	91	76	81	80
Gross tertiary enrollment ratio (% of relevant age group)	..	..	..	..
Primary completion rate (% of relevant age group)	91	95	91	98
Progression to secondary school (%)	..	..	..	..
Lower secondary completion rate (% of relevant age group)	101	83	..	..
Gross tertiary graduation ratio (%)	..	..	..	..
Female share of graduates in eng., manf. and constr. (%, tertiary)	..		..	
Youth literacy rate (% of population ages 15–24)	..	..	..	..
Health and related services				
Sex ratio at birth (male births per female births)	1.05		1.05	
Under-five mortality rate (per 1,000 live births)	15	17	11	13
Life expectancy at birth (years)	73	68	75	70
Pregnant women receiving prenatal care (%)	85		..	
Births attended by skilled health staff (% of total)	100		99	
Maternal mortality ratio (per 100,000 live births)	29		23	
Women's share of population ages 15+ living with HIV (%)	..		..	
Prevalence of HIV (% ages 15–24)	..	..	..	..
Economic structure, participation, and access to resources				
Labor force participation rate (% of population ages 15+)	..			..
Labor force participation rate (% of ages 15–24)	..			..
Wage and salaried workers (% of employed ages 15+)	75	69	..	..
Self-employed workers (% of employed ages 15+)	23	25	..	..
Unpaid family workers (% of employed ages 15+)	1.7	0.7	..	..
Employment in agriculture (% of employed ages 15+)	10	17	..	..
Employment in industry (% of employed ages 15+)	12	32	..	..
Employment in services (% of employed ages 15+)	77	46	..	..
Women in wage employment in the nonagricultural sector (%)	43		..	
Women's share of part-time employment (% of total)	46		..	
Maternity leave (days paid)			90	
Maternity leave benefits (% of wages paid)			88	
Employment to population ratio (% ages 15+)	..	..	..	..
Employment to population ratio (% ages 15–24)	..	..	..	..
Firms with female participation in ownership (%)			57	
Firms with a female top manager (%)			24	
Children in employment (% of children ages 7–14)	..	..	..	..
Unemployment rate (% of labor force ages 15+)	..	..	..	..
Unemployment rate (% of labor force ages 15–24)	..	..	..	..
Internet users (%)	..	..	..	..
Account at a financial institution (% age 15+)	..	..	..	..
Mobile account (% age 15+)	..	..	..	..
Saved any money last year (% age 15+)	..	..	..	..
Public life and decision making				
Seats held by women in national parliament (%)	..		33	
Female legislators, senior officials and managers (% of total)	49		..	
Proportion of women in ministerial level positions (%)	..		46	
Agency				
Total fertility rate (births per woman)	2.6		2.2	
Adolescent fertility rate (births per 1,000 women ages 15–19)	55		31	
Women first married by age 18 (% of women ages 20–24)	..		..	

Guam

	High income
Population (thousands)	168
GNI, Atlas ($ millions)	..
GNI per capita, Atlas ($)	..
Population living below $1.90 a day (%)	..

	2000		2013	
	Female	Male	Female	Male
Education				
Net primary enrollment rate (%)	..	..	..	..
Net secondary enrollment rate (%)	..	..	..	..
Gross tertiary enrollment ratio (% of relevant age group)	..	..	..	..
Primary completion rate (% of relevant age group)	..	..	..	..
Progression to secondary school (%)	..	..	..	..
Lower secondary completion rate (% of relevant age group)	..	..	..	..
Gross tertiary graduation ratio (%)	..	..	..	..
Female share of graduates in eng., manf. and constr. (%, tertiary)	..		..	
Youth literacy rate (% of population ages 15–24)	..	..	..	..
Health and related services				
Sex ratio at birth (male births per female births)	*1.06*		1.06	
Under-five mortality rate (per 1,000 live births)	..		..	
Life expectancy at birth (years)	78	73	82	76
Pregnant women receiving prenatal care (%)	..		..	
Births attended by skilled health staff (% of total)	99		..	
Maternal mortality ratio (per 100,000 live births)	..		..	
Women's share of population ages 15+ living with HIV (%)	..		..	
Prevalence of HIV (% ages 15–24)	..	..	..	..
Economic structure, participation, and access to resources				
Labor force participation rate (% of population ages 15+)	56	74	56	69
Labor force participation rate (% of ages 15–24)	41	53	44	49
Wage and salaried workers (% of employed ages 15+)	..	..	..	..
Self-employed workers (% of employed ages 15+)	..	..	..	..
Unpaid family workers (% of employed ages 15+)	..	..	..	..
Employment in agriculture (% of employed ages 15+)	..	..	..	..
Employment in industry (% of employed ages 15+)	..	..	..	..
Employment in services (% of employed ages 15+)	..	..	..	..
Women in wage employment in the nonagricultural sector (%)	46		44	
Women's share of part-time employment (% of total)	..		..	
Maternity leave (days paid)	..		..	
Maternity leave benefits (% of wages paid)	..		..	
Employment to population ratio (% ages 15+)	..	..	..	..
Employment to population ratio (% ages 15–24)	..	..	..	..
Firms with female participation in ownership (%)	..		..	
Firms with a female top manager (%)	..		..	
Children in employment (% of children ages 7–14)	..	..	..	..
Unemployment rate (% of labor force ages 15+)	..	..	..	..
Unemployment rate (% of labor force ages 15–24)	..	..	..	..
Internet users (%)	..	..	..	..
Account at a financial institution (% age 15+)	..	..	..	..
Mobile account (% age 15+)	..	..	..	..
Saved any money last year (% age 15+)	..	..	..	..
Public life and decision making				
Seats held by women in national parliament (%)	..		..	
Female legislators, senior officials and managers (% of total)	..		..	
Proportion of women in ministerial level positions (%)	..		..	
Agency				
Total fertility rate (births per woman)	2.8		2.4	
Adolescent fertility rate (births per 1,000 women ages 15–19)	62		49	
Women first married by age 18 (% of women ages 20–24)	..		..	

Guatemala

Latin America & the Caribbean   **Lower middle income**

Population (millions)	16
GNI, Atlas ($ billions)	55
GNI per capita, Atlas ($)	3,410
Population living below $1.90 a day (%)	*12*

	2000 Female	2000 Male	2013 Female	2013 Male
Education				
Net primary enrollment rate (%)	82	89	85	86
Net secondary enrollment rate (%)	26	28	45	49
Gross tertiary enrollment ratio (% of relevant age group)	8	*11*	19	18
Primary completion rate (% of relevant age group)	52	63	84	87
Progression to secondary school (%)	94	95	87	98
Lower secondary completion rate (% of relevant age group)	30	33	56	61
Gross tertiary graduation ratio (%)	2	2	..	..
Female share of graduates in eng., manf. and constr. (%, tertiary)	25		..	
Youth literacy rate (% of population ages 15–24)	78	86	90	94
Health and related services				
Sex ratio at birth (male births per female births)	*1.05*		1.05	
Under-five mortality rate (per 1,000 live births)	46	55	26	32
Life expectancy at birth (years)	71	64	76	69
Pregnant women receiving prenatal care (%)	*60*		..	
Births attended by skilled health staff (% of total)	41		52	
Maternal mortality ratio (per 100,000 live births)	160		140	
Women's share of population ages 15+ living with HIV (%)	26		39	
Prevalence of HIV (% ages 15–24)	0.2	0.5	0.2	0.2
Economic structure, participation, and access to resources				
Labor force participation rate (% of population ages 15+)	42	86	49	88
Labor force participation rate (% of ages 15–24)	35	78	43	80
Wage and salaried workers (% of employed ages 15+)	43	54	..	..
Self-employed workers (% of employed ages 15+)	57	46	..	..
Unpaid family workers (% of employed ages 15+)	15.1	15.1	..	..
Employment in agriculture (% of employed ages 15+)	19	52	*13*	*44*
Employment in industry (% of employed ages 15+)	24	22	*16*	*22*
Employment in services (% of employed ages 15+)	57	27	*72*	*35*
Women in wage employment in the nonagricultural sector (%)	*32*		37	
Women's share of part-time employment (% of total)	70		..	
Maternity leave (days paid)	..		84	
Maternity leave benefits (% of wages paid)	..		100	
Employment to population ratio (% ages 15+)	41	85	47	86
Employment to population ratio (% ages 15–24)	34	76	40	77
Firms with female participation in ownership (%)	..		44	
Firms with a female top manager (%)	..		16	
Children in employment (% of children ages 7–14)	..	..	11	27
Unemployment rate (% of labor force ages 15+)	2	1	4	2
Unemployment rate (% of labor force ages 15–24)	4	2	8	3
Internet users (%)	..	..	..	..
Account at a financial institution (% age 15+)	..	..	35	48
Mobile account (% age 15+)	..	..	0.1	3.6
Saved any money last year (% age 15+)	..	..	52	60
Public life and decision making				
Seats held by women in national parliament (%)	..		13	
Female legislators, senior officials and managers (% of total)	..		..	
Proportion of women in ministerial level positions (%)	..		20	
Agency				
Total fertility rate (births per woman)	4.8		3.8	
Adolescent fertility rate (births per 1,000 women ages 15–19)	108		81	
Women first married by age 18 (% of women ages 20–24)	*34*		..	

Guinea

Sub-Saharan Africa				Low income
Population (millions)				12
GNI, Atlas ($ billions)				6
GNI per capita, Atlas ($)				470
Population living below $1.90 a day (%)				35

	2000		2013	
	Female	Male	Female	Male
Education				
Net primary enrollment rate (%)	38	52	69	81
Net secondary enrollment rate (%)	9	22	23	37
Gross tertiary enrollment ratio (% of relevant age group)	0	2	6	14
Primary completion rate (% of relevant age group)	19	43	56	68
Progression to secondary school (%)	78	76	47	61
Lower secondary completion rate (% of relevant age group)	6	16	29	44
Gross tertiary graduation ratio (%)	..	..	..	..
Female share of graduates in eng., manf. and constr. (%, tertiary)	..		..	
Youth literacy rate (% of population ages 15–24)	..	..	22	38
Health and related services				
Sex ratio at birth (male births per female births)	1.02		1.02	
Under-five mortality rate (per 1,000 live births)	162	178	88	99
Life expectancy at birth (years)	51	51	57	55
Pregnant women receiving prenatal care (%)	71		85	
Births attended by skilled health staff (% of total)	35		45	
Maternal mortality ratio (per 100,000 live births)	950		650	
Women's share of population ages 15+ living with HIV (%)	60		61	
Prevalence of HIV (% ages 15–24)	1.0	0.4	0.7	0.4
Economic structure, participation, and access to resources				
Labor force participation rate (% of population ages 15+)	63	78	66	78
Labor force participation rate (% of ages 15–24)	50	57	52	57
Wage and salaried workers (% of employed ages 15+)	..	..	..	..
Self-employed workers (% of employed ages 15+)	..	..	..	..
Unpaid family workers (% of employed ages 15+)	..	..	..	..
Employment in agriculture (% of employed ages 15+)	..	..	..	..
Employment in industry (% of employed ages 15+)	..	..	..	..
Employment in services (% of employed ages 15+)	..	..	..	..
Women in wage employment in the nonagricultural sector (%)	..		18	
Women's share of part-time employment (% of total)	..		..	
Maternity leave (days paid)			98	
Maternity leave benefits (% of wages paid)	..		100	
Employment to population ratio (% ages 15+)	62	77	65	77
Employment to population ratio (% ages 15–24)	50	55	52	56
Firms with female participation in ownership (%)	..		..	
Firms with a female top manager (%)	..		..	
Children in employment (% of children ages 7–14)	..	..	36	40
Unemployment rate (% of labor force ages 15+)	2	2	2	2
Unemployment rate (% of labor force ages 15–24)	1	3	1	2
Internet users (%)	..	..	..	..
Account at a financial institution (% age 15+)	..	..	4	9
Mobile account (% age 15+)	..	..	0.6	2.4
Saved any money last year (% age 15+)	..	..	46	45
Public life and decision making				
Seats held by women in national parliament (%)	..		22	
Female legislators, senior officials and managers (% of total)	..		..	
Proportion of women in ministerial level positions (%)	..		15	
Agency				
Total fertility rate (births per woman)	5.9		4.9	
Adolescent fertility rate (births per 1,000 women ages 15–19)	169		142	
Women first married by age 18 (% of women ages 20–24)	65		52	

Guinea-Bissau

| Sub-Saharan Africa | | | Low income | |

Population (millions)			1.8
GNI, Atlas ($ millions)			995
GNI per capita, Atlas ($)			550
Population living below $1.90 a day (%)			67

	2000		2013	
	Female	Male	Female	Male
Education				
Net primary enrollment rate (%)	41	58	68	71
Net secondary enrollment rate (%)	6	11	..	..
Gross tertiary enrollment ratio (% of relevant age group)	..	..	..	..
Primary completion rate (% of relevant age group)	21	37	57	71
Progression to secondary school (%)	..	..	..	..
Lower secondary completion rate (% of relevant age group)	9	17	29	44
Gross tertiary graduation ratio (%)	..	..		
Female share of graduates in eng., manf. and constr. (%, tertiary)	..			
Youth literacy rate (% of population ages 15–24)	46	75	71	80
Health and related services				
Sex ratio at birth (male births per female births)	1.03		1.03	
Under-five mortality rate (per 1,000 live births)	164	190	85	100
Life expectancy at birth (years)	53	50	56	53
Pregnant women receiving prenatal care (%)	62		93	
Births attended by skilled health staff (% of total)	35		43	
Maternal mortality ratio (per 100,000 live births)	840		560	
Women's share of population ages 15+ living with HIV (%)	56		59	
Prevalence of HIV (% ages 15–24)	1.5	0.8	1.5	0.8
Economic structure, participation, and access to resources				
Labor force participation rate (% of population ages 15+)	63	79	68	79
Labor force participation rate (% of ages 15–24)	50	57	54	57
Wage and salaried workers (% of employed ages 15+)	..	..	..	..
Self-employed workers (% of employed ages 15+)	..	..	..	..
Unpaid family workers (% of employed ages 15+)	..	..	..	..
Employment in agriculture (% of employed ages 15+)	..	..	..	..
Employment in industry (% of employed ages 15+)	..	..	..	..
Employment in services (% of employed ages 15+)	..	..	..	..
Women in wage employment in the nonagricultural sector (%)	..		..	
Women's share of part-time employment (% of total)	..		..	
Maternity leave (days paid)	..			
Maternity leave benefits (% of wages paid)	..		..	
Employment to population ratio (% ages 15+)	59	73	63	73
Employment to population ratio (% ages 15–24)	44	51	48	51
Firms with female participation in ownership (%)	..		..	
Firms with a female top manager (%)	..		..	
Children in employment (% of children ages 7–14)	68	67	..	..
Unemployment rate (% of labor force ages 15+)	7	7	7	7
Unemployment rate (% of labor force ages 15–24)	11	10	12	11
Internet users (%)	..	..	..	..
Account at a financial institution (% age 15+)	..	..	..	..
Mobile account (% age 15+)	..	..	..	..
Saved any money last year (% age 15+)	..	..	..	..
Public life and decision making				
Seats held by women in national parliament (%)	..		14	
Female legislators, senior officials and managers (% of total)	..		..	
Proportion of women in ministerial level positions (%)	..		31	
Agency				
Total fertility rate (births per woman)	5.8		4.9	
Adolescent fertility rate (births per 1,000 women ages 15–19)	130		91	
Women first married by age 18 (% of women ages 20–24)	..		22	

Guyana

Latin America & the Caribbean			Lower middle income	
Population (thousands)				764
GNI, Atlas ($ billions)				3
GNI per capita, Atlas ($)				4,170
Population living below $1.90 a day (%)				..

	2000		2013	
	Female	Male	Female	Male
Education				
Net primary enrollment rate (%)	..	..	76	67
Net secondary enrollment rate (%)	73	73	100	86
Gross tertiary enrollment ratio (% of relevant age group)	..	..	18	8
Primary completion rate (% of relevant age group)	104	99	90	81
Progression to secondary school (%)	72	66	..	..
Lower secondary completion rate (% of relevant age group)	95	89	98	78
Gross tertiary graduation ratio (%)	..	..	4	2
Female share of graduates in eng., manf. and constr. (%, tertiary)	..		18	
Youth literacy rate (% of population ages 15–24)	..	..	..	..
Health and related services				
Sex ratio at birth (male births per female births)	1.05		1.05	
Under-five mortality rate (per 1,000 live births)	41	52	34	44
Life expectancy at birth (years)	67	60	69	64
Pregnant women receiving prenatal care (%)	81		..	
Births attended by skilled health staff (% of total)	86			
Maternal mortality ratio (per 100,000 live births)	240		250	
Women's share of population ages 15+ living with HIV (%)	63		58	
Prevalence of HIV (% ages 15–24)	0.9	0.4	1.2	0.7
Economic structure, participation, and access to resources				
Labor force participation rate (% of population ages 15+)	39	81	43	81
Labor force participation rate (% of population ages 15–24)	31	68	31	61
Wage and salaried workers (% of employed ages 15+)	..	..	..	..
Self-employed workers (% of employed ages 15+)	..	..	..	..
Unpaid family workers (% of employed ages 15+)	..	..	..	..
Employment in agriculture (% of employed ages 15+)	16	34	..	..
Employment in industry (% of employed ages 15+)	20	24	..	..
Employment in services (% of employed ages 15+)	61	42	..	..
Women in wage employment in the nonagricultural sector (%)	35		..	
Women's share of part-time employment (% of total)	..		..	
Maternity leave (days paid)			91	
Maternity leave benefits (% of wages paid)	..		70	
Employment to population ratio (% ages 15+)	33	73	37	73
Employment to population ratio (% ages 15–24)	20	54	21	49
Firms with female participation in ownership (%)			58	
Firms with a female top manager (%)	..		18	
Children in employment (% of children ages 7–14)	..	..	..	..
Unemployment rate (% of labor force ages 15+)	15	10	14	10
Unemployment rate (% of labor force ages 15–24)	33	21	32	20
Internet users (%)	..	..	..	..
Account at a financial institution (% age 15+)	..	..	..	..
Mobile account (% age 15+)	..	..	..	..
Saved any money last year (% age 15+)	..	..	..	..
Public life and decision making				
Seats held by women in national parliament (%)	..		35	
Female legislators, senior officials and managers (% of total)	25		..	
Proportion of women in ministerial level positions (%)	..		29	
Agency				
Total fertility rate (births per woman)	2.6		2.5	
Adolescent fertility rate (births per 1,000 women ages 15–19)	98		88	
Women first married by age 18 (% of women ages 20–24)	..		..	

Haiti

Latin America & the Caribbean	**Low income**
Population (millions)	11
GNI, Atlas ($ billions)	9
GNI per capita, Atlas ($)	820
Population living below $1.90 a day (%)	54

	2000		2013	
	Female	Male	Female	Male
Education				
Net primary enrollment rate (%)	..	..	..	..
Net secondary enrollment rate (%)	..	..	..	..
Gross tertiary enrollment ratio (% of relevant age group)	..	..	..	..
Primary completion rate (% of relevant age group)	..	..	..	..
Progression to secondary school (%)	..	..	..	..
Lower secondary completion rate (% of relevant age group)	..	..	..	..
Gross tertiary graduation ratio (%)	..	..	..	..
Female share of graduates in eng., manf. and constr. (%, tertiary)	..		..	
Youth literacy rate (% of population ages 15-24)	..	..	..	..
Health and related services				
Sex ratio at birth (male births per female births)	1.05		1.05	
Under-five mortality rate (per 1,000 live births)	98	112	63	75
Life expectancy at birth (years)	59	56	65	61
Pregnant women receiving prenatal care (%)	79		90	
Births attended by skilled health staff (% of total)	24		37	
Maternal mortality ratio (per 100,000 live births)	510		380	
Women's share of population ages 15+ living with HIV (%)	57		59	
Prevalence of HIV (% ages 15-24)	1.4	0.7	0.8	0.5
Economic structure, participation, and access to resources				
Labor force participation rate (% of population ages 15+)	57	69	61	71
Labor force participation rate (% of ages 15-24)	31	37	33	39
Wage and salaried workers (% of employed ages 15+)	..	..	..	..
Self-employed workers (% of employed ages 15+)	..	..	..	..
Unpaid family workers (% of employed ages 15+)	..	..	..	..
Employment in agriculture (% of employed ages 15+)	37	63	..	..
Employment in industry (% of employed ages 15+)	6	15	..	..
Employment in services (% of employed ages 15+)	57	22	..	..
Women in wage employment in the nonagricultural sector (%)	..		..	
Women's share of part-time employment (% of total)	..		..	
Maternity leave (days paid)	..		42	
Maternity leave benefits (% of wages paid)	..		100	
Employment to population ratio (% ages 15+)	52	65	56	67
Employment to population ratio (% ages 15-24)	24	32	26	33
Firms with female participation in ownership (%)	..			
Firms with a female top manager (%)	..		..	
Children in employment (% of children ages 7-14)	..	..	35	40
Unemployment rate (% of labor force ages 15+)	8	6	8	6
Unemployment rate (% of labor force ages 15-24)	21	15	21	15
Internet users (%)	..	..	..	..
Account at a financial institution (% age 15+)	..	..	14	21
Mobile account (% age 15+)	..	..	3.8	3.8
Saved any money last year (% age 15+)	..	..	45	44
Public life and decision making				
Seats held by women in national parliament (%)	..		4	
Female legislators, senior officials and managers (% of total)	..		..	
Proportion of women in ministerial level positions (%)	..		20	
Agency				
Total fertility rate (births per woman)	4.3		3.1	
Adolescent fertility rate (births per 1,000 women ages 15-19)	56		40	
Women first married by age 18 (% of women ages 20-24)	24		18	

Honduras

Latin America & the Caribbean **Lower middle income**

Population (millions)	8
GNI, Atlas ($ billions)	18
GNI per capita, Atlas ($)	2,280
Population living below $1.90 a day (%)	19

	2000		2013	
	Female	Male	Female	Male
Education				
Net primary enrollment rate (%)	89	88	90	89
Net secondary enrollment rate (%)	..	..	53	45
Gross tertiary enrollment ratio (% of relevant age group)	15	12	25	18
Primary completion rate (% of relevant age group)	70	75	96	90
Progression to secondary school (%)	..	..	60	58
Lower secondary completion rate (% of relevant age group)	..	..	47	38
Gross tertiary graduation ratio (%)	3	1	12	7
Female share of graduates in eng., manf. and constr. (%, tertiary)	..		37	
Youth literacy rate (% of population ages 15–24)	91	87	96[a]	95[a]
Health and related services				
Sex ratio at birth (male births per female births)	1.05		1.05	
Under-five mortality rate (per 1,000 live births)	34	41	18	23
Life expectancy at birth (years)	73	68	76	72
Pregnant women receiving prenatal care (%)	83		97	
Births attended by skilled health staff (% of total)	56		83	
Maternal mortality ratio (per 100,000 live births)	150		120	
Women's share of population ages 15+ living with HIV (%)	50		44	
Prevalence of HIV (% ages 15–24)	0.6	0.5	0.2	0.2
Economic structure, participation, and access to resources				
Labor force participation rate (% of population ages 15+)	44	88	43	83
Labor force participation rate (% of ages 15–24)	37	79	31	67
Wage and salaried workers (% of employed ages 15+)	50	48	41	46
Self-employed workers (% of employed ages 15+)	50	52	59	54
Unpaid family workers (% of employed ages 15+)	11.3	12.8	11.9	13.3
Employment in agriculture (% of employed ages 15+)	7	52	9	49
Employment in industry (% of employed ages 15+)	25	21	21	19
Employment in services (% of employed ages 15+)	68	28	70	31
Women in wage employment in the nonagricultural sector (%)	42		..	
Women's share of part-time employment (% of total)	57		..	
Maternity leave (days paid)	..		84	
Maternity leave benefits (% of wages paid)	..		100	
Employment to population ratio (% ages 15+)	43	85	40	80
Employment to population ratio (% ages 15–24)	34	74	28	63
Firms with female participation in ownership (%)	..		43	
Firms with a female top manager (%)	..		32	
Children in employment (% of children ages 7–14)	..	..	4	15
Unemployment rate (% of labor force ages 15+)	4	4	6	3
Unemployment rate (% of labor force ages 15–24)	8	7	12	6
Internet users (%)	..	..	..	..
Account at a financial institution (% age 15+)	..	..	25	35
Mobile account (% age 15+)	..	..	3.0	3.9
Saved any money last year (% age 15+)	..	..	37	42
Public life and decision making				
Seats held by women in national parliament (%)			26	
Female legislators, senior officials and managers (% of total)	..		..	
Proportion of women in ministerial level positions (%)	..		17	
Agency				
Total fertility rate (births per woman)	4.0		3.0	
Adolescent fertility rate (births per 1,000 women ages 15–19)	106		66	
Women first married by age 18 (% of women ages 20–24)	..		34	

Hong Kong SAR, China

High income

Population (millions)	7
GNI, Atlas ($ billions)	292
GNI per capita, Atlas ($)	40,320
Population living below $1.90 a day (%)	..

	2000 Female	2000 Male	2013 Female	2013 Male
Education				
Net primary enrollment rate (%)	..	..	93	94
Net secondary enrollment rate (%)	69	69	87	87
Gross tertiary enrollment ratio (% of relevant age group)	..	..	71	63
Primary completion rate (% of relevant age group)	..	..	95	97
Progression to secondary school (%)	100	100	100	100
Lower secondary completion rate (% of relevant age group)	..	..	93	94
Gross tertiary graduation ratio (%)	..		..	
Female share of graduates in eng., manf. and constr. (%, tertiary)	..		..	
Youth literacy rate (% of population ages 15–24)	..	..	..	..
Health and related services				
Sex ratio at birth (male births per female births)	1.07		1.07	
Under-five mortality rate (per 1,000 live births)	..	..	..	..
Life expectancy at birth (years)	84	78	87	81
Pregnant women receiving prenatal care (%)	..		..	
Births attended by skilled health staff (% of total)	..		..	
Maternal mortality ratio (per 100,000 live births)	..		..	
Women's share of population ages 15+ living with HIV (%)	..		..	
Prevalence of HIV (% ages 15–24)	..	..	..	..
Economic structure, participation, and access to resources				
Labor force participation rate (% of population ages 15+)	49	73	51	68
Labor force participation rate (% of ages 15–24)	45	47	38	38
Wage and salaried workers (% of employed ages 15+)	95	86	94	86
Self-employed workers (% of employed ages 15+)	5	15	6	14
Unpaid family workers (% of employed ages 15+)	1.2	0.1	0.8	0.1
Employment in agriculture (% of employed ages 15+)	0	0	..	..
Employment in industry (% of employed ages 15+)	10	28	4	19
Employment in services (% of employed ages 15+)	89	72	96	80
Women in wage employment in the nonagricultural sector (%)	45		50	
Women's share of part-time employment (% of total)	..		56	
Maternity leave (days paid)	..		70	
Maternity leave benefits (% of wages paid)	..		80	
Employment to population ratio (% ages 15+)	47	69	50	65
Employment to population ratio (% ages 15–24)	40	41	35	34
Firms with female participation in ownership (%)	..		..	
Firms with a female top manager (%)	..		..	
Children in employment (% of children ages 7–14)	..	..	..	..
Unemployment rate (% of labor force ages 15+)	4	6	3	4
Unemployment rate (% of labor force ages 15–24)	10	12	8	11
Internet users (%)	..	..	72	77
Account at a financial institution (% age 15+)	..	..	96	96
Mobile account (% age 15+)	..	..	..	..
Saved any money last year (% age 15+)	..	..	65	70
Public life and decision making				
Seats held by women in national parliament (%)	..		..	
Female legislators, senior officials and managers (% of total)	24		32	
Proportion of women in ministerial level positions (%)	..		..	
Agency				
Total fertility rate (births per woman)	1.0		1.1	
Adolescent fertility rate (births per 1,000 women ages 15–19)	4		3	
Women first married by age 18 (% of women ages 20–24)	..		..	

Hungary

	High income
Population (millions)	10
GNI, Atlas ($ billions)	133
GNI per capita, Atlas ($)	13,470
Population living below $1.90 a day (%)	<2

	2000		2013	
	Female	Male	Female	Male
Education				
Net primary enrollment rate (%)	88	88	90	92
Net secondary enrollment rate (%)	85	85	92	92
Gross tertiary enrollment ratio (% of relevant age group)	40	32	64	50
Primary completion rate (% of relevant age group)	96	97	98	98
Progression to secondary school (%)	100	100	99	99
Lower secondary completion rate (% of relevant age group)	..	..	95	94
Gross tertiary graduation ratio (%)	34	22	37	23
Female share of graduates in eng., manf. and constr. (%, tertiary)	21		22	
Youth literacy rate (% of population ages 15–24)	..	..	99	99
Health and related services				
Sex ratio at birth (male births per female births)	1.06		1.06	
Under-five mortality rate (per 1,000 live births)	10	12	5	6
Life expectancy at birth (years)	76	67	79	72
Pregnant women receiving prenatal care (%)	..		..	
Births attended by skilled health staff (% of total)	100		99	
Maternal mortality ratio (per 100,000 live births)	10		14	
Women's share of population ages 15+ living with HIV (%)	..		..	
Prevalence of HIV (% ages 15–24)	..	..	..	..
Economic structure, participation, and access to resources				
Labor force participation rate (% of population ages 15+)	41	58	45	60
Labor force participation rate (% of ages 15–24)	33	43	24	29
Wage and salaried workers (% of employed ages 15+)	90	81	92	86
Self-employed workers (% of employed ages 15+)	11	19	8	14
Unpaid family workers (% of employed ages 15+)	1.0	0.4	0.5	0.2
Employment in agriculture (% of employed ages 15+)	4	9	3	7
Employment in industry (% of employed ages 15+)	25	41	19	39
Employment in services (% of employed ages 15+)	71	50	78	54
Women in wage employment in the nonagricultural sector (%)	49		48	
Women's share of part-time employment (% of total)	71		65	
Maternity leave (days paid)	..		168	
Maternity leave benefits (% of wages paid)	..		70	
Employment to population ratio (% ages 15+)	39	54	40	54
Employment to population ratio (% ages 15–24)	29	37	17	21
Firms with female participation in ownership (%)	..		47	
Firms with a female top manager (%)	..		20	
Children in employment (% of children ages 7–14)	..	..	..	..
Unemployment rate (% of labor force ages 15+)	6	7	10	10
Unemployment rate (% of labor force ages 15–24)	11	14	28	26
Internet users (%)	..	..	72	74
Account at a financial institution (% age 15+)	..	..	72	72
Mobile account (% age 15+)	..	..	..	..
Saved any money last year (% age 15+)	..	..	37	40
Public life and decision making				
Seats held by women in national parliament (%)	..		10	
Female legislators, senior officials and managers (% of total)	34		40	
Proportion of women in ministerial level positions (%)	..		0	
Agency				
Total fertility rate (births per woman)	1.3		1.3	
Adolescent fertility rate (births per 1,000 women ages 15–19)	23		18	
Women first married by age 18 (% of women ages 20–24)	..		..	

Iceland

High income

Population (thousands)	328
GNI, Atlas ($ billions)	16
GNI per capita, Atlas ($)	47,640
Population living below $1.90 a day (%)	..

	2000		2013	
	Female	**Male**	**Female**	**Male**
Education				
Net primary enrollment rate (%)	*99*	*99*	98	98
Net secondary enrollment rate (%)	85	81	89	89
Gross tertiary enrollment ratio (% of relevant age group)	57	34	*103*	60
Primary completion rate (% of relevant age group)	94	101	*100*	93
Progression to secondary school (%)	100	100	99	100
Lower secondary completion rate (% of relevant age group)	94	95	97	99
Gross tertiary graduation ratio (%)	46	22	*80*	41
Female share of graduates in eng., manf. and constr. (%, tertiary)	25		33	
Youth literacy rate (% of population ages 15–24)	..	..	..	..
Health and related services				
Sex ratio at birth (male births per female births)	*1.04*		1.05	
Under-five mortality rate (per 1,000 live births)	4	4	2	2
Life expectancy at birth (years)	82	78	85	82
Pregnant women receiving prenatal care (%)	..		..	
Births attended by skilled health staff (% of total)	..		..	
Maternal mortality ratio (per 100,000 live births)	6		4	
Women's share of population ages 15+ living with HIV (%)	..		..	
Prevalence of HIV (% ages 15–24)	..	..	..	..
Economic structure, participation, and access to resources				
Labor force participation rate (% of population ages 15+)	72	82	71	77
Labor force participation rate (% of ages 15–24)	73	70	74	70
Wage and salaried workers (% of employed ages 15+)	89	77	91	83
Self-employed workers (% of employed ages 15+)	11	23	8	16
Unpaid family workers (% of employed ages 15+)	0.6	0.2	0.0	0.0
Employment in agriculture (% of employed ages 15+)	4	12	2	9
Employment in industry (% of employed ages 15+)	11	33	8	28
Employment in services (% of employed ages 15+)	85	55	90	63
Women in wage employment in the nonagricultural sector (%)	52		51	
Women's share of part-time employment (% of total)	77		66	
Maternity leave (days paid)	..		90	
Maternity leave benefits (% of wages paid)	..		49	
Employment to population ratio (% ages 15+)	70	81	67	73
Employment to population ratio (% ages 15–24)	71	66	68	60
Firms with female participation in ownership (%)	..		..	
Firms with a female top manager (%)	..		..	
Children in employment (% of children ages 7–14)	..	..	5	..
Unemployment rate (% of labor force ages 15+)	3	2	5	6
Unemployment rate (% of labor force ages 15–24)	4	6	8	14
Internet users (%)	..	..	96	98
Account at a financial institution (% age 15+)	..	..	..	..
Mobile account (% age 15+)	..	..	..	..
Saved any money last year (% age 15+)	..	..	..	..
Public life and decision making				
Seats held by women in national parliament (%)	..		41	
Female legislators, senior officials and managers (% of total)	29		*40*	
Proportion of women in ministerial level positions (%)	..		*44*	
Agency				
Total fertility rate (births per woman)	2.1		2.0	
Adolescent fertility rate (births per 1,000 women ages 15–19)	20		6	
Women first married by age 18 (% of women ages 20–24)	..		..	

India

South Asia			**Lower middle income**

Population (millions)	1,295
GNI, Atlas ($ billions)	2,036
GNI per capita, Atlas ($)	1,570
Population living below $1.90 a day (%)	*21*

	2000		2013	
	Female	**Male**	**Female**	**Male**
Education				
Net primary enrollment rate (%)	74	88	..	..
Net secondary enrollment rate (%)	..	..	..	..
Gross tertiary enrollment ratio (% of relevant age group)	7	11	24	26
Primary completion rate (% of relevant age group)	64	81	97	96
Progression to secondary school (%)	88	92	92	92
Lower secondary completion rate (% of relevant age group)	*47*	*62*	*78*	*80*
Gross tertiary graduation ratio (%)	..	..	..	..
Female share of graduates in eng., manf. and constr. (%, tertiary)	..		..	
Youth literacy rate (% of population ages 15–24)	68	84	82	90
Health and related services				
Sex ratio at birth (male births per female births)	*1.11*		*1.11*	
Under-five mortality rate (per 1,000 live births)	96	87	49	46
Life expectancy at birth (years)	63	61	68	65
Pregnant women receiving prenatal care (%)	62		..	
Births attended by skilled health staff (% of total)	43		..	
Maternal mortality ratio (per 100,000 live births)	370		190	
Women's share of population ages 15+ living with HIV (%)	..		..	
Prevalence of HIV (% ages 15–24)	..	..	..	..
Economic structure, participation, and access to resources				
Labor force participation rate (% of population ages 15+)	34	83	27	80
Labor force participation rate (% of ages 15–24)	26	65	18	51
Wage and salaried workers (% of employed ages 15+)	46	4	15	19
Self-employed workers (% of employed ages 15+)	91	82	86	81
Unpaid family workers (% of employed ages 15+)	37.8	12.8	33.9	11.0
Employment in agriculture (% of employed ages 15+)	75	54	60	43
Employment in industry (% of employed ages 15+)	12	18	21	26
Employment in services (% of employed ages 15+)	14	28	20	31
Women in wage employment in the nonagricultural sector (%)	17		19	
Women's share of part-time employment (% of total)	..		..	
Maternity leave (days paid)	..		84	
Maternity leave benefits (% of wages paid)	..		100	
Employment to population ratio (% ages 15+)	33	79	26	77
Employment to population ratio (% ages 15–24)	24	58	16	46
Firms with female participation in ownership (%)			11[a]	
Firms with a female top manager (%)	..		9[a]	
Children in employment (% of children ages 7–14)	5	5	2	2
Unemployment rate (% of labor force ages 15+)	4	4	4	4
Unemployment rate (% of labor force ages 15–24)	10	10	11	10
Internet users (%)	..	..	..	..
Account at a financial institution (% age 15+)	..	..	43	62
Mobile account (% age 15+)	..	..	1.2	3.5
Saved any money last year (% age 15+)	..	..	34	42
Public life and decision making				
Seats held by women in national parliament (%)	..		12	
Female legislators, senior officials and managers (% of total)	14		*14*	
Proportion of women in ministerial level positions (%)	..		22	
Agency				
Total fertility rate (births per woman)	3.1		2.5	
Adolescent fertility rate (births per 1,000 women ages 15–19)	67		26	
Women first married by age 18 (% of women ages 20–24)	*50*		..	

Indonesia

East Asia & Pacific	Lower middle income
Population (millions)	254
GNI, Atlas ($ billions)	924
GNI per capita, Atlas ($)	3,630
Population living below $1.90 a day (%)	16

	2000 Female	2000 Male	2013 Female	2013 Male
Education				
Net primary enrollment rate (%)	93	94	93	92
Net secondary enrollment rate (%)	50	51	76	77
Gross tertiary enrollment ratio (% of relevant age group)	14	16	32	31
Primary completion rate (% of relevant age group)	95	95	107	103
Progression to secondary school (%)	79	78	96	97
Lower secondary completion rate (% of relevant age group)	71	69	86	81
Gross tertiary graduation ratio (%)	6	7	15	16
Female share of graduates in eng., manf. and constr. (%, tertiary)	..		..	
Youth literacy rate (% of population ages 15-24)	..	..	99	99
Health and related services				
Sex ratio at birth (male births per female births)	1.05		1.05	
Under-five mortality rate (per 1,000 live births)	47	57	24	30
Life expectancy at birth (years)	69	65	73	69
Pregnant women receiving prenatal care (%)	88		96	
Births attended by skilled health staff (% of total)	67		83	
Maternal mortality ratio (per 100,000 live births)	310		190	
Women's share of population ages 15+ living with HIV (%)	23		37	
Prevalence of HIV (% ages 15-24)	0.1	0.1	0.4	0.4
Economic structure, participation, and access to resources				
Labor force participation rate (% of population ages 15+)	50	85	51	84
Labor force participation rate (% of ages 15-24)	44	67	40	60
Wage and salaried workers (% of employed ages 15+)	29	36	33	39
Self-employed workers (% of employed ages 15+)	71	64	60	50
Unpaid family workers (% of employed ages 15+)	38.6	8.1	30.9	6.9
Employment in agriculture (% of employed ages 15+)	47	44	34	35
Employment in industry (% of employed ages 15+)	15	19	16	25
Employment in services (% of employed ages 15+)	38	37	49	39
Women in wage employment in the nonagricultural sector (%)	32		35	
Women's share of part-time employment (% of total)	47		..	
Maternity leave (days paid)	..		90	
Maternity leave benefits (% of wages paid)	..		100	
Employment to population ratio (% ages 15+)	47	80	48	80
Employment to population ratio (% ages 15-24)	36	55	31	47
Firms with female participation in ownership (%)	..		..	
Firms with a female top manager (%)	..		..	
Children in employment (% of children ages 7-14)	9	9	3	4
Unemployment rate (% of labor force ages 15+)	7	6	7	6
Unemployment rate (% of labor force ages 15-24)	18	18	22	21
Internet users (%)	..	..	9	11
Account at a financial institution (% age 15+)	..	..	37	35
Mobile account (% age 15+)	..	..	0.7	0.2
Saved any money last year (% age 15+)	..	..	70	68
Public life and decision making				
Seats held by women in national parliament (%)	..		17	
Female legislators, senior officials and managers (% of total)	..		23	
Proportion of women in ministerial level positions (%)	..		23	
Agency				
Total fertility rate (births per woman)	2.5		2.3	
Adolescent fertility rate (births per 1,000 women ages 15-19)	50		50	
Women first married by age 18 (% of women ages 20-24)	..		17	

Iran, Islamic Rep.

Middle East & North Africa	Upper middle income
Population (millions)	78
GNI, Atlas ($ billions)	528
GNI per capita, Atlas ($)	6,840
Population living below $1.90 a day (%)	<2

	2000 Female	2000 Male	2013 Female	2013 Male
Education				
Net primary enrollment rate (%)	84	87	..	..
Net secondary enrollment rate (%)	..	..	79	84
Gross tertiary enrollment ratio (% of relevant age group)	18	21	56	60
Primary completion rate (% of relevant age group)	90	95	105	103
Progression to secondary school (%)	92	93	97	97
Lower secondary completion rate (% of relevant age group)	79	79	93	96
Gross tertiary graduation ratio (%)	..	..	18	20
Female share of graduates in eng., manf. and constr. (%, tertiary)		..	25	
Youth literacy rate (% of population ages 15-24)	96	98	98	98
Health and related services				
Sex ratio at birth (male births per female births)	1.05		1.05	
Under-five mortality rate (per 1,000 live births)	34	36	15	16
Life expectancy at birth (years)	71	69	76	72
Pregnant women receiving prenatal care (%)	..		97	
Births attended by skilled health staff (% of total)	90		96	
Maternal mortality ratio (per 100,000 live births)	44		23	
Women's share of population ages 15+ living with HIV (%)	10		13	
Prevalence of HIV (% ages 15-24)	0.1	0.1	0.1	0.1
Economic structure, participation, and access to resources				
Labor force participation rate (% of population ages 15+)	14	74	17	74
Labor force participation rate (% of ages 15-24)	13	52	13	49
Wage and salaried workers (% of employed ages 15+)	..	..	..	..
Self-employed workers (% of employed ages 15+)	..	..	..	..
Unpaid family workers (% of employed ages 15+)	..	..	..	..
Employment in agriculture (% of employed ages 15+)	..	..	..	..
Employment in industry (% of employed ages 15+)	..	..	..	..
Employment in services (% of employed ages 15+)	..	..	..	..
Women in wage employment in the nonagricultural sector (%)	14		15	
Women's share of part-time employment (% of total)	..		..	
Maternity leave (days paid)	..		270	
Maternity leave benefits (% of wages paid)	..		67	
Employment to population ratio (% ages 15+)	11	65	13	65
Employment to population ratio (% ages 15-24)	8	40	8	36
Firms with female participation in ownership (%)			..	
Firms with a female top manager (%)			..	
Children in employment (% of children ages 7-14)	..	..	..	..
Unemployment rate (% of labor force ages 15+)	21	12	20	12
Unemployment rate (% of labor force ages 15-24)	35	24	42	26
Internet users (%)	..	..	26	34
Account at a financial institution (% age 15+)	..	..	87	97
Mobile account (% age 15+)	..	..	4.0	5.0
Saved any money last year (% age 15+)	..	..	40	44
Public life and decision making				
Seats held by women in national parliament (%)	..		3	
Female legislators, senior officials and managers (% of total)	..		..	
Proportion of women in ministerial level positions (%)	..		10	
Agency				
Total fertility rate (births per woman)	2.2		1.9	
Adolescent fertility rate (births per 1,000 women ages 15-19)	40		27	
Women first married by age 18 (% of women ages 20-24)	..		17	

Iraq

Middle East & North Africa	**Upper middle income**
Population (millions)	35
GNI, Atlas ($ billions)	220
GNI per capita, Atlas ($)	6,320
Population living below $1.90 a day (%)	..

	2000		2013	
	Female	Male	Female	Male
Education				
Net primary enrollment rate (%)	82	94	..	..
Net secondary enrollment rate (%)	25	38	..	..
Gross tertiary enrollment ratio (% of relevant age group)	8	15	..	..
Primary completion rate (% of relevant age group)	50	61	..	..
Progression to secondary school (%)	67	85	..	..
Lower secondary completion rate (% of relevant age group)	24	33	..	..
Gross tertiary graduation ratio (%)	..	..	..	..
Female share of graduates in eng., manf. and constr. (%, tertiary)	..		..	
Youth literacy rate (% of population ages 15–24)	80	89	81	83
Health and related services				
Sex ratio at birth (male births per female births)	1.07		1.07	
Under-five mortality rate (per 1,000 live births)	41	48	29	35
Life expectancy at birth (years)	73	69	73	66
Pregnant women receiving prenatal care (%)	77		78	
Births attended by skilled health staff (% of total)	72		91	
Maternal mortality ratio (per 100,000 live births)	71		67	
Women's share of population ages 15+ living with HIV (%)	..		..	
Prevalence of HIV (% ages 15–24)	..	..	..	..
Economic structure, participation, and access to resources				
Labor force participation rate (% of population ages 15+)	13	70	15	70
Labor force participation rate (% of ages 15–24)	8	52	8	48
Wage and salaried workers (% of employed ages 15+)	..	..	..	..
Self-employed workers (% of employed ages 15+)	..	..	..	..
Unpaid family workers (% of employed ages 15+)	..	..	..	..
Employment in agriculture (% of employed ages 15+)	..	..	..	..
Employment in industry (% of employed ages 15+)	..	..	..	..
Employment in services (% of employed ages 15+)	..	..	..	..
Women in wage employment in the nonagricultural sector (%)	..		..	
Women's share of part-time employment (% of total)	..		..	
Maternity leave (days paid)			72	
Maternity leave benefits (% of wages paid)	..		100	
Employment to population ratio (% ages 15+)	9	59	11	60
Employment to population ratio (% ages 15–24)	3	35	3	34
Firms with female participation in ownership (%)	..		7	
Firms with a female top manager (%)	..		2	
Children in employment (% of children ages 7–14)	10	17	4	8
Unemployment rate (% of labor force ages 15+)	29	16	24	14
Unemployment rate (% of labor force ages 15–24)	67	33	59	30
Internet users (%)	..	..	..	..
Account at a financial institution (% age 15+)	..	..	7	15
Mobile account (% age 15+)	..	..	..	..
Saved any money last year (% age 15+)	..	..	44	53
Public life and decision making				
Seats held by women in national parliament (%)	..		27	
Female legislators, senior officials and managers (% of total)	..		..	
Proportion of women in ministerial level positions (%)	..		6	
Agency				
Total fertility rate (births per woman)	5.0		4.0	
Adolescent fertility rate (births per 1,000 women ages 15–19)	66		83	
Women first married by age 18 (% of women ages 20–24)	..		24	

Ireland

	High income
Population (millions)	5
GNI, Atlas ($ billions)	206
GNI per capita, Atlas ($)	44,660
Population living below $1.90 a day (%)	..

	2000 Female	2000 Male	2013 Female	2013 Male
Education				
Net primary enrollment rate (%)	94	95	95	96
Net secondary enrollment rate (%)	93	87	100	99
Gross tertiary enrollment ratio (% of relevant age group)	55	45	72	70
Primary completion rate (% of relevant age group)	95	94	..	..
Progression to secondary school (%)	..	..	..	..
Lower secondary completion rate (% of relevant age group)	95	93	102	101
Gross tertiary graduation ratio (%)	35	27	56	44
Female share of graduates in eng., manf. and constr. (%, tertiary)	17		17	
Youth literacy rate (% of population ages 15–24)	..	..	..	..
Health and related services				
Sex ratio at birth (male births per female births)	1.07		1.07	
Under-five mortality rate (per 1,000 live births)	6	8	3	4
Life expectancy at birth (years)	79	74	83	79
Pregnant women receiving prenatal care (%)	..		..	
Births attended by skilled health staff (% of total)	100		..	
Maternal mortality ratio (per 100,000 live births)	6		9	
Women's share of population ages 15+ living with HIV (%)	29		30	
Prevalence of HIV (% ages 15–24)	0.1	0.1	0.1	0.1
Economic structure, participation, and access to resources				
Labor force participation rate (% of population ages 15+)	47	71	53	68
Labor force participation rate (% of ages 15–24)	47	56	39	41
Wage and salaried workers (% of employed ages 15+)	91	74	92	75
Self-employed workers (% of employed ages 15+)	9	26	8	25
Unpaid family workers (% of employed ages 15+)	1.9	0.9	0.9	0.7
Employment in agriculture (% of employed ages 15+)	2	10	1	8
Employment in industry (% of employed ages 15+)	13	38	9	27
Employment in services (% of employed ages 15+)	85	52	90	65
Women in wage employment in the nonagricultural sector (%)	46		52	
Women's share of part-time employment (% of total)	75		69	
Maternity leave (days paid)	..		182	
Maternity leave benefits (% of wages paid)	..		35	
Employment to population ratio (% ages 15+)	45	68	47	58
Employment to population ratio (% ages 15–24)	44	53	30	29
Firms with female participation in ownership (%)	..		..	
Firms with a female top manager (%)	..		..	
Children in employment (% of children ages 7–14)	..	..	..	..
Unemployment rate (% of labor force ages 15+)	4	4	11	15
Unemployment rate (% of labor force ages 15–24)	7	6	23	30
Internet users (%)	..	..	79	78
Account at a financial institution (% age 15+)	..	..	95	95
Mobile account (% age 15+)	..	..	..	..
Saved any money last year (% age 15+)	..	..	65	75
Public life and decision making				
Seats held by women in national parliament (%)	..		16	
Female legislators, senior officials and managers (% of total)	26		33	
Proportion of women in ministerial level positions (%)	..		29	
Agency				
Total fertility rate (births per woman)	1.9		2.0	
Adolescent fertility rate (births per 1,000 women ages 15–19)	19		11	
Women first married by age 18 (% of women ages 20–24)	..		..	

Isle of Man

High income

Population (thousands)	87
GNI, Atlas ($ billions)	..
GNI per capita, Atlas ($)	..
Population living below $1.90 a day (%)	..

	2000		2013	
	Female	**Male**	**Female**	**Male**
Education				
Net primary enrollment rate (%)	..	..	..	..
Net secondary enrollment rate (%)	..	..	..	..
Gross tertiary enrollment ratio (% of relevant age group)	..	..	..	..
Primary completion rate (% of relevant age group)	..	..	..	..
Progression to secondary school (%)	..	..	..	..
Lower secondary completion rate (% of relevant age group)	..	..	..	..
Gross tertiary graduation ratio (%)	..	..	..	..
Female share of graduates in eng., manf. and constr. (%, tertiary)	..		..	
Youth literacy rate (% of population ages 15–24)	..	..	..	..
Health and related services				
Sex ratio at birth (male births per female births)	..		..	
Under-five mortality rate (per 1,000 live births)	..		..	
Life expectancy at birth (years)	82	75	..	..
Pregnant women receiving prenatal care (%)	..		..	
Births attended by skilled health staff (% of total)	..		..	
Maternal mortality ratio (per 100,000 live births)	..		..	
Women's share of population ages 15+ living with HIV (%)	..		..	
Prevalence of HIV (% ages 15–24)	..	..	..	..
Economic structure, participation, and access to resources				
Labor force participation rate (% of population ages 15+)	..	..	..	..
Labor force participation rate (% of ages 15–24)	..	..	..	..
Wage and salaried workers (% of employed ages 15+)	92	80	..	..
Self-employed workers (% of employed ages 15+)	8	20	..	..
Unpaid family workers (% of employed ages 15+)	..	..	..	..
Employment in agriculture (% of employed ages 15+)	1	2	..	..
Employment in industry (% of employed ages 15+)	6	25	..	..
Employment in services (% of employed ages 15+)	94	73	..	..
Women in wage employment in the nonagricultural sector (%)	..		..	
Women's share of part-time employment (% of total)	..		..	
Maternity leave (days paid)	..		..	
Maternity leave benefits (% of wages paid)	..		..	
Employment to population ratio (% ages 15+)	..	..	..	..
Employment to population ratio (% ages 15–24)	..	..	..	..
Firms with female participation in ownership (%)	..		..	
Firms with a female top manager (%)	..		..	
Children in employment (% of children ages 7–14)	..	..	..	..
Unemployment rate (% of labor force ages 15+)	..	..	..	..
Unemployment rate (% of labor force ages 15–24)	..	..	..	..
Internet users (%)	..	..	..	..
Account at a financial institution (% age 15+)	..	..	..	..
Mobile account (% age 15+)	..	..	..	..
Saved any money last year (% age 15+)	..	..	..	..
Public life and decision making				
Seats held by women in national parliament (%)	..		..	
Female legislators, senior officials and managers (% of total)	..		..	
Proportion of women in ministerial level positions (%)	..		..	
Agency				
Total fertility rate (births per woman)	1.7		..	
Adolescent fertility rate (births per 1,000 women ages 15–19)	..		..	
Women first married by age 18 (% of women ages 20–24)	..		..	

Israel

High income

Population (millions)	8
GNI, Atlas ($ billions)	287
GNI per capita, Atlas ($)	34,990
Population living below $1.90 a day (%)	..

	2000 Female	2000 Male	2013 Female	2013 Male
Education				
Net primary enrollment rate (%)	98	98	97	96
Net secondary enrollment rate (%)	99	97	100	97
Gross tertiary enrollment ratio (% of relevant age group)	59	41	76	57
Primary completion rate (% of relevant age group)	*104*	*105*	103	102
Progression to secondary school (%)	*100*	*100*	*100*	*100*
Lower secondary completion rate (% of relevant age group)	98	98	103	101
Gross tertiary graduation ratio (%)	37	22	*51*	*34*
Female share of graduates in eng., manf. and constr. (%, tertiary)	28		..	
Youth literacy rate (% of population ages 15–24)	..	..	..	..
Health and related services				
Sex ratio at birth (male births per female births)	*1.05*		1.05	
Under-five mortality rate (per 1,000 live births)	6	7	4	4
Life expectancy at birth (years)	81	77	84	80
Pregnant women receiving prenatal care (%)	..		..	
Births attended by skilled health staff (% of total)	..		..	
Maternal mortality ratio (per 100,000 live births)	9		2	
Women's share of population ages 15+ living with HIV (%)	..		..	
Prevalence of HIV (% ages 15–24)	..	..	..	..
Economic structure, participation, and access to resources				
Labor force participation rate (% of population ages 15+)	48	61	58	69
Labor force participation rate (% of ages 15–24)	36	33	48	49
Wage and salaried workers (% of employed ages 15+)	91	82	*92*	*84*
Self-employed workers (% of employed ages 15+)	9	18	8	17
Unpaid family workers (% of employed ages 15+)	0.8	0.2	*0.2*	*0.1*
Employment in agriculture (% of employed ages 15+)	1	3	..	..
Employment in industry (% of employed ages 15+)	12	34	..	..
Employment in services (% of employed ages 15+)	86	62	..	..
Women in wage employment in the nonagricultural sector (%)	48		51	
Women's share of part-time employment (% of total)	76		69	
Maternity leave (days paid)	..		98	
Maternity leave benefits (% of wages paid)	..		100	
Employment to population ratio (% ages 15+)	44	55	54	65
Employment to population ratio (% ages 15–24)	30	27	43	44
Firms with female participation in ownership (%)	..		27	
Firms with a female top manager (%)	..		10	
Children in employment (% of children ages 7–14)	..	..	..	..
Unemployment rate (% of labor force ages 15+)	9	9	6	6
Unemployment rate (% of labor force ages 15–24)	17	17	11	11
Internet users (%)	..	..	68	73
Account at a financial institution (% age 15+)	..	..	90	90
Mobile account (% age 15+)	..	..	..	..
Saved any money last year (% age 15+)	..	..	62	62
Public life and decision making				
Seats held by women in national parliament (%)	..		24	
Female legislators, senior officials and managers (% of total)	27		..	
Proportion of women in ministerial level positions (%)	..		18	
Agency				
Total fertility rate (births per woman)	3.0		3.0	
Adolescent fertility rate (births per 1,000 women ages 15–19)	17		10	
Women first married by age 18 (% of women ages 20–24)	..		..	

Italy

High income

Population (millions)	61
GNI, Atlas ($ billions)	2,103
GNI per capita, Atlas ($)	34,280
Population living below $1.90 a day (%)	..

	2000		2013	
	Female	Male	Female	Male
Education				
Net primary enrollment rate (%)	98	99	96	97
Net secondary enrollment rate (%)	86	88	92	91
Gross tertiary enrollment ratio (% of relevant age group)	55	43	74	52
Primary completion rate (% of relevant age group)	102	102	99	99
Progression to secondary school (%)	100	100	100	100
Lower secondary completion rate (% of relevant age group)	99	98	100	101
Gross tertiary graduation ratio (%)	25	19	42	27
Female share of graduates in eng., manf. and constr. (%, tertiary)	28		40	
Youth literacy rate (% of population ages 15–24)	100	100	100	100
Health and related services				
Sex ratio at birth (male births per female births)	1.06		1.06	
Under-five mortality rate (per 1,000 live births)	5	6	3	4
Life expectancy at birth (years)	83	77	85	80
Pregnant women receiving prenatal care (%)	..		..	
Births attended by skilled health staff (% of total)	..		..	
Maternal mortality ratio (per 100,000 live births)	4		4	
Women's share of population ages 15+ living with HIV (%)	..		..	
Prevalence of HIV (% ages 15–24)	..	..	..	..
Economic structure, participation, and access to resources				
Labor force participation rate (% of population ages 15+)	35	61	40	60
Labor force participation rate (% of ages 15–24)	34	42	24	33
Wage and salaried workers (% of employed ages 15+)	78	68	82	71
Self-employed workers (% of employed ages 15+)	22	32	18	29
Unpaid family workers (% of employed ages 15+)	5.8	2.8	2.0	1.0
Employment in agriculture (% of employed ages 15+)	4	6	3	5
Employment in industry (% of employed ages 15+)	21	38	14	38
Employment in services (% of employed ages 15+)	75	56	84	58
Women in wage employment in the nonagricultural sector (%)	40		46	
Women's share of part-time employment (% of total)	73		76	
Maternity leave (days paid)	..		150	
Maternity leave benefits (% of wages paid)	..		80	
Employment to population ratio (% ages 15+)	30	56	34	53
Employment to population ratio (% ages 15–24)	22	30	14	20
Firms with female participation in ownership (%)	..		..	
Firms with a female top manager (%)	..		..	
Children in employment (% of children ages 7–14)	..	..	..	..
Unemployment rate (% of labor force ages 15+)	15	8	13	12
Unemployment rate (% of labor force ages 15–24)	35	28	41	39
Internet users (%)	..	..	54	63
Account at a financial institution (% age 15+)	..	..	83	92
Mobile account (% age 15+)	..	..	..	..
Saved any money last year (% age 15+)	..	..	49	65
Public life and decision making				
Seats held by women in national parliament (%)	..		31	
Female legislators, senior officials and managers (% of total)	14		25	
Proportion of women in ministerial level positions (%)	..		44	
Agency				
Total fertility rate (births per woman)	1.3		1.4	
Adolescent fertility rate (births per 1,000 women ages 15–19)	7		6	
Women first married by age 18 (% of women ages 20–24)	..		..	

Jamaica

Latin America & the Caribbean	Upper middle income

Population (millions)	3
GNI, Atlas ($ billions)	14
GNI per capita, Atlas ($)	5,220
Population living below $1.90 a day (%)	..

	2000 Female	2000 Male	2013 Female	2013 Male
Education				
Net primary enrollment rate (%)	92	93	..	..
Net secondary enrollment rate (%)	79	76	76	72
Gross tertiary enrollment ratio (% of relevant age group)	20	11	40	18
Primary completion rate (% of relevant age group)	90	85	..	..
Progression to secondary school (%)	96	100	93	88
Lower secondary completion rate (% of relevant age group)	100	99	82	85
Gross tertiary graduation ratio (%)	..	..	..	..
Female share of graduates in eng., manf. and constr. (%, tertiary)	..		..	
Youth literacy rate (% of population ages 15-24)	96	87	99	94
Health and related services				
Sex ratio at birth (male births per female births)	1.05		1.05	
Under-five mortality rate (per 1,000 live births)	19	25	14	18
Life expectancy at birth (years)	73	68	76	71
Pregnant women receiving prenatal care (%)	67		98	
Births attended by skilled health staff (% of total)	96		99	
Maternal mortality ratio (per 100,000 live births)	88		80	
Women's share of population ages 15+ living with HIV (%)	38		38	
Prevalence of HIV (% ages 15-24)	1.3	1.5	0.6	0.8
Economic structure, participation, and access to resources				
Labor force participation rate (% of population ages 15+)	59	78	56	71
Labor force participation rate (% of ages 15-24)	42	56	31	40
Wage and salaried workers (% of employed ages 15+)	65	55	67	53
Self-employed workers (% of employed ages 15+)	35	45	33	47
Unpaid family workers (% of employed ages 15+)	3.0	1.3	1.5	0.6
Employment in agriculture (% of employed ages 15+)	9	29	8	26
Employment in industry (% of employed ages 15+)	6	24	7	22
Employment in services (% of employed ages 15+)	84	47	86	52
Women in wage employment in the nonagricultural sector (%)	45		48	
Women's share of part-time employment (% of total)	54		..	
Maternity leave (days paid)	..		56	
Maternity leave benefits (% of wages paid)	..		100	
Employment to population ratio (% ages 15+)	46	70	45	63
Employment to population ratio (% ages 15-24)	23	42	17	29
Firms with female participation in ownership (%)	..		38	
Firms with a female top manager (%)	..		24	
Children in employment (% of children ages 7-14)	1	2	6	6
Unemployment rate (% of labor force ages 15+)	22	10	20	11
Unemployment rate (% of labor force ages 15-24)	46	25	45	28
Internet users (%)	..	..	37	31
Account at a financial institution (% age 15+)	..	..	78	79
Mobile account (% age 15+)	..	..	1.4	0.4
Saved any money last year (% age 15+)	..	..	71	78
Public life and decision making				
Seats held by women in national parliament (%)	..		13	
Female legislators, senior officials and managers (% of total)	..		..	
Proportion of women in ministerial level positions (%)	..		20	
Agency				
Total fertility rate (births per woman)	2.6		2.3	
Adolescent fertility rate (births per 1,000 women ages 15-19)	87		61	
Women first married by age 18 (% of women ages 20-24)	..		8	

Japan

High income

Population (millions)	127
GNI, Atlas ($ billions)	5,339
GNI per capita, Atlas ($)	42,000
Population living below $1.90 a day (%)	..

	2000 Female	2000 Male	2013 Female	2013 Male
Education				
Net primary enrollment rate (%)	..	..	100	100
Net secondary enrollment rate (%)	..	..	100	99
Gross tertiary enrollment ratio (% of relevant age group)	45	52	58	65
Primary completion rate (% of relevant age group)	102	102	102	102
Progression to secondary school (%)	..	..	..	..
Lower secondary completion rate (% of relevant age group)	..	..	..	..
Gross tertiary graduation ratio (%)	25	40	40	48
Female share of graduates in eng., manf. and constr. (%, tertiary)	11		12	
Youth literacy rate (% of population ages 15-24)	..	..	..	..
Health and related services				
Sex ratio at birth (male births per female births)	1.06		1.06	
Under-five mortality rate (per 1,000 live births)	4	5	3	3
Life expectancy at birth (years)	85	78	87	80
Pregnant women receiving prenatal care (%)	..		..	
Births attended by skilled health staff (% of total)	..		..	
Maternal mortality ratio (per 100,000 live births)	10		6	
Women's share of population ages 15+ living with HIV (%)	..		..	
Prevalence of HIV (% ages 15-24)	..	..	..	..
Economic structure, participation, and access to resources				
Labor force participation rate (% of population ages 15+)	49	76	49	70
Labor force participation rate (% of ages 15-24)	46	47	44	42
Wage and salaried workers (% of employed ages 15+)	81	84	89	87
Self-employed workers (% of employed ages 15+)	18	16	11	13
Unpaid family workers (% of employed ages 15+)	10.6	1.7	5.6	1.0
Employment in agriculture (% of employed ages 15+)	6	5	4	4
Employment in industry (% of employed ages 15+)	22	38	15	33
Employment in services (% of employed ages 15+)	72	57	80	62
Women in wage employment in the nonagricultural sector (%)	40		43	
Women's share of part-time employment (% of total)	71		71	
Maternity leave (days paid)	..		98	
Maternity leave benefits (% of wages paid)	..		67	
Employment to population ratio (% ages 15+)	47	73	47	67
Employment to population ratio (% ages 15-24)	43	42	41	39
Firms with female participation in ownership (%)	..		..	
Firms with a female top manager (%)	..		..	
Children in employment (% of children ages 7-14)	..	..	..	..
Unemployment rate (% of labor force ages 15+)	5	5	4	4
Unemployment rate (% of labor force ages 15-24)	8	10	6	8
Internet users (%)	..	..	78	85
Account at a financial institution (% age 15+)	..	..	97	96
Mobile account (% age 15+)	..	..	..	..
Saved any money last year (% age 15+)	..	..	75	69
Public life and decision making				
Seats held by women in national parliament (%)	..		9	
Female legislators, senior officials and managers (% of total)	..		..	
Proportion of women in ministerial level positions (%)	..		22	
Agency				
Total fertility rate (births per woman)	1.4		1.4	
Adolescent fertility rate (births per 1,000 women ages 15-19)	5		4	
Women first married by age 18 (% of women ages 20-24)	..		..	

Jordan

Middle East & North Africa			Upper middle income	
Population (millions)				7
GNI, Atlas ($ billions)				34
GNI per capita, Atlas ($)				5,160
Population living below $1.90 a day (%)				<2

	2000		2013	
	Female	Male	Female	Male
Education				
Net primary enrollment rate (%)	95	93	96	98
Net secondary enrollment rate (%)	81	77	89	86
Gross tertiary enrollment ratio (% of relevant age group)	30	26	50	43
Primary completion rate (% of relevant age group)	103	100	92	94
Progression to secondary school (%)	99	98	99	99
Lower secondary completion rate (% of relevant age group)	91	88	91	90
Gross tertiary graduation ratio (%)	20	20	46	40
Female share of graduates in eng., manf. and constr. (%, tertiary)	..		13	
Youth literacy rate (% of population ages 15–24)	..	..	99	99
Health and related services				
Sex ratio at birth (male births per female births)	1.05		1.05	
Under-five mortality rate (per 1,000 live births)	26	29	17	19
Life expectancy at birth (years)	73	70	76	72
Pregnant women receiving prenatal care (%)	99		99	
Births attended by skilled health staff (% of total)	100		100	
Maternal mortality ratio (per 100,000 live births)	65		50	
Women's share of population ages 15+ living with HIV (%)	..		..	
Prevalence of HIV (% ages 15–24)	..	..	..	..
Economic structure, participation, and access to resources				
Labor force participation rate (% of population ages 15+)	13	69	16	67
Labor force participation rate (% of ages 15–24)	9	46	10	39
Wage and salaried workers (% of employed ages 15+)	91	79	96	82
Self-employed workers (% of employed ages 15+)	8	21	4	18
Unpaid family workers (% of employed ages 15+)	2.1	1.9	0.3	0.4
Employment in agriculture (% of employed ages 15+)	4	5	1	2
Employment in industry (% of employed ages 15+)	12	23	8	19
Employment in services (% of employed ages 15+)	85	72	91	79
Women in wage employment in the nonagricultural sector (%)	14		..	
Women's share of part-time employment (% of total)	..		..	
Maternity leave (days paid)	..		70	
Maternity leave benefits (% of wages paid)	..		100	
Employment to population ratio (% ages 15+)	10	60	12	60
Employment to population ratio (% ages 15–24)	5	34	5	28
Firms with female participation in ownership (%)	..		16	
Firms with a female top manager (%)	..		2	
Children in employment (% of children ages 7–14)	..	..	..	..
Unemployment rate (% of labor force ages 15+)	22	12	22	11
Unemployment rate (% of labor force ages 15–24)	41	26	56	28
Internet users (%)	..	..	..	..
Account at a financial institution (% age 15+)	..	..	16	33
Mobile account (% age 15+)	..	..	0.4	0.5
Saved any money last year (% age 15+)	..	..	29	29
Public life and decision making				
Seats held by women in national parliament (%)	..		12	
Female legislators, senior officials and managers (% of total)	..		..	
Proportion of women in ministerial level positions (%)	..		11	
Agency				
Total fertility rate (births per woman)	4.1		3.2	
Adolescent fertility rate (births per 1,000 women ages 15–19)	36		24	
Women first married by age 18 (% of women ages 20–24)	11		8	

Kazakhstan

Europe & Central Asia

Upper middle income

Population (millions)	17
GNI, Atlas ($ billions)	202
GNI per capita, Atlas ($)	11,670
Population living below $1.90 a day (%)	<2

	2000		2013	
	Female	Male	Female	Male
Education				
Net primary enrollment rate (%)	89	88	86	86
Net secondary enrollment rate (%)	93	88	92	91
Gross tertiary enrollment ratio (% of relevant age group)	35	30	63	48
Primary completion rate (% of relevant age group)	95	94	103	101
Progression to secondary school (%)	98	100.	*100*	*100*
Lower secondary completion rate (% of relevant age group)	102	93	101	102
Gross tertiary graduation ratio (%)	24	20	..	..
Female share of graduates in eng., manf. and constr. (%, tertiary)	..		31	
Youth literacy rate (% of population ages 15-24)	*100*	*100*	..	..
Health and related services				
Sex ratio at birth (male births per female births)	*1.07*		*1.07*	
Under-five mortality rate (per 1,000 live births)	37	50	12	16
Life expectancy at birth (years)	71	60	75	66
Pregnant women receiving prenatal care (%)	*94*		*99*	
Births attended by skilled health staff (% of total)	98		100	
Maternal mortality ratio (per 100,000 live births)	71		26	
Women's share of population ages 15+ living with HIV (%)	36		37	
Prevalence of HIV (% ages 15-24)	0.1	0.1	0.1	0.1
Economic structure, participation, and access to resources				
Labor force participation rate (% of population ages 15+)	65	76	68	78
Labor force participation rate (% of ages 15-24)	49	55	44	51
Wage and salaried workers (% of employed ages 15+)	54	61	70	69
Self-employed workers (% of employed ages 15+)	*46*	*39*	30	31
Unpaid family workers (% of employed ages 15+)	*1.2*	*0.9*	0.4	0.4
Employment in agriculture (% of employed ages 15+)	*34*	*37*	..	..
Employment in industry (% of employed ages 15+)	*10*	*23*	..	..
Employment in services (% of employed ages 15+)	*56*	*41*	..	..
Women in wage employment in the nonagricultural sector (%)	*49*		51	
Women's share of part-time employment (% of total)	..		..	
Maternity leave (days paid)	..		126	
Maternity leave benefits (% of wages paid)	..		100	
Employment to population ratio (% ages 15+)	55	69	64	75
Employment to population ratio (% ages 15-24)	40	49	42	49
Firms with female participation in ownership (%)	..		28	
Firms with a female top manager (%)	..		19	
Children in employment (% of children ages 7-14)	..	..	..	..
Unemployment rate (% of labor force ages 15+)	16	10	6	4
Unemployment rate (% of labor force ages 15-24)	18	12	5	4
Internet users (%)	..	..	..	..
Account at a financial institution (% age 15+)	..	..	56	52
Mobile account (% age 15+)	..	..	..	..
Saved any money last year (% age 15+)	..	..	30	31
Public life and decision making				
Seats held by women in national parliament (%)	..		26	
Female legislators, senior officials and managers (% of total)	*33*		..	
Proportion of women in ministerial level positions (%)	..		13	
Agency				
Total fertility rate (births per woman)	1.8		2.6	
Adolescent fertility rate (births per 1,000 women ages 15-19)	34		29	
Women first married by age 18 (% of women ages 20-24)	*14*		6	

Kenya

| Sub-Saharan Africa | | | Lower middle income | |

Population (millions)				45
GNI, Atlas ($ billions)				58
GNI per capita, Atlas ($)				1,290
Population living below $1.90 a day (%)				..

	2000		2013	
	Female	Male	Female	Male
Education				
Net primary enrollment rate (%)	66	65	85	82
Net secondary enrollment rate (%)	33	34	55	57
Gross tertiary enrollment ratio (% of relevant age group)	2	4	..	..
Primary completion rate (% of relevant age group)	..	..	..	..
Progression to secondary school	..	..	..	..
Lower secondary completion rate (% of relevant age group)	..	..	..	..
Gross tertiary graduation ratio (%)	1	2	..	..
Female share of graduates in eng., manf. and constr. (%, tertiary)	13		..	
Youth literacy rate (% of population ages 15–24)	92	93	..	..
Health and related services				
Sex ratio at birth (male births per female births)	*1.03*		1.03	
Under-five mortality rate (per 1,000 live births)	102	114	45	53
Life expectancy at birth (years)	54	52	64	60
Pregnant women receiving prenatal care (%)	76		..	
Births attended by skilled health staff (% of total)	44		..	
Maternal mortality ratio (per 100,000 live births)	570		400	
Women's share of population ages 15+ living with HIV (%)	57		58	
Prevalence of HIV (% ages 15–24)	..	..	..	..
Economic structure, participation, and access to resources				
Labor force participation rate (% of population ages 15+)	63	73	62	72
Labor force participation rate (% of ages 15–24)	41	48	36	43
Wage and salaried workers (% of employed ages 15+)	19	46	..	..
Self-employed workers (% of employed ages 15+)	*78*	*50*	..	..
Unpaid family workers (% of employed ages 15+)	*53.2*	*26.9*	..	..
Employment in agriculture (% of employed ages 15+)	..	..	..	..
Employment in industry (% of employed ages 15+)	..	..	..	..
Employment in services (% of employed ages 15+)	..	..	..	..
Women in wage employment in the nonagricultural sector (%)	..		36	
Women's share of part-time employment (% of total)	..		..	
Maternity leave (days paid)	..		90	
Maternity leave benefits (% of wages paid)	..		100	
Employment to population ratio (% ages 15+)	56	67	56	67
Employment to population ratio (% ages 15–24)	34	40	30	36
Firms with female participation in ownership (%)	..		49	
Firms with a female top manager (%)	..		13	
Children in employment (% of children ages 7–14)	35	40	..	..
Unemployment rate (% of labor force ages 15+)	11	9	11	8
Unemployment rate (% of labor force ages 15–24)	18	17	17	17
Internet users (%)	..	..	..	..
Account at a financial institution (% age 15+)	..	..	52	59
Mobile account (% age 15+)	..	..	54.9	62.4
Saved any money last year (% age 15+)	..	..	72	80
Public life and decision making				
Seats held by women in national parliament (%)	..		20	
Female legislators, senior officials and managers (% of total)	..		..	
Proportion of women in ministerial level positions (%)	..		30	
Agency				
Total fertility rate (births per woman)	5.0		4.4	
Adolescent fertility rate (births per 1,000 women ages 15–19)	105		92	
Women first married by age 18 (% of women ages 20–24)	25		..	

Kiribati

East Asia & Pacific	Lower middle income
Population (thousands)	110
GNI, Atlas ($ millions)	237
GNI per capita, Atlas ($)	2,150
Population living below $1.90 a day (%)	..

	2000		2013	
	Female	Male	Female	Male
Education				
Net primary enrollment rate (%)	..	..	..	..
Net secondary enrollment rate (%)	..	..	..	..
Gross tertiary enrollment ratio (% of relevant age group)	..	..	..	..
Primary completion rate (% of relevant age group)	98	106	..	..
Progression to secondary school (%)	..	..	..	..
Lower secondary completion rate (% of relevant age group)	..	..	..	..
Gross tertiary graduation ratio (%)	..	..	..	..
Female share of graduates in eng., manf. and constr. (%, tertiary)	..		..	
Youth literacy rate (% of population ages 15-24)	..	..	..	..
Health and related services				
Sex ratio at birth (male births per female births)	*1.07*		1.07	
Under-five mortality rate (per 1,000 live births)	65	76	51	61
Life expectancy at birth (years)	68	62	72	66
Pregnant women receiving prenatal care (%)	..		..	
Births attended by skilled health staff (% of total)	89		..	
Maternal mortality ratio (per 100,000 live births)	200		130	
Women's share of population ages 15+ living with HIV (%)	..		..	
Prevalence of HIV (% ages 15-24)	..	..	..	..
Economic structure, participation, and access to resources				
Labor force participation rate (% of population ages 15+)	..	..	..	..
Labor force participation rate (% of ages 15-24)	..	..	..	..
Wage and salaried workers (% of employed ages 15+)	..	..	..	..
Self-employed workers (% of employed ages 15+)	..	..	..	..
Unpaid family workers (% of employed ages 15+)	..	..	..	..
Employment in agriculture (% of employed ages 15+)	1	4	..	..
Employment in industry (% of employed ages 15+)	3	10	..	..
Employment in services (% of employed ages 15+)	96	81	..	..
Women in wage employment in the nonagricultural sector (%)	37		44	
Women's share of part-time employment (% of total)	..		..	
Maternity leave (days paid)	..		..	
Maternity leave benefits (% of wages paid)	..		..	
Employment to population ratio (% ages 15+)	..	..	..	..
Employment to population ratio (% ages 15-24)	..	..	..	..
Firms with female participation in ownership (%)	..		..	
Firms with a female top manager (%)	..		..	
Children in employment (% of children ages 7-14)	..	..	..	..
Unemployment rate (% of labor force ages 15+)	..	..	..	..
Unemployment rate (% of labor force ages 15-24)	..	..	..	..
Internet users (%)	..	..	..	..
Account at a financial institution (% age 15+)	..	..	..	..
Mobile account (% age 15+)	..	..	..	..
Saved any money last year (% age 15+)	..	..	..	..
Public life and decision making				
Seats held by women in national parliament (%)	..		9	
Female legislators, senior officials and managers (% of total)	..		*36*	
Proportion of women in ministerial level positions (%)	..		21	
Agency				
Total fertility rate (births per woman)	3.9		3.0	
Adolescent fertility rate (births per 1,000 women ages 15-19)	37		18	
Women first married by age 18 (% of women ages 20-24)	..		..	

Korea, Dem. People's Rep.

East Asia & Pacific	Low income
Population (millions)	25
GNI, Atlas ($ millions)	..
GNI per capita, Atlas ($)	..
Population living below $1.90 a day (%)	..

	2000		2013	
	Female	Male	Female	Male
Education				
Net primary enrollment rate (%)	..	..	..	..
Net secondary enrollment rate (%)	..	..	..	..
Gross tertiary enrollment ratio (% of relevant age group)	..	..	..	..
Primary completion rate (% of relevant age group)	..	..	..	..
Progression to secondary school (%)	..	..	..	..
Lower secondary completion rate (% of relevant age group)	..	..	..	..
Gross tertiary graduation ratio (%)	..		..	
Female share of graduates in eng., manf. and constr. (%, tertiary)	..		..	
Youth literacy rate (% of population ages 15–24)	..	..	..	..
Health and related services				
Sex ratio at birth (male births per female births)	*1.05*		1.05	
Under-five mortality rate (per 1,000 live births)	55	65	22	28
Life expectancy at birth (years)	69	61	73	66
Pregnant women receiving prenatal care (%)	97		..	
Births attended by skilled health staff (% of total)	97		..	
Maternal mortality ratio (per 100,000 live births)	120		87	
Women's share of population ages 15+ living with HIV (%)	..		..	
Prevalence of HIV (% ages 15–24)	..	..	..	..
Economic structure, participation, and access to resources				
Labor force participation rate (% of population ages 15+)	75	88	72	84
Labor force participation rate (% of ages 15–24)	74	71	65	60
Wage and salaried workers (% of employed ages 15+)	..	..	..	..
Self-employed workers (% of employed ages 15+)	..	..	..	..
Unpaid family workers (% of employed ages 15+)	..	..	..	..
Employment in agriculture (% of employed ages 15+)	..	..	..	..
Employment in industry (% of employed ages 15+)	..	..	..	..
Employment in services (% of employed ages 15+)	..	..	..	..
Women in wage employment in the nonagricultural sector (%)	..		..	
Women's share of part-time employment (% of total)	..		..	
Maternity leave (days paid)	..		..	
Maternity leave benefits (% of wages paid)	..		..	
Employment to population ratio (% ages 15+)	72	83	69	80
Employment to population ratio (% ages 15–24)	68	63	59	54
Firms with female participation in ownership (%)	..		..	
Firms with a female top manager (%)	..		..	
Children in employment (% of children ages 7–14)	..	..	..	..
Unemployment rate (% of labor force ages 15+)	4	5	4	5
Unemployment rate (% of labor force ages 15–24)	9	11	9	11
Internet users (%)	..	..	..	..
Account at a financial institution (% age 15+)	..	..	..	..
Mobile account (% age 15+)	..	..	..	..
Saved any money last year (% age 15+)	..	..	..	..
Public life and decision making				
Seats held by women in national parliament (%)	..		16	
Female legislators, senior officials and managers (% of total)	..		..	
Proportion of women in ministerial level positions (%)	..		6	
Agency				
Total fertility rate (births per woman)	2.0		2.0	
Adolescent fertility rate (births per 1,000 women ages 15–19)	1		1	
Women first married by age 18 (% of women ages 20–24)	..		..	

Korea, Rep.

High income

Population (millions)	50
GNI, Atlas ($ billions)	1,366
GNI per capita, Atlas ($)	27,090
Population living below $1.90 a day (%)	..

	2000		2013	
	Female	Male	Female	Male
Education				
Net primary enrollment rate (%)	100	99	97[a]	98[a]
Net secondary enrollment rate (%)	95	96	97[a]	98[a]
Gross tertiary enrollment ratio (% of relevant age group)	59	96	82[a]	109[a]
Primary completion rate (% of relevant age group)	105	104	104[a]	105[a]
Progression to secondary school (%)	99	99	100	100
Lower secondary completion rate (% of relevant age group)	99	99	98[a]	99[a]
Gross tertiary graduation ratio (%)	28	28	50	47
Female share of graduates in eng., manf. and constr. (%, tertiary)	28		24	
Youth literacy rate (% of population ages 15-24)	..	..	..	..
Health and related services				
Sex ratio at birth (male births per female births)	*1.10*		1.07	
Under-five mortality rate (per 1,000 live births)	6	6	3	4
Life expectancy at birth (years)	80	72	85	78
Pregnant women receiving prenatal care (%)	..		..	
Births attended by skilled health staff (% of total)	..		..	
Maternal mortality ratio (per 100,000 live births)	19		27	
Women's share of population ages 15+ living with HIV (%)	..		..	
Prevalence of HIV (% ages 15-24)	..	..	..	..
Economic structure, participation, and access to resources				
Labor force participation rate (% of population ages 15+)	49	73	50	72
Labor force participation rate (% of ages 15-24)	37	33	30	24
Wage and salaried workers (% of employed ages 15+)	62	64	74	70
Self-employed workers (% of employed ages 15+)	39	36	26	30
Unpaid family workers (% of employed ages 15+)	19.2	2.0	10.7	1.2
Employment in agriculture (% of employed ages 15+)	12	10	7	6
Employment in industry (% of employed ages 15+)	19	35	13	20
Employment in services (% of employed ages 15+)	69	56	81	73
Women in wage employment in the nonagricultural sector (%)	40		43	
Women's share of part-time employment (% of total)	58		61	
Maternity leave (days paid)	..		90	
Maternity leave benefits (% of wages paid)	..		100	
Employment to population ratio (% ages 15+)	47	70	49	70
Employment to population ratio (% ages 15-24)	34	29	28	22
Firms with female participation in ownership (%)	..		..	
Firms with a female top manager (%)	..			
Children in employment (% of children ages 7-14)	..	..	..	..
Unemployment rate (% of labor force ages 15+)	4	5	3	3
Unemployment rate (% of labor force ages 15-24)	9	13	9	10
Internet users (%)	..	..	81	89
Account at a financial institution (% age 15+)	..	..	93	95
Mobile account (% age 15+)	..	..	..	..
Saved any money last year (% age 15+)	..	..	72	76
Public life and decision making				
Seats held by women in national parliament (%)	..		16	
Female legislators, senior officials and managers (% of total)	5		..	
Proportion of women in ministerial level positions (%)	..		6	
Agency				
Total fertility rate (births per woman)	1.5		1.2	
Adolescent fertility rate (births per 1,000 women ages 15-19)	3		2	
Women first married by age 18 (% of women ages 20-24)	..		..	

Kosovo

Europe & Central Asia	Lower middle income
Population (millions)	1.8
GNI, Atlas ($ billions)	7
GNI per capita, Atlas ($)	4,000
Population living below $1.90 a day (%)	<2

	2000		2013	
	Female	Male	Female	Male
Education				
Net primary enrollment rate (%)	..	..	..	..
Net secondary enrollment rate (%)	..	..	..	..
Gross tertiary enrollment ratio (% of relevant age group)	..	..	..	..
Primary completion rate (% of relevant age group)	..	..	..	..
Progression to secondary school (%)	..	..	..	..
Lower secondary completion rate (% of relevant age group)	..	..	..	..
Gross tertiary graduation ratio (%)	..	..	..	..
Female share of graduates in eng., manf. and constr. (%, tertiary)			..	
Youth literacy rate (% of population ages 15–24)	..	..	..	..
Health and related services				
Sex ratio at birth (male births per female births)	..		..	
Under-five mortality rate (per 1,000 live births)		..	..	
Life expectancy at birth (years)	70	66	73	69
Pregnant women receiving prenatal care (%)	..		..	
Births attended by skilled health staff (% of total)	..		..	
Maternal mortality ratio (per 100,000 live births)	..		..	
Women's share of population ages 15+ living with HIV (%)	..		..	
Prevalence of HIV (% ages 15–24)	..	..	..	..
Economic structure, participation, and access to resources				
Labor force participation rate (% of population ages 15+)	..	..	..	..
Labor force participation rate (% of ages 15–24)	..	..	..	..
Wage and salaried workers (% of employed ages 15+)	..	..	86	71
Self-employed workers (% of employed ages 15+)	..	..	14	29
Unpaid family workers (% of employed ages 15+)	..	..	5.4	5.8
Employment in agriculture (% of employed ages 15+)	..	..	5	4
Employment in industry (% of employed ages 15+)	..	..	10	33
Employment in services (% of employed ages 15+)	..	..	85	62
Women in wage employment in the nonagricultural sector (%)	..		..	
Women's share of part-time employment (% of total)	..			
Maternity leave (days paid)	..		270	
Maternity leave benefits (% of wages paid)	..		63	
Employment to population ratio (% ages 15+)	..	..	..	..
Employment to population ratio (% ages 15–24)	..	..	..	..
Firms with female participation in ownership (%)	..		11	
Firms with a female top manager (%)	..		7	
Children in employment (% of children ages 7–14)	..	..	..	..
Unemployment rate (% of labor force ages 15+)	..	..	..	..
Unemployment rate (% of labor force ages 15–24)	..	..	..	..
Internet users (%)	..	..	..	..
Account at a financial institution (% age 15+)	..	..	36	59
Mobile account (% age 15+)	..	..	..	..
Saved any money last year (% age 15+)	..	..	30	41
Public life and decision making				
Seats held by women in national parliament (%)	..		..	
Female legislators, senior officials and managers (% of total)	..		15	
Proportion of women in ministerial level positions (%)	..		..	
Agency				
Total fertility rate (births per woman)	3.0		2.2	
Adolescent fertility rate (births per 1,000 women ages 15–19)	..		..	
Women first married by age 18 (% of women ages 20–24)	..		..	

Kuwait

High income

Population (millions)	4
GNI, Atlas ($ billions)	187
GNI per capita, Atlas ($)	52,000
Population living below $1.90 a day (%)	..

	2000		2013	
	Female	Male	Female	Male
Education				
Net primary enrollment rate (%)	93	94	..	..
Net secondary enrollment rate (%)	99	100	..	..
Gross tertiary enrollment ratio (% of relevant age group)	*31*	*17*	41	18
Primary completion rate (% of relevant age group)	115	114	..	..
Progression to secondary school (%)	100	100	*100*	99
Lower secondary completion rate (% of relevant age group)	110	111	..	..
Gross tertiary graduation ratio (%)	..	..	23	6
Female share of graduates in eng., manf. and constr. (%, tertiary)	..		25	
Youth literacy rate (% of population ages 15-24)	..	..	99	99
Health and related services				
Sex ratio at birth (male births per female births)	*1.04*		1.04	
Under-five mortality rate (per 1,000 live births)	12	14	8	9
Life expectancy at birth (years)	74	72	76	73
Pregnant women receiving prenatal care (%)	..		..	
Births attended by skilled health staff (% of total)	100		..	
Maternal mortality ratio (per 100,000 live births)	8		14	
Women's share of population ages 15+ living with HIV (%)	..		..	
Prevalence of HIV (% ages 15-24)	..	..	..	..
Economic structure, participation, and access to resources				
Labor force participation rate (% of population ages 15+)	44	82	44	83
Labor force participation rate (% of ages 15-24)	27	47	24	43
Wage and salaried workers (% of employed ages 15+)	..	..	98	96
Self-employed workers (% of employed ages 15+)	..	..	2	4
Unpaid family workers (% of employed ages 15+)	..	..	0.6	0.4
Employment in agriculture (% of employed ages 15+)	..	..	..	..
Employment in industry (% of employed ages 15+)	..	..	..	..
Employment in services (% of employed ages 15+)	..	..	..	..
Women in wage employment in the nonagricultural sector (%)	23		..	
Women's share of part-time employment (% of total)	..		..	
Maternity leave (days paid)			70	
Maternity leave benefits (% of wages paid)	..		100	
Employment to population ratio (% ages 15+)	44	82	43	80
Employment to population ratio (% ages 15-24)	26	44	21	33
Firms with female participation in ownership (%)	..		..	
Firms with a female top manager (%)	..		..	
Children in employment (% of children ages 7-14)	..		..	
Unemployment rate (% of labor force ages 15+)	1	1	2	3
Unemployment rate (% of labor force ages 15-24)	3	5	13	23
Internet users (%)	..		..	..
Account at a financial institution (% age 15+)	..	..	64	79
Mobile account (% age 15+)	..	..	..	..
Saved any money last year (% age 15+)	..	..	60	62
Public life and decision making				
Seats held by women in national parliament (%)	..		2	
Female legislators, senior officials and managers (% of total)	..		..	
Proportion of women in ministerial level positions (%)	..		7	
Agency				
Total fertility rate (births per woman)	2.9		2.6	
Adolescent fertility rate (births per 1,000 women ages 15-19)	22		10	
Women first married by age 18 (% of women ages 20-24)	..		..	

Kyrgyz Republic

Europe & Central Asia			Lower middle income	

Population (millions)	6
GNI, Atlas ($ billions)	7
GNI per capita, Atlas ($)	1,250
Population living below $1.90 a day (%)	3

	2000		2013	
	Female	Male	Female	Male
Education				
Net primary enrollment rate (%)	85	87	89	92
Net secondary enrollment rate (%)	..	..	83	82
Gross tertiary enrollment ratio (% of relevant age group)	35	35	59	37
Primary completion rate (% of relevant age group)	93	94	102	104
Progression to secondary school (%)	97	100	100	100
Lower secondary completion rate (% of relevant age group)	27	24	89	90
Gross tertiary graduation ratio (%)	21	18	38	28
Female share of graduates in eng., manf. and constr. (%, tertiary)	36		26	
Youth literacy rate (% of population ages 15–24)	100	100	..	..
Health and related services				
Sex ratio at birth (male births per female births)	1.05		1.06	
Under-five mortality rate (per 1,000 live births)	44	53	19	24
Life expectancy at birth (years)	72	65	74	66
Pregnant women receiving prenatal care (%)	..		97	
Births attended by skilled health staff (% of total)	99		99	
Maternal mortality ratio (per 100,000 live births)	100		75	
Women's share of population ages 15+ living with HIV (%)	47		43	
Prevalence of HIV (% ages 15–24)	0.1	0.1	0.1	0.1
Economic structure, participation, and access to resources				
Labor force participation rate (% of population ages 15+)	56	74	56	80
Labor force participation rate (% of ages 15–24)	42	55	37	59
Wage and salaried workers (% of employed ages 15+)	44	42	..	..
Self-employed workers (% of employed ages 15+)	56	58	..	..
Unpaid family workers (% of employed ages 15+)	15.9	6.5	..	..
Employment in agriculture (% of employed ages 15+)	55	52	..	..
Employment in industry (% of employed ages 15+)	7	13	..	..
Employment in services (% of employed ages 15+)	38	35	..	..
Women in wage employment in the nonagricultural sector (%)	45		42	
Women's share of part-time employment (% of total)	..			
Maternity leave (days paid)	..		126	
Maternity leave benefits (% of wages paid)	..		19	
Employment to population ratio (% ages 15+)	52	69	51	74
Employment to population ratio (% ages 15–24)	36	48	31	51
Firms with female participation in ownership (%)	..		49	
Firms with a female top manager (%)	..		29	
Children in employment (% of children ages 7–14)	8	10	..	..
Unemployment rate (% of labor force ages 15+)	8	7	9	7
Unemployment rate (% of labor force ages 15–24)	15	12	18	14
Internet users (%)	..	..	..	..
Account at a financial institution (% age 15+)	..	..	19	18
Mobile account (% age 15+)	..	..	..	..
Saved any money last year (% age 15+)	..	..	34	39
Public life and decision making				
Seats held by women in national parliament (%)	..		23	
Female legislators, senior officials and managers (% of total)	28		..	
Proportion of women in ministerial level positions (%)	..		15	
Agency				
Total fertility rate (births per woman)	2.4		3.2	
Adolescent fertility rate (births per 1,000 women ages 15–19)	46		40	
Women first married by age 18 (% of women ages 20–24)	..		8	

Lao PDR

East Asia & Pacific   **Lower middle income**

Population (millions)	7
GNI, Atlas ($ billions)	11
GNI per capita, Atlas ($)	1,650
Population living below $1.90 a day (%)	*30*

	2000 Female	Male	2013 Female	Male
Education				
Net primary enrollment rate (%)	72	78	96	98
Net secondary enrollment rate (%)	24	31	43	46
Gross tertiary enrollment ratio (% of relevant age group)	2	4	17	19
Primary completion rate (% of relevant age group)	61	73	100	102
Progression to secondary school (%)	74	81	85	88
Lower secondary completion rate (% of relevant age group)	30	41	44	50
Gross tertiary graduation ratio (%)	1	1	10	13
Female share of graduates in eng., manf. and constr. (%, tertiary)	12		11	
Youth literacy rate (% of population ages 15-24)	74	88	..	..
Health and related services				
Sex ratio at birth (male births per female births)	*1.05*		1.05	
Under-five mortality rate (per 1,000 live births)	109	126	61	73
Life expectancy at birth (years)	63	60	70	67
Pregnant women receiving prenatal care (%)	*27*		54	
Births attended by skilled health staff (% of total)	19		42	
Maternal mortality ratio (per 100,000 live births)	600		220	
Women's share of population ages 15+ living with HIV (%)	41		46	
Prevalence of HIV (% ages 15-24)	0.1	0.1	0.2	0.1
Economic structure, participation, and access to resources				
Labor force participation rate (% of population ages 15+)	79	81	76	79
Labor force participation rate (% of ages 15-24)	77	64	68	59
Wage and salaried workers (% of employed ages 15+)	..	..	..	..
Self-employed workers (% of employed ages 15+)	..	..	..	..
Unpaid family workers (% of employed ages 15+)	..	..	..	..
Employment in agriculture (% of employed ages 15+)	..	..	..	..
Employment in industry (% of employed ages 15+)	..	..	..	..
Employment in services (% of employed ages 15+)	..	..	..	..
Women in wage employment in the nonagricultural sector (%)	..		35	
Women's share of part-time employment (% of total)	..			
Maternity leave (days paid)	..		105	
Maternity leave benefits (% of wages paid)	..		100	
Employment to population ratio (% ages 15+)	78	79	75	78
Employment to population ratio (% ages 15-24)	75	60	66	56
Firms with female participation in ownership (%)	..		42	
Firms with a female top manager (%)	..		32	
Children in employment (% of children ages 7-14)	..	..	10	8
Unemployment rate (% of labor force ages 15+)	2	2	1	2
Unemployment rate (% of labor force ages 15-24)	3	6	3	4
Internet users (%)	..	..	..	..
Account at a financial institution (% age 15+)	..	..	26	27
Mobile account (% age 15+)	..	..	..	..
Saved any money last year (% age 15+)	..	..	..	..
Public life and decision making				
Seats held by women in national parliament (%)	..		25	
Female legislators, senior officials and managers (% of total)	..		..	
Proportion of women in ministerial level positions (%)	..		10	
Agency				
Total fertility rate (births per woman)	4.2		3.0	
Adolescent fertility rate (births per 1,000 women ages 15-19)	80		65	
Women first married by age 18 (% of women ages 20-24)	..		35	

Latvia

Population (millions)	2
GNI, Atlas ($ billions)	31
GNI per capita, Atlas ($)	15,660
Population living below $1.90 a day (%)	<2

	2000 Female	2000 Male	2013 Female	2013 Male
Education				
Net primary enrollment rate (%)	94	97	97	96
Net secondary enrollment rate (%)	..	..	88	86
Gross tertiary enrollment ratio (% of relevant age group)	73	41	80	53
Primary completion rate (% of relevant age group)	95	97	106	106
Progression to secondary school (%)	99	100	98	98
Lower secondary completion rate (% of relevant age group)	..	..	96	100
Gross tertiary graduation ratio (%)	56	29	60	26
Female share of graduates in eng., manf. and constr. (%, tertiary)	16		27	
Youth literacy rate (% of population ages 15–24)	100	100	100	100
Health and related services				
Sex ratio at birth (male births per female births)	1.05		1.05	
Under-five mortality rate (per 1,000 live births)	15	19	7	9
Life expectancy at birth (years)	76	65	79	69
Pregnant women receiving prenatal care (%)	..		..	
Births attended by skilled health staff (% of total)	100		..	
Maternal mortality ratio (per 100,000 live births)	42		13	
Women's share of population ages 15+ living with HIV (%)	..		..	
Prevalence of HIV (% ages 15–24)	..	..	..	..
Economic structure, participation, and access to resources				
Labor force participation rate (% of population ages 15+)	49	65	55	68
Labor force participation rate (% of ages 15–24)	32	45	37	45
Wage and salaried workers (% of employed ages 15+)	86	84	91	86
Self-employed workers (% of employed ages 15+)	14	16	9	14
Unpaid family workers (% of employed ages 15+)	4.8	3.4	0.6	1.1
Employment in agriculture (% of employed ages 15+)	12	16	5	12
Employment in industry (% of employed ages 15+)	18	34	14	33
Employment in services (% of employed ages 15+)	69	49	81	55
Women in wage employment in the nonagricultural sector (%)	51		53	
Women's share of part-time employment (% of total)	54		63	
Maternity leave (days paid)	..		112	
Maternity leave benefits (% of wages paid)	..		80	
Employment to population ratio (% ages 15+)	42	55	49	60
Employment to population ratio (% ages 15–24)	25	35	29	36
Firms with female participation in ownership (%)	..		36	
Firms with a female top manager (%)	..		32	
Children in employment (% of children ages 7–14)	..	..	..	..
Unemployment rate (% of labor force ages 15+)	13	15	11	12
Unemployment rate (% of labor force ages 15–24)	22	21	22	19
Internet users (%)	..	..	75	76
Account at a financial institution (% age 15+)	..	..	90	90
Mobile account (% age 15+)	..	..	..	..
Saved any money last year (% age 15+)	..	..	45	43
Public life and decision making				
Seats held by women in national parliament (%)	..		18	
Female legislators, senior officials and managers (% of total)	37		45	
Proportion of women in ministerial level positions (%)	..		23	
Agency				
Total fertility rate (births per woman)	1.3		1.4	
Adolescent fertility rate (births per 1,000 women ages 15–19)	19		14	
Women first married by age 18 (% of women ages 20–24)	..		..	

Lebanon

Middle East & North Africa	**Upper middle income**
Population (millions)	5
GNI, Atlas ($ billions)	45
GNI per capita, Atlas ($)	9,800
Population living below $1.90 a day (%)	..

	2000		2013	
	Female	Male	Female	Male
Education				
Net primary enrollment rate (%)	..	..	90	97
Net secondary enrollment rate (%)	..	..	68	67
Gross tertiary enrollment ratio (% of relevant age group)	41	36	50	46
Primary completion rate (% of relevant age group)	117	114	87	91
Progression to secondary school (%)	100	93	99	97
Lower secondary completion rate (% of relevant age group)	96	79	69	62
Gross tertiary graduation ratio (%)	20	14	30	26
Female share of graduates in eng., manf. and constr. (%, tertiary)	24		17	
Youth literacy rate (% of population ages 15–24)	..	..	..	..
Health and related services				
Sex ratio at birth (male births per female births)	1.05		1.05	
Under-five mortality rate (per 1,000 live births)	19	21	8	9
Life expectancy at birth (years)	76	73	82	78
Pregnant women receiving prenatal care (%)	96		..	
Births attended by skilled health staff (% of total)	..		..	
Maternal mortality ratio (per 100,000 live births)	37		16	
Women's share of population ages 15+ living with HIV (%)	9		11	
Prevalence of HIV (% ages 15–24)	0.1	0.1	0.1	0.1
Economic structure, participation, and access to resources				
Labor force participation rate (% of population ages 15+)	19	71	23	71
Labor force participation rate (% of ages 15–24)	18	44	19	42
Wage and salaried workers (% of employed ages 15+)	..	..	..	..
Self-employed workers (% of employed ages 15+)	..	..	..	..
Unpaid family workers (% of employed ages 15+)	..	..	..	..
Employment in agriculture (% of employed ages 15+)	..	..	..	..
Employment in industry (% of employed ages 15+)	..	..	..	..
Employment in services (% of employed ages 15+)	..	..	..	..
Women in wage employment in the nonagricultural sector (%)	..		..	
Women's share of part-time employment (% of total)	..		..	
Maternity leave (days paid)	..		70	
Maternity leave benefits (% of wages paid)	..		100	
Employment to population ratio (% ages 15+)	17	65	21	67
Employment to population ratio (% ages 15–24)	14	34	14	34
Firms with female participation in ownership (%)	..		44	
Firms with a female top manager (%)	..		4	
Children in employment (% of children ages 7–14)	..		..	..
Unemployment rate (% of labor force ages 15+)	11	8	11	5
Unemployment rate (% of labor force ages 15–24)	21	22	24	19
Internet users (%)	..		..	..
Account at a financial institution (% age 15+)	..	..	33	62
Mobile account (% age 15+)	..	..	0.3	1.1
Saved any money last year (% age 15+)	..	..	43	51
Public life and decision making				
Seats held by women in national parliament (%)	..		3	
Female legislators, senior officials and managers (% of total)	..		..	
Proportion of women in ministerial level positions (%)	..		4	
Agency				
Total fertility rate (births per woman)	2.2		1.5	
Adolescent fertility rate (births per 1,000 women ages 15–19)	23		13	
Women first married by age 18 (% of women ages 20–24)	..		..	

Lesotho

Sub-Saharan Africa **Lower middle income**

Population (millions)	2
GNI, Atlas ($ billions)	3
GNI per capita, Atlas ($)	1,340
Population living below $1.90 a day (%)	60

	2000		2013	
	Female	**Male**	**Female**	**Male**
Education				
Net primary enrollment rate (%)	84	77	81	78
Net secondary enrollment rate (%)	26	15	42	27
Gross tertiary enrollment ratio (% of relevant age group)	3	2	12	8
Primary completion rate (% of relevant age group)	75	53	84	64
Progression to secondary school (%)	67	70	86	83
Lower secondary completion rate (% of relevant age group)	32	23	48	34
Gross tertiary graduation ratio (%)	..	..	4	2
Female share of graduates in eng., manf. and constr. (%, tertiary)	..		28	
Youth literacy rate (% of population ages 15-24)	97	85	..	..
Health and related services				
Sex ratio at birth (male births per female births)	1.03		1.03	
Under-five mortality rate (per 1,000 live births)	109	125	83	97
Life expectancy at birth (years)	48	47	50	49
Pregnant women receiving prenatal care (%)	85		..	
Births attended by skilled health staff (% of total)	60		..	
Maternal mortality ratio (per 100,000 live births)	680		490	
Women's share of population ages 15+ living with HIV (%)	57		58	
Prevalence of HIV (% ages 15-24)	13.8	7.8	10.2	5.9
Economic structure, participation, and access to resources				
Labor force participation rate (% of population ages 15+)	68	80	59	74
Labor force participation rate (% of ages 15-24)	57	69	37	52
Wage and salaried workers (% of employed ages 15+)	30	23	..	..
Self-employed workers (% of employed ages 15+)	64	74	..	..
Unpaid family workers (% of employed ages 15+)	..	..	..	..
Employment in agriculture (% of employed ages 15+)	65	78	..	..
Employment in industry (% of employed ages 15+)	10	9	..	..
Employment in services (% of employed ages 15+)	25	13	..	..
Women in wage employment in the nonagricultural sector (%)	51		..	
Women's share of part-time employment (% of total)	..		..	
Maternity leave (days paid)	..		84	
Maternity leave benefits (% of wages paid)	..		100	
Employment to population ratio (% ages 15+)	37	57	42	58
Employment to population ratio (% ages 15-24)	25	44	22	38
Firms with female participation in ownership (%)	..		..	
Firms with a female top manager (%)	..		..	
Children in employment (% of children ages 7-14)	28	34	..	..
Unemployment rate (% of labor force ages 15+)	45	29	28	22
Unemployment rate (% of labor force ages 15-24)	56	36	41	28
Internet users (%)	..	..	..	..
Account at a financial institution (% age 15+)	..	..	17	20
Mobile account (% age 15+)	..	..	..	..
Saved any money last year (% age 15+)	..	..	..	..
Public life and decision making				
Seats held by women in national parliament (%)	..		25	
Female legislators, senior officials and managers (% of total)	52		..	
Proportion of women in ministerial level positions (%)	..		22	
Agency				
Total fertility rate (births per woman)	4.1		3.0	
Adolescent fertility rate (births per 1,000 women ages 15-19)	91		92	
Women first married by age 18 (% of women ages 20-24)	..		..	

Liberia

Sub-Saharan Africa   **Low income**

Population (millions)	4
GNI, Atlas ($ billions)	1.6
GNI per capita, Atlas ($)	370
Population living below $1.90 a day (%)	..

	2000		2013	
	Female	Male	Female	Male
Education				
Net primary enrollment rate (%)	41	52	37[a]	39[a]
Net secondary enrollment rate (%)	..	..	15[a]	18[a]
Gross tertiary enrollment ratio (% of relevant age group)	14	25	9	14
Primary completion rate (% of relevant age group)	..	..	54[a]	63[a]
Progression to secondary school (%)	..	..	..	..
Lower secondary completion rate (% of relevant age group)	31	45	32[a]	42[a]
Gross tertiary graduation ratio (%)	4	5	..	..
Female share of graduates in eng., manf. and constr. (%, tertiary)	32		25	
Youth literacy rate (% of population ages 15-24)	..	..	..	..
Health and related services				
Sex ratio at birth (male births per female births)	1.05		1.05	
Under-five mortality rate (per 1,000 live births)	173	191	65	75
Life expectancy at birth (years)	53	52	62	60
Pregnant women receiving prenatal care (%)	84		96	
Births attended by skilled health staff (% of total)	51		61	
Maternal mortality ratio (per 100,000 live births)	1,100		640	
Women's share of population ages 15+ living with HIV (%)	58		59	
Prevalence of HIV (% ages 15-24)	1.3	0.7	0.4	0.3
Economic structure, participation, and access to resources				
Labor force participation rate (% of population ages 15+)	58	62	58	65
Labor force participation rate (% of ages 15-24)	35	36	35	36
Wage and salaried workers (% of employed ages 15+)	..	..	9	28
Self-employed workers (% of employed ages 15+)	..	..	91	72
Unpaid family workers (% of employed ages 15+)	..	..	19.7	12.5
Employment in agriculture (% of employed ages 15+)	..	..	48	50
Employment in industry (% of employed ages 15+)	..	..	5	14
Employment in services (% of employed ages 15+)	..	..	47	37
Women in wage employment in the nonagricultural sector (%)	..		24	
Women's share of part-time employment (% of total)	..		..	
Maternity leave (days paid)	..		90	
Maternity leave benefits (% of wages paid)	..		100	
Employment to population ratio (% ages 15+)	56	60	56	63
Employment to population ratio (% ages 15-24)	32	34	33	34
Firms with female participation in ownership (%)	..		..	
Firms with a female top manager (%)	..		..	
Children in employment (% of children ages 7-14)	..	..	15	22
Unemployment rate (% of labor force ages 15+)	4	4	4	4
Unemployment rate (% of labor force ages 15-24)	6	4	6	3
Internet users (%)	..	..	..	..
Account at a financial institution (% age 15+)	..	..	15	23
Mobile account (% age 15+)	..	..	..	..
Saved any money last year (% age 15+)	..	..	..	..
Public life and decision making				
Seats held by women in national parliament (%)	..		11	
Female legislators, senior officials and managers (% of total)	..		..	
Proportion of women in ministerial level positions (%)	..		20	
Agency				
Total fertility rate (births per woman)	5.9		4.8	
Adolescent fertility rate (births per 1,000 women ages 15-19)	149		111	
Women first married by age 18 (% of women ages 20-24)	..		36	

Libya

Middle East & North Africa	Upper middle income
Population (millions)	6
GNI, Atlas ($ billions)	50
GNI per capita, Atlas ($)	7,910
Population living below $1.90 a day (%)	..

	2000		2013	
	Female	Male	Female	Male
Education				
Net primary enrollment rate (%)	..	..	..	..
Net secondary enrollment rate (%)	..	..	..	..
Gross tertiary enrollment ratio (% of relevant age group)	50	51	..	..
Primary completion rate (% of relevant age group)	..	..	..	..
Progression to secondary school (%)	..	..	..	..
Lower secondary completion rate (% of relevant age group)	..	..	..	..
Gross tertiary graduation ratio (%)	..	..	..	..
Female share of graduates in eng., manf. and constr. (%, tertiary)	..		..	
Youth literacy rate (% of population ages 15–24)	..	..	100	100
Health and related services				
Sex ratio at birth (male births per female births)	1.06		1.06	
Under-five mortality rate (per 1,000 live births)	25	31	12	15
Life expectancy at birth (years)	74	70	77	73
Pregnant women receiving prenatal care (%)	..		..	
Births attended by skilled health staff (% of total)	99		..	
Maternal mortality ratio (per 100,000 live births)	21		15	
Women's share of population ages 15+ living with HIV (%)	..		..	
Prevalence of HIV (% ages 15–24)	..	..	..	..
Economic structure, participation, and access to resources				
Labor force participation rate (% of population ages 15+)	27	74	30	76
Labor force participation rate (% of ages 15–24)	22	49	24	49
Wage and salaried workers (% of employed ages 15+)	..	..	..	..
Self-employed workers (% of employed ages 15+)	..	..	..	..
Unpaid family workers (% of employed ages 15+)	..	..	..	..
Employment in agriculture (% of employed ages 15+)	..	..	..	..
Employment in industry (% of employed ages 15+)	..	..	..	..
Employment in services (% of employed ages 15+)	..	..	..	..
Women in wage employment in the nonagricultural sector (%)	16		..	
Women's share of part-time employment (% of total)	..		..	
Maternity leave (days paid)	..		..	
Maternity leave benefits (% of wages paid)	..		..	
Employment to population ratio (% ages 15+)	19	61	21	65
Employment to population ratio (% ages 15–24)	9	31	6	30
Firms with female participation in ownership (%)	..		..	
Firms with a female top manager (%)	..		..	
Children in employment (% of children ages 7–14)	..	..	..	..
Unemployment rate (% of labor force ages 15+)	29	17	30	15
Unemployment rate (% of labor force ages 15–24)	61	37	77	39
Internet users (%)	..	..	..	..
Account at a financial institution (% age 15+)	..	..	..	..
Mobile account (% age 15+)	..	..	..	..
Saved any money last year (% age 15+)	..	..	..	..
Public life and decision making				
Seats held by women in national parliament (%)	..		16	
Female legislators, senior officials and managers (% of total)	..		..	
Proportion of women in ministerial level positions (%)	..		4	
Agency				
Total fertility rate (births per woman)	3.1		2.4	
Adolescent fertility rate (births per 1,000 women ages 15–19)	7		6	
Women first married by age 18 (% of women ages 20–24)	..		..	

Liechtenstein

High income

Population (thousands)		37
GNI, Atlas ($ billions)		..
GNI per capita, Atlas ($)		..
Population living below $1.90 a day (%)		..

	2000		2013	
	Female	Male	Female	Male
Education				
Net primary enrollment rate (%)	..	..	..	..
Net secondary enrollment rate (%)	..	..	87	97
Gross tertiary enrollment ratio (% of relevant age group)	..	..	30	54
Primary completion rate (% of relevant age group)	..	..	99	105
Progression to secondary school (%)	..	..	100	100
Lower secondary completion rate (% of relevant age group)	..	..	110	100
Gross tertiary graduation ratio (%)	..	..	15	24
Female share of graduates in eng., manf. and constr. (%, tertiary)	..		41	
Youth literacy rate (% of population ages 15–24)	..	..	..	..
Health and related services				
Sex ratio at birth (male births per female births)			..	
Under-five mortality rate (per 1,000 live births)		..	..	..
Life expectancy at birth (years)	80	74	85	80
Pregnant women receiving prenatal care (%)	..		..	
Births attended by skilled health staff (% of total)	..		..	
Maternal mortality ratio (per 100,000 live births)	..		..	
Women's share of population ages 15+ living with HIV (%)	..		..	
Prevalence of HIV (% ages 15–24)	..	..	..	..
Economic structure, participation, and access to resources				
Labor force participation rate (% of population ages 15+)	..	..	..	..
Labor force participation rate (% of ages 15–24)	..	..	..	..
Wage and salaried workers (% of employed ages 15+)	..	..	..	..
Self-employed workers (% of employed ages 15+)	..	..	..	..
Unpaid family workers (% of employed ages 15+)	..	..	..	..
Employment in agriculture (% of employed ages 15+)	..	..	..	..
Employment in industry (% of employed ages 15+)	..	..	..	..
Employment in services (% of employed ages 15+)	..		..	..
Women in wage employment in the nonagricultural sector (%)	39		44	
Women's share of part-time employment (% of total)	..		..	
Maternity leave (days paid)	..		..	
Maternity leave benefits (% of wages paid)	..		..	
Employment to population ratio (% ages 15+)	..	..	..	..
Employment to population ratio (% ages 15–24)	..	..	..	..
Firms with female participation in ownership (%)	..		..	
Firms with a female top manager (%)	..		..	
Children in employment (% of children ages 7–14)	..	..	..	..
Unemployment rate (% of labor force ages 15+)	..	..	..	..
Unemployment rate (% of labor force ages 15–24)	..	..	..	..
Internet users (%)	..	..	..	..
Account at a financial institution (% age 15+)	..	..	..	..
Mobile account (% age 15+)	..	..	..	..
Saved any money last year (% age 15+)	..	..	..	..
Public life and decision making				
Seats held by women in national parliament (%)	..		20	
Female legislators, senior officials and managers (% of total)	..		..	
Proportion of women in ministerial level positions (%)	..		50	
Agency				
Total fertility rate (births per woman)	1.6		1.5	
Adolescent fertility rate (births per 1,000 women ages 15–19)	..		..	
Women first married by age 18 (% of women ages 20–24)	..		..	

Lithuania

High income

Population (millions)	3
GNI, Atlas ($ billions)	45
GNI per capita, Atlas ($)	15,380
Population living below $1.90 a day (%)	<2

	2000 Female	2000 Male	2013 Female	2013 Male
Education				
Net primary enrollment rate (%)	96	96	95	96
Net secondary enrollment rate (%)	92	91	96	97
Gross tertiary enrollment ratio (% of relevant age group)	61	40	83	57
Primary completion rate (% of relevant age group)	97	98	96	97
Progression to secondary school (%)	100	100	100	99
Lower secondary completion rate (% of relevant age group)	88	78	103	104
Gross tertiary graduation ratio (%)	26	18	82	48
Female share of graduates in eng., manf. and constr. (%, tertiary)	35		22	
Youth literacy rate (% of population ages 15-24)	100	100	100	100
Health and related services				
Sex ratio at birth (male births per female births)	1.06		1.05	
Under-five mortality rate (per 1,000 live births)	11	13	5	6
Life expectancy at birth (years)	78	67	80	69
Pregnant women receiving prenatal care (%)	..		..	
Births attended by skilled health staff (% of total)	100		..	
Maternal mortality ratio (per 100,000 live births)	20		11	
Women's share of population ages 15+ living with HIV (%)	..		..	
Prevalence of HIV (% ages 15-24)	..	..	..	..
Economic structure, participation, and access to resources				
Labor force participation rate (% of population ages 15+)	55	66	56	67
Labor force participation rate (% of ages 15-24)	33	42	28	37
Wage and salaried workers (% of employed ages 15+)	83	77	90	86
Self-employed workers (% of employed ages 15+)	17	23	10	14
Unpaid family workers (% of employed ages 15+)	3.5	2.5	1.4	0.9
Employment in agriculture (% of employed ages 15+)	15	22	6	12
Employment in industry (% of employed ages 15+)	20	34	16	34
Employment in services (% of employed ages 15+)	65	44	77	54
Women in wage employment in the nonagricultural sector (%)	54		53	
Women's share of part-time employment (% of total)	57		62	
Maternity leave (days paid)	..		126	
Maternity leave benefits (% of wages paid)	..		100	
Employment to population ratio (% ages 15+)	47	54	50	58
Employment to population ratio (% ages 15-24)	24	29	22	28
Firms with female participation in ownership (%)	..		36	
Firms with a female top manager (%)	..		21	
Children in employment (% of children ages 7-14)	..	..	..	..
Unemployment rate (% of labor force ages 15+)	14	18	11	13
Unemployment rate (% of labor force ages 15-24)	27	30	20	23
Internet users (%)	..	..	68	69
Account at a financial institution (% age 15+)	..	..	78	78
Mobile account (% age 15+)	..	..	..	..
Saved any money last year (% age 15+)	..	..	54	53
Public life and decision making				
Seats held by women in national parliament (%)	..		23	
Female legislators, senior officials and managers (% of total)	43		38	
Proportion of women in ministerial level positions (%)	..		21	
Agency				
Total fertility rate (births per woman)	1.4		1.6	
Adolescent fertility rate (births per 1,000 women ages 15-19)	25		12	
Women first married by age 18 (% of women ages 20-24)	..		..	

Luxembourg

High income

Population (thousands)	556
GNI, Atlas ($ billions)	*38*
GNI per capita, Atlas ($)	*69,880*
Population living below $1.90 a day (%)	..

	2000 Female	2000 Male	2013 Female	2013 Male
Education				
Net primary enrollment rate (%)	97	95	*93*	*92*
Net secondary enrollment rate (%)	86	82	87	84
Gross tertiary enrollment ratio (% of relevant age group)	*11*	*9*	*21*	*19*
Primary completion rate (% of relevant age group)	..	..	86	84
Progression to secondary school (%)	..	..	..	..
Lower secondary completion rate (% of relevant age group)	..	..	110	109
Gross tertiary graduation ratio (%)	..	..	13	7
Female share of graduates in eng., manf. and constr. (%, tertiary)	..		22	
Youth literacy rate (% of population ages 15–24)	..	..	..	..
Health and related services				
Sex ratio at birth (male births per female births)	*1.05*		*1.05*	
Under-five mortality rate (per 1,000 live births)	4	5	2	2
Life expectancy at birth (years)	81	75	84	80
Pregnant women receiving prenatal care (%)	..		..	
Births attended by skilled health staff (% of total)	100		..	
Maternal mortality ratio (per 100,000 live births)	11		11	
Women's share of population ages 15+ living with HIV (%)	..		..	
Prevalence of HIV (% ages 15–24)	..	..	..	..
Economic structure, participation, and access to resources				
Labor force participation rate (% of population ages 15+)	41	66	51	65
Labor force participation rate (% of ages 15–24)	31	37	25	29
Wage and salaried workers (% of employed ages 15+)	93	89	92	90
Self-employed workers (% of employed ages 15+)	7	11	8	10
Unpaid family workers (% of employed ages 15+)	1.3	0.1	0.6	0.2
Employment in agriculture (% of employed ages 15+)	2	3	1	2
Employment in industry (% of employed ages 15+)	7	30	4	19
Employment in services (% of employed ages 15+)	92	67	93	77
Women in wage employment in the nonagricultural sector (%)	..	45		
Women's share of part-time employment (% of total)	90	81		
Maternity leave (days paid)		112		
Maternity leave benefits (% of wages paid)	..	100		
Employment to population ratio (% ages 15+)	40	65	47	61
Employment to population ratio (% ages 15–24)	28	35	20	24
Firms with female participation in ownership (%)	..		..	
Firms with a female top manager (%)	..		..	
Children in employment (% of children ages 7–14)	..	..	..	..
Unemployment rate (% of labor force ages 15+)	3	2	7	5
Unemployment rate (% of labor force ages 15–24)	7	6	19	20
Internet users (%)	..	..	92	96
Account at a financial institution (% age 15+)	..	..	97	96
Mobile account (% age 15+)	..	..	..	..
Saved any money last year (% age 15+)	..	..	79	76
Public life and decision making				
Seats held by women in national parliament (%)	..		28	
Female legislators, senior officials and managers (% of total)	27		24	
Proportion of women in ministerial level positions (%)	..		27	
Agency				
Total fertility rate (births per woman)	1.8		1.6	
Adolescent fertility rate (births per 1,000 women ages 15–19)	11		6	
Women first married by age 18 (% of women ages 20–24)	..		..	

Macao SAR, China

	High income
Population (thousands)	578
GNI, Atlas ($ billions)	40
GNI per capita, Atlas ($)	71,060
Population living below $1.90 a day (%)	..

	2000		2013	
	Female	**Male**	**Female**	**Male**
Education				
Net primary enrollment rate (%)	87	83	..	..
Net secondary enrollment rate (%)	71	66	80	77
Gross tertiary enrollment ratio (% of relevant age group)	25	27	70	55
Primary completion rate (% of relevant age group)	101	99	..	..
Progression to secondary school (%)	91	94	100	99
Lower secondary completion rate (% of relevant age group)	83	69	90	93
Gross tertiary graduation ratio (%)	12	12	52	36
Female share of graduates in eng., manf. and constr. (%, tertiary)	..		20	
Youth literacy rate (% of population ages 15-24)	100	99	100	100
Health and related services				
Sex ratio at birth (male births per female births)	1.05		1.05	
Under-five mortality rate (per 1,000 live births)	..	..		
Life expectancy at birth (years)	80	75	83	78
Pregnant women receiving prenatal care (%)	..		..	
Births attended by skilled health staff (% of total)	..		..	
Maternal mortality ratio (per 100,000 live births)	..		..	
Women's share of population ages 15+ living with HIV (%)	..		..	
Prevalence of HIV (% ages 15-24)	..	..	..	..
Economic structure, participation, and access to resources				
Labor force participation rate (% of population ages 15+)	56	76	66	78
Labor force participation rate (% of ages 15-24)	45	42	53	50
Wage and salaried workers (% of employed ages 15+)	92	85	96	90
Self-employed workers (% of employed ages 15+)	8	15	4	11
Unpaid family workers (% of employed ages 15+)	2.9	0.2	0.6	0.1
Employment in agriculture (% of employed ages 15+)	0	0	..	..
Employment in industry (% of employed ages 15+)	30	27	..	..
Employment in services (% of employed ages 15+)	70	73	..	..
Women in wage employment in the nonagricultural sector (%)	49		48	
Women's share of part-time employment (% of total)	50		..	
Maternity leave (days paid)	..		..	
Maternity leave benefits (% of wages paid)	..		..	
Employment to population ratio (% ages 15+)	53	69	65	76
Employment to population ratio (% ages 15-24)	42	36	51	48
Firms with female participation in ownership (%)	..		..	
Firms with a female top manager (%)	..		..	
Children in employment (% of children ages 7-14)	..	..	2	2
Unemployment rate (% of labor force ages 15+)	5	9	2	2
Unemployment rate (% of labor force ages 15-24)	7	14	4	3
Internet users (%)	..	..	65	66
Account at a financial institution (% age 15+)	..	..	..	..
Mobile account (% age 15+)	..	..	..	..
Saved any money last year (% age 15+)	..	..	..	..
Public life and decision making				
Seats held by women in national parliament (%)	..		..	
Female legislators, senior officials and managers (% of total)	19		32	
Proportion of women in ministerial level positions (%)	..		..	
Agency				
Total fertility rate (births per woman)	0.9		1.1	
Adolescent fertility rate (births per 1,000 women ages 15-19)	5		3	
Women first married by age 18 (% of women ages 20-24)	..		..	

Macedonia, FYR

Europe & Central Asia **Upper middle income**

Population (millions)	2
GNI, Atlas ($ billions)	11
GNI per capita, Atlas ($)	5,150
Population living below $1.90 a day (%)	..

	2000		2013	
	Female	**Male**	**Female**	**Male**
Education				
Net primary enrollment rate (%)	89	90	87	87
Net secondary enrollment rate (%)	..	..	..	..
Gross tertiary enrollment ratio (% of relevant age group)	26	20	42	35
Primary completion rate (% of relevant age group)	95	96	..	..
Progression to secondary school (%)	98	100	..	..
Lower secondary completion rate (% of relevant age group)	92	94	86	89
Gross tertiary graduation ratio (%)	13	7	33	25
Female share of graduates in eng., manf. and constr. (%, tertiary)	33		39	
Youth literacy rate (% of population ages 15–24)	98	99	98	99
Health and related services				
Sex ratio at birth (male births per female births)	1.05		1.05	
Under-five mortality rate (per 1,000 live births)	15	17	5	6
Life expectancy at birth (years)	76	71	78	73
Pregnant women receiving prenatal care (%)	81		99	
Births attended by skilled health staff (% of total)	98		98	
Maternal mortality ratio (per 100,000 live births)	15		7	
Women's share of population ages 15+ living with HIV (%)	..		..	
Prevalence of HIV (% ages 15–24)	..	..	..	..
Economic structure, participation, and access to resources				
Labor force participation rate (% of population ages 15+)	41	66	43	68
Labor force participation rate (% of ages 15–24)	31	46	27	41
Wage and salaried workers (% of employed ages 15+)	76	74	75	70
Self-employed workers (% of employed ages 15+)	24	27	25	30
Unpaid family workers (% of employed ages 15+)	16.5	7.4	14.4	5.4
Employment in agriculture (% of employed ages 15+)	25	23	18	17
Employment in industry (% of employed ages 15+)	30	36	24	33
Employment in services (% of employed ages 15+)	46	41	58	49
Women in wage employment in the nonagricultural sector (%)	42		42	
Women's share of part-time employment (% of total)	46		45	
Maternity leave (days paid)	..		270	
Maternity leave benefits (% of wages paid)	..		100	
Employment to population ratio (% ages 15+)	27	46	31	48
Employment to population ratio (% ages 15–24)	12	19	13	19
Firms with female participation in ownership (%)	..		30	
Firms with a female top manager (%)	..		26	
Children in employment (% of children ages 7–14)	..	..	19	20
Unemployment rate (% of labor force ages 15+)	35	31	29	29
Unemployment rate (% of labor force ages 15–24)	63	58	51	53
Internet users (%)	..	..	54	61
Account at a financial institution (% age 15+)	..	..	64	80
Mobile account (% age 15+)	..	..	..	..
Saved any money last year (% age 15+)	..	..	35	44
Public life and decision making				
Seats held by women in national parliament (%)	..		33	
Female legislators, senior officials and managers (% of total)	19		28	
Proportion of women in ministerial level positions (%)	..		8	
Agency				
Total fertility rate (births per woman)	1.7		1.4	
Adolescent fertility rate (births per 1,000 women ages 15–19)	28		18	
Women first married by age 18 (% of women ages 20–24)	..		7	

Madagascar

Sub-Saharan Africa	Low income
Population (millions)	24
GNI, Atlas ($ billions)	10
GNI per capita, Atlas ($)	440
Population living below $1.90 a day (%)	82

	2000		2013	
	Female	Male	Female	Male
Education				
Net primary enrollment rate (%)	65	65	..	..
Net secondary enrollment rate (%)	..	..	31	30
Gross tertiary enrollment ratio (% of relevant age group)	2	2	4	4
Primary completion rate (% of relevant age group)	36	36	70	67
Progression to secondary school (%)	62	63	73	73
Lower secondary completion rate (% of relevant age group)	14	14	37	39
Gross tertiary graduation ratio (%)	1	1	3	3
Female share of graduates in eng., manf. and constr. (%, tertiary)	..		24	
Youth literacy rate (% of population ages 15–24)	68	73	..	..
Health and related services				
Sex ratio at birth (male births per female births)	1.02		1.03	
Under-five mortality rate (per 1,000 live births)	103	115	45	54
Life expectancy at birth (years)	60	57	66	63
Pregnant women receiving prenatal care (%)	71		82	
Births attended by skilled health staff (% of total)	46		44	
Maternal mortality ratio (per 100,000 live births)	550		440	
Women's share of population ages 15+ living with HIV (%)	49		46	
Prevalence of HIV (% ages 15–24)	0.4	0.3	0.1	0.2
Economic structure, participation, and access to resources				
Labor force participation rate (% of population ages 15+)	84	90	87	91
Labor force participation rate (% of ages 15–24)	74	76	78	79
Wage and salaried workers (% of employed ages 15+)	..	..	7	12
Self-employed workers (% of employed ages 15+)	..	..	93	88
Unpaid family workers (% of employed ages 15+)	..	..	63.4	30.7
Employment in agriculture (% of employed ages 15+)	..	..	..	..
Employment in industry (% of employed ages 15+)	..	..	..	..
Employment in services (% of employed ages 15+)	..	..	..	..
Women in wage employment in the nonagricultural sector (%)	..		37	
Women's share of part-time employment (% of total)	59		..	
Maternity leave (days paid)			98	
Maternity leave benefits (% of wages paid)	..		100	
Employment to population ratio (% ages 15+)	81	88	83	88
Employment to population ratio (% ages 15–24)	72	74	74	76
Firms with female participation in ownership (%)	..		42	
Firms with a female top manager (%)	..		28	
Children in employment (% of children ages 7–14)	25	26	..	..
Unemployment rate (% of labor force ages 15+)	4	2	5	3
Unemployment rate (% of labor force ages 15–24)	3	2	6	5
Internet users (%)	..	..	..	..
Account at a financial institution (% age 15+)	..	..	6	6
Mobile account (% age 15+)	..	..	4.2	4.5
Saved any money last year (% age 15+)	..	..	37	42
Public life and decision making				
Seats held by women in national parliament (%)			21	
Female legislators, senior officials and managers (% of total)	..		25	
Proportion of women in ministerial level positions (%)	..		20	
Agency				
Total fertility rate (births per woman)	5.5		4.5	
Adolescent fertility rate (births per 1,000 women ages 15–19)	152		117	
Women first married by age 18 (% of women ages 20–24)	..		41	

Malawi

Sub-Saharan Africa	Low income
Population (millions)	17
GNI, Atlas ($ billions)	4
GNI per capita, Atlas ($)	250
Population living below $1.90 a day (%)	71

	2000		2013	
	Female	Male	Female	Male
Education				
Net primary enrollment rate (%)	..	..		
Net secondary enrollment rate (%)	27	36	30	32
Gross tertiary enrollment ratio (% of relevant age group)	0	0	1	1
Primary completion rate (% of relevant age group)	62	69	75	75
Progression to secondary school (%)	84	91	84	88
Lower secondary completion rate (% of relevant age group)	26	40	20	21
Gross tertiary graduation ratio (%)	..	..	..	..
Female share of graduates in eng., manf. and constr. (%, tertiary)	..		..	
Youth literacy rate (% of population ages 15–24)	71	82	70	74
Health and related services				
Sex ratio at birth (male births per female births)	1.03		1.03	
Under-five mortality rate (per 1,000 live births)	167	182	60	68
Life expectancy at birth (years)	46	46	55	55
Pregnant women receiving prenatal care (%)	91		95	
Births attended by skilled health staff (% of total)	56		71	
Maternal mortality ratio (per 100,000 live births)	750		510	
Women's share of population ages 15+ living with HIV (%)	59		60	
Prevalence of HIV (% ages 15–24)	8.5	3.3	4.1	2.4
Economic structure, participation, and access to resources				
Labor force participation rate (% of population ages 15+)	77	81	85	82
Labor force participation rate (% of ages 15–24)	62	56	65	55
Wage and salaried workers (% of employed ages 15+)	..	..	..	..
Self-employed workers (% of employed ages 15+)	..	..	..	..
Unpaid family workers (% of employed ages 15+)	..	..	..	..
Employment in agriculture (% of employed ages 15+)	..	..	..	..
Employment in industry (% of employed ages 15+)	..	..	..	..
Employment in services (% of employed ages 15+)	..	..	..	..
Women in wage employment in the nonagricultural sector (%)	..		..	
Women's share of part-time employment (% of total)	..		..	
Maternity leave (days paid)	..		56	
Maternity leave benefits (% of wages paid)	..		100	
Employment to population ratio (% ages 15+)	70	76	77	76
Employment to population ratio (% ages 15–24)	53	49	56	48
Firms with female participation in ownership (%)	..		..	
Firms with a female top manager (%)	..		..	
Children in employment (% of children ages 7–14)	..	..	24	26
Unemployment rate (% of labor force ages 15+)	9	6	9	6
Unemployment rate (% of labor force ages 15–24)	15	13	14	13
Internet users (%)	..	..	..	..
Account at a financial institution (% age 15+)	..	..	13	19
Mobile account (% age 15+)	..	..	2.5	5.2
Saved any money last year (% age 15+)	..	..	59	60
Public life and decision making				
Seats held by women in national parliament (%)	..		17	
Female legislators, senior officials and managers (% of total)	..		..	
Proportion of women in ministerial level positions (%)	..		11	
Agency				
Total fertility rate (births per woman)	6.3		5.4	
Adolescent fertility rate (births per 1,000 women ages 15–19)	161		137	
Women first married by age 18 (% of women ages 20–24)	47		50	

Malaysia

East Asia & Pacific	Upper middle income
Population (millions)	30
GNI, Atlas ($ billions)	322
GNI per capita, Atlas ($)	10,760
Population living below $1.90 a day (%)	..

	2000		2013	
	Female	Male	Female	Male
Education				
Net primary enrollment rate (%)	98	98	..	..
Net secondary enrollment rate (%)	69	63	67	71
Gross tertiary enrollment ratio (% of relevant age group)	26	25	41	34
Primary completion rate (% of relevant age group)	94	95	..	..
Progression to secondary school (%)	100	98	99	100
Lower secondary completion rate (% of relevant age group)	91	84	86	91
Gross tertiary graduation ratio (%)	12	9	25	18
Female share of graduates in eng., manf. and constr. (%, tertiary)	..		39	
Youth literacy rate (% of population ages 15-24)	97	97	98	98
Health and related services				
Sex ratio at birth (male births per female births)	1.06		1.06	
Under-five mortality rate (per 1,000 live births)	9	11	6	8
Life expectancy at birth (years)	75	71	77	73
Pregnant women receiving prenatal care (%)	..		97	
Births attended by skilled health staff (% of total)	97		99	
Maternal mortality ratio (per 100,000 live births)	40		29	
Women's share of population ages 15+ living with HIV (%)	12		20	
Prevalence of HIV (% ages 15-24)	0.1	0.3	0.1	0.1
Economic structure, participation, and access to resources				
Labor force participation rate (% of population ages 15+)	45	81	44	76
Labor force participation rate (% of ages 15-24)	41	57	33	48
Wage and salaried workers (% of employed ages 15+)	76	73	75	73
Self-employed workers (% of employed ages 15+)	24	27	25	27
Unpaid family workers (% of employed ages 15+)	11.1	2.7	8.4	2.5
Employment in agriculture (% of employed ages 15+)	14	21	8	15
Employment in industry (% of employed ages 15+)	29	34	20	33
Employment in services (% of employed ages 15+)	57	45	72	52
Women in wage employment in the nonagricultural sector (%)	38		39	
Women's share of part-time employment (% of total)	..		..	
Maternity leave (days paid)	..		60	
Maternity leave benefits (% of wages paid)	..		100	
Employment to population ratio (% ages 15+)	43	78	43	73
Employment to population ratio (% ages 15-24)	37	53	29	43
Firms with female participation in ownership (%)	..		..	
Firms with a female top manager (%)	..		..	
Children in employment (% of children ages 7-14)	..	..	..	..
Unemployment rate (% of labor force ages 15+)	3	3	3	3
Unemployment rate (% of labor force ages 15-24)	9	9	12	11
Internet users (%)	..	..	..	..
Account at a financial institution (% age 15+)	..	..	78	83
Mobile account (% age 15+)	..	..	2.6	3.1
Saved any money last year (% age 15+)	..	..	84	80
Public life and decision making				
Seats held by women in national parliament (%)	..		10	
Female legislators, senior officials and managers (% of total)	22		25	
Proportion of women in ministerial level positions (%)	..		6	
Agency				
Total fertility rate (births per woman)	2.8		2.0	
Adolescent fertility rate (births per 1,000 women ages 15-19)	14		13	
Women first married by age 18 (% of women ages 20-24)	..		..	

Maldives

South Asia			Upper middle income	

				357
Population (thousands)				357
GNI, Atlas ($ billions)				3
GNI per capita, Atlas ($)				7,170
Population living below $1.90 a day (%)				..

	2000		2013	
	Female	**Male**	**Female**	**Male**
Education				
Net primary enrollment rate (%)	99	98	..	..
Net secondary enrollment rate (%)	42	36	..	..
Gross tertiary enrollment ratio (% of relevant age group)	..	..	..	..
Primary completion rate (% of relevant age group)	190	178	..	..
Progression to secondary school (%)	67	57	..	..
Lower secondary completion rate (% of relevant age group)	..	..	99	88
Gross tertiary graduation ratio (%)	..			
Female share of graduates in eng., manf. and constr. (%, tertiary)	..		..	
Youth literacy rate (% of population ages 15–24)	98	98	..	..
Health and related services				
Sex ratio at birth (male births per female births)	1.06		1.06	
Under-five mortality rate (per 1,000 live births)	40	49	8	9
Life expectancy at birth (years)	70	69	79	77
Pregnant women receiving prenatal care (%)	81		..	
Births attended by skilled health staff (% of total)	70		99	
Maternal mortality ratio (per 100,000 live births)	110		31	
Women's share of population ages 15+ living with HIV (%)	..		..	
Prevalence of HIV (% ages 15–24)	..	..	..	..
Economic structure, participation, and access to resources				
Labor force participation rate (% of population ages 15+)	38	71	56	78
Labor force participation rate (% of ages 15–24)	30	48	49	59
Wage and salaried workers (% of employed ages 15+)	29	21	..	..
Self-employed workers (% of employed ages 15+)	41	71	..	..
Unpaid family workers (% of employed ages 15+)	3.4	1.3	..	..
Employment in agriculture (% of employed ages 15+)	5	18	..	..
Employment in industry (% of employed ages 15+)	24	16	..	..
Employment in services (% of employed ages 15+)	39	56	..	..
Women in wage employment in the nonagricultural sector (%)	41		41	
Women's share of part-time employment (% of total)	..		..	
Maternity leave (days paid)			60	
Maternity leave benefits (% of wages paid)	..		100	
Employment to population ratio (% ages 15+)	30	67	46	72
Employment to population ratio (% ages 15–24)	20	39	31	48
Firms with female participation in ownership (%)	..		..	
Firms with a female top manager (%)	..		..	
Children in employment (% of children ages 7–14)	..	..	..	..
Unemployment rate (% of labor force ages 15+)	19	7	18	7
Unemployment rate (% of labor force ages 15–24)	35	17	36	19
Internet users (%)	..	..	..	..
Account at a financial institution (% age 15+)	..	..	..	..
Mobile account (% age 15+)	..	..	..	..
Saved any money last year (% age 15+)	..	..	..	..
Public life and decision making				
Seats held by women in national parliament (%)	..		6	
Female legislators, senior officials and managers (% of total)	15		..	
Proportion of women in ministerial level positions (%)	..		13	
Agency				
Total fertility rate (births per woman)	3.3		2.3	
Adolescent fertility rate (births per 1,000 women ages 15–19)	34		7	
Women first married by age 18 (% of women ages 20–24)	..		..	

Mali

Sub-Saharan Africa	Low income
Population (millions)	17
GNI, Atlas ($ billions)	11
GNI per capita, Atlas ($)	660
Population living below $1.90 a day (%)	..

	2000 Female	2000 Male	2013 Female	2013 Male
Education				
Net primary enrollment rate (%)	40	54	64	73
Net secondary enrollment rate (%)	..	..	32	39
Gross tertiary enrollment ratio (% of relevant age group)	1	3	4	10
Primary completion rate (% of relevant age group)	26	40	54	63
Progression to secondary school (%)	71	82	92	94
Lower secondary completion rate (% of relevant age group)	12	22	28	36
Gross tertiary graduation ratio (%)	..	..	..	..
Female share of graduates in eng., manf. and constr. (%, tertiary)	..		..	
Youth literacy rate (% of population ages 15–24)	17	32	39	56
Health and related services				
Sex ratio at birth (male births per female births)	1.05		1.05	
Under-five mortality rate (per 1,000 live births)	211	228	108	120
Life expectancy at birth (years)	49	49	55	55
Pregnant women receiving prenatal care (%)	57		74	
Births attended by skilled health staff (% of total)	41		59	
Maternal mortality ratio (per 100,000 live births)	860		550	
Women's share of population ages 15+ living with HIV (%)	59		59	
Prevalence of HIV (% ages 15–24)	0.7	0.3	0.7	0.5
Economic structure, participation, and access to resources				
Labor force participation rate (% of population ages 15+)	37	66	51	81
Labor force participation rate (% of ages 15–24)	31	50	47	68
Wage and salaried workers (% of employed ages 15+)	..	..	..	..
Self-employed workers (% of employed ages 15+)	..	..	..	..
Unpaid family workers (% of employed ages 15+)	..	..	..	..
Employment in agriculture (% of employed ages 15+)	..	..	..	..
Employment in industry (% of employed ages 15+)	..	..	..	..
Employment in services (% of employed ages 15+)	..	..	..	..
Women in wage employment in the nonagricultural sector (%)	..		..	
Women's share of part-time employment (% of total)	..			
Maternity leave (days paid)			98	
Maternity leave benefits (% of wages paid)	..		100	
Employment to population ratio (% ages 15+)	32	62	45	76
Employment to population ratio (% ages 15–24)	27	46	40	63
Firms with female participation in ownership (%)	..		58	
Firms with a female top manager (%)	..		21	
Children in employment (% of children ages 7–14)	..	..	27	32
Unemployment rate (% of labor force ages 15+)	12	6	11	6
Unemployment rate (% of labor force ages 15–24)	15	8	14	8
Internet users (%)	..	..	..	..
Account at a financial institution (% age 15+)	..	..	11	16
Mobile account (% age 15+)	..	..	9.0	14.4
Saved any money last year (% age 15+)	..	..	45	45
Public life and decision making				
Seats held by women in national parliament (%)	..		9	
Female legislators, senior officials and managers (% of total)	..		..	
Proportion of women in ministerial level positions (%)	..		16	
Agency				
Total fertility rate (births per woman)	6.8		6.8	
Adolescent fertility rate (births per 1,000 women ages 15–19)	188		175	
Women first married by age 18 (% of women ages 20–24)	65		60	

Malta

High income

Population (thousands)	427
GNI, Atlas ($ billions)	9
GNI per capita, Atlas ($)	*21,000*
Population living below $1.90 a day (%)	..

	2000		2013	
	Female	**Male**	**Female**	**Male**
Education				
Net primary enrollment rate (%)	..	..	95	95
Net secondary enrollment rate (%)	73	73	84	80
Gross tertiary enrollment ratio (% of relevant age group)	22	18	47	36
Primary completion rate (% of relevant age group)	96	93	87	88
Progression to secondary school (%)	99	98	100	99
Lower secondary completion rate (% of relevant age group)	83	68	95	91
Gross tertiary graduation ratio (%)	15	13	40	25
Female share of graduates in eng., manf. and constr. (%, tertiary)	13		20	
Youth literacy rate (% of population ages 15–24)	..	..	99	98
Health and related services				
Sex ratio at birth (male births per female births)	*1.06*		1.06	
Under-five mortality rate (per 1,000 live births)	7	8	6	7
Life expectancy at birth (years)	80	76	83	79
Pregnant women receiving prenatal care (%)	..		..	
Births attended by skilled health staff (% of total)	..		..	
Maternal mortality ratio (per 100,000 live births)	11		9	
Women's share of population ages 15+ living with HIV (%)	..		..	
Prevalence of HIV (% ages 15–24)	..	..	..	..
Economic structure, participation, and access to resources				
Labor force participation rate (% of population ages 15+)	30	72	38	66
Labor force participation rate (% of ages 15–24)	59	60	48	53
Wage and salaried workers (% of employed ages 15+)	95	85	94	82
Self-employed workers (% of employed ages 15+)	6	15	6	19
Unpaid family workers (% of employed ages 15+)	0.0	0.1	0.1	0.0
Employment in agriculture (% of employed ages 15+)	1	2	1	1
Employment in industry (% of employed ages 15+)	25	36	11	28
Employment in services (% of employed ages 15+)	74	61	88	70
Women in wage employment in the nonagricultural sector (%)	33		41	
Women's share of part-time employment (% of total)	64		69	
Maternity leave (days paid)	..		126	
Maternity leave benefits (% of wages paid)	..		82	
Employment to population ratio (% ages 15+)	28	67	35	62
Employment to population ratio (% ages 15–24)	53	52	42	45
Firms with female participation in ownership (%)	..		..	
Firms with a female top manager (%)	..		..	
Children in employment (% of children ages 7–14)	..	..	..	..
Unemployment rate (% of labor force ages 15+)	7	6	7	7
Unemployment rate (% of labor force ages 15–24)	10	13	12	16
Internet users (%)	..	..	67	71
Account at a financial institution (% age 15+)	..	..	96	97
Mobile account (% age 15+)	..	..	..	..
Saved any money last year (% age 15+)	..	..	67	76
Public life and decision making				
Seats held by women in national parliament (%)	..		13	
Female legislators, senior officials and managers (% of total)	18		23	
Proportion of women in ministerial level positions (%)	..		7	
Agency				
Total fertility rate (births per woman)	1.7		1.4	
Adolescent fertility rate (births per 1,000 women ages 15–19)	20		17	
Women first married by age 18 (% of women ages 20–24)	..		..	

Marshall Islands

East Asia & Pacific	Upper middle income
Population (thousands)	53
GNI, Atlas ($ millions)	227
GNI per capita, Atlas ($)	4,300
Population living below $1.90 a day (%)	..

	2000		2013	
	Female	Male	Female	Male
Education				
Net primary enrollment rate (%)	95	97	..	..
Net secondary enrollment rate (%)	64	61	..	..
Gross tertiary enrollment ratio (% of relevant age group)	18	14	41	45
Primary completion rate (% of relevant age group)	84	100	104	96
Progression to secondary school (%)	86	87	..	..
Lower secondary completion rate (% of relevant age group)	106	96	134	134
Gross tertiary graduation ratio (%)	..	..	..	..
Female share of graduates in eng., manf. and constr. (%, tertiary)		..		..
Youth literacy rate (% of population ages 15–24)	..	..	..	..
Health and related services				
Sex ratio at birth (male births per female births)		..		..
Under-five mortality rate (per 1,000 live births)	37	46	32	40
Life expectancy at birth (years)	68	63	..	..
Pregnant women receiving prenatal care (%)		..		..
Births attended by skilled health staff (% of total)		95		99
Maternal mortality ratio (per 100,000 live births)		..		..
Women's share of population ages 15+ living with HIV (%)		..		..
Prevalence of HIV (% ages 15–24)	..	..	..	..
Economic structure, participation, and access to resources				
Labor force participation rate (% of population ages 15+)	..	..	..	..
Labor force participation rate (% of ages 15–24)	..	..	..	..
Wage and salaried workers (% of employed ages 15+)	68	73	..	..
Self-employed workers (% of employed ages 15+)	29	27	..	..
Unpaid family workers (% of employed ages 15+)	0.0	1.4	..	..
Employment in agriculture (% of employed ages 15+)	7	27	..	..
Employment in industry (% of employed ages 15+)	23	16	..	..
Employment in services (% of employed ages 15+)	68	56	..	..
Women in wage employment in the nonagricultural sector (%)	29		..	
Women's share of part-time employment (% of total)	..		..	
Maternity leave (days paid)	..		..	
Maternity leave benefits (% of wages paid)	..		..	
Employment to population ratio (% ages 15+)	..	..	..	..
Employment to population ratio (% ages 15–24)	..	..	..	..
Firms with female participation in ownership (%)	..		..	
Firms with a female top manager (%)	..		..	
Children in employment (% of children ages 7–14)	..	..	..	..
Unemployment rate (% of labor force ages 15+)	..	..	..	..
Unemployment rate (% of labor force ages 15–24)	..	..	..	..
Internet users (%)	..	..	..	..
Account at a financial institution (% age 15+)	..	..	..	..
Mobile account (% age 15+)	..	..	..	..
Saved any money last year (% age 15+)	..	..	..	..
Public life and decision making				
Seats held by women in national parliament (%)		..		3
Female legislators, senior officials and managers (% of total)		..		..
Proportion of women in ministerial level positions (%)		..		10
Agency				
Total fertility rate (births per woman)	5.7		4.1	
Adolescent fertility rate (births per 1,000 women ages 15–19)	..		..	
Women first married by age 18 (% of women ages 20–24)	..		..	

Mauritania

Sub-Saharan Africa	Lower middle income
Population (millions)	4
GNI, Atlas ($ billions)	5
GNI per capita, Atlas ($)	1,270
Population living below $1.90 a day (%)	..

	2000		2013	
	Female	Male	Female	Male
Education				
Net primary enrollment rate (%)	59	61	75	71
Net secondary enrollment rate (%)	12	15	20	23
Gross tertiary enrollment ratio (% of relevant age group)	1	6	3	7
Primary completion rate (% of relevant age group)	42	48	72	70
Progression to secondary school (%)	49	54	54	61
Lower secondary completion rate (% of relevant age group)	16	19	21	19
Gross tertiary graduation ratio (%)	..	..	..	..
Female share of graduates in eng., manf. and constr. (%, tertiary)	..		..	
Youth literacy rate (% of population ages 15–24)	55	68	..	..
Health and related services				
Sex ratio at birth (male births per female births)	1.05		1.05	
Under-five mortality rate (per 1,000 live births)	104	123	80	96
Life expectancy at birth (years)	61	58	63	60
Pregnant women receiving prenatal care (%)	64		84	
Births attended by skilled health staff (% of total)	57		65	
Maternal mortality ratio (per 100,000 live births)	480		320	
Women's share of population ages 15+ living with HIV (%)	53		54	
Prevalence of HIV (% ages 15–24)	0.8	0.5	0.4	0.2
Economic structure, participation, and access to resources				
Labor force participation rate (% of population ages 15+)	23	78	29	79
Labor force participation rate (% of ages 15–24)	18	57	23	57
Wage and salaried workers (% of employed ages 15+)	..	..	..	..
Self-employed workers (% of employed ages 15+)	..	..	..	..
Unpaid family workers (% of employed ages 15+)	..	..	..	..
Employment in agriculture (% of employed ages 15+)	..	..	..	..
Employment in industry (% of employed ages 15+)	..	..	..	..
Employment in services (% of employed ages 15+)	..	..	..	..
Women in wage employment in the nonagricultural sector (%)	36		..	
Women's share of part-time employment (% of total)	..		..	
Maternity leave (days paid)			98	
Maternity leave benefits (% of wages paid)	..		100	
Employment to population ratio (% ages 15+)	16	52	21	54
Employment to population ratio (% ages 15–24)	11	31	14	32
Firms with female participation in ownership (%)	..		15[a]	
Firms with a female top manager (%)	..		5[a]	
Children in employment (% of children ages 7–14)	..	..	..	..
Unemployment rate (% of labor force ages 15+)	29	33	28	32
Unemployment rate (% of labor force ages 15–24)	40	46	39	45
Internet users (%)	..	..	..	..
Account at a financial institution (% age 15+)	..	..	19	22
Mobile account (% age 15+)	..	..	6.6	6.3
Saved any money last year (% age 15+)	..	..	41	42
Public life and decision making				
Seats held by women in national parliament (%)	..		25	
Female legislators, senior officials and managers (% of total)	..		..	
Proportion of women in ministerial level positions (%)	..		27	
Agency				
Total fertility rate (births per woman)	5.4		4.7	
Adolescent fertility rate (births per 1,000 women ages 15–19)	97		79	
Women first married by age 18 (% of women ages 20–24)	37		34	

Mauritius

Sub-Saharan Africa	Upper middle income
Population (millions)	1.3
GNI, Atlas ($ billions)	12
GNI per capita, Atlas ($)	9,710
Population living below $1.90 a day (%)	<2

	2000 Female	2000 Male	2013 Female	2013 Male
Education				
Net primary enrollment rate (%)	93	93	98	98
Net secondary enrollment rate (%)	68	69	..	..
Gross tertiary enrollment ratio (% of relevant age group)	10	12	45	37
Primary completion rate (% of relevant age group)	102	104	103	100
Progression to secondary school (%)	84	78	83	73
Lower secondary completion rate (% of relevant age group)	78	73	90	84
Gross tertiary graduation ratio (%)	..		..	
Female share of graduates in eng., manf. and constr. (%, tertiary)	..		..	
Youth literacy rate (% of population ages 15–24)	95	94	99	98
Health and related services				
Sex ratio at birth (male births per female births)	*1.04*		1.04	
Under-five mortality rate (per 1,000 live births)	16	21	12	15
Life expectancy at birth (years)	75	68	78	71
Pregnant women receiving prenatal care (%)	..		..	
Births attended by skilled health staff (% of total)	99		..	
Maternal mortality ratio (per 100,000 live births)	28		73	
Women's share of population ages 15+ living with HIV (%)	29		29	
Prevalence of HIV (% ages 15–24)	0.3	0.4	0.2	0.2
Economic structure, participation, and access to resources				
Labor force participation rate (% of population ages 15+)	41	80	44	74
Labor force participation rate (% of ages 15–24)	36	63	37	49
Wage and salaried workers (% of employed ages 15+)	91	79	83	77
Self-employed workers (% of employed ages 15+)	9	21	17	23
Unpaid family workers (% of employed ages 15+)	1.7	0.5	4.4	0.9
Employment in agriculture (% of employed ages 15+)	11	13	7	9
Employment in industry (% of employed ages 15+)	43	37	20	32
Employment in services (% of employed ages 15+)	46	50	73	60
Women in wage employment in the nonagricultural sector (%)	39		38	
Women's share of part-time employment (% of total)	42		..	
Maternity leave (days paid)	..		84	
Maternity leave benefits (% of wages paid)	..		100	
Employment to population ratio (% ages 15+)	36	75	38	70
Employment to population ratio (% ages 15–24)	27	52	25	40
Firms with female participation in ownership (%)	..		..	
Firms with a female top manager (%)	..		..	
Children in employment (% of children ages 7–14)	..	..	..	..
Unemployment rate (% of labor force ages 15+)	12	6	14	5
Unemployment rate (% of labor force ages 15–24)	25	17	32	17
Internet users (%)	..	..	34	37
Account at a financial institution (% age 15+)	..	..	80	85
Mobile account (% age 15+)	..	..	0.2	1.6
Saved any money last year (% age 15+)	..	..	53	55
Public life and decision making				
Seats held by women in national parliament (%)	..		12	
Female legislators, senior officials and managers (% of total)	22		..	
Proportion of women in ministerial level positions (%)	..		12	
Agency				
Total fertility rate (births per woman)	2.0		1.4	
Adolescent fertility rate (births per 1,000 women ages 15–19)	36		29	
Women first married by age 18 (% of women ages 20–24)	..		..	

Mexico

Latin America & the Caribbean	Upper middle income
Population (millions)	125
GNI, Atlas ($ billions)	1,236
GNI per capita, Atlas ($)	9,860
Population living below $1.90 a day (%)	3

	2000		2013	
	Female	Male	Female	Male
Education				
Net primary enrollment rate (%)	94	98	97	95
Net secondary enrollment rate (%)	54	55	69	66
Gross tertiary enrollment ratio (% of relevant age group)	19	20	29	31
Primary completion rate (% of relevant age group)	93	97	105	102
Progression to secondary school (%)	89	92	96	97
Lower secondary completion rate (% of relevant age group)	68	69	83	78
Gross tertiary graduation ratio (%)	16	14	20	18
Female share of graduates in eng., manf. and constr. (%, tertiary)	22		28	
Youth literacy rate (% of population ages 15–24)	96	97	99	99
Health and related services				
Sex ratio at birth (male births per female births)	1.05		1.05	
Under-five mortality rate (per 1,000 live births)	23	28	12	14
Life expectancy at birth (years)	77	72	80	75
Pregnant women receiving prenatal care (%)	..		98	
Births attended by skilled health staff (% of total)	..		96	
Maternal mortality ratio (per 100,000 live births)	67		49	
Women's share of population ages 15+ living with HIV (%)	16		21	
Prevalence of HIV (% ages 15–24)	0.1	0.3	0.1	0.1
Economic structure, participation, and access to resources				
Labor force participation rate (% of population ages 15+)	39	82	45	80
Labor force participation rate (% of ages 15–24)	37	69	35	61
Wage and salaried workers (% of employed ages 15+)	65	64	65	67
Self-employed workers (% of employed ages 15+)	35	37	35	33
Unpaid family workers (% of employed ages 15+)	12.6	6.1	9.1	4.3
Employment in agriculture (% of employed ages 15+)	7	24	4	19
Employment in industry (% of employed ages 15+)	22	29	16	29
Employment in services (% of employed ages 15+)	71	47	80	51
Women in wage employment in the nonagricultural sector (%)	37		40	
Women's share of part-time employment (% of total)	65		57	
Maternity leave (days paid)	..		84	
Maternity leave benefits (% of wages paid)	..		100	
Employment to population ratio (% ages 15+)	38	81	43	76
Employment to population ratio (% ages 15–24)	34	66	31	56
Firms with female participation in ownership (%)	..		26	
Firms with a female top manager (%)	..		15	
Children in employment (% of children ages 7–14)	..	..	4	9
Unemployment rate (% of labor force ages 15+)	3	2	5	5
Unemployment rate (% of labor force ages 15–24)	6	5	11	9
Internet users (%)	..	..	42	45
Account at a financial institution (% age 15+)	..	..	39	39
Mobile account (% age 15+)	..	..	2.8	4.1
Saved any money last year (% age 15+)	..	..	54	63
Public life and decision making				
Seats held by women in national parliament (%)	..		38	
Female legislators, senior officials and managers (% of total)	24		..	
Proportion of women in ministerial level positions (%)	..		18	
Agency				
Total fertility rate (births per woman)	2.7		2.2	
Adolescent fertility rate (births per 1,000 women ages 15–19)	80		63	
Women first married by age 18 (% of women ages 20–24)	..		..	

Micronesia, Fed. Sts.

East Asia & Pacific	Lower middle income
Population (thousands)	104
GNI, Atlas ($ millions)	339
GNI per capita, Atlas ($)	3,270
Population living below $1.90 a day (%)	..

	2000 Female	Male	2013 Female	Male
Education				
Net primary enrollment rate (%)	..	..	84[a]	82[a]
Net secondary enrollment rate (%)	..	..	..	..
Gross tertiary enrollment ratio (% of relevant age group)	..	..	..	..
Primary completion rate (% of relevant age group)	..	..	..	..
Progression to secondary school (%)	..	..	..	..
Lower secondary completion rate (% of relevant age group)	..	..	..	..
Gross tertiary graduation ratio (%)	..	..	..	..
Female share of graduates in eng., manf. and constr. (%, tertiary)	..		..	
Youth literacy rate (% of population ages 15–24)	..	..	..	..
Health and related services				
Sex ratio at birth (male births per female births)	1.07		1.07	
Under-five mortality rate (per 1,000 live births)	49	58	31	38
Life expectancy at birth (years)	68	67	70	68
Pregnant women receiving prenatal care (%)	..		..	
Births attended by skilled health staff (% of total)	88		..	
Maternal mortality ratio (per 100,000 live births)	130		96	
Women's share of population ages 15+ living with HIV (%)	..		..	
Prevalence of HIV (% ages 15–24)	..	..	..	..
Economic structure, participation, and access to resources				
Labor force participation rate (% of population ages 15+)	..	..	..	..
Labor force participation rate (% of ages 15–24)	..	..	..	..
Wage and salaried workers (% of employed ages 15+)	..	..	..	..
Self-employed workers (% of employed ages 15+)	..	..	..	..
Unpaid family workers (% of employed ages 15+)	..	..	..	..
Employment in agriculture (% of employed ages 15+)	..	..	..	..
Employment in industry (% of employed ages 15+)	..	..	..	..
Employment in services (% of employed ages 15+)	..	..	..	..
Women in wage employment in the nonagricultural sector (%)	..		..	
Women's share of part-time employment (% of total)	..		..	
Maternity leave (days paid)	..		..	
Maternity leave benefits (% of wages paid)	..		..	
Employment to population ratio (% ages 15+)	..	..	..	..
Employment to population ratio (% ages 15–24)	..	..	..	..
Firms with female participation in ownership (%)	..		..	
Firms with a female top manager (%)	..		..	
Children in employment (% of children ages 7–14)	..	..	..	..
Unemployment rate (% of labor force ages 15+)	..	..	..	..
Unemployment rate (% of labor force ages 15–24)	..	..	..	..
Internet users (%)	..	..	..	..
Account at a financial institution (% age 15+)	..	..	..	..
Mobile account (% age 15+)	..	..	..	..
Saved any money last year (% age 15+)	..	..	..	..
Public life and decision making				
Seats held by women in national parliament (%)	..		0	
Female legislators, senior officials and managers (% of total)	..		..	
Proportion of women in ministerial level positions (%)	..		25	
Agency				
Total fertility rate (births per woman)	4.3		3.3	
Adolescent fertility rate (births per 1,000 women ages 15–19)	38		16	
Women first married by age 18 (% of women ages 20–24)	..		..	

Moldova

Population (millions)	4
GNI, Atlas ($ billions)	9
GNI per capita, Atlas ($)	2,550
Population living below $1.90 a day (%)	<2

	2000		2013	
	Female	Male	Female	Male
Education				
Net primary enrollment rate (%)	89	90	88	88
Net secondary enrollment rate (%)	79	77	78	77
Gross tertiary enrollment ratio (% of relevant age group)	37	28	47	36
Primary completion rate (% of relevant age group)	96	98	93	93
Progression to secondary school (%)	98	98	98	98
Lower secondary completion rate (% of relevant age group)	84	80	83	84
Gross tertiary graduation ratio (%)	..	..	42	28
Female share of graduates in eng., manf. and constr. (%, tertiary)	..		31	
Youth literacy rate (% of population ages 15-24)	100	99	100	100
Health and related services				
Sex ratio at birth (male births per female births)	1.06		1.06	
Under-five mortality rate (per 1,000 live births)	28	35	14	18
Life expectancy at birth (years)	71	63	73	65
Pregnant women receiving prenatal care (%)	..		99	
Births attended by skilled health staff (% of total)	98		99	
Maternal mortality ratio (per 100,000 live births)	39		21	
Women's share of population ages 15+ living with HIV (%)	35		43	
Prevalence of HIV (% ages 15-24)	..	..	..	..
Economic structure, participation, and access to resources				
Labor force participation rate (% of population ages 15+)	56	64	38	44
Labor force participation rate (% of ages 15-24)	33	40	19	23
Wage and salaried workers (% of employed ages 15+)	62	64	73	65
Self-employed workers (% of employed ages 15+)	38	36	27	35
Unpaid family workers (% of employed ages 15+)	8.8	5.5	3.0	1.3
Employment in agriculture (% of employed ages 15+)	50	52	23	30
Employment in industry (% of employed ages 15+)	10	18	13	26
Employment in services (% of employed ages 15+)	36	26	64	45
Women in wage employment in the nonagricultural sector (%)	53		55	
Women's share of part-time employment (% of total)	59		58	
Maternity leave (days paid)	..		126	
Maternity leave benefits (% of wages paid)	..		100	
Employment to population ratio (% ages 15+)	52	58	36	41
Employment to population ratio (% ages 15-24)	28	33	16	19
Firms with female participation in ownership (%)	..		47	
Firms with a female top manager (%)	..		26	
Children in employment (% of children ages 7-14)	33	34	..	..
Unemployment rate (% of labor force ages 15+)	7	10	4	6
Unemployment rate (% of labor force ages 15-24)	15	17	13	16
Internet users (%)	..	..	..	..
Account at a financial institution (% age 15+)	..	..	19	16
Mobile account (% age 15+)	..	..	..	..
Saved any money last year (% age 15+)	..	..	45	43
Public life and decision making				
Seats held by women in national parliament (%)	..		22	
Female legislators, senior officials and managers (% of total)	33		44	
Proportion of women in ministerial level positions (%)	..		28	
Agency				
Total fertility rate (births per woman)	1.6		1.5	
Adolescent fertility rate (births per 1,000 women ages 15-19)	42		23	
Women first married by age 18 (% of women ages 20-24)	..		..	

Monaco

Population (thousands)	38
GNI, Atlas ($ billions)	..
GNI per capita, Atlas ($)	..
Population living below $1.90 a day (%)	..

	2000 Female	Male	2013 Female	Male
Education				
Net primary enrollment rate (%)	..	..	..	..
Net secondary enrollment rate (%)	..	..	..	..
Gross tertiary enrollment ratio (% of relevant age group)	..	..	..	..
Primary completion rate (% of relevant age group)	..	..	..	..
Progression to secondary school (%)	..	..	..	..
Lower secondary completion rate (% of relevant age group)	..	..	..	..
Gross tertiary graduation ratio (%)	..		..	
Female share of graduates in eng., manf. and constr. (%, tertiary)	..		..	
Youth literacy rate (% of population ages 15-24)	..	..	..	..
Health and related services				
Sex ratio at birth (male births per female births)	..		..	
Under-five mortality rate (per 1,000 live births)	5	6	3	4
Life expectancy at birth (years)	..	..	..	..
Pregnant women receiving prenatal care (%)	..		..	
Births attended by skilled health staff (% of total)	..		..	
Maternal mortality ratio (per 100,000 live births)	..		..	
Women's share of population ages 15+ living with HIV (%)	..		..	
Prevalence of HIV (% ages 15-24)	..	..	..	..
Economic structure, participation, and access to resources				
Labor force participation rate (% of population ages 15+)	..	..	..	..
Labor force participation rate (% of ages 15-24)	..	..	..	..
Wage and salaried workers (% of employed ages 15+)	..	..	..	..
Self-employed workers (% of employed ages 15+)	..	..	..	..
Unpaid family workers (% of employed ages 15+)	..	..	..	..
Employment in agriculture (% of employed ages 15+)	..	..	..	..
Employment in industry (% of employed ages 15+)	..	..	..	..
Employment in services (% of employed ages 15+)	..	..	..	..
Women in wage employment in the nonagricultural sector (%)	39		..	
Women's share of part-time employment (% of total)	..		..	
Maternity leave (days paid)	..		..	
Maternity leave benefits (% of wages paid)	..		..	
Employment to population ratio (% ages 15+)	..	..	..	..
Employment to population ratio (% ages 15-24)	..	..	..	..
Firms with female participation in ownership (%)	..		..	
Firms with a female top manager (%)	..		..	
Children in employment (% of children ages 7-14)	..	..	..	..
Unemployment rate (% of labor force ages 15+)	..	..	..	..
Unemployment rate (% of labor force ages 15-24)	..	..	..	..
Internet users (%)	..	..	..	..
Account at a financial institution (% age 15+)	..	..	..	..
Mobile account (% age 15+)	..	..	..	..
Saved any money last year (% age 15+)	..	..	..	..
Public life and decision making				
Seats held by women in national parliament (%)	..		21	
Female legislators, senior officials and managers (% of total)	..		..	
Proportion of women in ministerial level positions (%)	..		20	
Agency				
Total fertility rate (births per woman)	..		..	
Adolescent fertility rate (births per 1,000 women ages 15-19)	..		..	
Women first married by age 18 (% of women ages 20-24)	..		..	

Mongolia

East Asia & Pacific	Upper middle income
Population (millions)	3
GNI, Atlas ($ billions)	12
GNI per capita, Atlas ($)	4,280
Population living below $1.90 a day (%)	<2

	2000		2013	
	Female	Male	Female	Male
Education				
Net primary enrollment rate (%)	91	89	94	96
Net secondary enrollment rate (%)	69	56	..	..
Gross tertiary enrollment ratio (% of relevant age group)	39	22	73	51
Primary completion rate (% of relevant age group)	89	85	..	..
Progression to secondary school (%)	99	96	..	..
Lower secondary completion rate (% of relevant age group)	71	54	109	104
Gross tertiary graduation ratio (%)	25	13	81	44
Female share of graduates in eng., manf. and constr. (%, tertiary)	46		38	
Youth literacy rate (% of population ages 15-24)	98	97	99	98
Health and related services				
Sex ratio at birth (male births per female births)	1.03		1.03	
Under-five mortality rate (per 1,000 live births)	52	73	18	27
Life expectancy at birth (years)	66	60	72	64
Pregnant women receiving prenatal care (%)	97		99	
Births attended by skilled health staff (% of total)	97		99	
Maternal mortality ratio (per 100,000 live births)	120		68	
Women's share of population ages 15+ living with HIV (%)	..		..	
Prevalence of HIV (% ages 15-24)	..	..	..	..
Economic structure, participation, and access to resources				
Labor force participation rate (% of population ages 15+)	56	66	57	69
Labor force participation rate (% of ages 15-24)	38	47	31	41
Wage and salaried workers (% of employed ages 15+)	44	39	49	46
Self-employed workers (% of employed ages 15+)	56	60	50	54
Unpaid family workers (% of employed ages 15+)	38.6	14.0	6.0	2.7
Employment in agriculture (% of employed ages 15+)	47	51	32	33
Employment in industry (% of employed ages 15+)	11	17	12	22
Employment in services (% of employed ages 15+)	42	33	55	44
Women in wage employment in the nonagricultural sector (%)	49		50	
Women's share of part-time employment (% of total)	..		..	
Maternity leave (days paid)			120	
Maternity leave benefits (% of wages paid)			100	
Employment to population ratio (% ages 15+)	52	62	54	66
Employment to population ratio (% ages 15-24)	34	42	28	38
Firms with female participation in ownership (%)			38	
Firms with a female top manager (%)			36	
Children in employment (% of children ages 7-14)	21	23	16	17
Unemployment rate (% of labor force ages 15+)	6	6	5	5
Unemployment rate (% of labor force ages 15-24)	11	10	10	9
Internet users (%)	..	..	..	..
Account at a financial institution (% age 15+)	..	..	93	90
Mobile account (% age 15+)	..	..	5.1	4.9
Saved any money last year (% age 15+)	..	..	51	43
Public life and decision making				
Seats held by women in national parliament (%)			15	
Female legislators, senior officials and managers (% of total)	30		..	
Proportion of women in ministerial level positions (%)	..		11	
Agency				
Total fertility rate (births per woman)	2.1		2.4	
Adolescent fertility rate (births per 1,000 women ages 15-19)	26		16	
Women first married by age 18 (% of women ages 20-24)	..		5	

Montenegro

Europe & Central Asia	Upper middle income
Population (thousands)	622
GNI, Atlas ($ billions)	5
GNI per capita, Atlas ($)	7,240
Population living below $1.90 a day (%)	<2

	2000		2013	
	Female	Male	Female	Male
Education				
Net primary enrollment rate (%)	..	..	99	98
Net secondary enrollment rate (%)	..	..	..	..
Gross tertiary enrollment ratio (% of relevant age group)	19	14	62	49
Primary completion rate (% of relevant age group)	..	..	102	100
Progression to secondary school (%)	..	..	..	..
Lower secondary completion rate (% of relevant age group)	..	..	93	93
Gross tertiary graduation ratio (%)	..	..	..	..
Female share of graduates in eng., manf. and constr. (%, tertiary)	..		..	
Youth literacy rate (% of population ages 15–24)	..	..	99	99
Health and related services				
Sex ratio at birth (male births per female births)	1.08		1.07	
Under-five mortality rate (per 1,000 live births)	13	15	4	5
Life expectancy at birth (years)	77	71	77	72
Pregnant women receiving prenatal care (%)	..		..	
Births attended by skilled health staff (% of total)	99		..	
Maternal mortality ratio (per 100,000 live births)	10		7	
Women's share of population ages 15+ living with HIV (%)	..		..	
Prevalence of HIV (% ages 15–24)	..	..	..	..
Economic structure, participation, and access to resources				
Labor force participation rate (% of population ages 15+)	43	60	43	57
Labor force participation rate (% of ages 15–24)	28	41	28	33
Wage and salaried workers (% of employed ages 15+)	..	..	88	78
Self-employed workers (% of employed ages 15+)	..	..	12	22
Unpaid family workers (% of employed ages 15+)	..	..	2.2	1.5
Employment in agriculture (% of employed ages 15+)	..	..	5	6
Employment in industry (% of employed ages 15+)	..	..	8	26
Employment in services (% of employed ages 15+)	..	..	87	68
Women in wage employment in the nonagricultural sector (%)	44		47	
Women's share of part-time employment (% of total)	..		44	
Maternity leave (days paid)	..		45	
Maternity leave benefits (% of wages paid)	..		100	
Employment to population ratio (% ages 15+)	34	49	34	46
Employment to population ratio (% ages 15–24)	18	26	17	19
Firms with female participation in ownership (%)	..		24	
Firms with a female top manager (%)	..		19	
Children in employment (% of children ages 7–14)	..	..	..	..
Unemployment rate (% of labor force ages 15+)	21	19	21	19
Unemployment rate (% of labor force ages 15–24)	35	36	41	42
Internet users (%)	..	..	33	39
Account at a financial institution (% age 15+)	..	..	58	62
Mobile account (% age 15+)	..	..	..	..
Saved any money last year (% age 15+)	..	..	26	27
Public life and decision making				
Seats held by women in national parliament (%)	..		17	
Female legislators, senior officials and managers (% of total)	..		30	
Proportion of women in ministerial level positions (%)	..		17	
Agency				
Total fertility rate (births per woman)	1.8		1.7	
Adolescent fertility rate (births per 1,000 women ages 15–19)	19		12	
Women first married by age 18 (% of women ages 20–24)	..		..	

Morocco

Population (millions)	34
GNI, Atlas ($ billions)	103
GNI per capita, Atlas ($)	2,980
Population living below $1.90 a day (%)	..

	2000		2013	
	Female	Male	Female	Male
Education				
Net primary enrollment rate (%)	71	80	98[a]	99[a]
Net secondary enrollment rate (%)	..	..	53	59
Gross tertiary enrollment ratio (% of relevant age group)	8	11	13	15
Primary completion rate (% of relevant age group)	51	64	100[a]	102[a]
Progression to secondary school (%)	87	88	85	92
Lower secondary completion rate (% of relevant age group)	30	35	66[a]	70[a]
Gross tertiary graduation ratio (%)	4	6	..	..
Female share of graduates in eng., manf. and constr. (%, tertiary)	19		26	
Youth literacy rate (% of population ages 15-24)	..	..	74	89
Health and related services				
Sex ratio at birth (male births per female births)	1.06		1.06	
Under-five mortality rate (per 1,000 live births)	46	54	25	30
Life expectancy at birth (years)	70	67	73	69
Pregnant women receiving prenatal care (%)	..		77	
Births attended by skilled health staff (% of total)	..		74	
Maternal mortality ratio (per 100,000 live births)	200		120	
Women's share of population ages 15+ living with HIV (%)	40		30	
Prevalence of HIV (% ages 15-24)	0.1	0.1	0.1	0.1
Economic structure, participation, and access to resources				
Labor force participation rate (% of population ages 15+)	29	79	27	76
Labor force participation rate (% of ages 15-24)	28	65	19	53
Wage and salaried workers (% of employed ages 15+)	28	43	..	..
Self-employed workers (% of employed ages 15+)	70	53	..	..
Unpaid family workers (% of employed ages 15+)	54.9	21.4	..	..
Employment in agriculture (% of employed ages 15+)	5	5	..	..
Employment in industry (% of employed ages 15+)	39	30	..	..
Employment in services (% of employed ages 15+)	56	65	..	..
Women in wage employment in the nonagricultural sector (%)	22		22	
Women's share of part-time employment (% of total)	..		..	
Maternity leave (days paid)	..		98	
Maternity leave benefits (% of wages paid)	..		67	
Employment to population ratio (% ages 15+)	25	69	24	69
Employment to population ratio (% ages 15-24)	24	51	16	43
Firms with female participation in ownership (%)	..		..	
Firms with a female top manager (%)	..			
Children in employment (% of children ages 7-14)	13	14	10	..
Unemployment rate (% of labor force ages 15+)	13	14	10	9
Unemployment rate (% of labor force ages 15-24)	16	21	17	19
Internet users (%)	..	..	45	58
Account at a financial institution (% age 15+)	..	..	27	52
Mobile account (% age 15+)	..	..	..	..
Saved any money last year (% age 15+)	..	..	..	..
Public life and decision making				
Seats held by women in national parliament (%)	..		17	
Female legislators, senior officials and managers (% of total)	..		..	
Proportion of women in ministerial level positions (%)	..		16	
Agency				
Total fertility rate (births per woman)	2.7		2.7	
Adolescent fertility rate (births per 1,000 women ages 15-19)	34		32	
Women first married by age 18 (% of women ages 20-24)	..		..	

Mozambique

Sub-Saharan Africa	Low income
Population (millions)	27
GNI, Atlas ($ billions)	17
GNI per capita, Atlas ($)	620
Population living below $1.90 a day (%)	..

	2000 Female	2000 Male	2013 Female	2013 Male
Education				
Net primary enrollment rate (%)	50	62	85	90
Net secondary enrollment rate (%)	3	4	18	19
Gross tertiary enrollment ratio (% of relevant age group)	..	..	4	6
Primary completion rate (% of relevant age group)	12	20	46	53
Progression to secondary school (%)	59	56	63	58
Lower secondary completion rate (% of relevant age group)	3	5	23	24
Gross tertiary graduation ratio (%)	..	..	..	..
Female share of graduates in eng., manf. and constr. (%, tertiary)	..		34	
Youth literacy rate (% of population ages 15–24)	..	..	..	..
Health and related services				
Sex ratio at birth (male births per female births)	*1.03*		1.03	
Under-five mortality rate (per 1,000 live births)	165	177	74	83
Life expectancy at birth (years)	49	46	51	49
Pregnant women receiving prenatal care (%)	76		*91*	
Births attended by skilled health staff (% of total)	..		54	
Maternal mortality ratio (per 100,000 live births)	870		480	
Women's share of population ages 15+ living with HIV (%)	58		60	
Prevalence of HIV (% ages 15–24)	..	..	..	..
Economic structure, participation, and access to resources				
Labor force participation rate (% of population ages 15+)	88	83	86	83
Labor force participation rate (% of ages 15–24)	79	64	71	60
Wage and salaried workers (% of employed ages 15+)	..	..	..	..
Self-employed workers (% of employed ages 15+)	..	..	..	..
Unpaid family workers (% of employed ages 15+)	..	..	..	..
Employment in agriculture (% of employed ages 15+)	..	..	..	..
Employment in industry (% of employed ages 15+)	..	..	..	..
Employment in services (% of employed ages 15+)	..	..	..	..
Women in wage employment in the nonagricultural sector (%)	..			
Women's share of part-time employment (% of total)	..		..	
Maternity leave (days paid)	..		60	
Maternity leave benefits (% of wages paid)	..		100	
Employment to population ratio (% ages 15+)	79	77	78	77
Employment to population ratio (% ages 15–24)	67	55	60	52
Firms with female participation in ownership (%)	..		..	
Firms with a female top manager (%)	..		..	
Children in employment (% of children ages 7–14)	..	..	..	..
Unemployment rate (% of labor force ages 15+)	10	7	9	7
Unemployment rate (% of labor force ages 15–24)	15	14	15	14
Internet users (%)	..	..	..	..
Account at a financial institution (% age 15+)	..	..	..	..
Mobile account (% age 15+)	..	..	..	..
Saved any money last year (% age 15+)	..	..	..	..
Public life and decision making				
Seats held by women in national parliament (%)	..		40	
Female legislators, senior officials and managers (% of total)	..		..	
Proportion of women in ministerial level positions (%)	..		29	
Agency				
Total fertility rate (births per woman)	5.8		5.2	
Adolescent fertility rate (births per 1,000 women ages 15–19)	185		143	
Women first married by age 18 (% of women ages 20–24)	..		48	

Myanmar

East Asia & Pacific	Lower middle income
Population (millions)	53
GNI, Atlas ($ billions)	68
GNI per capita, Atlas ($)	1,270
Population living below $1.90 a day (%)	..

	2000 Female	Male	2013 Female	Male
Education				
Net primary enrollment rate (%)	..	..	..	..
Net secondary enrollment rate (%)	33	31	48	46
Gross tertiary enrollment ratio (% of relevant age group)	8	5	15	12
Primary completion rate (% of relevant age group)	74	78	97	93
Progression to secondary school (%)	65	67	..	..
Lower secondary completion rate (% of relevant age group)	32	32	47	44
Gross tertiary graduation ratio (%)	..	..	36	20
Female share of graduates in eng., manf. and constr. (%, tertiary)	..		65	
Youth literacy rate (% of population ages 15-24)	93	96	96	96
Health and related services				
Sex ratio at birth (male births per female births)	1.03		1.03	
Under-five mortality rate (per 1,000 live births)	76	89	45	55
Life expectancy at birth (years)	64	60	67	63
Pregnant women receiving prenatal care (%)	76		83	
Births attended by skilled health staff (% of total)	57		71	
Maternal mortality ratio (per 100,000 live births)	360		200	
Women's share of population ages 15+ living with HIV (%)	23		35	
Prevalence of HIV (% ages 15-24)	0.4	0.9	0.3	0.4
Economic structure, participation, and access to resources				
Labor force participation rate (% of population ages 15+)	73	80	75	82
Labor force participation rate (% of ages 15-24)	57	57	57	58
Wage and salaried workers (% of employed ages 15+)	..	..	..	..
Self-employed workers (% of employed ages 15+)	..	..	..	..
Unpaid family workers (% of employed ages 15+)	..	..	..	..
Employment in agriculture (% of employed ages 15+)	..	..	..	..
Employment in industry (% of employed ages 15+)	..	..	..	..
Employment in services (% of employed ages 15+)	..	..	..	..
Women in wage employment in the nonagricultural sector (%)	36		..	
Women's share of part-time employment (% of total)	..		..	
Maternity leave (days paid)	..		98	
Maternity leave benefits (% of wages paid)	..		70	
Employment to population ratio (% ages 15+)	71	78	72	80
Employment to population ratio (% ages 15-24)	51	53	51	53
Firms with female participation in ownership (%)	..		27[a]	
Firms with a female top manager (%)	..		30[a]	
Children in employment (% of children ages 7-14)	..	..	..	..
Unemployment rate (% of labor force ages 15+)	4	3	4	3
Unemployment rate (% of labor force ages 15-24)	10	8	11	9
Internet users (%)	..	..	..	..
Account at a financial institution (% age 15+)	..	..	17	29
Mobile account (% age 15+)	..	..	0.3	0.0
Saved any money last year (% age 15+)	..	..	46	48
Public life and decision making				
Seats held by women in national parliament (%)	..		6	
Female legislators, senior officials and managers (% of total)	..		..	
Proportion of women in ministerial level positions (%)	..		5	
Agency				
Total fertility rate (births per woman)	2.4		1.9	
Adolescent fertility rate (births per 1,000 women ages 15-19)	25		17	
Women first married by age 18 (% of women ages 20-24)	..		..	

Namibia

Sub-Saharan Africa	Upper middle income
Population (millions)	2
GNI, Atlas ($ billions)	14
GNI per capita, Atlas ($)	5,680
Population living below $1.90 a day (%)	..

	2000		2013	
	Female	Male	Female	Male
Education				
Net primary enrollment rate (%)	90	85	89	86
Net secondary enrollment rate (%)	48	38	..	..
Gross tertiary enrollment ratio (% of relevant age group)	6	8	..	..
Primary completion rate (% of relevant age group)	97	86	88	83
Progression to secondary school (%)	100	96	..	..
Lower secondary completion rate (% of relevant age group)	55	51	62	55
Gross tertiary graduation ratio (%)	8	7	..	
Female share of graduates in eng., manf. and constr. (%, tertiary)	0		..	
Youth literacy rate (% of population ages 15–24)	93	91	..	..
Health and related services				
Sex ratio at birth (male births per female births)	1.03		1.03	
Under-five mortality rate (per 1,000 live births)	70	81	41	49
Life expectancy at birth (years)	57	53	67	62
Pregnant women receiving prenatal care (%)	91		..	
Births attended by skilled health staff (% of total)	76		..	
Maternal mortality ratio (per 100,000 live births)	270		130	
Women's share of population ages 15+ living with HIV (%)	58		54	
Prevalence of HIV (% ages 15–24)	10.2	5.2	5.0	2.9
Economic structure, participation, and access to resources				
Labor force participation rate (% of population ages 15+)	49	65	55	64
Labor force participation rate (% of ages 15–24)	28	34	29	35
Wage and salaried workers (% of employed ages 15+)	56	68	55	72
Self-employed workers (% of employed ages 15+)	42	30	45	27
Unpaid family workers (% of employed ages 15+)	4.1	2.6	5.5	3.8
Employment in agriculture (% of employed ages 15+)	29	33	27	28
Employment in industry (% of employed ages 15+)	7	17	5	22
Employment in services (% of employed ages 15+)	63	50	68	50
Women in wage employment in the nonagricultural sector (%)	43		43	
Women's share of part-time employment (% of total)	..		..	
Maternity leave (days paid)	..		84	
Maternity leave benefits (% of wages paid)	..		100	
Employment to population ratio (% ages 15+)	38	52	45	54
Employment to population ratio (% ages 15–24)	15	19	18	24
Firms with female participation in ownership (%)	..		41[a]	
Firms with a female top manager (%)	..		27[a]	
Children in employment (% of children ages 7–14)	15	16	..	..
Unemployment rate (% of labor force ages 15+)	22	19	19	15
Unemployment rate (% of labor force ages 15–24)	46	42	39	30
Internet users (%)	..	..	..	..
Account at a financial institution (% age 15+)	..	..	56	60
Mobile account (% age 15+)	..	..	8.4	12.5
Saved any money last year (% age 15+)	..	..	53	62
Public life and decision making				
Seats held by women in national parliament (%)	..		41	
Female legislators, senior officials and managers (% of total)	30		43	
Proportion of women in ministerial level positions (%)	..		22	
Agency				
Total fertility rate (births per woman)	4.0		3.1	
Adolescent fertility rate (births per 1,000 women ages 15–19)	85		77	
Women first married by age 18 (% of women ages 20–24)	10		..	

Nepal

South Asia	**Low income**
Population (millions)	28
GNI, Atlas ($ billions)	21
GNI per capita, Atlas ($)	730
Population living below $1.90 a day (%)	15

	2000		2013	
	Female	Male	Female	Male
Education				
Net primary enrollment rate (%)	68	84	97	98
Net secondary enrollment rate (%)	..	..	62[a]	58[a]
Gross tertiary enrollment ratio (% of relevant age group)	2	7	16	19
Primary completion rate (% of relevant age group)	59	79	107[a]	97[a]
Progression to secondary school	81	79	87	88
Lower secondary completion rate (% of relevant age group)	36	52	86[a]	79[a]
Gross tertiary graduation ratio (%)	..	..	9	11
Female share of graduates in eng., manf. and constr. (%, tertiary)	..		14	
Youth literacy rate (% of population ages 15–24)	60	81	80	90
Health and related services				
Sex ratio at birth (male births per female births)	1.07		1.07	
Under-five mortality rate (per 1,000 live births)	79	82	34	38
Life expectancy at birth (years)	63	61	70	67
Pregnant women receiving prenatal care (%)	27		58	
Births attended by skilled health staff (% of total)	12		36	
Maternal mortality ratio (per 100,000 live births)	430		190	
Women's share of population ages 15+ living with HIV (%)	13		34	
Prevalence of HIV (% ages 15–24)	0.1	0.1	0.1	0.1
Economic structure, participation, and access to resources				
Labor force participation rate (% of population ages 15+)	82	90	80	87
Labor force participation rate (% of ages 15–24)	80	83	75	76
Wage and salaried workers (% of employed ages 15+)	13	34	..	..
Self-employed workers (% of employed ages 15+)	87	66	..	..
Unpaid family workers (% of employed ages 15+)	12.9	5.7	..	..
Employment in agriculture (% of employed ages 15+)	73	60	..	..
Employment in industry (% of employed ages 15+)	14	13	..	..
Employment in services (% of employed ages 15+)	13	26	..	..
Women in wage employment in the nonagricultural sector (%)	14		..	
Women's share of part-time employment (% of total)	..			
Maternity leave (days paid)			52	
Maternity leave benefits (% of wages paid)	..		100	
Employment to population ratio (% ages 15+)	80	88	78	85
Employment to population ratio (% ages 15–24)	77	78	72	72
Firms with female participation in ownership (%)	..		22	
Firms with a female top manager (%)	..		17	
Children in employment (% of children ages 7–14)	52	42	..	..
Unemployment rate (% of labor force ages 15+)	2	3	2	3
Unemployment rate (% of labor force ages 15–24)	3	6	3	6
Internet users (%)	..			
Account at a financial institution (% age 15+)	..	..	31	37
Mobile account (% age 15+)	..	..	0.3	0.4
Saved any money last year (% age 15+)	..	..	44	46
Public life and decision making				
Seats held by women in national parliament (%)	..		30	
Female legislators, senior officials and managers (% of total)	14		..	
Proportion of women in ministerial level positions (%)	..		14	
Agency				
Total fertility rate (births per woman)	4.1		2.3	
Adolescent fertility rate (births per 1,000 women ages 15–19)	118		73	
Women first married by age 18 (% of women ages 20–24)	56		41	

Netherlands

High income				
Population (millions)				17
GNI, Atlas ($ billions)				863
GNI per capita, Atlas ($)				51,210
Population living below $1.90 a day (%)				..

	2000		2013	
	Female	Male	Female	Male
Education				
Net primary enrollment rate (%)	99	100	97	97
Net secondary enrollment rate (%)	92	91	93	92
Gross tertiary enrollment ratio (% of relevant age group)	53	52	*81*	*74*
Primary completion rate (% of relevant age group)	98	99	..	..
Progression to secondary school (%)	..	..	..	..
Lower secondary completion rate (% of relevant age group)	60	64	..	..
Gross tertiary graduation ratio (%)	41	34	57	*42*
Female share of graduates in eng., manf. and constr. (%, tertiary)	13		21	
Youth literacy rate (% of population ages 15–24)	..	..	..	..
Health and related services				
Sex ratio at birth (male births per female births)	*1.06*		*1.05*	
Under-five mortality rate (per 1,000 live births)	6	7	3	4
Life expectancy at birth (years)	81	76	83	79
Pregnant women receiving prenatal care (%)	..		..	
Births attended by skilled health staff (% of total)	100		..	
Maternal mortality ratio (per 100,000 live births)	15		6	
Women's share of population ages 15+ living with HIV (%)	..		..	
Prevalence of HIV (% ages 15–24)	..	..	..	..
Economic structure, participation, and access to resources				
Labor force participation rate (% of population ages 15+)	53	73	59	71
Labor force participation rate (% of ages 15–24)	71	73	72	69
Wage and salaried workers (% of employed ages 15+)	90	87	88	81
Self-employed workers (% of employed ages 15+)	9	13	12	19
Unpaid family workers (% of employed ages 15+)	1.6	0.3	0.8	0.3
Employment in agriculture (% of employed ages 15+)	2	4	2	*3*
Employment in industry (% of employed ages 15+)	9	29	6	*23*
Employment in services (% of employed ages 15+)	82	62	*84*	*61*
Women in wage employment in the nonagricultural sector (%)	44		49	
Women's share of part-time employment (% of total)	73		72	
Maternity leave (days paid)	..		112	
Maternity leave benefits (% of wages paid)	..		100	
Employment to population ratio (% ages 15+)	52	71	55	66
Employment to population ratio (% ages 15–24)	67	70	64	61
Firms with female participation in ownership (%)	..		..	
Firms with a female top manager (%)	..		..	
Children in employment (% of children ages 7–14)	..	..	6	..
Unemployment rate (% of labor force ages 15+)	3	2	6	7
Unemployment rate (% of labor force ages 15–24)	6	5	11	11
Internet users (%)	..	..	93	95
Account at a financial institution (% age 15+)	..	..	99	99
Mobile account (% age 15+)	..	..	..	..
Saved any money last year (% age 15+)	..	..	72	77
Public life and decision making				
Seats held by women in national parliament (%)	..		37	
Female legislators, senior officials and managers (% of total)	25		*30*	
Proportion of women in ministerial level positions (%)	..		47	
Agency				
Total fertility rate (births per woman)	1.7		1.7	
Adolescent fertility rate (births per 1,000 women ages 15–19)	7		4	
Women first married by age 18 (% of women ages 20–24)	..		..	

New Caledonia

Population (thousands)	266
GNI, Atlas ($ billions)	..
GNI per capita, Atlas ($)	..
Population living below $1.90 a day (%)	..

	2000		2013	
	Female	Male	Female	Male
Education				
Net primary enrollment rate (%)	..	..	..	..
Net secondary enrollment rate (%)	..	..	..	..
Gross tertiary enrollment ratio (% of relevant age group)	..	..	..	..
Primary completion rate (% of relevant age group)	..	..	..	..
Progression to secondary school (%)	..	..	..	..
Lower secondary completion rate (% of relevant age group)	..	..	..	..
Gross tertiary graduation ratio (%)	..	..	..	..
Female share of graduates in eng., manf. and constr. (%, tertiary)	..		..	
Youth literacy rate (% of population ages 15-24)	..	..	100	100
Health and related services				
Sex ratio at birth (male births per female births)	*1.05*		1.05	
Under-five mortality rate (per 1,000 live births)	..	..	..	..
Life expectancy at birth (years)	79	72	80	74
Pregnant women receiving prenatal care (%)	..		..	
Births attended by skilled health staff (% of total)	..		..	
Maternal mortality ratio (per 100,000 live births)	..		..	
Women's share of population ages 15+ living with HIV (%)	..		..	
Prevalence of HIV (% ages 15-24)	..	..	..	..
Economic structure, participation, and access to resources				
Labor force participation rate (% of population ages 15+)	48	71	46	67
Labor force participation rate (% of ages 15-24)	45	58	45	58
Wage and salaried workers (% of employed ages 15+)	..	..	..	..
Self-employed workers (% of employed ages 15+)	..	..	..	..
Unpaid family workers (% of employed ages 15+)	..	..	..	..
Employment in agriculture (% of employed ages 15+)	..	..	..	..
Employment in industry (% of employed ages 15+)	..	..	..	..
Employment in services (% of employed ages 15+)	..	..	..	..
Women in wage employment in the nonagricultural sector (%)	..		..	
Women's share of part-time employment (% of total)	..		..	
Maternity leave (days paid)	..		..	
Maternity leave benefits (% of wages paid)	..		..	
Employment to population ratio (% ages 15+)	..		..	..
Employment to population ratio (% ages 15-24)	..		..	..
Firms with female participation in ownership (%)	..		..	
Firms with a female top manager (%)	..		..	
Children in employment (% of children ages 7-14)	..	..	..	..
Unemployment rate (% of labor force ages 15+)	..	..	..	..
Unemployment rate (% of labor force ages 15-24)	..	..	..	..
Internet users (%)	..	..	..	..
Account at a financial institution (% age 15+)	..	..	..	..
Mobile account (% age 15+)	..	..	..	..
Saved any money last year (% age 15+)	..	..	..	..
Public life and decision making				
Seats held by women in national parliament (%)	..		..	
Female legislators, senior officials and managers (% of total)	..		..	
Proportion of women in ministerial level positions (%)	..		..	
Agency				
Total fertility rate (births per woman)	2.6		2.3	
Adolescent fertility rate (births per 1,000 women ages 15-19)	18		19	
Women first married by age 18 (% of women ages 20-24)	..		..	

New Zealand

	High income
Population (millions)	5
GNI, Atlas ($ billions)	175
GNI per capita, Atlas ($)	39,300
Population living below $1.90 a day (%)	..

	2000 Female	2000 Male	2013 Female	2013 Male
Education				
Net primary enrollment rate (%)	99	99	98	98
Net secondary enrollment rate (%)	92	91	98	97
Gross tertiary enrollment ratio (% of relevant age group)	79	54	94	65
Primary completion rate (% of relevant age group)	..	..	..	..
Progression to secondary school (%)	..	..	..	..
Lower secondary completion rate (% of relevant age group)	..	..	..	..
Gross tertiary graduation ratio (%)	53	30	73	43
Female share of graduates in eng., manf. and constr. (%, tertiary)	32		27	
Youth literacy rate (% of population ages 15-24)	..	..	..	..
Health and related services				
Sex ratio at birth (male births per female births)	1.05		1.06	
Under-five mortality rate (per 1,000 live births)	7	8	5	6
Life expectancy at birth (years)	81	76	83	80
Pregnant women receiving prenatal care (%)	..		..	
Births attended by skilled health staff (% of total)	97		..	
Maternal mortality ratio (per 100,000 live births)	12		8	
Women's share of population ages 15+ living with HIV (%)	..		..	
Prevalence of HIV (% ages 15-24)	..	..	..	..
Economic structure, participation, and access to resources				
Labor force participation rate (% of population ages 15+)	57	73	62	74
Labor force participation rate (% of ages 15-24)	60	66	58	62
Wage and salaried workers (% of employed ages 15+)	85	74	88	80
Self-employed workers (% of employed ages 15+)	15	26	12	20
Unpaid family workers (% of employed ages 15+)	1.3	0.5	1.3	0.7
Employment in agriculture (% of employed ages 15+)	6	11	..	..
Employment in industry (% of employed ages 15+)	12	32	..	..
Employment in services (% of employed ages 15+)	81	56	..	..
Women in wage employment in the nonagricultural sector (%)	47		47	
Women's share of part-time employment (% of total)	73		74	
Maternity leave (days paid)	..		112	
Maternity leave benefits (% of wages paid)	..		47	
Employment to population ratio (% ages 15+)	53	69	58	70
Employment to population ratio (% ages 15-24)	52	56	49	53
Firms with female participation in ownership (%)	..		..	
Firms with a female top manager (%)	..		..	
Children in employment (% of children ages 7-14)	..	..	..	..
Unemployment rate (% of labor force ages 15+)	6	6	7	6
Unemployment rate (% of labor force ages 15-24)	13	15	16	15
Internet users (%)	..	..	..	..
Account at a financial institution (% age 15+)	..	..	99	100
Mobile account (% age 15+)	..	..	..	..
Saved any money last year (% age 15+)	..	..	86	88
Public life and decision making				
Seats held by women in national parliament (%)	..		31	
Female legislators, senior officials and managers (% of total)	38		..	
Proportion of women in ministerial level positions (%)	..		33	
Agency				
Total fertility rate (births per woman)	2.0		2.0	
Adolescent fertility rate (births per 1,000 women ages 15-19)	28		24	
Women first married by age 18 (% of women ages 20-24)	..		..	

Nicaragua

Latin America & the Caribbean	Lower middle income
Population (millions)	6
GNI, Atlas ($ billions)	11
GNI per capita, Atlas ($)	1,870
Population living below $1.90 a day (%)	..

	2000		2013	
	Female	Male	Female	Male
Education				
Net primary enrollment rate (%)	79	78	92	91
Net secondary enrollment rate (%)	37	32	49	42
Gross tertiary enrollment ratio (% of relevant age group)	18	16	..	..
Primary completion rate (% of relevant age group)	70	62	83	77
Progression to secondary school (%)	98	100	..	..
Lower secondary completion rate (% of relevant age group)	49	40	68	57
Gross tertiary graduation ratio (%)	4	3	..	..
Female share of graduates in eng., manf. and constr. (%, tertiary)	..		..	
Youth literacy rate (% of population ages 15–24)	89	84	..	..
Health and related services				
Sex ratio at birth (male births per female births)	1.05		1.05	
Under-five mortality rate (per 1,000 live births)	36	44	20	25
Life expectancy at birth (years)	72	67	78	72
Pregnant women receiving prenatal care (%)	86		95	
Births attended by skilled health staff (% of total)	67		88	
Maternal mortality ratio (per 100,000 live births)	140		100	
Women's share of population ages 15+ living with HIV (%)	37		28	
Prevalence of HIV (% ages 15–24)	0.2	0.3	0.1	0.2
Economic structure, participation, and access to resources				
Labor force participation rate (% of population ages 15+)	38	83	47	80
Labor force participation rate (% of ages 15–24)	28	68	32	64
Wage and salaried workers (% of employed ages 15+)	52	51	42	49
Self-employed workers (% of employed ages 15+)	48	49	59	51
Unpaid family workers (% of employed ages 15+)	11.0	13.1	19.7	15.8
Employment in agriculture (% of employed ages 15+)	..	..	15	44
Employment in industry (% of employed ages 15+)	..	..	15	18
Employment in services (% of employed ages 15+)	..	..	70	38
Women in wage employment in the nonagricultural sector (%)	..		..	
Women's share of part-time employment (% of total)	49		59	
Maternity leave (days paid)	..		84	
Maternity leave benefits (% of wages paid)	..		100	
Employment to population ratio (% ages 15+)	37	76	44	75
Employment to population ratio (% ages 15–24)	27	66	28	58
Firms with female participation in ownership (%)	..		62	
Firms with a female top manager (%)	..		32	
Children in employment (% of children ages 7–14)	6	18	21	41
Unemployment rate (% of labor force ages 15+)	4	7	8	7
Unemployment rate (% of labor force ages 15–24)	5	3	14	9
Internet users (%)	..	..	..	..
Account at a financial institution (% age 15+)	..	..	14	24
Mobile account (% age 15+)	..	..	1.1	1.0
Saved any money last year (% age 15+)	..	..	48	55
Public life and decision making				
Seats held by women in national parliament (%)	..		41	
Female legislators, senior officials and managers (% of total)	..		..	
Proportion of women in ministerial level positions (%)	..		47	
Agency				
Total fertility rate (births per woman)	3.3		2.5	
Adolescent fertility rate (births per 1,000 women ages 15–19)	118		90	
Women first married by age 18 (% of women ages 20–24)	43		..	

Niger

Sub-Saharan Africa				**Low income**
Population (millions)				19
GNI, Atlas ($ billions)				8
GNI per capita, Atlas ($)				420
Population living below $1.90 a day (%)				50

	2000		2013	
	Female	Male	Female	Male
Education				
Net primary enrollment rate (%)	23	33	58	69
Net secondary enrollment rate (%)	4	7	10	15
Gross tertiary enrollment ratio (% of relevant age group)	..	..	1	3
Primary completion rate (% of relevant age group)	15	23	44	55
Progression to secondary school (%)	50	50	69	71
Lower secondary completion rate (% of relevant age group)	4	6	10	15
Gross tertiary graduation ratio (%)	0	0	1	2
Female share of graduates in eng., manf. and constr. (%, tertiary)	..		..	
Youth literacy rate (% of population ages 15–24)	14	26	15	35
Health and related services				
Sex ratio at birth (male births per female births)	1.05		1.05	
Under-five mortality rate (per 1,000 live births)	222	232	91	100
Life expectancy at birth (years)	51	51	59	58
Pregnant women receiving prenatal care (%)	41		83	
Births attended by skilled health staff (% of total)	16		29	
Maternal mortality ratio (per 100,000 live births)	850		630	
Women's share of population ages 15+ living with HIV (%)	52		57	
Prevalence of HIV (% ages 15–24)	1.1	0.7	0.2	0.1
Economic structure, participation, and access to resources				
Labor force participation rate (% of population ages 15+)	38	89	40	90
Labor force participation rate (% of ages 15–24)	34	77	36	80
Wage and salaried workers (% of employed ages 15+)	..	..	..	..
Self-employed workers (% of employed ages 15+)	..	..	..	..
Unpaid family workers (% of employed ages 15+)	..	..	..	..
Employment in agriculture (% of employed ages 15+)	..	..	..	..
Employment in industry (% of employed ages 15+)	..	..	..	..
Employment in services (% of employed ages 15+)	..	..	..	..
Women in wage employment in the nonagricultural sector (%)	..		..	
Women's share of part-time employment (% of total)	..		..	
Maternity leave (days paid)	..		98	
Maternity leave benefits (% of wages paid)	..		100	
Employment to population ratio (% ages 15+)	36	84	38	85
Employment to population ratio (% ages 15–24)	32	71	33	74
Firms with female participation in ownership (%)	..		..	
Firms with a female top manager (%)	..		..	
Children in employment (% of children ages 7–14)	..	..	47	50
Unemployment rate (% of labor force ages 15+)	5	5	5	5
Unemployment rate (% of labor force ages 15–24)	6	7	6	7
Internet users (%)	..	..	..	..
Account at a financial institution (% age 15+)	..	..	3	4
Mobile account (% age 15+)	..	..	2.2	5.5
Saved any money last year (% age 15+)	..	..	62	60
Public life and decision making				
Seats held by women in national parliament (%)	..		13	
Female legislators, senior officials and managers (% of total)	..		..	
Proportion of women in ministerial level positions (%)	..		13	
Agency				
Total fertility rate (births per woman)	7.7		7.6	
Adolescent fertility rate (births per 1,000 women ages 15–19)	219		204	
Women first married by age 18 (% of women ages 20–24)	77		76	

Nigeria

Sub-Saharan Africa	Lower middle income
Population (millions)	177
GNI, Atlas ($ billions)	526
GNI per capita, Atlas ($)	2,970
Population living below $1.90 a day (%)	..

	2000		2013	
	Female	**Male**	**Female**	**Male**
Education				
Net primary enrollment rate (%)	59	70	58	69
Net secondary enrollment rate (%)	..	..	..	..
Gross tertiary enrollment ratio (% of relevant age group)	5	7	..	..
Primary completion rate (% of relevant age group)	..	..	72	80
Progression to secondary school (%)	..	..	..	..
Lower secondary completion rate (% of relevant age group)	..	..	..	..
Gross tertiary graduation ratio (%)	2	2	..	..
Female share of graduates in eng., manf. and constr. (%, tertiary)	..		..	
Youth literacy rate (% of population ages 15–24)	..	..	..	..
Health and related services				
Sex ratio at birth (male births per female births)	1.06		1.06	
Under-five mortality rate (per 1,000 live births)	178	196	102	115
Life expectancy at birth (years)	47	46	53	52
Pregnant women receiving prenatal care (%)	64		61	
Births attended by skilled health staff (% of total)	42		38	
Maternal mortality ratio (per 100,000 live births)	950		560	
Women's share of population ages 15+ living with HIV (%)	57		58	
Prevalence of HIV (% ages 15–24)	2.1	1.0	1.3	0.7
Economic structure, participation, and access to resources				
Labor force participation rate (% of population ages 15+)	45	67	48	64
Labor force participation rate (% of ages 15–24)	31	40	35	40
Wage and salaried workers (% of employed ages 15+)	..	..	..	..
Self-employed workers (% of employed ages 15+)	..	..	..	..
Unpaid family workers (% of employed ages 15+)	..	..	..	..
Employment in agriculture (% of employed ages 15+)	..	..	..	..
Employment in industry (% of employed ages 15+)	..	..	..	..
Employment in services (% of employed ages 15+)	..	..	..	..
Women in wage employment in the nonagricultural sector (%)	19		..	
Women's share of part-time employment (% of total)	..		..	
Maternity leave (days paid)	..		84	
Maternity leave benefits (% of wages paid)	..		50	
Employment to population ratio (% ages 15+)	42	62	45	59
Employment to population ratio (% ages 15–24)	27	35	30	35
Firms with female participation in ownership (%)	..		18[a]	
Firms with a female top manager (%)	..		17[a]	
Children in employment (% of children ages 7–14)	..	..	19	23
Unemployment rate (% of labor force ages 15+)	7	8	7	8
Unemployment rate (% of labor force ages 15–24)	13	14	13	14
Internet users (%)	..	..	..	..
Account at a financial institution (% age 15+)	..	..	34	54
Mobile account (% age 15+)	..	..	2.1	2.5
Saved any money last year (% age 15+)	..	..	66	72
Public life and decision making				
Seats held by women in national parliament (%)	..		6	
Female legislators, senior officials and managers (% of total)	..		..	
Proportion of women in ministerial level positions (%)	..		24	
Agency				
Total fertility rate (births per woman)	6.1		6.0	
Adolescent fertility rate (births per 1,000 women ages 15–19)	133		112	
Women first married by age 18 (% of women ages 20–24)	40		43	

Northern Mariana Islands

High income

Population (thousands)	55
GNI, Atlas ($ millions)	..
GNI per capita, Atlas ($)	..
Population living below $1.90 a day (%)	..

	2000		2013	
	Female	**Male**	**Female**	**Male**
Education				
Net primary enrollment rate (%)	..	..	..	..
Net secondary enrollment rate (%)	..	..	..	..
Gross tertiary enrollment ratio (% of relevant age group)	..	..	..	..
Primary completion rate (% of relevant age group)	..	..	..	..
Progression to secondary school (%)	..	..	..	..
Lower secondary completion rate (% of relevant age group)	..	..	..	..
Gross tertiary graduation ratio (%)	..	..	..	..
Female share of graduates in eng., manf. and constr. (%, tertiary)	..		..	
Youth literacy rate (% of population ages 15–24)	..	..	..	..
Health and related services				
Sex ratio at birth (male births per female births)	..		..	
Under-five mortality rate (per 1,000 live births)	..	..	..	..
Life expectancy at birth (years)	..		..	
Pregnant women receiving prenatal care (%)	..		..	
Births attended by skilled health staff (% of total)	100		..	
Maternal mortality ratio (per 100,000 live births)	..		..	
Women's share of population ages 15+ living with HIV (%)	..		..	
Prevalence of HIV (% ages 15–24)	..	..	..	..
Economic structure, participation, and access to resources				
Labor force participation rate (% of population ages 15+)	..	..	..	..
Labor force participation rate (% of ages 15–24)	..	..	..	..
Wage and salaried workers (% of employed ages 15+)	..	..	..	..
Self-employed workers (% of employed ages 15+)	..	..	..	..
Unpaid family workers (% of employed ages 15+)	..	..	..	..
Employment in agriculture (% of employed ages 15+)	..	..	..	..
Employment in industry (% of employed ages 15+)	..	..	..	..
Employment in services (% of employed ages 15+)	..	..	..	..
Women in wage employment in the nonagricultural sector (%)	..		..	
Women's share of part-time employment (% of total)	..		..	
Maternity leave (days paid)	..		..	
Maternity leave benefits (% of wages paid)	..		..	
Employment to population ratio (% ages 15+)	..	..	..	..
Employment to population ratio (% ages 15–24)	..	..	..	..
Firms with female participation in ownership (%)	..		..	
Firms with a female top manager (%)	..		..	
Children in employment (% of children ages 7–14)	..	..	..	..
Unemployment rate (% of labor force ages 15+)	..	..	..	..
Unemployment rate (% of labor force ages 15–24)	..	..	..	..
Internet users (%)	..	..	..	..
Account at a financial institution (% age 15+)	..	..	..	..
Mobile account (% age 15+)	..	..	..	..
Saved any money last year (% age 15+)	..	..	..	..
Public life and decision making				
Seats held by women in national parliament (%)	..		..	
Female legislators, senior officials and managers (% of total)	..		..	
Proportion of women in ministerial level positions (%)	..		..	
Agency				
Total fertility rate (births per woman)	..		..	
Adolescent fertility rate (births per 1,000 women ages 15–19)	..		..	
Women first married by age 18 (% of women ages 20–24)	..		..	

Norway

High income

Population (millions)	5
GNI, Atlas ($ billions)	529
GNI per capita, Atlas ($)	103,050
Population living below $1.90 a day (%)	..

	2000 Female	2000 Male	2013 Female	2013 Male
Education				
Net primary enrollment rate (%)	100	100	100	100
Net secondary enrollment rate (%)	95	94	95	95
Gross tertiary enrollment ratio (% of relevant age group)	82	57	94	63
Primary completion rate (% of relevant age group)	99	97	100	101
Progression to secondary school (%)	100	100	*98*	*100*
Lower secondary completion rate (% of relevant age group)	98	97	100	100
Gross tertiary graduation ratio (%)	52	28	61	34
Female share of graduates in eng., manf. and constr. (%, tertiary)	23		20	
Youth literacy rate (% of population ages 15–24)	..	..	..	..
Health and related services				
Sex ratio at birth (male births per female births)	*1.05*		1.06	
Under-five mortality rate (per 1,000 live births)	4	5	2	3
Life expectancy at birth (years)	81	76	84	80
Pregnant women receiving prenatal care (%)	..		..	
Births attended by skilled health staff (% of total)	..		..	
Maternal mortality ratio (per 100,000 live births)	8		4	
Women's share of population ages 15+ living with HIV (%)	29		29	
Prevalence of HIV (% ages 15–24)	0.1	0.1	0.1	0.1
Economic structure, participation, and access to resources				
Labor force participation rate (% of population ages 15+)	60	72	61	69
Labor force participation rate (% of ages 15–24)	60	67	58	56
Wage and salaried workers (% of employed ages 15+)	95	90	96	91
Self-employed workers (% of employed ages 15+)	5	10	4	9
Unpaid family workers (% of employed ages 15+)	0.5	0.3	0.2	0.2
Employment in agriculture (% of employed ages 15+)	2	6	*1*	*4*
Employment in industry (% of employed ages 15+)	9	33	8	*32*
Employment in services (% of employed ages 15+)	88	61	92	65
Women in wage employment in the nonagricultural sector (%)	48		49	
Women's share of part-time employment (% of total)	77		69	
Maternity leave (days paid)[c]	..		..	
Maternity leave benefits (% of wages paid)	..		..	
Employment to population ratio (% ages 15+)	58	70	59	66
Employment to population ratio (% ages 15–24)	54	61	54	50
Firms with female participation in ownership (%)	..		..	
Firms with a female top manager (%)	..		..	
Children in employment (% of children ages 7–14)	..	..	..	..
Unemployment rate (% of labor force ages 15+)	3	4	3	4
Unemployment rate (% of labor force ages 15–24)	11	9	8	11
Internet users (%)	..	..	94	96
Account at a financial institution (% age 15+)	..	..	100	100
Mobile account (% age 15+)	..	..	..	..
Saved any money last year (% age 15+)	..	..	91	89
Public life and decision making				
Seats held by women in national parliament (%)	..		40	
Female legislators, senior officials and managers (% of total)	25		*31*	
Proportion of women in ministerial level positions (%)	..		47	
Agency				
Total fertility rate (births per woman)	1.9		1.9	
Adolescent fertility rate (births per 1,000 women ages 15–19)	11		6	
Women first married by age 18 (% of women ages 20–24)	..		..	

Oman

Population (millions)	4
GNI, Atlas ($ billions)	66
GNI per capita, Atlas ($)	16,870
Population living below $1.90 a day (%)	..

	2000		2013	
	Female	Male	Female	Male
Education				
Net primary enrollment rate (%)	84	84	94	93
Net secondary enrollment rate (%)	69	69	91	77
Gross tertiary enrollment ratio (% of relevant age group)	8	8	34	24
Primary completion rate (% of relevant age group)	83	84	101	95
Progression to secondary school (%)	100	100	100	99
Lower secondary completion rate (% of relevant age group)	79	70	94	79
Gross tertiary graduation ratio (%)	..	..	24	10
Female share of graduates in eng., manf. and constr. (%, tertiary)	..		53	
Youth literacy rate (% of population ages 15–24)	..	..	99[a]	99[a]
Health and related services				
Sex ratio at birth (male births per female births)	1.05		1.05	
Under-five mortality rate (per 1,000 live births)	15	18	10	13
Life expectancy at birth (years)	74	70	79	75
Pregnant women receiving prenatal care (%)	100		..	
Births attended by skilled health staff (% of total)	95		..	
Maternal mortality ratio (per 100,000 live births)	22		11	
Women's share of population ages 15+ living with HIV (%)	28		27	
Prevalence of HIV (% ages 15–24)	0.1	0.1	0.1	0.1
Economic structure, participation, and access to resources				
Labor force participation rate (% of population ages 15+)	23	78	29	83
Labor force participation rate (% of ages 15–24)	23	50	25	58
Wage and salaried workers (% of employed ages 15+)	88	88	95	97
Self-employed workers (% of employed ages 15+)	10	12	4	3
Unpaid family workers (% of employed ages 15+)	..	..	..	..
Employment in agriculture (% of employed ages 15+)	5	7	1	6
Employment in industry (% of employed ages 15+)	14	11	6	43
Employment in services (% of employed ages 15+)	80	82	93	51
Women in wage employment in the nonagricultural sector (%)	25		..	
Women's share of part-time employment (% of total)	..		..	
Maternity leave (days paid)	..		50	
Maternity leave benefits (% of wages paid)	..		100	
Employment to population ratio (% ages 15+)	19	73	25	77
Employment to population ratio (% ages 15–24)	15	41	17	48
Firms with female participation in ownership (%)	..		..	
Firms with a female top manager (%)	..		..	
Children in employment (% of children ages 7–14)	..	..	..	..
Unemployment rate (% of labor force ages 15+)	18	7	15	7
Unemployment rate (% of labor force ages 15–24)	31	18	32	18
Internet users (%)	..	..	60	71
Account at a financial institution (% age 15+)	..	..	64	84
Mobile account (% age 15+)	..	..	..	..
Saved any money last year (% age 15+)	..	..	..	..
Public life and decision making				
Seats held by women in national parliament (%)	..		1	
Female legislators, senior officials and managers (% of total)	9		..	
Proportion of women in ministerial level positions (%)	..		7	
Agency				
Total fertility rate (births per woman)	3.7		2.9	
Adolescent fertility rate (births per 1,000 women ages 15–19)	30		9	
Women first married by age 18 (% of women ages 20–24)	..		..	

Pakistan

Population (millions)	185
GNI, Atlas ($ billions)	260
GNI per capita, Atlas ($)	1,410
Population living below $1.90 a day (%)	8

	2000		2013	
	Female	Male	Female	Male
Education				
Net primary enrollment rate (%)	45	66	67	77
Net secondary enrollment rate (%)	..	..	32	43
Gross tertiary enrollment ratio (% of relevant age group)	..	..	10	10
Primary completion rate (% of relevant age group)	..	..	67	79
Progression to secondary school (%)	..	..	75	79
Lower secondary completion rate (% of relevant age group)	..	..	41	51
Gross tertiary graduation ratio (%)	..		..	
Female share of graduates in eng., manf. and constr. (%, tertiary)	..		..	
Youth literacy rate (% of population ages 15–24)	43	67	64	80
Health and related services				
Sex ratio at birth (male births per female births)	1.10		1.09	
Under-five mortality rate (per 1,000 live births)	109	115	77	85
Life expectancy at birth (years)	65	63	68	66
Pregnant women receiving prenatal care (%)	43		73	
Births attended by skilled health staff (% of total)	23		52	
Maternal mortality ratio (per 100,000 live births)	280		170	
Women's share of population ages 15+ living with HIV (%)	27		28	
Prevalence of HIV (% ages 15–24)	0.1	0.1	0.1	0.1
Economic structure, participation, and access to resources				
Labor force participation rate (% of population ages 15+)	16	84	25	83
Labor force participation rate (% of ages 15–24)	10	71	22	67
Wage and salaried workers (% of employed ages 15+)	33	36	..	..
Self-employed workers (% of employed ages 15+)	67	64	..	..
Unpaid family workers (% of employed ages 15+)	50.1	16.7	..	..
Employment in agriculture (% of employed ages 15+)	73	44	76	35
Employment in industry (% of employed ages 15+)	9	20	11	25
Employment in services (% of employed ages 15+)	18	36	13	36
Women in wage employment in the nonagricultural sector (%)	13		..	
Women's share of part-time employment (% of total)	..		..	
Maternity leave (days paid)			84	
Maternity leave benefits (% of wages paid)	..		100	
Employment to population ratio (% ages 15+)	14	79	22	80
Employment to population ratio (% ages 15–24)	7	63	19	62
Firms with female participation in ownership (%)	..		12	
Firms with a female top manager (%)	..		6	
Children in employment (% of children ages 7–14)	..	..	14	13
Unemployment rate (% of labor force ages 15+)	16	6	9	4
Unemployment rate (% of labor force ages 15–24)	29	11	12	8
Internet users (%)	..	..		
Account at a financial institution (% age 15+)	..	..	3	14
Mobile account (% age 15+)	..	..	2.2	9.3
Saved any money last year (% age 15+)	..	..	24	39
Public life and decision making				
Seats held by women in national parliament (%)	..		21	
Female legislators, senior officials and managers (% of total)	3		..	
Proportion of women in ministerial level positions (%)	..		0	
Agency				
Total fertility rate (births per woman)	4.5		3.2	
Adolescent fertility rate (births per 1,000 women ages 15–19)	51		39	
Women first married by age 18 (% of women ages 20–24)	..		21	

Palau

East Asia & Pacific	Upper middle income
Population (thousands)	21
GNI, Atlas ($ millions)	234
GNI per capita, Atlas ($)	11,110
Population living below $1.90 a day (%)	..

	2000		2013	
	Female	Male	Female	Male
Education				
Net primary enrollment rate (%)	..	..	..	..
Net secondary enrollment rate (%)	..	..	99[a]	90[a]
Gross tertiary enrollment ratio (% of relevant age group)	58	25	76	49
Primary completion rate (% of relevant age group)	90	107	94[a]	97[a]
Progression to secondary school (%)	..	..	95	98
Lower secondary completion rate (% of relevant age group)	..	..	107[a]	102[a]
Gross tertiary graduation ratio (%)	..		38	26
Female share of graduates in eng., manf. and constr. (%, tertiary)	..		8	
Youth literacy rate (% of population ages 15-24)	..	..	100	100
Health and related services				
Sex ratio at birth (male births per female births)	..			
Under-five mortality rate (per 1,000 live births)	24	30	15	18
Life expectancy at birth (years)	75	67	..	..
Pregnant women receiving prenatal care (%)	..		90	
Births attended by skilled health staff (% of total)	100		100	
Maternal mortality ratio (per 100,000 live births)	..		..	
Women's share of population ages 15+ living with HIV (%)	..		..	
Prevalence of HIV (% ages 15-24)	..	..	..	..
Economic structure, participation, and access to resources				
Labor force participation rate (% of population ages 15+)	..	..	..	..
Labor force participation rate (% of ages 15-24)	..	..	..	..
Wage and salaried workers (% of employed ages 15+)	..	..	..	..
Self-employed workers (% of employed ages 15+)	..	..	..	..
Unpaid family workers (% of employed ages 15+)	..	..	..	..
Employment in agriculture (% of employed ages 15+)	..	..	..	..
Employment in industry (% of employed ages 15+)	..	..	..	..
Employment in services (% of employed ages 15+)	..	..	..	..
Women in wage employment in the nonagricultural sector (%)	40		..	
Women's share of part-time employment (% of total)	..		..	
Maternity leave (days paid)	..			
Maternity leave benefits (% of wages paid)	..			
Employment to population ratio (% ages 15+)	..	..	..	..
Employment to population ratio (% ages 15-24)	..	..	..	..
Firms with female participation in ownership (%)	..		..	
Firms with a female top manager (%)	..		..	
Children in employment (% of children ages 7-14)	..	..	..	..
Unemployment rate (% of labor force ages 15+)	..	..	..	..
Unemployment rate (% of labor force ages 15-24)	..	..	..	..
Internet users (%)	..		..	
Account at a financial institution (% age 15+)	..	..	..	..
Mobile account (% age 15+)	..	..	..	..
Saved any money last year (% age 15+)	..	..	..	..
Public life and decision making				
Seats held by women in national parliament (%)	..		0	
Female legislators, senior officials and managers (% of total)	..		..	
Proportion of women in ministerial level positions (%)	..		13	
Agency				
Total fertility rate (births per woman)	1.5		..	
Adolescent fertility rate (births per 1,000 women ages 15-19)	..		..	
Women first married by age 18 (% of women ages 20-24)	..		..	

Panama

Latin America & the Caribbean **Upper middle income**

Population (millions)	4
GNI, Atlas ($ billions)	43
GNI per capita, Atlas ($)	11,130
Population living below $1.90 a day (%)	3

	2000		2013	
	Female	Male	Female	Male
Education				
Net primary enrollment rate (%)	94	94	90	91
Net secondary enrollment rate (%)	61	55	79	74
Gross tertiary enrollment ratio (% of relevant age group)	52	30	53	34
Primary completion rate (% of relevant age group)	91	92	96	97
Progression to secondary school (%)	..	..	97	100
Lower secondary completion rate (% of relevant age group)	..	..	77	69
Gross tertiary graduation ratio (%)	30	13	31	16
Female share of graduates in eng., manf. and constr. (%, tertiary)	36		36	
Youth literacy rate (% of population ages 15–24)	96	97	97	98
Health and related services				
Sex ratio at birth (male births per female births)	1.05		1.05	
Under-five mortality rate (per 1,000 live births)	23	29	15	19
Life expectancy at birth (years)	78	73	81	75
Pregnant women receiving prenatal care (%)	72		..	
Births attended by skilled health staff (% of total)	90		94	
Maternal mortality ratio (per 100,000 live births)	79		85	
Women's share of population ages 15+ living with HIV (%)	18		25	
Prevalence of HIV (% ages 15–24)	0.4	1.2	0.1	0.2
Economic structure, participation, and access to resources				
Labor force participation rate (% of population ages 15+)	45	82	49	82
Labor force participation rate (% of ages 15–24)	36	64	33	63
Wage and salaried workers (% of employed ages 15+)	79	60	71	66
Self-employed workers (% of employed ages 15+)	21	40	29	34
Unpaid family workers (% of employed ages 15+)	1.8	3.0	7.2	3.3
Employment in agriculture (% of employed ages 15+)	2	25	9	22
Employment in industry (% of employed ages 15+)	9	22	9	24
Employment in services (% of employed ages 15+)	89	54	83	54
Women in wage employment in the nonagricultural sector (%)	43		44	
Women's share of part-time employment (% of total)	48		48	
Maternity leave (days paid)	..		98	
Maternity leave benefits (% of wages paid)	..		100	
Employment to population ratio (% ages 15+)	37	73	47	79
Employment to population ratio (% ages 15–24)	23	48	29	58
Firms with female participation in ownership (%)	..		25	
Firms with a female top manager (%)	..		24	
Children in employment (% of children ages 7–14)	..	..	4	5
Unemployment rate (% of labor force ages 15+)	18	11	5	3
Unemployment rate (% of labor force ages 15–24)	37	25	14	9
Internet users (%)	..	..	42	39
Account at a financial institution (% age 15+)	..	..	40	47
Mobile account (% age 15+)	..	..	1.1	2.0
Saved any money last year (% age 15+)	..	..	62	63
Public life and decision making				
Seats held by women in national parliament (%)	..		19	
Female legislators, senior officials and managers (% of total)	40		46	
Proportion of women in ministerial level positions (%)	..		28	
Agency				
Total fertility rate (births per woman)	2.8		2.5	
Adolescent fertility rate (births per 1,000 women ages 15–19)	89		75	
Women first married by age 18 (% of women ages 20–24)	..		..	

Papua New Guinea

East Asia & Pacific	Lower middle income
Population (millions)	7
GNI, Atlas ($ billions)	15
GNI per capita, Atlas ($)	2,030
Population living below $1.90 a day (%)	..

	2000 Female	2000 Male	2013 Female	2013 Male
Education				
Net primary enrollment rate (%)	..	..	82	89
Net secondary enrollment rate (%)	..	..	..	..
Gross tertiary enrollment ratio (% of relevant age group)	1	2	..	..
Primary completion rate (% of relevant age group)	51	59	72	84
Progression to secondary school (%)	..	..	..	..
Lower secondary completion rate (% of relevant age group)	13	18	57	67
Gross tertiary graduation ratio (%)	1	2	..	..
Female share of graduates in eng., manf. and constr. (%, tertiary)	..		..	
Youth literacy rate (% of population ages 15-24)	64	69	77	67
Health and related services				
Sex ratio at birth (male births per female births)	1.08		1.08	
Under-five mortality rate (per 1,000 live births)	73	84	53	62
Life expectancy at birth (years)	61	57	65	60
Pregnant women receiving prenatal care (%)	..		..	
Births attended by skilled health staff (% of total)	41		..	
Maternal mortality ratio (per 100,000 live births)	340		220	
Women's share of population ages 15+ living with HIV (%)	54		57	
Prevalence of HIV (% ages 15-24)	0.6	0.3	0.2	0.2
Economic structure, participation, and access to resources				
Labor force participation rate (% of population ages 15+)	71	74	71	74
Labor force participation rate (% of ages 15-24)	61	58	59	57
Wage and salaried workers (% of employed ages 15+)	..	..	..	..
Self-employed workers (% of employed ages 15+)	..	..	..	..
Unpaid family workers (% of employed ages 15+)	..	..	..	..
Employment in agriculture (% of employed ages 15+)	..	..	..	..
Employment in industry (% of employed ages 15+)	..	..	..	..
Employment in services (% of employed ages 15+)	..	..	..	..
Women in wage employment in the nonagricultural sector (%)	32		..	
Women's share of part-time employment (% of total)	..		..	
Maternity leave (days paid)	..		0	
Maternity leave benefits (% of wages paid)	..		..	
Employment to population ratio (% ages 15+)	68	72	69	73
Employment to population ratio (% ages 15-24)	57	55	55	55
Firms with female participation in ownership (%)	..		..	
Firms with a female top manager (%)	..		..	
Children in employment (% of children ages 7-14)	..	..	..	..
Unemployment rate (% of labor force ages 15+)	3	2	3	2
Unemployment rate (% of labor force ages 15-24)	7	5	5	4
Internet users (%)	..	..	..	..
Account at a financial institution (% age 15+)	..	..	..	..
Mobile account (% age 15+)	..	..	..	..
Saved any money last year (% age 15+)	..	..	..	..
Public life and decision making				
Seats held by women in national parliament (%)	..		3	
Female legislators, senior officials and managers (% of total)	..		..	
Proportion of women in ministerial level positions (%)	..		3	
Agency				
Total fertility rate (births per woman)	4.5		3.8	
Adolescent fertility rate (births per 1,000 women ages 15-19)	66		55	
Women first married by age 18 (% of women ages 20-24)	..		..	

Paraguay

Latin America & the Caribbean	Upper middle income
Population (millions)	7
GNI, Atlas ($ billions)	29
GNI per capita, Atlas ($)	4,380
Population living below $1.90 a day (%)	2

	2000		2013	
	Female	Male	Female	Male
Education				
Net primary enrollment rate (%)	98	97	80	81
Net secondary enrollment rate (%)	53	50	68	63
Gross tertiary enrollment ratio (% of relevant age group)	18	13	40	29
Primary completion rate (% of relevant age group)	93	91	84	83
Progression to secondary school (%)	92	94	94	95
Lower secondary completion rate (% of relevant age group)	72	69	76	70
Gross tertiary graduation ratio (%)	9	5	..	..
Female share of graduates in eng., manf. and constr. (%, tertiary)	..			
Youth literacy rate (% of population ages 15–24)	..	..	98[a]	99[a]
Health and related services				
Sex ratio at birth (male births per female births)	1.05		1.05	
Under-five mortality rate (per 1,000 live births)	30	37	18	23
Life expectancy at birth (years)	72	68	75	70
Pregnant women receiving prenatal care (%)	89		..	
Births attended by skilled health staff (% of total)	61		96	
Maternal mortality ratio (per 100,000 live births)	120		110	
Women's share of population ages 15+ living with HIV (%)	29		34	
Prevalence of HIV (% ages 15–24)	0.1	0.1	0.2	0.3
Economic structure, participation, and access to resources				
Labor force participation rate (% of population ages 15+)	51	87	56	85
Labor force participation rate (% of ages 15–24)	45	77	46	74
Wage and salaried workers (% of employed ages 15+)	45	45	49	53
Self-employed workers (% of employed ages 15+)	55	55	53	47
Unpaid family workers (% of employed ages 15+)	10.3	13.4	8.7	8.8
Employment in agriculture (% of employed ages 15+)	20	39	23	30
Employment in industry (% of employed ages 15+)	10	21	8	22
Employment in services (% of employed ages 15+)	69	40	69	48
Women in wage employment in the nonagricultural sector (%)	39		44	
Women's share of part-time employment (% of total)	59		58	
Maternity leave (days paid)	..		63	
Maternity leave benefits (% of wages paid)	..		50	
Employment to population ratio (% ages 15+)	46	81	52	81
Employment to population ratio (% ages 15–24)	37	68	39	67
Firms with female participation in ownership (%)	..		52	
Firms with a female top manager (%)	..		23	
Children in employment (% of children ages 7–14)	..	..	..	..
Unemployment rate (% of labor force ages 15+)	9	7	7	4
Unemployment rate (% of labor force ages 15–24)	17	12	15	9
Internet users (%)	..	..	36	38
Account at a financial institution (% age 15+)	..	..	23	21
Mobile account (% age 15+)	..	..	..	..
Saved any money last year (% age 15+)	..	..	..	..
Public life and decision making				
Seats held by women in national parliament (%)	..		15	
Female legislators, senior officials and managers (% of total)	..		32	
Proportion of women in ministerial level positions (%)	..		8	
Agency				
Total fertility rate (births per woman)	3.7		2.9	
Adolescent fertility rate (births per 1,000 women ages 15–19)	83		58	
Women first married by age 18 (% of women ages 20–24)	..		..	

Peru

Latin America & the Caribbean	Upper middle income
Population (millions)	31
GNI, Atlas ($ billions)	197
GNI per capita, Atlas ($)	6,370
Population living below $1.90 a day (%)	4

	2000		2013	
	Female	Male	Female	Male
Education				
Net primary enrollment rate (%)	97	98	92	92
Net secondary enrollment rate (%)	64	66	77	76
Gross tertiary enrollment ratio (% of relevant age group)	31	31	42	39
Primary completion rate (% of relevant age group)	100	104	93	92
Progression to secondary school (%)	96	99	98	100
Lower secondary completion rate (% of relevant age group)	77	81	85	82
Gross tertiary graduation ratio (%)	..	..	..	..
Female share of graduates in eng., manf. and constr. (%, tertiary)	..		..	
Youth literacy rate (% of population ages 15–24)	..	..	99	99
Health and related services				
Sex ratio at birth (male births per female births)	1.05		1.05	
Under-five mortality rate (per 1,000 live births)	35	42	15	18
Life expectancy at birth (years)	73	68	78	72
Pregnant women receiving prenatal care (%)	84		96	
Births attended by skilled health staff (% of total)	59		87	
Maternal mortality ratio (per 100,000 live births)	160		89	
Women's share of population ages 15+ living with HIV (%)	30		30	
Prevalence of HIV (% ages 15–24)	0.2	0.4	0.1	0.1
Economic structure, participation, and access to resources				
Labor force participation rate (% of population ages 15+)	58	83	68	84
Labor force participation rate (% of ages 15–24)	48	66	55	67
Wage and salaried workers (% of employed ages 15+)	33	52	44	52
Self-employed workers (% of employed ages 15+)	55	45	56	48
Unpaid family workers (% of employed ages 15+)	10.7	4.9	18.1	6.5
Employment in agriculture (% of employed ages 15+)	0	1	23	28
Employment in industry (% of employed ages 15+)	14	27	10	23
Employment in services (% of employed ages 15+)	86	72	67	49
Women in wage employment in the nonagricultural sector (%)	31		37	
Women's share of part-time employment (% of total)	..		..	
Maternity leave (days paid)			90	
Maternity leave benefits (% of wages paid)	..		100	
Employment to population ratio (% ages 15+)	54	78	65	81
Employment to population ratio (% ages 15–24)	42	58	50	62
Firms with female participation in ownership (%)	..		29	
Firms with a female top manager (%)	..		14	
Children in employment (% of children ages 7–14)	22	26	19	22
Unemployment rate (% of labor force ages 15+)	7	6	4	4
Unemployment rate (% of labor force ages 15–24)	13	12	9	9
Internet users (%)	..	..	36	42
Account at a financial institution (% age 15+)	..	..	22	36
Mobile account (% age 15+)	..	..	0.0	0.0
Saved any money last year (% age 15+)	..	..	36	43
Public life and decision making				
Seats held by women in national parliament (%)	..		22	
Female legislators, senior officials and managers (% of total)	28		30	
Proportion of women in ministerial level positions (%)	..		22	
Agency				
Total fertility rate (births per woman)	2.9		2.4	
Adolescent fertility rate (births per 1,000 women ages 15–19)	65		50	
Women first married by age 18 (% of women ages 20–24)	19		19	

Philippines

East Asia & Pacific	Lower middle income
Population (millions)	99
GNI, Atlas ($ billions)	344
GNI per capita, Atlas ($)	3,470
Population living below $1.90 a day (%)	*13*

	2000 Female	2000 Male	2013 Female	2013 Male
Education				
Net primary enrollment rate (%)	*91*	*89*	90	90
Net secondary enrollment rate (%)	*55*	*47*	70	60
Gross tertiary enrollment ratio (% of relevant age group)	*32*	*29*	38	30
Primary completion rate (% of relevant age group)	*105*	*96*	96	92
Progression to secondary school (%)	*98*	*99*	..	..
Lower secondary completion rate (% of relevant age group)	*73*	*63*	84	76
Gross tertiary graduation ratio (%)	*23*	*14*	..	..
Female share of graduates in eng., manf. and constr. (%, tertiary)	..		30	
Youth literacy rate (% of population ages 15-24)	96	94	..	..
Health and related services				
Sex ratio at birth (male births per female births)	*1.06*		1.06	
Under-five mortality rate (per 1,000 live births)	35	44	25	31
Life expectancy at birth (years)	70	64	72	65
Pregnant women receiving prenatal care (%)	86		96	
Births attended by skilled health staff (% of total)	58		73	
Maternal mortality ratio (per 100,000 live births)	120		120	
Women's share of population ages 15+ living with HIV (%)	35		12	
Prevalence of HIV (% ages 15-24)	0.1	0.1	0.1	0.1
Economic structure, participation, and access to resources				
Labor force participation rate (% of population ages 15+)	49	82	51	80
Labor force participation rate (% of ages 15-24)	38	59	37	58
Wage and salaried workers (% of employed ages 15+)	51	51	..	..
Self-employed workers (% of employed ages 15+)	49	49	..	..
Unpaid family workers (% of employed ages 15+)	16.8	9.4	..	..
Employment in agriculture (% of employed ages 15+)	24	45	20	38
Employment in industry (% of employed ages 15+)	13	18	10	19
Employment in services (% of employed ages 15+)	63	37	70	43
Women in wage employment in the nonagricultural sector (%)	41		42	
Women's share of part-time employment (% of total)	..		..	
Maternity leave (days paid)	..		60	
Maternity leave benefits (% of wages paid)	..		100	
Employment to population ratio (% ages 15+)	43	73	48	74
Employment to population ratio (% ages 15-24)	28	46	30	49
Firms with female participation in ownership (%)	..		..	
Firms with a female top manager (%)	..		..	
Children in employment (% of children ages 7-14)	*10*	*16*	7	11
Unemployment rate (% of labor force ages 15+)	11	11	7	7
Unemployment rate (% of labor force ages 15-24)	26	21	19	15
Internet users (%)	..	..	..	..
Account at a financial institution (% age 15+)	..	..	34	22
Mobile account (% age 15+)	..	..	4.9	3.5
Saved any money last year (% age 15+)	..	..	66	69
Public life and decision making				
Seats held by women in national parliament (%)	..		27	
Female legislators, senior officials and managers (% of total)	59		..	
Proportion of women in ministerial level positions (%)	..		20	
Agency				
Total fertility rate (births per woman)	3.8		3.0	
Adolescent fertility rate (births per 1,000 women ages 15-19)	52		61	
Women first married by age 18 (% of women ages 20-24)	*15*		*15*	

Poland

		High income
Population (millions)		38
GNI, Atlas ($ billions)		522
GNI per capita, Atlas ($)		13,730
Population living below $1.90 a day (%)		<2

	2000		2013	
	Female	Male	Female	Male
Education				
Net primary enrollment rate (%)	97	97	97	97
Net secondary enrollment rate (%)	92	89	93	92
Gross tertiary enrollment ratio (% of relevant age group)	59	42	87	56
Primary completion rate (% of relevant age group)	..	..	98	98
Progression to secondary school (%)	..	..	98	100
Lower secondary completion rate (% of relevant age group)	..	..	95	96
Gross tertiary graduation ratio (%)	51	30	71	39
Female share of graduates in eng., manf. and constr. (%, tertiary)	..		36	
Youth literacy rate (% of population ages 15–24)	..	..	100	100
Health and related services				
Sex ratio at birth (male births per female births)	1.06		1.06	
Under-five mortality rate (per 1,000 live births)	8	10	5	6
Life expectancy at birth (years)	78	70	81	73
Pregnant women receiving prenatal care (%)	..		..	
Births attended by skilled health staff (% of total)	100		..	
Maternal mortality ratio (per 100,000 live births)	8		3	
Women's share of population ages 15+ living with HIV (%)	..		..	
Prevalence of HIV (% ages 15–24)	0.1	0.1	0.1	0.1
Economic structure, participation, and access to resources				
Labor force participation rate (% of population ages 15+)	49	64	49	65
Labor force participation rate (% of ages 15–24)	33	40	29	39
Wage and salaried workers (% of employed ages 15+)	75	71	82	76
Self-employed workers (% of employed ages 15+)	25	29	18	25
Unpaid family workers (% of employed ages 15+)	6.6	3.4	4.7	2.2
Employment in agriculture (% of employed ages 15+)	18	19	12	13
Employment in industry (% of employed ages 15+)	19	41	16	42
Employment in services (% of employed ages 15+)	63	40	72	45
Women in wage employment in the nonagricultural sector (%)	47		47	
Women's share of part-time employment (% of total)	62		68	
Maternity leave (days paid)	..		182	
Maternity leave benefits (% of wages paid)	..		100	
Employment to population ratio (% ages 15+)	40	54	43	59
Employment to population ratio (% ages 15–24)	21	27	20	29
Firms with female participation in ownership (%)	..		40	
Firms with a female top manager (%)	..		21	
Children in employment (% of children ages 7–14)	..	..	..	..
Unemployment rate (% of labor force ages 15+)	18	15	11	10
Unemployment rate (% of labor force ages 15–24)	37	33	30	25
Internet users (%)	..	..	62	64
Account at a financial institution (% age 15+)	..	..	73	83
Mobile account (% age 15+)	..	..	..	..
Saved any money last year (% age 15+)	..	..	41	53
Public life and decision making				
Seats held by women in national parliament (%)	..		24	
Female legislators, senior officials and managers (% of total)	33		38	
Proportion of women in ministerial level positions (%)	..		28	
Agency				
Total fertility rate (births per woman)	1.4		1.3	
Adolescent fertility rate (births per 1,000 women ages 15–19)	17		14	
Women first married by age 18 (% of women ages 20–24)	..		..	

Portugal

High income

Population (millions)	10
GNI, Atlas ($ billions)	222
GNI per capita, Atlas ($)	21,320
Population living below $1.90 a day (%)	..

	2000 Female	Male	2013 Female	Male
Education				
Net primary enrollment rate (%)	99	99	96	95
Net secondary enrollment rate (%)	85	79	97	93
Gross tertiary enrollment ratio (% of relevant age group)	55	41	72	61
Primary completion rate (% of relevant age group)	..	..	..	..
Progression to secondary school (%)	..	..	..	..
Lower secondary completion rate (% of relevant age group)	..	..	..	..
Gross tertiary graduation ratio (%)	..	..	62	43
Female share of graduates in eng., manf. and constr. (%, tertiary)	35		33	
Youth literacy rate (% of population ages 15–24)	..	..	99	99
Health and related services				
Sex ratio at birth (male births per female births)	1.06		1.06	
Under-five mortality rate (per 1,000 live births)	7	8	3	4
Life expectancy at birth (years)	80	73	84	77
Pregnant women receiving prenatal care (%)	..		..	
Births attended by skilled health staff (% of total)	100		..	
Maternal mortality ratio (per 100,000 live births)	11		8	
Women's share of population ages 15+ living with HIV (%)	..		..	
Prevalence of HIV (% ages 15–24)	..	..	..	..
Economic structure, participation, and access to resources				
Labor force participation rate (% of population ages 15+)	53	70	55	66
Labor force participation rate (% of ages 15–24)	41	51	34	37
Wage and salaried workers (% of employed ages 15+)	74	72	83	74
Self-employed workers (% of employed ages 15+)	24	27	17	26
Unpaid family workers (% of employed ages 15+)	3.3	1.4	0.8	0.6
Employment in agriculture (% of employed ages 15+)	14	11	9	12
Employment in industry (% of employed ages 15+)	23	44	15	35
Employment in services (% of employed ages 15+)	63	45	76	53
Women in wage employment in the nonagricultural sector (%)	46		50	
Women's share of part-time employment (% of total)	72		58	
Maternity leave (days paid)[c]	..		..	
Maternity leave benefits (% of wages paid)	..		..	
Employment to population ratio (% ages 15+)	50	68	46	55
Employment to population ratio (% ages 15–24)	36	47	21	23
Firms with female participation in ownership (%)	..		..	
Firms with a female top manager (%)	..		..	
Children in employment (% of children ages 7–14)	3	5	..	..
Unemployment rate (% of labor force ages 15+)	5	3	17	16
Unemployment rate (% of labor force ages 15–24)	12	6	40	36
Internet users (%)	..	..	58	66
Account at a financial institution (% age 15+)	..	..	86	89
Mobile account (% age 15+)	..	..	..	..
Saved any money last year (% age 15+)	..	..	53	54
Public life and decision making				
Seats held by women in national parliament (%)	..		31	
Female legislators, senior officials and managers (% of total)	31		33	
Proportion of women in ministerial level positions (%)	..		29	
Agency				
Total fertility rate (births per woman)	1.6		1.3	
Adolescent fertility rate (births per 1,000 women ages 15–19)	20		10	
Women first married by age 18 (% of women ages 20–24)	..		..	

Puerto Rico

High income	
Population (millions)	4
GNI, Atlas ($ billions)	69
GNI per capita, Atlas ($)	*19,310*
Population living below $1.90 a day (%)	..

	2000		2013	
	Female	**Male**	**Female**	**Male**
Education				
Net primary enrollment rate (%)	..	..	83	80
Net secondary enrollment rate (%)	..	..	77	72
Gross tertiary enrollment ratio (% of relevant age group)	..	..	100	70
Primary completion rate (% of relevant age group)	..	..	..	..
Progression to secondary school (%)	..	..	..	..
Lower secondary completion rate (% of relevant age group)	..	..	..	..
Gross tertiary graduation ratio (%)	..	..	..	..
Female share of graduates in eng., manf. and constr. (%, tertiary)	..		23	
Youth literacy rate (% of population ages 15–24)	..	..	99	99
Health and related services				
Sex ratio at birth (male births per female births)	*1.05*		1.05	
Under-five mortality rate (per 1,000 live births)	..	..	..	
Life expectancy at birth (years)	81	73	83	75
Pregnant women receiving prenatal care (%)	..		..	
Births attended by skilled health staff (% of total)	..		..	
Maternal mortality ratio (per 100,000 live births)	24		20	
Women's share of population ages 15+ living with HIV (%)	..		..	
Prevalence of HIV (% ages 15–24)	..	..	..	..
Economic structure, participation, and access to resources				
Labor force participation rate (% of population ages 15+)	35	60	34	52
Labor force participation rate (% of ages 15–24)	27	43	20	29
Wage and salaried workers (% of employed ages 15+)	93	80	91	79
Self-employed workers (% of employed ages 15+)	7	20	9	21
Unpaid family workers (% of employed ages 15+)	1.0	0.1	..	..
Employment in agriculture (% of employed ages 15+)	0	3	0	3
Employment in industry (% of employed ages 15+)	15	28	8	19
Employment in services (% of employed ages 15+)	85	69	92	79
Women in wage employment in the nonagricultural sector (%)	40		46	
Women's share of part-time employment (% of total)	..		..	
Maternity leave (days paid)	..		56	
Maternity leave benefits (% of wages paid)	..		100	
Employment to population ratio (% ages 15+)	32	52	30	44
Employment to population ratio (% ages 15–24)	23	33	15	20
Firms with female participation in ownership (%)	..		..	
Firms with a female top manager (%)	..		..	
Children in employment (% of children ages 7–14)	..	..	..	..
Unemployment rate (% of labor force ages 15+)	8	12	12	16
Unemployment rate (% of labor force ages 15–24)	17	24	24	30
Internet users (%)	..	..	..	..
Account at a financial institution (% age 15+)	..	..	66	74
Mobile account (% age 15+)	..	..	..	..
Saved any money last year (% age 15+)	..	..	40	49
Public life and decision making				
Seats held by women in national parliament (%)	..		..	
Female legislators, senior officials and managers (% of total)	37		..	
Proportion of women in ministerial level positions (%)	..		..	
Agency				
Total fertility rate (births per woman)	2.0		1.6	
Adolescent fertility rate (births per 1,000 women ages 15–19)	68		43	
Women first married by age 18 (% of women ages 20–24)	..		..	

Qatar

High income

Population (millions)	2
GNI, Atlas ($ billions)	205
GNI per capita, Atlas ($)	94,410
Population living below $1.90 a day (%)	..

	2000		2013	
	Female	Male	Female	Male
Education				
Net primary enrollment rate (%)	100	92	..	..
Net secondary enrollment rate (%)	79	67	100	91
Gross tertiary enrollment ratio (% of relevant age group)	31	9	44	7
Primary completion rate (% of relevant age group)	98	87	..	..
Progression to secondary school (%)	..	..	100	99
Lower secondary completion rate (% of relevant age group)	..	..	110	110
Gross tertiary graduation ratio (%)	29	9	14	1
Female share of graduates in eng., manf. and constr. (%, tertiary)	54		27	
Youth literacy rate (% of population ages 15–24)	..	..	100[a]	98[a]
Health and related services				
Sex ratio at birth (male births per female births)	1.05		1.05	
Under-five mortality rate (per 1,000 live births)	11	13	7	9
Life expectancy at birth (years)	78	76	79	78
Pregnant women receiving prenatal care (%)	..		..	
Births attended by skilled health staff (% of total)	100		..	
Maternal mortality ratio (per 100,000 live births)	9		6	
Women's share of population ages 15+ living with HIV (%)	..		..	
Prevalence of HIV (% ages 15–24)	..	..	..	..
Economic structure, participation, and access to resources				
Labor force participation rate (% of population ages 15+)	38	92	51	96
Labor force participation rate (% of ages 15–24)	26	60	32	78
Wage and salaried workers (% of employed ages 15+)	..	..	99	99
Self-employed workers (% of employed ages 15+)	..	..	0	1
Unpaid family workers (% of employed ages 15+)	..	..	0.0	0.1
Employment in agriculture (% of employed ages 15+)	0	3	0	2
Employment in industry (% of employed ages 15+)	3	44	4	59
Employment in services (% of employed ages 15+)	96	53	96	40
Women in wage employment in the nonagricultural sector (%)	15		13	
Women's share of part-time employment (% of total)	..		..	
Maternity leave (days paid)	..		50	
Maternity leave benefits (% of wages paid)	..		100	
Employment to population ratio (% ages 15+)	36	92	49	95
Employment to population ratio (% ages 15–24)	23	60	29	78
Firms with female participation in ownership (%)	..		..	
Firms with a female top manager (%)	..		..	
Children in employment (% of children ages 7–14)	..	..	..	..
Unemployment rate (% of labor force ages 15+)	5	0	3	0
Unemployment rate (% of labor force ages 15–24)	13	1	10	1
Internet users (%)	..	..	..	..
Account at a financial institution (% age 15+)	..	..	62	69
Mobile account (% age 15+)	..	..	..	..
Saved any money last year (% age 15+)	..	..	..	..
Public life and decision making				
Seats held by women in national parliament (%)	..		0	
Female legislators, senior officials and managers (% of total)	5		12	
Proportion of women in ministerial level positions (%)	..		5	
Agency				
Total fertility rate (births per woman)	3.2		2.0	
Adolescent fertility rate (births per 1,000 women ages 15–19)	21		11	
Women first married by age 18 (% of women ages 20–24)	..		..	

Romania

Europe & Central Asia		**Upper middle income**	
Population (millions)			20
GNI, Atlas ($ billions)			187
GNI per capita, Atlas ($)			9,370
Population living below $1.90 a day (%)			<2

	2000		2013	
	Female	Male	Female	Male
Education				
Net primary enrollment rate (%)	85	86	85	86
Net secondary enrollment rate (%)	..	..	..	..
Gross tertiary enrollment ratio (% of relevant age group)	25	23	59	44
Primary completion rate (% of relevant age group)	90	90	93	94
Progression to secondary school (%)	99	100	99	100
Lower secondary completion rate (% of relevant age group)	86	83	85	86
Gross tertiary graduation ratio (%)	17	15	58	36
Female share of graduates in eng., manf. and constr. (%, tertiary)	25		37	
Youth literacy rate (% of population ages 15–24)	98	98	99	99
Health and related services				
Sex ratio at birth (male births per female births)	1.06		1.06	
Under-five mortality rate (per 1,000 live births)	24	30	10	12
Life expectancy at birth (years)	75	68	78	71
Pregnant women receiving prenatal care (%)	..		..	
Births attended by skilled health staff (% of total)	99		99	
Maternal mortality ratio (per 100,000 live births)	53		33	
Women's share of population ages 15+ living with HIV (%)	..		..	
Prevalence of HIV (% ages 15–24)	..	..	..	..
Economic structure, participation, and access to resources				
Labor force participation rate (% of population ages 15+)	59	72	49	65
Labor force participation rate (% of ages 15–24)	38	48	26	35
Wage and salaried workers (% of employed ages 15+)	52	56	68	68
Self-employed workers (% of employed ages 15+)	49	44	32	32
Unpaid family workers (% of employed ages 15+)	31.1	11.4	18.9	6.9
Employment in agriculture (% of employed ages 15+)	46	40	30	28
Employment in industry (% of employed ages 15+)	21	31	20	35
Employment in services (% of employed ages 15+)	33	29	50	37
Women in wage employment in the nonagricultural sector (%)	46		46	
Women's share of part-time employment (% of total)	54		49	
Maternity leave (days paid)	..		126	
Maternity leave benefits (% of wages paid)	..		85	
Employment to population ratio (% ages 15+)	55	66	46	60
Employment to population ratio (% ages 15–24)	32	39	20	27
Firms with female participation in ownership (%)	..		47	
Firms with a female top manager (%)	..		20	
Children in employment (% of children ages 7–14)	1	2	..	..
Unemployment rate (% of labor force ages 15+)	6	8	7	8
Unemployment rate (% of labor force ages 15–24)	16	19	24	24
Internet users (%)	..	..	48	52
Account at a financial institution (% age 15+)	..	..	57	65
Mobile account (% age 15+)	..	..	0.4	0.6
Saved any money last year (% age 15+)	..	..	34	39
Public life and decision making				
Seats held by women in national parliament (%)	..		14	
Female legislators, senior officials and managers (% of total)	27		31	
Proportion of women in ministerial level positions (%)	..		14	
Agency				
Total fertility rate (births per woman)	1.3		1.5	
Adolescent fertility rate (births per 1,000 women ages 15–19)	39		35	
Women first married by age 18 (% of women ages 20–24)	..		..	

Russian Federation

High income

Population (millions)				144
GNI, Atlas ($ billions)				1,930
GNI per capita, Atlas ($)				13,210
Population living below $1.90 a day (%)				<2

	2000		2013	
	Female	Male	Female	Male
Education				
Net primary enrollment rate (%)	..	..	96	96
Net secondary enrollment rate (%)	..	..	..	..
Gross tertiary enrollment ratio (% of relevant age group)	69	53	85	68
Primary completion rate (% of relevant age group)	..	..	..	..
Progression to secondary school (%)	..	..	..	..
Lower secondary completion rate (% of relevant age group)	..	..	..	..
Gross tertiary graduation ratio (%)	..	..	76	48
Female share of graduates in eng., manf. and constr. (%, tertiary)	..		..	
Youth literacy rate (% of population ages 15–24)	100	100	100	100
Health and related services				
Sex ratio at birth (male births per female births)	1.06		1.06	
Under-five mortality rate (per 1,000 live births)	20	26	8	11
Life expectancy at birth (years)	72	59	76	66
Pregnant women receiving prenatal care (%)	..		..	
Births attended by skilled health staff (% of total)	99		100	
Maternal mortality ratio (per 100,000 live births)	57		24	
Women's share of population ages 15+ living with HIV (%)	..		..	
Prevalence of HIV (% ages 15–24)	..	..	..	..
Economic structure, participation, and access to resources				
Labor force participation rate (% of population ages 15+)	54	68	57	72
Labor force participation rate (% of ages 15–24)	39	47	35	44
Wage and salaried workers (% of employed ages 15+)	90	90	..	..
Self-employed workers (% of employed ages 15+)	10	11	..	..
Unpaid family workers (% of employed ages 15+)	0.1	0.2	..	..
Employment in agriculture (% of employed ages 15+)	12	17	..	..
Employment in industry (% of employed ages 15+)	22	35	..	..
Employment in services (% of employed ages 15+)	67	48	..	..
Women in wage employment in the nonagricultural sector (%)	50		50	
Women's share of part-time employment (% of total)	66		65	
Maternity leave (days paid)	..		140	
Maternity leave benefits (% of wages paid)	..		100	
Employment to population ratio (% ages 15+)	49	61	54	67
Employment to population ratio (% ages 15–24)	31	38	30	38
Firms with female participation in ownership (%)	..		29	
Firms with a female top manager (%)	..		20	
Children in employment (% of children ages 7–14)	..	..	..	..
Unemployment rate (% of labor force ages 15+)	10	11	5	6
Unemployment rate (% of labor force ages 15–24)	22	20	15	14
Internet users (%)	..	..	67	69
Account at a financial institution (% age 15+)	..	..	70	64
Mobile account (% age 15+)	..	..	..	..
Saved any money last year (% age 15+)	..	..	41	40
Public life and decision making				
Seats held by women in national parliament (%)	..		14	
Female legislators, senior officials and managers (% of total)	36		..	
Proportion of women in ministerial level positions (%)	..		7	
Agency				
Total fertility rate (births per woman)	1.2		1.7	
Adolescent fertility rate (births per 1,000 women ages 15–19)	31		24	
Women first married by age 18 (% of women ages 20–24)	..		..	

Rwanda

Population (millions)	11
GNI, Atlas ($ billions)	8
GNI per capita, Atlas ($)	700
Population living below $1.90 a day (%)	60

	2000		2013	
	Female	Male	Female	Male
Education				
Net primary enrollment rate (%)	82	83	95	92
Net secondary enrollment rate (%)	..	..	..	..
Gross tertiary enrollment ratio (% of relevant age group)	1	2	7	9
Primary completion rate (% of relevant age group)	21	25	64	54
Progression to secondary school (%)	..	..	74	76
Lower secondary completion rate (% of relevant age group)	..	..	29	26
Gross tertiary graduation ratio (%)	..	..	2	4
Female share of graduates in eng., manf. and constr. (%, tertiary)	..		20	
Youth literacy rate (% of population ages 15-24)	77	79	83	81
Health and related services				
Sex ratio at birth (male births per female births)	1.01		1.02	
Under-five mortality rate (per 1,000 live births)	175	193	38	45
Life expectancy at birth (years)	49	47	66	62
Pregnant women receiving prenatal care (%)	92		98	
Births attended by skilled health staff (% of total)	31		69	
Maternal mortality ratio (per 100,000 live births)	1,000		320	
Women's share of population ages 15+ living with HIV (%)	59		61	
Prevalence of HIV (% ages 15-24)	2.1	1.0	1.3	1.0
Economic structure, participation, and access to resources				
Labor force participation rate (% of population ages 15+)	86	85	86	85
Labor force participation rate (% of ages 15-24)	77	75	74	71
Wage and salaried workers (% of employed ages 15+)	..	..	..	..
Self-employed workers (% of employed ages 15+)	..	..	..	..
Unpaid family workers (% of employed ages 15+)	..	..	..	..
Employment in agriculture (% of employed ages 15+)	..	..	..	..
Employment in industry (% of employed ages 15+)	..	..	..	..
Employment in services (% of employed ages 15+)	..	..	..	..
Women in wage employment in the nonagricultural sector (%)	33		34	
Women's share of part-time employment (% of total)	..		..	
Maternity leave (days paid)	..		84	
Maternity leave benefits (% of wages paid)	..		60	
Employment to population ratio (% ages 15+)	86	84	86	85
Employment to population ratio (% ages 15-24)	77	74	74	70
Firms with female participation in ownership (%)	..		43	
Firms with a female top manager (%)	..		20	
Children in employment (% of children ages 7-14)	30	36	20	18
Unemployment rate (% of labor force ages 15+)	0	1	0	1
Unemployment rate (% of labor force ages 15-24)	1	1	1	1
Internet users (%)	..	..	..	..
Account at a financial institution (% age 15+)	..	..	31	46
Mobile account (% age 15+)	..	..	16.1	20.1
Saved any money last year (% age 15+)	..	..	52	58
Public life and decision making				
Seats held by women in national parliament (%)			64	
Female legislators, senior officials and managers (% of total)	..		..	
Proportion of women in ministerial level positions (%)	..		36	
Agency				
Total fertility rate (births per woman)	5.9		4.5	
Adolescent fertility rate (births per 1,000 women ages 15-19)	49		27	
Women first married by age 18 (% of women ages 20-24)	20		8	

Samoa

East Asia & Pacific	Lower middle income
Population (thousands)	192
GNI, Atlas ($ millions)	777
GNI per capita, Atlas ($)	4,050
Population living below $1.90 a day (%)	..

	2000		2013	
	Female	Male	Female	Male
Education				
Net primary enrollment rate (%)	91	88	96	94
Net secondary enrollment rate (%)	69	60	84	75
Gross tertiary enrollment ratio (% of relevant age group)	7	8	..	..
Primary completion rate (% of relevant age group)	95	93	100	105
Progression to secondary school (%)	100	96	97	98
Lower secondary completion rate (% of relevant age group)	101	93	103	102
Gross tertiary graduation ratio (%)	2	2	..	..
Female share of graduates in eng., manf. and constr. (%, tertiary)	0		..	
Youth literacy rate (% of population ages 15–24)	..	..	99	99
Health and related services				
Sex ratio at birth (male births per female births)	1.08		1.08	
Under-five mortality rate (per 1,000 live births)	20	24	16	19
Life expectancy at birth (years)	73	66	77	70
Pregnant women receiving prenatal care (%)	..		..	
Births attended by skilled health staff (% of total)	100		..	
Maternal mortality ratio (per 100,000 live births)	89		58	
Women's share of population ages 15+ living with HIV (%)	..		..	
Prevalence of HIV (% ages 15–24)	..	..	..	..
Economic structure, participation, and access to resources				
Labor force participation rate (% of population ages 15+)	33	74	24	58
Labor force participation rate (% of ages 15–24)	25	52	17	40
Wage and salaried workers (% of employed ages 15+)	59	44	75	43
Self-employed workers (% of employed ages 15+)	..	..	25	57
Unpaid family workers (% of employed ages 15+)	35.7	51.2	..	..
Employment in agriculture (% of employed ages 15+)	16	50	..	..
Employment in industry (% of employed ages 15+)	31	15	..	..
Employment in services (% of employed ages 15+)	51	33	..	..
Women in wage employment in the nonagricultural sector (%)	37		37	
Women's share of part-time employment (% of total)	..		..	
Maternity leave (days paid)	..			
Maternity leave benefits (% of wages paid)	..			
Employment to population ratio (% ages 15+)	..	..	..	..
Employment to population ratio (% ages 15–24)	..	..	..	..
Firms with female participation in ownership (%)	..			
Firms with a female top manager (%)	..			
Children in employment (% of children ages 7–14)	..	..	..	..
Unemployment rate (% of labor force ages 15+)	..	..	..	..
Unemployment rate (% of labor force ages 15–24)	..	..	..	..
Internet users (%)	..	..	..	..
Account at a financial institution (% age 15+)	..	..	..	..
Mobile account (% age 15+)	..	..	..	..
Saved any money last year (% age 15+)	..	..	..	..
Public life and decision making				
Seats held by women in national parliament (%)	..		6	
Female legislators, senior officials and managers (% of total)	29		36	
Proportion of women in ministerial level positions (%)	..		8	
Agency				
Total fertility rate (births per woman)	4.5		4.1	
Adolescent fertility rate (births per 1,000 women ages 15–19)	40		26	
Women first married by age 18 (% of women ages 20–24)	..		..	

San Marino

Population (thousands)	32
GNI, Atlas ($ billions)	..
GNI per capita, Atlas ($)	..
Population living below $1.90 a day (%)	..

	2000		2013	
	Female	**Male**	**Female**	**Male**
Education				
Net primary enrollment rate (%)	..	..	92	93
Net secondary enrollment rate (%)	..	..	..	..
Gross tertiary enrollment ratio (% of relevant age group)	..	..	70	50
Primary completion rate (% of relevant age group)	..	..	93	98
Progression to secondary school (%)	..	..	100	98
Lower secondary completion rate (% of relevant age group)	..	..	93	91
Gross tertiary graduation ratio (%)	..	..	..	
Female share of graduates in eng., manf. and constr. (%, tertiary)	..		..	
Youth literacy rate (% of population ages 15–24)	..	..	..	..
Health and related services				
Sex ratio at birth (male births per female births)				
Under-five mortality rate (per 1,000 live births)	5	6	3	3
Life expectancy at birth (years)	84	77	86	80
Pregnant women receiving prenatal care (%)	..		..	
Births attended by skilled health staff (% of total)	..		..	
Maternal mortality ratio (per 100,000 live births)	..		..	
Women's share of population ages 15+ living with HIV (%)	..		..	
Prevalence of HIV (% ages 15–24)	..	..	..	..
Economic structure, participation, and access to resources				
Labor force participation rate (% of population ages 15+)	..	..	..	..
Labor force participation rate (% of ages 15–24)	..		..	
Wage and salaried workers (% of employed ages 15+)	91	87	..	..
Self-employed workers (% of employed ages 15+)	9	13	..	..
Unpaid family workers (% of employed ages 15+)	0.0	0.0	..	..
Employment in agriculture (% of employed ages 15+)	0	1	..	..
Employment in industry (% of employed ages 15+)	24	53	..	..
Employment in services (% of employed ages 15+)	75	47	..	..
Women in wage employment in the nonagricultural sector (%)	42		43	
Women's share of part-time employment (% of total)	..		..	
Maternity leave (days paid)	..		..	
Maternity leave benefits (% of wages paid)	..		..	
Employment to population ratio (% ages 15+)	..	..	..	..
Employment to population ratio (% ages 15–24)	..	..	..	..
Firms with female participation in ownership (%)	..		..	
Firms with a female top manager (%)	..		..	
Children in employment (% of children ages 7–14)	..	..	..	..
Unemployment rate (% of labor force ages 15+)	..	..	..	..
Unemployment rate (% of labor force ages 15–24)	..	..	..	..
Internet users (%)	..	..	..	..
Account at a financial institution (% age 15+)	..	..	..	..
Mobile account (% age 15+)	..	..	..	..
Saved any money last year (% age 15+)	..	..	..	..
Public life and decision making				
Seats held by women in national parliament (%)	..		17	
Female legislators, senior officials and managers (% of total)	18		..	
Proportion of women in ministerial level positions (%)	..		11	
Agency				
Total fertility rate (births per woman)	..		1.3	
Adolescent fertility rate (births per 1,000 women ages 15–19)	..		..	
Women first married by age 18 (% of women ages 20–24)	..		..	

São Tomé and Príncipe

Sub-Saharan Africa	Lower middle income
Population (thousands)	186
GNI, Atlas ($ millions)	311
GNI per capita, Atlas ($)	1,670
Population living below $1.90 a day (%)	*34*

	2000		2013	
	Female	Male	Female	Male
Education				
Net primary enrollment rate (%)	79	81	92[a]	93[a]
Net secondary enrollment rate (%)	..	..	53	46
Gross tertiary enrollment ratio (% of relevant age group)	..	..	7	8
Primary completion rate (% of relevant age group)	45	40	98[a]	90[a]
Progression to secondary school (%)	79	65	81	76
Lower secondary completion rate (% of relevant age group)	..	..	73[a]	61[a]
Gross tertiary graduation ratio (%)	..		..	
Female share of graduates in eng., manf. and constr. (%, tertiary)	..		..	
Youth literacy rate (% of population ages 15–24)	95	96	..	..
Health and related services				
Sex ratio at birth (male births per female births)	*1.03*		1.03	
Under-five mortality rate (per 1,000 live births)	84	95	43	52
Life expectancy at birth (years)	65	62	68	64
Pregnant women receiving prenatal care (%)	91		..	
Births attended by skilled health staff (% of total)	79		..	
Maternal mortality ratio (per 100,000 live births)	300		210	
Women's share of population ages 15+ living with HIV (%)	33		39	
Prevalence of HIV (% ages 15–24)	0.8	1.3	0.2	0.2
Economic structure, participation, and access to resources				
Labor force participation rate (% of population ages 15+)	39	73	45	78
Labor force participation rate (% of ages 15–24)	26	55	27	55
Wage and salaried workers (% of employed ages 15+)	..	..	..	..
Self-employed workers (% of employed ages 15+)	..	..	..	..
Unpaid family workers (% of employed ages 15+)	..	..	..	..
Employment in agriculture (% of employed ages 15+)	23	31	..	..
Employment in industry (% of employed ages 15+)	6	26	..	..
Employment in services (% of employed ages 15+)	71	43	..	..
Women in wage employment in the nonagricultural sector (%)	..		..	
Women's share of part-time employment (% of total)	..		..	
Maternity leave (days paid)			90	
Maternity leave benefits (% of wages paid)			100	
Employment to population ratio (% ages 15+)	..	..	..	..
Employment to population ratio (% ages 15–24)	..	..	..	..
Firms with female participation in ownership (%)	..		..	
Firms with a female top manager (%)	..		..	
Children in employment (% of children ages 7–14)	..	..	..	..
Unemployment rate (% of labor force ages 15+)	..	..	..	..
Unemployment rate (% of labor force ages 15–24)	..	..	..	..
Internet users (%)	..	..	..	..
Account at a financial institution (% age 15+)	..	..	..	..
Mobile account (% age 15+)	..	..	..	..
Saved any money last year (% age 15+)	..	..	..	..
Public life and decision making				
Seats held by women in national parliament (%)	..		18	
Female legislators, senior officials and managers (% of total)	..		24	
Proportion of women in ministerial level positions (%)	..		8	
Agency				
Total fertility rate (births per woman)	4.7		4.1	
Adolescent fertility rate (births per 1,000 women ages 15–19)	103		85	
Women first married by age 18 (% of women ages 20–24)	..		..	

Saudi Arabia

High income

Population (millions)	31
GNI, Atlas ($ billions)	759
GNI per capita, Atlas ($)	25,140
Population living below $1.90 a day (%)	..

	2000 Female	2000 Male	2013 Female	2013 Male
Education				
Net primary enrollment rate (%)	..	..	99[a]	96[a]
Net secondary enrollment rate (%)	..	..	100[a]	99[a]
Gross tertiary enrollment ratio (% of relevant age group)	25	20	59	56
Primary completion rate (% of relevant age group)	..	..	121[a]	113[a]
Progression to secondary school (%)	..	..	92	100
Lower secondary completion rate (% of relevant age group)	..	..	120[a]	110[a]
Gross tertiary graduation ratio (%)	14	11	27	15
Female share of graduates in eng., manf. and constr. (%, tertiary)	1		3	
Youth literacy rate (% of population ages 15–24)	94	98	99	99
Health and related services				
Sex ratio at birth (male births per female births)	1.03		1.03	
Under-five mortality rate (per 1,000 live births)	21	24	14	16
Life expectancy at birth (years)	74	71	78	74
Pregnant women receiving prenatal care (%)	..			
Births attended by skilled health staff (% of total)	..		..	
Maternal mortality ratio (per 100,000 live births)	24		16	
Women's share of population ages 15+ living with HIV (%)	..		..	
Prevalence of HIV (% ages 15–24)	..	..	..	..
Economic structure, participation, and access to resources				
Labor force participation rate (% of population ages 15+)	16	74	20	78
Labor force participation rate (% of ages 15–24)	8	31	10	28
Wage and salaried workers (% of employed ages 15+)	..	..	..	..
Self-employed workers (% of employed ages 15+)	..	..	..	..
Unpaid family workers (% of employed ages 15+)	..	..	..	..
Employment in agriculture (% of employed ages 15+)	2	7	0	5
Employment in industry (% of employed ages 15+)	2	23	2	28
Employment in services (% of employed ages 15+)	96	71	98	67
Women in wage employment in the nonagricultural sector (%)	14		14	
Women's share of part-time employment (% of total)	..		..	
Maternity leave (days paid)	..		70	
Maternity leave benefits (% of wages paid)	..		100	
Employment to population ratio (% ages 15+)	15	71	16	76
Employment to population ratio (% ages 15–24)	5	25	4	22
Firms with female participation in ownership (%)	..		..	
Firms with a female top manager (%)	..		..	
Children in employment (% of children ages 7–14)	..	..	..	..
Unemployment rate (% of labor force ages 15+)	9	4	21	3
Unemployment rate (% of labor force ages 15–24)	31	22	55	21
Internet users (%)	..	..	..	..
Account at a financial institution (% age 15+)	..		61	75
Mobile account (% age 15+)	..		..	..
Saved any money last year (% age 15+)	..	..	36	52
Public life and decision making				
Seats held by women in national parliament (%)	..		20	
Female legislators, senior officials and managers (% of total)	..		7	
Proportion of women in ministerial level positions (%)	..		0	
Agency				
Total fertility rate (births per woman)	4.0		2.6	
Adolescent fertility rate (births per 1,000 women ages 15–19)	27		9	
Women first married by age 18 (% of women ages 20–24)	..		..	

Senegal

Sub-Saharan Africa   **Lower middle income**

Population (millions)	15
GNI, Atlas ($ billions)	15
GNI per capita, Atlas ($)	1,040
Population living below $1.90 a day (%)	*38*

	2000		2013	
	Female	**Male**	**Female**	**Male**
Education				
Net primary enrollment rate (%)	54	61	77[a]	70[a]
Net secondary enrollment rate (%)	..	..	..	..
Gross tertiary enrollment ratio (% of relevant age group)	..	..	6	*10*
Primary completion rate (% of relevant age group)	33	45	65[a]	57[a]
Progression to secondary school (%)	53	57	92	94
Lower secondary completion rate (% of relevant age group)	11	17	41[a]	41[a]
Gross tertiary graduation ratio (%)	..	..	..	..
Female share of graduates in eng., manf. and constr. (%, tertiary)	..		..	
Youth literacy rate (% of population ages 15–24)	41	58	51	61
Health and related services				
Sex ratio at birth (male births per female births)	*1.04*		1.04	
Under-five mortality rate (per 1,000 live births)	129	141	44	54
Life expectancy at birth (years)	59	56	65	62
Pregnant women receiving prenatal care (%)	79		95	
Births attended by skilled health staff (% of total)	58		65	
Maternal mortality ratio (per 100,000 live births)	480		320	
Women's share of population ages 15+ living with HIV (%)	30		43	
Prevalence of HIV (% ages 15–24)	0.4	0.7	0.1	0.1
Economic structure, participation, and access to resources				
Labor force participation rate (% of population ages 15+)	64	88	66	88
Labor force participation rate (% of ages 15–24)	54	81	53	79
Wage and salaried workers (% of employed ages 15+)	*15*	*26*	*14*	*29*
Self-employed workers (% of employed ages 15+)	*84*	*73*	*68*	*51*
Unpaid family workers (% of employed ages 15+)	*24.7*	*23.5*	*30.1*	*18.2*
Employment in agriculture (% of employed ages 15+)	*44*	*47*	..	..
Employment in industry (% of employed ages 15+)	*8*	*16*	..	..
Employment in services (% of employed ages 15+)	*43*	*32*	..	..
Women in wage employment in the nonagricultural sector (%)	*11*		*27*	
Women's share of part-time employment (% of total)	..		..	
Maternity leave (days paid)	..		98	
Maternity leave benefits (% of wages paid)	..		100	
Employment to population ratio (% ages 15+)	56	81	57	81
Employment to population ratio (% ages 15–24)	44	72	43	70
Firms with female participation in ownership (%)	..		23[a]	
Firms with a female top manager (%)	..		14[a]	
Children in employment (% of children ages 7–14)	..	..	9	18
Unemployment rate (% of labor force ages 15+)	13	8	13	8
Unemployment rate (% of labor force ages 15–24)	19	11	19	11
Internet users (%)	..	..	..	..
Account at a financial institution (% age 15+)	..	..	8	16
Mobile account (% age 15+)	..	..	4.7	7.8
Saved any money last year (% age 15+)	..	..	57	61
Public life and decision making				
Seats held by women in national parliament (%)	..		43	
Female legislators, senior officials and managers (% of total)	..		..	
Proportion of women in ministerial level positions (%)	..		20	
Agency				
Total fertility rate (births per woman)	5.6		4.9	
Adolescent fertility rate (births per 1,000 women ages 15–19)	107		80	
Women first married by age 18 (% of women ages 20–24)	..		*33*	

Serbia

Europe & Central Asia	Upper middle income
Population (millions)	7
GNI, Atlas ($ billions)	42
GNI per capita, Atlas ($)	5,820
Population living below $1.90 a day (%)	<2

	2000		2013	
	Female	Male	Female	Male
Education				
Net primary enrollment rate (%)	..	..	95	95
Net secondary enrollment rate (%)	..	..	94	92
Gross tertiary enrollment ratio (% of relevant age group)	*41*	*34*	65	49
Primary completion rate (% of relevant age group)	..	..	99	99
Progression to secondary school (%)	..	..	99	100
Lower secondary completion rate (% of relevant age group)	..	..	97	95
Gross tertiary graduation ratio (%)	..	..	27	20
Female share of graduates in eng., manf. and constr. (%, tertiary)	..		35	
Youth literacy rate (% of population ages 15-24)	..	..	99	*99*
Health and related services				
Sex ratio at birth (male births per female births)	*1.05*		1.05	
Under-five mortality rate (per 1,000 live births)	11	14	6	7
Life expectancy at birth (years)	74	69	78	73
Pregnant women receiving prenatal care (%)	..		99	
Births attended by skilled health staff (% of total)	98		*100*	
Maternal mortality ratio (per 100,000 live births)	7		16	
Women's share of population ages 15+ living with HIV (%)	..		..	
Prevalence of HIV (% ages 15-24)	..	..	..	..
Economic structure, participation, and access to resources				
Labor force participation rate (% of population ages 15+)	45	65	45	61
Labor force participation rate (% of ages 15-24)	31	45	23	35
Wage and salaried workers (% of employed ages 15+)	..	..	72	65
Self-employed workers (% of employed ages 15+)	..	..	28	36
Unpaid family workers (% of employed ages 15+)	..	..	13.0	3.8
Employment in agriculture (% of employed ages 15+)	..	..	*19*	*23*
Employment in industry (% of employed ages 15+)	..	..	*17*	*33*
Employment in services (% of employed ages 15+)	..	..	*64*	*44*
Women in wage employment in the nonagricultural sector (%)	44		45	
Women's share of part-time employment (% of total)	..		..	
Maternity leave (days paid)			135	
Maternity leave benefits (% of wages paid)	..		100	
Employment to population ratio (% ages 15+)	38	58	33	49
Employment to population ratio (% ages 15-24)	22	34	10	19
Firms with female participation in ownership (%)	..		30	
Firms with a female top manager (%)	..		14	
Children in employment (% of children ages 7-14)	..	..	..	..
Unemployment rate (% of labor force ages 15+)	15	11	26	19
Unemployment rate (% of labor force ages 15-24)	31	26	56	44
Internet users (%)	..	..		
Account at a financial institution (% age 15+)	..	..	83	83
Mobile account (% age 15+)	..	..	..	..
Saved any money last year (% age 15+)	..	..	26	29
Public life and decision making				
Seats held by women in national parliament (%)	..		34	
Female legislators, senior officials and managers (% of total)	..		*33*	
Proportion of women in ministerial level positions (%)	..		22	
Agency				
Total fertility rate (births per woman)	1.5		1.5	
Adolescent fertility rate (births per 1,000 women ages 15-19)	28		19	
Women first married by age 18 (% of women ages 20-24)	..		5	

Seychelles

High income

Population (thousands)	92
GNI, Atlas ($ billions)	1.3
GNI per capita, Atlas ($)	13,990
Population living below $1.90 a day (%)	..

	2000		2013	
	Female	Male	Female	Male
Education				
Net primary enrollment rate (%)	90	87	..	..
Net secondary enrollment rate (%)	72	66	66	61
Gross tertiary enrollment ratio (% of relevant age group)	..	..	5	2
Primary completion rate (% of relevant age group)	104	101	97	101
Progression to secondary school (%)	99	98	..	..
Lower secondary completion rate (% of relevant age group)	102	107	99	103
Gross tertiary graduation ratio (%)	..	..	9	1
Female share of graduates in eng., manf. and constr. (%, tertiary)	..		0	
Youth literacy rate (% of population ages 15-24)	99	99	99	99
Health and related services				
Sex ratio at birth (male births per female births)	1.06		1.06	
Under-five mortality rate (per 1,000 live births)	13	15	12	15
Life expectancy at birth (years)	77	69	79	69
Pregnant women receiving prenatal care (%)	..		..	
Births attended by skilled health staff (% of total)	..		..	
Maternal mortality ratio (per 100,000 live births)	..		..	
Women's share of population ages 15+ living with HIV (%)	..		..	
Prevalence of HIV (% ages 15-24)	..	..	..	..
Economic structure, participation, and access to resources				
Labor force participation rate (% of population ages 15+)	..	..	..	..
Labor force participation rate (% of ages 15-24)	..	..	..	..
Wage and salaried workers (% of employed ages 15+)	..	..	..	..
Self-employed workers (% of employed ages 15+)	..	..	..	..
Unpaid family workers (% of employed ages 15+)	..	..	..	..
Employment in agriculture (% of employed ages 15+)	..	..	..	..
Employment in industry (% of employed ages 15+)	..	..	..	..
Employment in services (% of employed ages 15+)	..	..	..	..
Women in wage employment in the nonagricultural sector (%)	..	53		
Women's share of part-time employment (% of total)	..			
Maternity leave (days paid)	..	98		
Maternity leave benefits (% of wages paid)	..	100		
Employment to population ratio (% ages 15+)	..	..	..	..
Employment to population ratio (% ages 15-24)	..	..	..	..
Firms with female participation in ownership (%)	..			
Firms with a female top manager (%)	..			
Children in employment (% of children ages 7-14)	..	..	..	..
Unemployment rate (% of labor force ages 15+)	..	..	..	..
Unemployment rate (% of labor force ages 15-24)	..	..	..	..
Internet users (%)	..	..	..	..
Account at a financial institution (% age 15+)	..	..	..	..
Mobile account (% age 15+)	..	..	..	..
Saved any money last year (% age 15+)	..	..	..	..
Public life and decision making				
Seats held by women in national parliament (%)	..	44		
Female legislators, senior officials and managers (% of total)	..		..	
Proportion of women in ministerial level positions (%)	..	25		
Agency				
Total fertility rate (births per woman)	2.1		2.4	
Adolescent fertility rate (births per 1,000 women ages 15-19)	58		58	
Women first married by age 18 (% of women ages 20-24)	..		..	

Sierra Leone

Population (millions)	6
GNI, Atlas ($ billions)	4
GNI per capita, Atlas ($)	710
Population living below $1.90 a day (%)	52

	2000 Female	2000 Male	2013 Female	2013 Male
Education				
Net primary enrollment rate (%)	..	..	..	..
Net secondary enrollment rate (%)	..	..	36	40
Gross tertiary enrollment ratio (% of relevant age group)	1	2	..	..
Primary completion rate (% of relevant age group)	..	..	69	73
Progression to secondary school (%)	..	..	88	88
Lower secondary completion rate (% of relevant age group)	19	26	50	58
Gross tertiary graduation ratio (%)	2	2	..	..
Female share of graduates in eng., manf. and constr. (%, tertiary)	25		..	
Youth literacy rate (% of population ages 15–24)	..	..	56	73
Health and related services				
Sex ratio at birth (male births per female births)	1.02		1.02	
Under-five mortality rate (per 1,000 live births)	225	246	113	127
Life expectancy at birth (years)	39	37	46	45
Pregnant women receiving prenatal care (%)	68		97	
Births attended by skilled health staff (% of total)	42		60	
Maternal mortality ratio (per 100,000 live births)	2,200		1,100	
Women's share of population ages 15+ living with HIV (%)	58		59	
Prevalence of HIV (% ages 15–24)	0.8	0.4	0.4	0.2
Economic structure, participation, and access to resources				
Labor force participation rate (% of population ages 15+)	66	62	66	69
Labor force participation rate (% of ages 15–24)	46	35	48	40
Wage and salaried workers (% of employed ages 15+)	..	..	..	..
Self-employed workers (% of employed ages 15+)	..	..	..	..
Unpaid family workers (% of employed ages 15+)	..	..	..	..
Employment in agriculture (% of employed ages 15+)	..	..	..	..
Employment in industry (% of employed ages 15+)	..	..	..	..
Employment in services (% of employed ages 15+)	..	..	..	..
Women in wage employment in the nonagricultural sector (%)	..		..	
Women's share of part-time employment (% of total)	..		..	
Maternity leave (days paid)			84	
Maternity leave benefits (% of wages paid)	..		100	
Employment to population ratio (% ages 15+)	65	59	64	66
Employment to population ratio (% ages 15–24)	44	33	47	38
Firms with female participation in ownership (%)	..		..	
Firms with a female top manager (%)	..		..	
Children in employment (% of children ages 7–14)	65	65	58	61
Unemployment rate (% of labor force ages 15+)	2	5	2	4
Unemployment rate (% of labor force ages 15–24)	4	7	3	7
Internet users (%)	..	..	..	..
Account at a financial institution (% age 15+)	..	..	11	18
Mobile account (% age 15+)	..	..	3.6	5.4
Saved any money last year (% age 15+)	..	..	64	67
Public life and decision making				
Seats held by women in national parliament (%)	..		12	
Female legislators, senior officials and managers (% of total)	..		..	
Proportion of women in ministerial level positions (%)	..		7	
Agency				
Total fertility rate (births per woman)	5.9		4.7	
Adolescent fertility rate (births per 1,000 women ages 15–19)	159		120	
Women first married by age 18 (% of women ages 20–24)	..		39	

Singapore

High income

Population (millions)	5
GNI, Atlas ($ billions)	302
GNI per capita, Atlas ($)	55,150
Population living below $1.90 a day (%)	..

	2000 Female	2000 Male	2013 Female	2013 Male
Education				
Net primary enrollment rate (%)	..	..	..	..
Net secondary enrollment rate (%)	..	..	..	..
Gross tertiary enrollment ratio (% of relevant age group)	..	..	..	..
Primary completion rate (% of relevant age group)	..	..	..	..
Progression to secondary school (%)	..	..	..	..
Lower secondary completion rate (% of relevant age group)	..	..	..	..
Gross tertiary graduation ratio (%)	..	..	..	..
Female share of graduates in eng., manf. and constr. (%, tertiary)	..		..	
Youth literacy rate (% of population ages 15–24)	100	99	100	100
Health and related services				
Sex ratio at birth (male births per female births)	1.07		1.07	
Under-five mortality rate (per 1,000 live births)	4	4	3	3
Life expectancy at birth (years)	80	76	85	80
Pregnant women receiving prenatal care (%)	..		..	
Births attended by skilled health staff (% of total)	100		..	
Maternal mortality ratio (per 100,000 live births)	19		6	
Women's share of population ages 15+ living with HIV (%)	..		..	
Prevalence of HIV (% ages 15–24)	..	..	..	..
Economic structure, participation, and access to resources				
Labor force participation rate (% of population ages 15+)	53	78	59	77
Labor force participation rate (% of ages 15–24)	50	47	38	40
Wage and salaried workers (% of employed ages 15+)	91	81	90	82
Self-employed workers (% of employed ages 15+)	9	19	11	19
Unpaid family workers (% of employed ages 15+)	2.0	0.4	0.8	0.3
Employment in agriculture (% of employed ages 15+)	1	1	..	..
Employment in industry (% of employed ages 15+)	21	29	..	..
Employment in services (% of employed ages 15+)	79	70	..	..
Women in wage employment in the nonagricultural sector (%)	44		47	
Women's share of part-time employment (% of total)	..		..	
Maternity leave (days paid)	..		105	
Maternity leave benefits (% of wages paid)	..		100	
Employment to population ratio (% ages 15+)	51	76	57	75
Employment to population ratio (% ages 15–24)	43	41	34	36
Firms with female participation in ownership (%)	..		..	
Firms with a female top manager (%)	..		..	
Children in employment (% of children ages 7–14)	..	..	3	..
Unemployment rate (% of labor force ages 15+)	4	3	3	3
Unemployment rate (% of labor force ages 15–24)	14	12	11	9
Internet users (%)	..	..	..	..
Account at a financial institution (% age 15+)	..	..	96	97
Mobile account (% age 15+)	..	..	5.2	7.1
Saved any money last year (% age 15+)	..	..	71	76
Public life and decision making				
Seats held by women in national parliament (%)	..		25	
Female legislators, senior officials and managers (% of total)	25		34	
Proportion of women in ministerial level positions (%)	..		6	
Agency				
Total fertility rate (births per woman)	1.4		1.2	
Adolescent fertility rate (births per 1,000 women ages 15–19)	8		4	
Women first married by age 18 (% of women ages 20–24)	..		..	

Sint Maarten (Dutch part)

High income

Population (thousands)	38
GNI, Atlas ($ millions)	..
GNI per capita, Atlas ($)	..
Population living below $1.90 a day (%)	..

	2000 Female	Male	2013 Female	Male
Education				
Net primary enrollment rate (%)	..	..	..	..
Net secondary enrollment rate (%)	..	..	..	..
Gross tertiary enrollment ratio (% of relevant age group)	..	..	..	..
Primary completion rate (% of relevant age group)	..	..	..	..
Progression to secondary school (%)	..	..	..	..
Lower secondary completion rate (% of relevant age group)	..	..	..	..
Gross tertiary graduation ratio (%)	..	..	..	..
Female share of graduates in eng., manf. and constr. (%, tertiary)	..		..	
Youth literacy rate (% of population ages 15–24)	..	..	..	..
Health and related services				
Sex ratio at birth (male births per female births)	..		..	
Under-five mortality rate (per 1,000 live births)	..	..	..	..
Life expectancy at birth (years)	..	..	..	73
Pregnant women receiving prenatal care (%)			..	
Births attended by skilled health staff (% of total)			..	
Maternal mortality ratio (per 100,000 live births)			..	
Women's share of population ages 15+ living with HIV (%)	..		..	
Prevalence of HIV (% ages 15–24)	..	..	..	..
Economic structure, participation, and access to resources				
Labor force participation rate (% of population ages 15+)	..	..	..	..
Labor force participation rate (% of ages 15–24)	..	..	..	..
Wage and salaried workers (% of employed ages 15+)	..	..	..	..
Self-employed workers (% of employed ages 15+)	..	..	..	..
Unpaid family workers (% of employed ages 15+)	..	..	..	..
Employment in agriculture (% of employed ages 15+)	..	..	..	..
Employment in industry (% of employed ages 15+)	..	..	..	..
Employment in services (% of employed ages 15+)	..	..	..	..
Women in wage employment in the nonagricultural sector (%)	..		..	
Women's share of part-time employment (% of total)	..		..	
Maternity leave (days paid)			..	
Maternity leave benefits (% of wages paid)			..	
Employment to population ratio (% ages 15+)	..	..	..	..
Employment to population ratio (% ages 15–24)	..	..	..	..
Firms with female participation in ownership (%)			..	
Firms with a female top manager (%)			..	
Children in employment (% of children ages 7–14)	..	..	..	..
Unemployment rate (% of labor force ages 15+)	..	..	..	..
Unemployment rate (% of labor force ages 15–24)	..	..	..	..
Internet users (%)	..	..	..	..
Account at a financial institution (% age 15+)	..	..	..	..
Mobile account (% age 15+)	..	..	..	..
Saved any money last year (% age 15+)	..	..	..	..
Public life and decision making				
Seats held by women in national parliament (%)	..		..	
Female legislators, senior officials and managers (% of total)	..		..	
Proportion of women in ministerial level positions (%)	..		..	
Agency				
Total fertility rate (births per woman)	*2.0*		*2.0*	
Adolescent fertility rate (births per 1,000 women ages 15–19)	..		..	
Women first married by age 18 (% of women ages 20–24)	..		..	

Slovak Republic

High income

Population (millions)	5
GNI, Atlas ($ billions)	96
GNI per capita, Atlas ($)	17,810
Population living below $1.90 a day (%)	<2

	2000		2013	
	Female	Male	Female	Male
Education				
Net primary enrollment rate (%)	..	..	..	..
Net secondary enrollment rate (%)	..	..	..	..
Gross tertiary enrollment ratio (% of relevant age group)	29	28	65	42
Primary completion rate (% of relevant age group)	96	97	96	96
Progression to secondary school (%)	100	99	99	99
Lower secondary completion rate (% of relevant age group)	..	..	81	82
Gross tertiary graduation ratio (%)	22	20	57	31
Female share of graduates in eng., manf. and constr. (%, tertiary)	30		31	
Youth literacy rate (% of population ages 15–24)	..	..	..	..
Health and related services				
Sex ratio at birth (male births per female births)	1.05		1.05	
Under-five mortality rate (per 1,000 live births)	11	13	7	8
Life expectancy at birth (years)	77	69	80	73
Pregnant women receiving prenatal care (%)	..		..	
Births attended by skilled health staff (% of total)	100		99	
Maternal mortality ratio (per 100,000 live births)	12		7	
Women's share of population ages 15+ living with HIV (%)	..		..	
Prevalence of HIV (% ages 15–24)	0.1	0.1	0.1	0.1
Economic structure, participation, and access to resources				
Labor force participation rate (% of population ages 15+)	53	68	51	69
Labor force participation rate (% of ages 15–24)	43	50	24	38
Wage and salaried workers (% of employed ages 15+)	95	89	90	80
Self-employed workers (% of employed ages 15+)	4	11	10	20
Unpaid family workers (% of employed ages 15+)	0.2	0.1	0.1	0.0
Employment in agriculture (% of employed ages 15+)	4	9	2	5
Employment in industry (% of employed ages 15+)	26	47	21	51
Employment in services (% of employed ages 15+)	71	44	77	45
Women in wage employment in the nonagricultural sector (%)	49		48	
Women's share of part-time employment (% of total)	71		59	
Maternity leave (days paid)	..		238	
Maternity leave benefits (% of wages paid)	..		65	
Employment to population ratio (% ages 15+)	43	55	44	59
Employment to population ratio (% ages 15–24)	28	30	17	25
Firms with female participation in ownership (%)	..		30	
Firms with a female top manager (%)	..		14	
Children in employment (% of children ages 7–14)	..	..	..	..
Unemployment rate (% of labor force ages 15+)	19	19	15	14
Unemployment rate (% of labor force ages 15–24)	34	40	31	35
Internet users (%)	..	..	78	78
Account at a financial institution (% age 15+)	..	..	80	74
Mobile account (% age 15+)	..	..	..	..
Saved any money last year (% age 15+)	..	..	67	58
Public life and decision making				
Seats held by women in national parliament (%)	..		19	
Female legislators, senior officials and managers (% of total)	31		31	
Proportion of women in ministerial level positions (%)	..		0	
Agency				
Total fertility rate (births per woman)	1.3		1.3	
Adolescent fertility rate (births per 1,000 women ages 15–19)	23		20	
Women first married by age 18 (% of women ages 20–24)	..		..	

Slovenia

High income

Population (millions)	2
GNI, Atlas ($ billions)	48
GNI per capita, Atlas ($)	23,220
Population living below $1.90 a day (%)	<2

	2000		2013	
	Female	**Male**	**Female**	**Male**
Education				
Net primary enrollment rate (%)	94	92	98	97
Net secondary enrollment rate (%)	93	90	95	94
Gross tertiary enrollment ratio (% of relevant age group)	64	47	101	69
Primary completion rate (% of relevant age group)	95	97	98	98
Progression to secondary school (%)	99	100	100	100
Lower secondary completion rate (% of relevant age group)	93	91	94	93
Gross tertiary graduation ratio (%)	21	12	67	34
Female share of graduates in eng., manf. and constr. (%, tertiary)	22		24	
Youth literacy rate (% of population ages 15–24)	..	..	100	100
Health and related services				
Sex ratio at birth (male births per female births)	1.05		1.05	
Under-five mortality rate (per 1,000 live births)	5	6	2	3
Life expectancy at birth (years)	79	72	83	77
Pregnant women receiving prenatal care (%)	..		..	
Births attended by skilled health staff (% of total)	100		100	
Maternal mortality ratio (per 100,000 live births)	12		7	
Women's share of population ages 15+ living with HIV (%)	9		9	
Prevalence of HIV (% ages 15–24)	0.1	0.1	0.1	0.1
Economic structure, participation, and access to resources				
Labor force participation rate (% of population ages 15+)	51	64	52	63
Labor force participation rate (% of ages 15–24)	34	41	31	37
Wage and salaried workers (% of employed ages 15+)	87	81	86	80
Self-employed workers (% of employed ages 15+)	13	19	14	20
Unpaid family workers (% of employed ages 15+)	6.6	3.3	6.0	3.8
Employment in agriculture (% of employed ages 15+)	10	9	8	9
Employment in industry (% of employed ages 15+)	28	45	18	42
Employment in services (% of employed ages 15+)	62	44	73	49
Women in wage employment in the nonagricultural sector (%)	48		47	
Women's share of part-time employment (% of total)	57		60	
Maternity leave (days paid)	..		105	
Maternity leave benefits (% of wages paid)	..		100	
Employment to population ratio (% ages 15+)	48	60	46	57
Employment to population ratio (% ages 15–24)	28	35	23	29
Firms with female participation in ownership (%)	..		35	
Firms with a female top manager (%)	..		19	
Children in employment (% of children ages 7–14)	..	..	..	..
Unemployment rate (% of labor force ages 15+)	7	7	11	9
Unemployment rate (% of labor force ages 15–24)	18	15	24	22
Internet users (%)	..	..	71	74
Account at a financial institution (% age 15+)	..	..	97	98
Mobile account (% age 15+)	..	..	..	..
Saved any money last year (% age 15+)	..	..	62	70
Public life and decision making				
Seats held by women in national parliament (%)	..		37	
Female legislators, senior officials and managers (% of total)	30		38	
Proportion of women in ministerial level positions (%)	..		44	
Agency				
Total fertility rate (births per woman)	1.3		1.6	
Adolescent fertility rate (births per 1,000 women ages 15–19)	7		4	
Women first married by age 18 (% of women ages 20–24)	..		..	

Solomon Islands

East Asia & Pacific	Lower middle income
Population (thousands)	572
GNI, Atlas ($ billions)	1.0
GNI per capita, Atlas ($)	1,830
Population living below $1.90 a day (%)	..

	2000		2013	
	Female	Male	Female	Male
Education				
Net primary enrollment rate (%)	..	..	..	..
Net secondary enrollment rate (%)	17	21	..	..
Gross tertiary enrollment ratio (% of relevant age group)	..	..	..	..
Primary completion rate (% of relevant age group)	..	..	86	86
Progression to secondary school (%)	..	..	..	..
Lower secondary completion rate (% of relevant age group)	26	37	63	64
Gross tertiary graduation ratio (%)	..		..	
Female share of graduates in eng., manf. and constr. (%, tertiary)	..		..	
Youth literacy rate (% of population ages 15–24)	80	90	..	..
Health and related services				
Sex ratio at birth (male births per female births)	1.07		1.07	
Under-five mortality rate (per 1,000 live births)	30	36	26	31
Life expectancy at birth (years)	64	62	69	66
Pregnant women receiving prenatal care (%)	..		..	
Births attended by skilled health staff (% of total)	85		..	
Maternal mortality ratio (per 100,000 live births)	210		130	
Women's share of population ages 15+ living with HIV (%)	..		..	
Prevalence of HIV (% ages 15–24)	..	..	..	..
Economic structure, participation, and access to resources				
Labor force participation rate (% of population ages 15+)	53	79	53	79
Labor force participation rate (% of ages 15–24)	42	57	42	56
Wage and salaried workers (% of employed ages 15+)	..	..	..	..
Self-employed workers (% of employed ages 15+)	..	..	..	..
Unpaid family workers (% of employed ages 15+)	..	..	..	..
Employment in agriculture (% of employed ages 15+)	..	..	..	..
Employment in industry (% of employed ages 15+)	..	..	..	..
Employment in services (% of employed ages 15+)	..	..	..	..
Women in wage employment in the nonagricultural sector (%)	31		..	
Women's share of part-time employment (% of total)	..		..	
Maternity leave (days paid)	..		..	
Maternity leave benefits (% of wages paid)	..		..	
Employment to population ratio (% ages 15+)	50	75	51	76
Employment to population ratio (% ages 15–24)	37	51	37	51
Firms with female participation in ownership (%)	..		..	
Firms with a female top manager (%)	..		..	
Children in employment (% of children ages 7–14)	..	..	..	..
Unemployment rate (% of labor force ages 15+)	5	5	4	4
Unemployment rate (% of labor force ages 15–24)	12	11	11	9
Internet users (%)	..	..	..	..
Account at a financial institution (% age 15+)	..	..	..	..
Mobile account (% age 15+)	..	..	..	..
Saved any money last year (% age 15+)	..	..	..	..
Public life and decision making				
Seats held by women in national parliament (%)	..		2	
Female legislators, senior officials and managers (% of total)	..		..	
Proportion of women in ministerial level positions (%)	..		4	
Agency				
Total fertility rate (births per woman)	4.7		4.0	
Adolescent fertility rate (births per 1,000 women ages 15–19)	71		49	
Women first married by age 18 (% of women ages 20–24)	..		..	

Somalia

Sub-Saharan Africa   Low income

Population (millions)	11
GNI, Atlas ($ millions)	..
GNI per capita, Atlas ($)	..
Population living below $1.90 a day (%)	..

	2000		2013	
	Female	Male	Female	Male
Education				
Net primary enrollment rate (%)	..	..	..	..
Net secondary enrollment rate (%)	..	..	..	..
Gross tertiary enrollment ratio (% of relevant age group)	..	..	..	..
Primary completion rate (% of relevant age group)	..	..	..	..
Progression to secondary school (%)	..	..	..	..
Lower secondary completion rate (% of relevant age group)	..	..	..	..
Gross tertiary graduation ratio (%)	..	..	..	..
Female share of graduates in eng., manf. and constr. (%, tertiary)	..		..	
Youth literacy rate (% of population ages 15–24)	..	..	..	..
Health and related services				
Sex ratio at birth (male births per female births)	*1.03*		1.03	
Under-five mortality rate (per 1,000 live births)	167	182	130	143
Life expectancy at birth (years)	52	49	57	53
Pregnant women receiving prenatal care (%)	*32*		..	
Births attended by skilled health staff (% of total)	*33*			
Maternal mortality ratio (per 100,000 live births)	1,200		850	
Women's share of population ages 15+ living with HIV (%)	48		51	
Prevalence of HIV (% ages 15–24)	0.3	0.3	0.2	0.2
Economic structure, participation, and access to resources				
Labor force participation rate (% of population ages 15+)	36	77	37	76
Labor force participation rate (% of ages 15–24)	33	61	32	58
Wage and salaried workers (% of employed ages 15+)	..	..	..	..
Self-employed workers (% of employed ages 15+)	..	..	..	..
Unpaid family workers (% of employed ages 15+)	..	..	..	..
Employment in agriculture (% of employed ages 15+)	..	..	..	..
Employment in industry (% of employed ages 15+)	..	..	..	..
Employment in services (% of employed ages 15+)	..	..	..	..
Women in wage employment in the nonagricultural sector (%)	..		..	
Women's share of part-time employment (% of total)	..		..	
Maternity leave (days paid)	..		..	
Maternity leave benefits (% of wages paid)	..		..	
Employment to population ratio (% ages 15+)	33	72	35	71
Employment to population ratio (% ages 15–24)	29	55	28	52
Firms with female participation in ownership (%)	..		..	
Firms with a female top manager (%)	..		..	
Children in employment (% of children ages 7–14)	..	..	..	..
Unemployment rate (% of labor force ages 15+)	7	7	7	7
Unemployment rate (% of labor force ages 15–24)	11	10	11	10
Internet users (%)	..	..	..	..
Account at a financial institution (% age 15+)	..	..	6	10
Mobile account (% age 15+)	..	..	32.1	42.0
Saved any money last year (% age 15+)	..	..	32	42
Public life and decision making				
Seats held by women in national parliament (%)			14	
Female legislators, senior officials and managers (% of total)	..		..	
Proportion of women in ministerial level positions (%)			8	
Agency				
Total fertility rate (births per woman)	7.6		6.6	
Adolescent fertility rate (births per 1,000 women ages 15–19)	127		105	
Women first married by age 18 (% of women ages 20–24)	..		..	

South Africa

Sub-Saharan Africa	Upper middle income
Population (millions)	54
GNI, Atlas ($ billions)	367
GNI per capita, Atlas ($)	6,800
Population living below $1.90 a day (%)	17

	2000 Female	2000 Male	2013 Female	2013 Male
Education				
Net primary enrollment rate (%)	90	90	..	..
Net secondary enrollment rate (%)	62	54	..	..
Gross tertiary enrollment ratio (% of relevant age group)	..	..	23	17
Primary completion rate (% of relevant age group)	88	86	..	..
Progression to secondary school (%)	99	97	..	..
Lower secondary completion rate (% of relevant age group)	80	71	..	..
Gross tertiary graduation ratio (%)	..	..	8	6
Female share of graduates in eng., manf. and constr. (%, tertiary)	..		29	
Youth literacy rate (% of population ages 15–24)	..	..	99	98
Health and related services				
Sex ratio at birth (male births per female births)	1.03		1.03	
Under-five mortality rate (per 1,000 live births)	69	81	37	47
Life expectancy at birth (years)	58	54	59	55
Pregnant women receiving prenatal care (%)	94		..	
Births attended by skilled health staff (% of total)	84		..	
Maternal mortality ratio (per 100,000 live births)	150		140	
Women's share of population ages 15+ living with HIV (%)	57		60	
Prevalence of HIV (% ages 15–24)	15.9	5.5	8.1	4.0
Economic structure, participation, and access to resources				
Labor force participation rate (% of population ages 15+)	50	65	45	61
Labor force participation rate (% of ages 15–24)	29	34	24	29
Wage and salaried workers (% of employed ages 15+)	..	..	86	83
Self-employed workers (% of employed ages 15+)	..	..	13	16
Unpaid family workers (% of employed ages 15+)	..	..	1.2	0.5
Employment in agriculture (% of employed ages 15+)	16	15	4	6
Employment in industry (% of employed ages 15+)	12	33	13	32
Employment in services (% of employed ages 15+)	71	50	83	62
Women in wage employment in the nonagricultural sector (%)	41		46	
Women's share of part-time employment (% of total)	66		65	
Maternity leave (days paid)	..		120	
Maternity leave benefits (% of wages paid)	..		38	
Employment to population ratio (% ages 15+)	35	49	32	47
Employment to population ratio (% ages 15–24)	15	19	10	15
Firms with female participation in ownership (%)	..		..	
Firms with a female top manager (%)	..		..	
Children in employment (% of children ages 7–14)	26	29	..	..
Unemployment rate (% of labor force ages 15+)	29	25	28	22
Unemployment rate (% of labor force ages 15–24)	48	43	59	49
Internet users (%)	..		..	
Account at a financial institution (% age 15+)	..	..	69	69
Mobile account (% age 15+)	..	..	13.9	15.0
Saved any money last year (% age 15+)	..	..	66	67
Public life and decision making				
Seats held by women in national parliament (%)	..		42	
Female legislators, senior officials and managers (% of total)	..		31	
Proportion of women in ministerial level positions (%)	..		42	
Agency				
Total fertility rate (births per woman)	2.9		2.4	
Adolescent fertility rate (births per 1,000 women ages 15–19)	75		47	
Women first married by age 18 (% of women ages 20–24)	8		..	

South Sudan

Sub-Saharan Africa				Low income
Population (millions)				12
GNI, Atlas ($ billions)				11
GNI per capita, Atlas ($)				940
Population living below $1.90 a day (%)				..

	2000		2013	
	Female	Male	Female	Male
Education				
Net primary enrollment rate (%)	..	..	34	48
Net secondary enrollment rate (%)	..	..	..	..
Gross tertiary enrollment ratio (% of relevant age group)	..	..	..	..
Primary completion rate (% of relevant age group)	..	..	27	47
Progression to secondary school (%)	..	..	..	..
Lower secondary completion rate (% of relevant age group)	..	..	12	22
Gross tertiary graduation ratio (%)	..	..	..	..
Female share of graduates in eng., manf. and constr. (%, tertiary)			..	
Youth literacy rate (% of population ages 15–24)	..	..	..	..
Health and related services				
Sex ratio at birth (male births per female births)	1.04		1.04	
Under-five mortality rate (per 1,000 live births)	174	190	87	98
Life expectancy at birth (years)	50	48	56	54
Pregnant women receiving prenatal care (%)	..		40	
Births attended by skilled health staff (% of total)	..		19	
Maternal mortality ratio (per 100,000 live births)	1,200		730	
Women's share of population ages 15+ living with HIV (%)	58		58	
Prevalence of HIV (% ages 15–24)	1.4	0.7	1.3	0.7
Economic structure, participation, and access to resources				
Labor force participation rate (% of population ages 15+)	..	..	..	..
Labor force participation rate (% of ages 15–24)	..	..	..	..
Wage and salaried workers (% of employed ages 15+)	..	..	..	..
Self-employed workers (% of employed ages 15+)	..	..	..	..
Unpaid family workers (% of employed ages 15+)	..	..	..	..
Employment in agriculture (% of employed ages 15+)	..	..	..	..
Employment in industry (% of employed ages 15+)	..	..	..	..
Employment in services (% of employed ages 15+)	..	..	..	..
Women in wage employment in the nonagricultural sector (%)	..		..	
Women's share of part-time employment (% of total)	..		..	
Maternity leave (days paid)	..		56	
Maternity leave benefits (% of wages paid)	..		100	
Employment to population ratio (% ages 15+)	..	..	..	..
Employment to population ratio (% ages 15–24)	..	..	..	..
Firms with female participation in ownership (%)	..		22[a]	
Firms with a female top manager (%)	..		9[a]	
Children in employment (% of children ages 7–14)	..	..	..	..
Unemployment rate (% of labor force ages 15+)	..	..	..	..
Unemployment rate (% of labor force ages 15–24)	..	..	..	..
Internet users (%)	..	..	..	..
Account at a financial institution (% age 15+)	..	..	..	..
Mobile account (% age 15+)	..	..	..	..
Saved any money last year (% age 15+)	..	..	..	..
Public life and decision making				
Seats held by women in national parliament (%)	..		27	
Female legislators, senior officials and managers (% of total)	..		..	
Proportion of women in ministerial level positions (%)	..		23	
Agency				
Total fertility rate (births per woman)	6.1		4.9	
Adolescent fertility rate (births per 1,000 women ages 15–19)	124		68	
Women first married by age 18 (% of women ages 20–24)	..		52	

Spain

	High income
Population (millions)	46
GNI, Atlas ($ billions)	1,396
GNI per capita, Atlas ($)	29,940
Population living below $1.90 a day (%)	..

	2000		2013	
	Female	Male	Female	Male
Education				
Net primary enrollment rate (%)	100	100	99	98
Net secondary enrollment rate (%)	91	88	97	95
Gross tertiary enrollment ratio (% of relevant age group)	64	54	95	78
Primary completion rate (% of relevant age group)	..	..	99	99
Progression to secondary school (%)	..	..	..	..
Lower secondary completion rate (% of relevant age group)	..	..	86	76
Gross tertiary graduation ratio (%)	39	26	53	37
Female share of graduates in eng., manf. and constr. (%, tertiary)	24		27	
Youth literacy rate (% of population ages 15–24)	..	..	100	100
Health and related services				
Sex ratio at birth (male births per female births)	1.06		1.06	
Under-five mortality rate (per 1,000 live births)	6	7	4	4
Life expectancy at birth (years)	83	76	86	80
Pregnant women receiving prenatal care (%)	..		..	
Births attended by skilled health staff (% of total)	..		..	
Maternal mortality ratio (per 100,000 live births)	5		4	
Women's share of population ages 15+ living with HIV (%)	..		..	
Prevalence of HIV (% ages 15–24)	..	..	..	..
Economic structure, participation, and access to resources				
Labor force participation rate (% of population ages 15+)	41	66	53	66
Labor force participation rate (% of ages 15–24)	41	51	35	38
Wage and salaried workers (% of employed ages 15+)	83	78	87	78
Self-employed workers (% of employed ages 15+)	17	22	13	22
Unpaid family workers (% of employed ages 15+)	3.7	1.2	0.8	0.6
Employment in agriculture (% of employed ages 15+)	5	8	3	6
Employment in industry (% of employed ages 15+)	15	40	9	31
Employment in services (% of employed ages 15+)	81	52	89	64
Women in wage employment in the nonagricultural sector (%)	39		47	
Women's share of part-time employment (% of total)	79		76	
Maternity leave (days paid)	..		112	
Maternity leave benefits (% of wages paid)	..		100	
Employment to population ratio (% ages 15+)	32	60	38	49
Employment to population ratio (% ages 15–24)	27	40	15	16
Firms with female participation in ownership (%)	..		..	
Firms with a female top manager (%)	..		..	
Children in employment (% of children ages 7–14)	..	..	..	..
Unemployment rate (% of labor force ages 15+)	21	10	27	26
Unemployment rate (% of labor force ages 15–24)	34	20	57	58
Internet users (%)	..	..	70	74
Account at a financial institution (% age 15+)	..	..	98	98
Mobile account (% age 15+)	..	..	..	..
Saved any money last year (% age 15+)	..	..	59	75
Public life and decision making				
Seats held by women in national parliament (%)	..		41	
Female legislators, senior officials and managers (% of total)	32		30	
Proportion of women in ministerial level positions (%)	..		31	
Agency				
Total fertility rate (births per woman)	1.2		1.3	
Adolescent fertility rate (births per 1,000 women ages 15–19)	9		9	
Women first married by age 18 (% of women ages 20–24)	..		..	

Sri Lanka

South Asia　　　　　　　　　　　　　**Lower middle income**

Population (millions)	21
GNI, Atlas ($ billions)	70
GNI per capita, Atlas ($)	3,400
Population living below $1.90 a day (%)	<2

	2000 Female	2000 Male	2013 Female	2013 Male
Education				
Net primary enrollment rate (%)	100	100	94	94
Net secondary enrollment rate (%)	..	..	87	83
Gross tertiary enrollment ratio (% of relevant age group)	..	..	23	14
Primary completion rate (% of relevant age group)	106	107	97	98
Progression to secondary school (%)	99	98	100	99
Lower secondary completion rate (% of relevant age group)	91	87	97	93
Gross tertiary graduation ratio (%)	2	2	9	6
Female share of graduates in eng., manf. and constr. (%, tertiary)	..		22	
Youth literacy rate (% of population ages 15-24)	96	95	99	98
Health and related services				
Sex ratio at birth (male births per female births)	1.05		1.04	
Under-five mortality rate (per 1,000 live births)	15	18	9	11
Life expectancy at birth (years)	75	68	77	71
Pregnant women receiving prenatal care (%)	95		..	
Births attended by skilled health staff (% of total)	96		..	
Maternal mortality ratio (per 100,000 live births)	55		29	
Women's share of population ages 15+ living with HIV (%)	28		32	
Prevalence of HIV (% ages 15-24)	0.1	0.1	0.1	0.1
Economic structure, participation, and access to resources				
Labor force participation rate (% of population ages 15+)	37	77	35	76
Labor force participation rate (% of ages 15-24)	31	57	26	49
Wage and salaried workers (% of employed ages 15+)	56	57	51	55
Self-employed workers (% of employed ages 15+)	45	43	49	45
Unpaid family workers (% of employed ages 15+)	26.5	6.5	22.7	3.5
Employment in agriculture (% of employed ages 15+)	40	32	35	42
Employment in industry (% of employed ages 15+)	24	22	25	14
Employment in services (% of employed ages 15+)	25	28	29	28
Women in wage employment in the nonagricultural sector (%)	32		32	
Women's share of part-time employment (% of total)	..		..	
Maternity leave (days paid)			84	
Maternity leave benefits (% of wages paid)	..		100	
Employment to population ratio (% ages 15+)	33	73	33	74
Employment to population ratio (% ages 15-24)	21	46	20	42
Firms with female participation in ownership (%)	..		26	
Firms with a female top manager (%)	..		9	
Children in employment (% of children ages 7-14)	13	20	..	..
Unemployment rate (% of labor force ages 15+)	12	6	7	3
Unemployment rate (% of labor force ages 15-24)	31	20	24	14
Internet users (%)	..	..	..	..
Account at a financial institution (% age 15+)	..	..	83	82
Mobile account (% age 15+)	..	..	0.0	0.1
Saved any money last year (% age 15+)	..	..	43	48
Public life and decision making				
Seats held by women in national parliament (%)	..		6	
Female legislators, senior officials and managers (% of total)	22		28	
Proportion of women in ministerial level positions (%)	..		7	
Agency				
Total fertility rate (births per woman)	2.2		2.3	
Adolescent fertility rate (births per 1,000 women ages 15-19)	28		15	
Women first married by age 18 (% of women ages 20-24)				

St. Kitts and Nevis

High income

Population (thousands)	55
GNI, Atlas ($ millions)	796
GNI per capita, Atlas ($)	14,490
Population living below $1.90 a day (%)	..

	2000 Female	2000 Male	2013 Female	2013 Male
Education				
Net primary enrollment rate (%)	..	..	81	78
Net secondary enrollment rate (%)	99	93	88	82
Gross tertiary enrollment ratio (% of relevant age group)	..	..	..	..
Primary completion rate (% of relevant age group)	110	97	93	86
Progression to secondary school (%)	96	89	..	..
Lower secondary completion rate (% of relevant age group)	106	100	97	91
Gross tertiary graduation ratio (%)	..	..	..	
Female share of graduates in eng., manf. and constr. (%, tertiary)	..		..	
Youth literacy rate (% of population ages 15–24)	..	..	..	..
Health and related services				
Sex ratio at birth (male births per female births)	..		..	
Under-five mortality rate (per 1,000 live births)	17	20	10	11
Life expectancy at birth (years)	74	69	..	..
Pregnant women receiving prenatal care (%)	78		..	
Births attended by skilled health staff (% of total)	99		100	
Maternal mortality ratio (per 100,000 live births)	..		..	
Women's share of population ages 15+ living with HIV (%)	..		..	
Prevalence of HIV (% ages 15–24)	..	..	..	..
Economic structure, participation, and access to resources				
Labor force participation rate (% of population ages 15+)	..	..		..
Labor force participation rate (% of ages 15–24)	..	..		..
Wage and salaried workers (% of employed ages 15+)	89	82	..	..
Self-employed workers (% of employed ages 15+)	9	15	..	..
Unpaid family workers (% of employed ages 15+)	0.8	0.5	..	..
Employment in agriculture (% of employed ages 15+)	0	0	..	..
Employment in industry (% of employed ages 15+)	45	52	..	..
Employment in services (% of employed ages 15+)	51	35	..	..
Women in wage employment in the nonagricultural sector (%)	..		..	
Women's share of part-time employment (% of total)	..		..	
Maternity leave (days paid)	..		91	
Maternity leave benefits (% of wages paid)	..		65	
Employment to population ratio (% ages 15+)	..	..	..	..
Employment to population ratio (% ages 15–24)	..	..	..	..
Firms with female participation in ownership (%)	..		58	
Firms with a female top manager (%)	..		21	
Children in employment (% of children ages 7–14)	..	..	..	..
Unemployment rate (% of labor force ages 15+)	..	..	..	..
Unemployment rate (% of labor force ages 15–24)	..	..	..	..
Internet users (%)	..	..	..	..
Account at a financial institution (% age 15+)	..	..	..	..
Mobile account (% age 15+)	..	..	..	..
Saved any money last year (% age 15+)	..	..	..	..
Public life and decision making				
Seats held by women in national parliament (%)	..		13	
Female legislators, senior officials and managers (% of total)	..		..	
Proportion of women in ministerial level positions (%)	..		13	
Agency				
Total fertility rate (births per woman)	2.1		..	
Adolescent fertility rate (births per 1,000 women ages 15–19)	..		..	
Women first married by age 18 (% of women ages 20–24)	..		..	

St. Lucia

Latin America & the Caribbean	Upper middle income
Population (thousands)	184
GNI, Atlas ($ billions)	1.3
GNI per capita, Atlas ($)	7,080
Population living below $1.90 a day (%)	..

	2000		2013	
	Female	**Male**	**Female**	**Male**
Education				
Net primary enrollment rate (%)	87	91	..	..
Net secondary enrollment rate (%)	70	55	81	80
Gross tertiary enrollment ratio (% of relevant age group)	..	..	19	9
Primary completion rate (% of relevant age group)	106	104	..	..
Progression to secondary school (%)	78	59	95	93
Lower secondary completion rate (% of relevant age group)	92	70	81	90
Gross tertiary graduation ratio (%)	..	..	..	..
Female share of graduates in eng., manf. and constr. (%, tertiary)	..		..	
Youth literacy rate (% of population ages 15–24)	..	..	..	..
Health and related services				
Sex ratio at birth (male births per female births)	1.03		1.03	
Under-five mortality rate (per 1,000 live births)	16	20	13	16
Life expectancy at birth (years)	73	70	78	72
Pregnant women receiving prenatal care (%)	48		97	
Births attended by skilled health staff (% of total)	100		99	
Maternal mortality ratio (per 100,000 live births)	44		34	
Women's share of population ages 15+ living with HIV (%)	..		..	
Prevalence of HIV (% ages 15–24)	..	..	..	..
Economic structure, participation, and access to resources				
Labor force participation rate (% of population ages 15+)	62	76	63	76
Labor force participation rate (% of ages 15–24)	54	62	50	59
Wage and salaried workers (% of employed ages 15+)	71	59	..	..
Self-employed workers (% of employed ages 15+)	28	39	..	..
Unpaid family workers (% of employed ages 15+)	1.4	0.5	..	..
Employment in agriculture (% of employed ages 15+)	14	26	..	..
Employment in industry (% of employed ages 15+)	15	25	..	..
Employment in services (% of employed ages 15+)	70	47	..	..
Women in wage employment in the nonagricultural sector (%)	49		..	
Women's share of part-time employment (% of total)	..		..	
Maternity leave (days paid)			91	
Maternity leave benefits (% of wages paid)			65	
Employment to population ratio (% ages 15+)	..		..	
Employment to population ratio (% ages 15–24)	..	..	..	..
Firms with female participation in ownership (%)			32	
Firms with a female top manager (%)			24	
Children in employment (% of children ages 7–14)	..	..	..	..
Unemployment rate (% of labor force ages 15+)	..	..	..	..
Unemployment rate (% of labor force ages 15–24)	..	..	..	..
Internet users (%)	..	..	..	..
Account at a financial institution (% age 15+)	..	..	..	..
Mobile account (% age 15+)	..	..	..	..
Saved any money last year (% age 15+)	..	..	..	..
Public life and decision making				
Seats held by women in national parliament (%)	..		17	
Female legislators, senior officials and managers (% of total)	55		..	
Proportion of women in ministerial level positions (%)	..		15	
Agency				
Total fertility rate (births per woman)	2.3		1.9	
Adolescent fertility rate (births per 1,000 women ages 15–19)	65		54	
Women first married by age 18 (% of women ages 20–24)	..		8	

St. Martin (French part)

	High income
Population (thousands)	32
GNI, Atlas ($ millions)	..
GNI per capita, Atlas ($)	..
Population living below $1.90 a day (%)	..

	2000		2013	
	Female	**Male**	**Female**	**Male**
Education				
Net primary enrollment rate (%)	..	..	..	..
Net secondary enrollment rate (%)	..	..	..	..
Gross tertiary enrollment ratio (% of relevant age group)	..	..	..	..
Primary completion rate (% of relevant age group)	..	..	..	..
Progression to secondary school (%)	..	..	..	..
Lower secondary completion rate (% of relevant age group)	..	..	..	..
Gross tertiary graduation ratio (%)	..	..	..	..
Female share of graduates in eng., manf. and constr. (%, tertiary)	..		..	
Youth literacy rate (% of population ages 15–24)	..	..	..	..
Health and related services				
Sex ratio at birth (male births per female births)		..		..
Under-five mortality rate (per 1,000 live births)	..	..	..	..
Life expectancy at birth (years)	80	74	83	76
Pregnant women receiving prenatal care (%)	..		..	
Births attended by skilled health staff (% of total)	..		..	
Maternal mortality ratio (per 100,000 live births)	..		..	
Women's share of population ages 15+ living with HIV (%)	..		..	
Prevalence of HIV (% ages 15–24)	..	..	..	..
Economic structure, participation, and access to resources				
Labor force participation rate (% of population ages 15+)	..	..	..	..
Labor force participation rate (% of ages 15–24)	..	..	..	..
Wage and salaried workers (% of employed ages 15+)	..	..	..	..
Self-employed workers (% of employed ages 15+)	..	..	..	..
Unpaid family workers (% of employed ages 15+)	..	..	..	..
Employment in agriculture (% of employed ages 15+)	..	..	..	..
Employment in industry (% of employed ages 15+)	..	..	..	..
Employment in services (% of employed ages 15+)	..	..	..	..
Women in wage employment in the nonagricultural sector (%)	..		..	
Women's share of part-time employment (% of total)	..		..	
Maternity leave (days paid)	..		..	
Maternity leave benefits (% of wages paid)	..		..	
Employment to population ratio (% ages 15+)	..	..	..	..
Employment to population ratio (% ages 15–24)	..	..	..	..
Firms with female participation in ownership (%)	..		..	
Firms with a female top manager (%)	..		..	
Children in employment (% of children ages 7–14)	..	..	..	..
Unemployment rate (% of labor force ages 15+)	..	..	..	..
Unemployment rate (% of labor force ages 15–24)	..	..	..	..
Internet users (%)	..	..	..	..
Account at a financial institution (% age 15+)	..	..	..	..
Mobile account (% age 15+)	..	..	..	..
Saved any money last year (% age 15+)	..	..	..	..
Public life and decision making				
Seats held by women in national parliament (%)	..		..	
Female legislators, senior officials and managers (% of total)	..		..	
Proportion of women in ministerial level positions (%)	..		..	
Agency				
Total fertility rate (births per woman)	1.8		1.8	
Adolescent fertility rate (births per 1,000 women ages 15–19)	..		..	
Women first married by age 18 (% of women ages 20–24)	..		..	

St. Vincent and the Grenadines

Latin America & the Caribbean　　　　　　**Upper middle income**

Population (thousands)	109
GNI, Atlas ($ millions)	717
GNI per capita, Atlas ($)	6,560
Population living below $1.90 a day (%)	..

	2000		2013	
	Female	**Male**	**Female**	**Male**
Education				
Net primary enrollment rate (%)	..	..	90	93
Net secondary enrollment rate (%)	78	58	87	84
Gross tertiary enrollment ratio (% of relevant age group)	..	..	..	..
Primary completion rate (% of relevant age group)	..	..	104	111
Progression to secondary school (%)	..	..	100	100
Lower secondary completion rate (% of relevant age group)	..	..	91	90
Gross tertiary graduation ratio (%)	..	..	..	..
Female share of graduates in eng., manf. and constr. (%, tertiary)	..		..	
Youth literacy rate (% of population ages 15–24)	..	..	..	..
Health and related services				
Sex ratio at birth (male births per female births)	1.03		1.03	
Under-five mortality rate (per 1,000 live births)	20	24	17	20
Life expectancy at birth (years)	73	68	75	70
Pregnant women receiving prenatal care (%)	99		..	
Births attended by skilled health staff (% of total)	100		99	
Maternal mortality ratio (per 100,000 live births)	75		45	
Women's share of population ages 15+ living with HIV (%)	..		..	
Prevalence of HIV (% ages 15–24)	..	..	..	..
Economic structure, participation, and access to resources				
Labor force participation rate (% of population ages 15+)	50	80	56	78
Labor force participation rate (% of ages 15–24)	43	68	43	61
Wage and salaried workers (% of employed ages 15+)	..	..	..	..
Self-employed workers (% of employed ages 15+)	..	..	..	..
Unpaid family workers (% of employed ages 15+)	..	..	..	..
Employment in agriculture (% of employed ages 15+)	8	20	..	..
Employment in industry (% of employed ages 15+)	8	27	..	..
Employment in services (% of employed ages 15+)	80	48	..	..
Women in wage employment in the nonagricultural sector (%)	..		..	
Women's share of part-time employment (% of total)	41		..	
Maternity leave (days paid)			91	
Maternity leave benefits (% of wages paid)	..		65	
Employment to population ratio (% ages 15+)	..	..	..	..
Employment to population ratio (% ages 15–24)	..	..	..	..
Firms with female participation in ownership (%)	..		76	
Firms with a female top manager (%)	..		39	
Children in employment (% of children ages 7–14)	..	..	..	..
Unemployment rate (% of labor force ages 15+)	..	..	..	..
Unemployment rate (% of labor force ages 15–24)	..	..	..	..
Internet users (%)	..	..	..	..
Account at a financial institution (% age 15+)	..	..	..	..
Mobile account (% age 15+)	..	..	..	..
Saved any money last year (% age 15+)	..	..	..	..
Public life and decision making				
Seats held by women in national parliament (%)	..		13	
Female legislators, senior officials and managers (% of total)	50		..	
Proportion of women in ministerial level positions (%)	..		9	
Agency				
Total fertility rate (births per woman)	2.4		2.0	
Adolescent fertility rate (births per 1,000 women ages 15–19)	69		52	
Women first married by age 18 (% of women ages 20–24)	..		..	

Sudan

| Sub-Saharan Africa | | | Lower middle income | |

Population (millions)		39
GNI, Atlas ($ billions)		67
GNI per capita, Atlas ($)		1,710
Population living below $1.90 a day (%)		..

	2000		2013	
	Female	Male	Female	Male
Education				
Net primary enrollment rate (%)	..	..	56	53
Net secondary enrollment rate (%)	..	..	..	..
Gross tertiary enrollment ratio (% of relevant age group)	7[b]	6[b]	18	16
Primary completion rate (% of relevant age group)	..	..	53	61
Progression to secondary school (%)	..	..	94	94
Lower secondary completion rate (% of relevant age group)	..	..	43	50
Gross tertiary graduation ratio (%)	..	..	11	9
Female share of graduates in eng., manf. and constr. (%, tertiary)			32	
Youth literacy rate (% of population ages 15–24)	72[b]	86[b]	86	91
Health and related services				
Sex ratio at birth (male births per female births)	1.04[b]		1.04	
Under-five mortality rate (per 1,000 live births)	100[b]	112[b]	65	75
Life expectancy at birth (years)	60[b]	56[b]	64	60
Pregnant women receiving prenatal care (%)	60		74	
Births attended by skilled health staff (% of total)	..		23	
Maternal mortality ratio (per 100,000 live births)	540[b]		360	
Women's share of population ages 15+ living with HIV (%)	52[b]		47	
Prevalence of HIV (% ages 15–24)	0.1[b]	0.1[b]	0.2	0.1
Economic structure, participation, and access to resources				
Labor force participation rate (% of population ages 15+)	29	75	31	76
Labor force participation rate (% of ages 15–24)	27	45	27	43
Wage and salaried workers (% of employed ages 15+)	..	..	..	..
Self-employed workers (% of employed ages 15+)	..	..	..	..
Unpaid family workers (% of employed ages 15+)	..	..	..	..
Employment in agriculture (% of employed ages 15+)	..	..	..	..
Employment in industry (% of employed ages 15+)	..	..	..	..
Employment in services (% of employed ages 15+)	..	..	..	..
Women in wage employment in the nonagricultural sector (%)	..		..	
Women's share of part-time employment (% of total)	..		..	
Maternity leave (days paid)	..		56	
Maternity leave benefits (% of wages paid)	..		100	
Employment to population ratio (% ages 15+)	23	65	25	66
Employment to population ratio (% ages 15–24)	20	35	20	34
Firms with female participation in ownership (%)	..		8[a]	
Firms with a female top manager (%)	..		3[a]	
Children in employment (% of children ages 7–14)	17[b]	21[b]	..	..
Unemployment rate (% of labor force ages 15+)	21	13	20	13
Unemployment rate (% of labor force ages 15–24)	27	22	28	23
Internet users (%)	..	..	..	..
Account at a financial institution (% age 15+)	..	..	10	20
Mobile account (% age 15+)	..	..	..	..
Saved any money last year (% age 15+)	..	..	41	41
Public life and decision making				
Seats held by women in national parliament (%)	..		31	
Female legislators, senior officials and managers (% of total)	..		..	
Proportion of women in ministerial level positions (%)	..		15	
Agency				
Total fertility rate (births per woman)	5.4[b]		4.4	
Adolescent fertility rate (births per 1,000 women ages 15–19)	116[b]		76	
Women first married by age 18 (% of women ages 20–24)	..		33	

Suriname

Latin America & the Caribbean **Upper middle income**

Population (thousands)	538
GNI, Atlas ($ billions)	5
GNI per capita, Atlas ($)	*9,470*
Population living below $1.90 a day (%)	..

	2000		2013	
	Female	**Male**	**Female**	**Male**
Education				
Net primary enrollment rate (%)	..	..	81	80
Net secondary enrollment rate (%)	..	..	57	48
Gross tertiary enrollment ratio (% of relevant age group)	*15*	*9*	..	..
Primary completion rate (% of relevant age group)	..	..	91	79
Progression to secondary school (%)	..	..	..	..
Lower secondary completion rate (% of relevant age group)	..	..	57	31
Gross tertiary graduation ratio (%)	..	..	..	..
Female share of graduates in eng., manf. and constr. (%, tertiary)	..		..	
Youth literacy rate (% of population ages 15–24)	..	..	99	98
Health and related services				
Sex ratio at birth (male births per female births)	*1.08*		*1.07*	
Under-five mortality rate (per 1,000 live births)	30	38	19	24
Life expectancy at birth (years)	71	65	74	68
Pregnant women receiving prenatal care (%)	91		*91*	
Births attended by skilled health staff (% of total)	85		91	
Maternal mortality ratio (per 100,000 live births)	120		130	
Women's share of population ages 15+ living with HIV (%)	43		46	
Prevalence of HIV (% ages 15–24)	0.8	0.7	0.5	0.3
Economic structure, participation, and access to resources				
Labor force participation rate (% of population ages 15+)	36	66	41	69
Labor force participation rate (% of ages 15–24)	14	39	17	39
Wage and salaried workers (% of employed ages 15+)	*87*	*78*	..	..
Self-employed workers (% of employed ages 15+)	*11*	*21*	..	..
Unpaid family workers (% of employed ages 15+)	*1.6*	*0.9*	..	..
Employment in agriculture (% of employed ages 15+)	*2*	*8*	..	..
Employment in industry (% of employed ages 15+)	*1*	*22*	..	..
Employment in services (% of employed ages 15+)	*97*	*64*	..	..
Women in wage employment in the nonagricultural sector (%)	*38*		..	
Women's share of part-time employment (% of total)	*59*		..	
Maternity leave (days paid)	..		*0*	
Maternity leave benefits (% of wages paid)	..		..	
Employment to population ratio (% ages 15+)	29	59	36	65
Employment to population ratio (% ages 15–24)	7	26	12	32
Firms with female participation in ownership (%)	..		*18*	
Firms with a female top manager (%)	..		*15*	
Children in employment (% of children ages 7–14)	..	..	..	..
Unemployment rate (% of labor force ages 15+)	21	12	11	6
Unemployment rate (% of labor force ages 15–24)	52	34	31	19
Internet users (%)	..	..	..	..
Account at a financial institution (% age 15+)	..	..	..	..
Mobile account (% age 15+)	..	..	..	..
Saved any money last year (% age 15+)	..	..	..	..
Public life and decision making				
Seats held by women in national parliament (%)	..		*12*[a]	
Female legislators, senior officials and managers (% of total)	..		36	
Proportion of women in ministerial level positions (%)	..		6	
Agency				
Total fertility rate (births per woman)	2.7		2.3	
Adolescent fertility rate (births per 1,000 women ages 15–19)	57		47	
Women first married by age 18 (% of women ages 20–24)	..		*19*	

Swaziland

Sub-Saharan Africa		Lower middle income

Population (millions)	1.3
GNI, Atlas ($ billions)	3
GNI per capita, Atlas ($)	2,700
Population living below $1.90 a day (%)	..

	2000		2013	
	Female	Male	Female	Male
Education				
Net primary enrollment rate (%)	73	71	..	..
Net secondary enrollment rate (%)	32	27	39	32
Gross tertiary enrollment ratio (% of relevant age group)	4	5	5	5
Primary completion rate (% of relevant age group)	63	59	79	76
Progression to secondary school (%)	87	84	96	97
Lower secondary completion rate (% of relevant age group)	32	33	45	47
Gross tertiary graduation ratio (%)	5	5	7	10
Female share of graduates in eng., manf. and constr. (%, tertiary)	33		15	
Youth literacy rate (% of population ages 15-24)	93	91	95	92
Health and related services				
Sex ratio at birth (male births per female births)	1.03		1.03	
Under-five mortality rate (per 1,000 live births)	121	135	56	65
Life expectancy at birth (years)	49	48	48	50
Pregnant women receiving prenatal care (%)	87		97	
Births attended by skilled health staff (% of total)	70		82	
Maternal mortality ratio (per 100,000 live births)	520		310	
Women's share of population ages 15+ living with HIV (%)	58		59	
Prevalence of HIV (% ages 15-24)	22.5	8.3	15.5	7.2
Economic structure, participation, and access to resources				
Labor force participation rate (% of population ages 15+)	43	72	44	72
Labor force participation rate (% of ages 15-24)	38	53	37	52
Wage and salaried workers (% of employed ages 15+)	..	..	..	..
Self-employed workers (% of employed ages 15+)	..	..	..	..
Unpaid family workers (% of employed ages 15+)	..	..	..	..
Employment in agriculture (% of employed ages 15+)	..	..	..	..
Employment in industry (% of employed ages 15+)	..	..	..	..
Employment in services (% of employed ages 15+)	..	..	..	..
Women in wage employment in the nonagricultural sector (%)	..		..	
Women's share of part-time employment (% of total)	..		..	
Maternity leave (days paid)			14	
Maternity leave benefits (% of wages paid)	..		100	
Employment to population ratio (% ages 15+)	32	57	33	57
Employment to population ratio (% ages 15-24)	21	32	20	31
Firms with female participation in ownership (%)	..		..	
Firms with a female top manager (%)	..		..	
Children in employment (% of children ages 7-14)	11	11	12	15
Unemployment rate (% of labor force ages 15+)	26	21	26	21
Unemployment rate (% of labor force ages 15-24)	46	39	46	40
Internet users (%)	..		..	..
Account at a financial institution (% age 15+)	..	..	27	30
Mobile account (% age 15+)	..	..	..	..
Saved any money last year (% age 15+)	..	..	..	..
Public life and decision making				
Seats held by women in national parliament (%)	..		6	
Female legislators, senior officials and managers (% of total)	..		..	
Proportion of women in ministerial level positions (%)	..		26	
Agency				
Total fertility rate (births per woman)	4.2		3.3	
Adolescent fertility rate (births per 1,000 women ages 15-19)	105		74	
Women first married by age 18 (% of women ages 20-24)	..		7	

Sweden

			High income
Population (millions)			10
GNI, Atlas ($ billions)			597
GNI per capita, Atlas ($)			61,600
Population living below $1.90 a day (%)			..

	2000		2013	
	Female	Male	Female	Male
Education				
Net primary enrollment rate (%)	99	100	99	99
Net secondary enrollment rate (%)	97	94	94	95
Gross tertiary enrollment ratio (% of relevant age group)	80	55	79	51
Primary completion rate (% of relevant age group)	100	99	101	102
Progression to secondary school (%)	100	100	*100*	*100*
Lower secondary completion rate (% of relevant age group)	..	..	97	98
Gross tertiary graduation ratio (%)	40	25	45	*23*
Female share of graduates in eng., manf. and constr. (%, tertiary)	25		29	
Youth literacy rate (% of population ages 15–24)	..	..	..	..
Health and related services				
Sex ratio at birth (male births per female births)	*1.06*		*1.06*	
Under-five mortality rate (per 1,000 live births)	4	5	3	3
Life expectancy at birth (years)	82	77	84	80
Pregnant women receiving prenatal care (%)	..		..	
Births attended by skilled health staff (% of total)	..		..	
Maternal mortality ratio (per 100,000 live births)	5		4	
Women's share of population ages 15+ living with HIV (%)	..		..	
Prevalence of HIV (% ages 15–24)	0.1	0.1	0.1	0.1
Economic structure, participation, and access to resources				
Labor force participation rate (% of population ages 15+)	58	68	60	68
Labor force participation rate (% of population ages 15–24)	49	52	55	54
Wage and salaried workers (% of employed ages 15+)	94	84	94	85
Self-employed workers (% of employed ages 15+)	6	16	6	15
Unpaid family workers (% of employed ages 15+)	0.3	0.7	0.2	0.2
Employment in agriculture (% of employed ages 15+)	1	4	*1*	*3*
Employment in industry (% of employed ages 15+)	11	37	*8*	*30*
Employment in services (% of employed ages 15+)	87	60	*91*	*66*
Women in wage employment in the nonagricultural sector (%)	51		50	
Women's share of part-time employment (% of total)	73		62	
Maternity leave (days paid)[c]	..		..	
Maternity leave benefits (% of wages paid)	..		..	
Employment to population ratio (% ages 15+)	55	64	56	62
Employment to population ratio (% ages 15–24)	43	46	43	40
Firms with female participation in ownership (%)	..		53[a]	
Firms with a female top manager (%)	..		13[a]	
Children in employment (% of children ages 7–14)	..	..	..	..
Unemployment rate (% of labor force ages 15+)	6	6	8	8
Unemployment rate (% of labor force ages 15–24)	12	12	23	25
Internet users (%)	..	..	95	95
Account at a financial institution (% age 15+)	..	..	100	100
Mobile account (% age 15+)	..	..	..	..
Saved any money last year (% age 15+)	..	..	84	85
Public life and decision making				
Seats held by women in national parliament (%)	..		44	
Female legislators, senior officials and managers (% of total)	31		35	
Proportion of women in ministerial level positions (%)	..		52	
Agency				
Total fertility rate (births per woman)	1.5		1.9	
Adolescent fertility rate (births per 1,000 women ages 15–19)	7		6	
Women first married by age 18 (% of women ages 20–24)	..		..	

Switzerland

	High income
Population (millions)	8
GNI, Atlas ($ billions)	733
GNI per capita, Atlas ($)	90,670
Population living below $1.90 a day (%)	..

	2000 Female	2000 Male	2013 Female	2013 Male
Education				
Net primary enrollment rate (%)	96	96	93	93
Net secondary enrollment rate (%)	82	87	80	82
Gross tertiary enrollment ratio (% of relevant age group)	32	43	56	57
Primary completion rate (% of relevant age group)	98	95	98	95
Progression to secondary school (%)	100	100	100	100
Lower secondary completion rate (% of relevant age group)	101	93	98	94
Gross tertiary graduation ratio (%)	19	27	48	50
Female share of graduates in eng., manf. and constr. (%, tertiary)	8		14	
Youth literacy rate (% of population ages 15–24)	..	..	..	..
Health and related services				
Sex ratio at birth (male births per female births)	1.05		1.05	
Under-five mortality rate (per 1,000 live births)	5	6	4	4
Life expectancy at birth (years)	83	77	85	81
Pregnant women receiving prenatal care (%)	..		..	
Births attended by skilled health staff (% of total)	..		..	
Maternal mortality ratio (per 100,000 live births)	7		6	
Women's share of population ages 15+ living with HIV (%)	..		..	
Prevalence of HIV (% ages 15–24)	..	..	..	..
Economic structure, participation, and access to resources				
Labor force participation rate (% of population ages 15+)	58	78	62	75
Labor force participation rate (% of ages 15–24)	66	70	67	68
Wage and salaried workers (% of employed ages 15+)	85	80	87	83
Self-employed workers (% of employed ages 15+)	15	20	13	17
Unpaid family workers (% of employed ages 15+)	3.6	1.7	2.6	1.7
Employment in agriculture (% of employed ages 15+)	4	5	3	4
Employment in industry (% of employed ages 15+)	13	36	10	29
Employment in services (% of employed ages 15+)	83	59	83	63
Women in wage employment in the nonagricultural sector (%)	46		48	
Women's share of part-time employment (% of total)	81		80	
Maternity leave (days paid)	..		98	
Maternity leave benefits (% of wages paid)	..		59	
Employment to population ratio (% ages 15+)	56	76	59	72
Employment to population ratio (% ages 15–24)	63	66	61	62
Firms with female participation in ownership (%)	..		..	
Firms with a female top manager (%)	..		..	
Children in employment (% of children ages 7–14)	..	..	..	..
Unemployment rate (% of labor force ages 15+)	3	2	5	4
Unemployment rate (% of labor force ages 15–24)	4	6	9	9
Internet users (%)	..	..	82	90
Account at a financial institution (% age 15+)	..	..	97	99
Mobile account (% age 15+)	..	..	..	..
Saved any money last year (% age 15+)	..	..	75	77
Public life and decision making				
Seats held by women in national parliament (%)	..		31	
Female legislators, senior officials and managers (% of total)	23		33	
Proportion of women in ministerial level positions (%)	..		43	
Agency				
Total fertility rate (births per woman)	1.5		1.5	
Adolescent fertility rate (births per 1,000 women ages 15–19)	5		3	
Women first married by age 18 (% of women ages 20–24)	..		..	

Syrian Arab Republic

Middle East & North Africa	Lower middle income
Population (millions)	22
GNI, Atlas ($ billions)	..
GNI per capita, Atlas ($)	..
Population living below $1.90 a day (%)	

	2000 Female	2000 Male	2013 Female	2013 Male
Education				
Net primary enrollment rate (%)	..	..	61	62
Net secondary enrollment rate (%)	38	41	44	44
Gross tertiary enrollment ratio (% of relevant age group)	11	13	31	31
Primary completion rate (% of relevant age group)	88	95	64	64
Progression to secondary school (%)	71	75	57	57
Lower secondary completion rate (% of relevant age group)	46	49	50	49
Gross tertiary graduation ratio (%)	4	5	12	12
Female share of graduates in eng., manf. and constr. (%, tertiary)	..		36	
Youth literacy rate (% of population ages 15–24)	93	97	95	97
Health and related services				
Sex ratio at birth (male births per female births)	1.05		1.05	
Under-five mortality rate (per 1,000 live births)	21	26	12	14
Life expectancy at birth (years)	75	72	78	72
Pregnant women receiving prenatal care (%)	71		..	
Births attended by skilled health staff (% of total)	..		..	
Maternal mortality ratio (per 100,000 live births)	75		49	
Women's share of population ages 15+ living with HIV (%)	20		20	
Prevalence of HIV (% ages 15–24)	0.1	0.1	0.1	0.1
Economic structure, participation, and access to resources				
Labor force participation rate (% of population ages 15+)	20	81	14	73
Labor force participation rate (% of ages 15–24)	19	64	10	49
Wage and salaried workers (% of employed ages 15+)	47	50	83	60
Self-employed workers (% of employed ages 15+)	53	50	9	38
Unpaid family workers (% of employed ages 15+)	44.2	10.8	8.2	2.4
Employment in agriculture (% of employed ages 15+)	62	26	22	13
Employment in industry (% of employed ages 15+)	8	30	9	36
Employment in services (% of employed ages 15+)	31	43	69	51
Women in wage employment in the nonagricultural sector (%)	16		16	
Women's share of part-time employment (% of total)	..		27	
Maternity leave (days paid)	..		120	
Maternity leave benefits (% of wages paid)	..		100	
Employment to population ratio (% ages 15+)	16	75	10	67
Employment to population ratio (% ages 15–24)	12	56	3	38
Firms with female participation in ownership (%)	..		..	
Firms with a female top manager (%)	..		..	
Children in employment (% of children ages 7–14)	..	..	..	..
Unemployment rate (% of labor force ages 15+)	22	6	28	8
Unemployment rate (% of labor force ages 15–24)	38	13	66	23
Internet users (%)	..	..	..	..
Account at a financial institution (% age 15+)	..	..	20	27
Mobile account (% age 15+)	..	..	..	..
Saved any money last year (% age 15+)	..	..	..	..
Public life and decision making				
Seats held by women in national parliament (%)	..		12	
Female legislators, senior officials and managers (% of total)	..		9	
Proportion of women in ministerial level positions (%)	..		6	
Agency				
Total fertility rate (births per woman)	4.0		3.0	
Adolescent fertility rate (births per 1,000 women ages 15–19)	58		40	
Women first married by age 18 (% of women ages 20–24)	..		..	

Tajikistan

Europe & Central Asia   **Lower middle income**

Population (millions)	8
GNI, Atlas ($ billions)	9
GNI per capita, Atlas ($)	1,080
Population living below $1.90 a day (%)	..

	2000 Female	2000 Male	2013 Female	2013 Male
Education				
Net primary enrollment rate (%)	90	97	95[a]	96[a]
Net secondary enrollment rate (%)	65	76	79	88
Gross tertiary enrollment ratio (% of relevant age group)	11	25	18[a]	30[a]
Primary completion rate (% of relevant age group)	..	..	98[a]	99[a]
Progression to secondary school (%)	..	..	98	100
Lower secondary completion rate (% of relevant age group)	..	..	90[a]	97[a]
Gross tertiary graduation ratio (%)	..	..	..	..
Female share of graduates in eng., manf. and constr. (%, tertiary)		..		
Youth literacy rate (% of population ages 15–24)	100	100	100	100
Health and related services				
Sex ratio at birth (male births per female births)	1.05		1.05	
Under-five mortality rate (per 1,000 live births)	85	101	40	50
Life expectancy at birth (years)	68	60	71	64
Pregnant women receiving prenatal care (%)	71		79	
Births attended by skilled health staff (% of total)	71		87	
Maternal mortality ratio (per 100,000 live births)	89		44	
Women's share of population ages 15+ living with HIV (%)	45		39	
Prevalence of HIV (% ages 15–24)	0.1	0.1	0.1	0.1
Economic structure, participation, and access to resources				
Labor force participation rate (% of population ages 15+)	58	75	59	77
Labor force participation rate (% of ages 15–24)	40	55	39	57
Wage and salaried workers (% of employed ages 15+)	..	..	..	..
Self-employed workers (% of employed ages 15+)	..	..	..	..
Unpaid family workers (% of employed ages 15+)	..	..	..	..
Employment in agriculture (% of employed ages 15+)	..	..	..	..
Employment in industry (% of employed ages 15+)	..	..	..	..
Employment in services (% of employed ages 15+)	..	..	..	..
Women in wage employment in the nonagricultural sector (%)	23		..	
Women's share of part-time employment (% of total)	..			
Maternity leave (days paid)	..		140	
Maternity leave benefits (% of wages paid)	..		100	
Employment to population ratio (% ages 15+)	52	65	53	68
Employment to population ratio (% ages 15–24)	34	43	34	47
Firms with female participation in ownership (%)	..		33	
Firms with a female top manager (%)	..		10	
Children in employment (% of children ages 7–14)	7	8	..	..
Unemployment rate (% of labor force ages 15+)	10	13	10	12
Unemployment rate (% of labor force ages 15–24)	14	22	12	18
Internet users (%)	..	..	..	..
Account at a financial institution (% age 15+)	..	..	9	14
Mobile account (% age 15+)	..	..	0.0	0.0
Saved any money last year (% age 15+)	..	..	27	36
Public life and decision making				
Seats held by women in national parliament (%)	..		19	
Female legislators, senior officials and managers (% of total)	..		..	
Proportion of women in ministerial level positions (%)	..		11	
Agency				
Total fertility rate (births per woman)	4.0		3.8	
Adolescent fertility rate (births per 1,000 women ages 15–19)	45		38	
Women first married by age 18 (% of women ages 20–24)	..		12	

Tanzania

Sub-Saharan Africa				Low income
Population (millions)				52
GNI, Atlas ($ billions)				46
GNI per capita, Atlas ($)				930
Population living below $1.90 a day (%)				47

	2000		2013	
	Female	Male	Female	Male
Education				
Net primary enrollment rate (%)	54	52	85	82
Net secondary enrollment rate (%)	..	..	..	..
Gross tertiary enrollment ratio (% of relevant age group)	0	1	3	5
Primary completion rate (% of relevant age group)	50	49	80	72
Progression to secondary school (%)	19	20	54	59
Lower secondary completion rate (% of relevant age group)	6	7	33	39
Gross tertiary graduation ratio (%)	0	0	..	..
Female share of graduates in eng., manf. and constr. (%, tertiary)	..		..	
Youth literacy rate (% of population ages 15-24)	76	81	85	87
Health and related services				
Sex ratio at birth (male births per female births)	1.03		1.03	
Under-five mortality rate (per 1,000 live births)	125	136	45	52
Life expectancy at birth (years)	51	49	63	60
Pregnant women receiving prenatal care (%)	49		88	
Births attended by skilled health staff (% of total)	36		49	
Maternal mortality ratio (per 100,000 live births)	770		410	
Women's share of population ages 15+ living with HIV (%)	58		59	
Prevalence of HIV (% ages 15-24)	3.8	2.0	2.1	1.4
Economic structure, participation, and access to resources				
Labor force participation rate (% of population ages 15+)	87	91	88	90
Labor force participation rate (% of ages 15-24)	82	82	81	80
Wage and salaried workers (% of employed ages 15+)	4	10	11	21
Self-employed workers (% of employed ages 15+)	96	90	81	71
Unpaid family workers (% of employed ages 15+)	4.6	3.0	38.4	25.6
Employment in agriculture (% of employed ages 15+)	84	80	..	..
Employment in industry (% of employed ages 15+)	1	4	..	..
Employment in services (% of employed ages 15+)	15	16	..	..
Women in wage employment in the nonagricultural sector (%)	..		33	
Women's share of part-time employment (% of total)	58		..	
Maternity leave (days paid)	..		84	
Maternity leave benefits (% of wages paid)	..		100	
Employment to population ratio (% ages 15+)	81	88	84	88
Employment to population ratio (% ages 15-24)	74	76	75	76
Firms with female participation in ownership (%)	..		25	
Firms with a female top manager (%)	..		14	
Children in employment (% of children ages 7-14)	39	41	28	31
Unemployment rate (% of labor force ages 15+)	7	4	5	2
Unemployment rate (% of labor force ages 15-24)	10	8	7	6
Internet users (%)	..	..	..	..
Account at a financial institution (% age 15+)	..	..	17	21
Mobile account (% age 15+)	..	..	26.6	38.4
Saved any money last year (% age 15+)	..	..	56	62
Public life and decision making				
Seats held by women in national parliament (%)	..		36	
Female legislators, senior officials and managers (% of total)	49		..	
Proportion of women in ministerial level positions (%)	..		32	
Agency				
Total fertility rate (births per woman)	5.7		5.2	
Adolescent fertility rate (births per 1,000 women ages 15-19)	133		119	
Women first married by age 18 (% of women ages 20-24)	39		37	

Thailand

East Asia & Pacific   **Upper middle income**

Population (millions)	68
GNI, Atlas ($ billions)	363
GNI per capita, Atlas ($)	5,370
Population living below $1.90 a day (%)	<2

	2000 Female	2000 Male	2013 Female	2013 Male
Education				
Net primary enrollment rate (%)	..	..	..	..
Net secondary enrollment rate (%)	..	..	82	77
Gross tertiary enrollment ratio (% of relevant age group)	38	32	59	44
Primary completion rate (% of relevant age group)	84	85	..	..
Progression to secondary school (%)	..	..	..	..
Lower secondary completion rate (% of relevant age group)	..	..	..	..
Gross tertiary graduation ratio (%)	17	13	..	..
Female share of graduates in eng., manf. and constr. (%, tertiary)	..		..	
Youth literacy rate (% of population ages 15–24)	98	98	97	97
Health and related services				
Sex ratio at birth (male births per female births)	*1.06*		1.06	
Under-five mortality rate (per 1,000 live births)	19	26	11	14
Life expectancy at birth (years)	75	67	78	71
Pregnant women receiving prenatal care (%)	92		98	
Births attended by skilled health staff (% of total)	99		100	
Maternal mortality ratio (per 100,000 live births)	40		26	
Women's share of population ages 15+ living with HIV (%)	29		43	
Prevalence of HIV (% ages 15–24)	1.3	0.7	0.2	0.3
Economic structure, participation, and access to resources				
Labor force participation rate (% of population ages 15+)	65	81	64	81
Labor force participation rate (% of ages 15–24)	49	57	40	56
Wage and salaried workers (% of employed ages 15+)	39	40	41	42
Self-employed workers (% of employed ages 15+)	61	60	59	58
Unpaid family workers (% of employed ages 15+)	39.8	16.4	30.4	16.1
Employment in agriculture (% of employed ages 15+)	48	50	38	41
Employment in industry (% of employed ages 15+)	17	20	18	23
Employment in services (% of employed ages 15+)	35	30	44	36
Women in wage employment in the nonagricultural sector (%)	44		45	
Women's share of part-time employment (% of total)	49		..	
Maternity leave (days paid)	..		90	
Maternity leave benefits (% of wages paid)	..		100	
Employment to population ratio (% ages 15+)	64	79	64	80
Employment to population ratio (% ages 15–24)	45	53	39	54
Firms with female participation in ownership (%)	..		..	
Firms with a female top manager (%)	..		..	
Children in employment (% of children ages 7–14)	..	..	1	..
Unemployment rate (% of labor force ages 15+)	2	3	1	1
Unemployment rate (% of labor force ages 15–24)	6	7	3	3
Internet users (%)	..	..	29	29
Account at a financial institution (% age 15+)	..	..	75	81
Mobile account (% age 15+)	..	..	1.7	0.8
Saved any money last year (% age 15+)	..	..	78	83
Public life and decision making				
Seats held by women in national parliament (%)	..		6	
Female legislators, senior officials and managers (% of total)	*26*		25	
Proportion of women in ministerial level positions (%)	..		4	
Agency				
Total fertility rate (births per woman)	1.7		1.4	
Adolescent fertility rate (births per 1,000 women ages 15–19)	43		45	
Women first married by age 18 (% of women ages 20–24)	..		22	

Timor-Leste

East Asia & Pacific			**Lower middle income**	
Population (millions)				1.2
GNI, Atlas ($ billions)				4
GNI per capita, Atlas ($)				3,120
Population living below $1.90 a day (%)				..

	2000		2013	
	Female	**Male**	**Female**	**Male**
Education				
Net primary enrollment rate (%)	..	..	90	92
Net secondary enrollment rate (%)	..	..	40	36
Gross tertiary enrollment ratio (% of relevant age group)	10	8	15	21
Primary completion rate (% of relevant age group)	..	..	72	70
Progression to secondary school (%)	..	..	95	94
Lower secondary completion rate (% of relevant age group)	..	..	61	60
Gross tertiary graduation ratio (%)	..	..	..	
Female share of graduates in eng., manf. and constr. (%, tertiary)	..		..	
Youth literacy rate (% of population ages 15–24)	..	..	79	80
Health and related services				
Sex ratio at birth (male births per female births)	1.05		1.05	
Under-five mortality rate (per 1,000 live births)	104	116	48	57
Life expectancy at birth (years)	61	58	69	66
Pregnant women receiving prenatal care (%)	43		84	
Births attended by skilled health staff (% of total)	24		29	
Maternal mortality ratio (per 100,000 live births)	680		270	
Women's share of population ages 15+ living with HIV (%)	..		..	
Prevalence of HIV (% ages 15–24)	..	..	..	..
Economic structure, participation, and access to resources				
Labor force participation rate (% of population ages 15+)	38	74	25	51
Labor force participation rate (% of ages 15–24)	33	48	11	18
Wage and salaried workers (% of employed ages 15+)	..	..	20	32
Self-employed workers (% of employed ages 15+)	..	..	..	..
Unpaid family workers (% of employed ages 15+)	..	..	32.4	27.3
Employment in agriculture (% of employed ages 15+)	..	..	50	51
Employment in industry (% of employed ages 15+)	..	..	7	10
Employment in services (% of employed ages 15+)	..	..	42	39
Women in wage employment in the nonagricultural sector (%)	..		23	
Women's share of part-time employment (% of total)	..		..	
Maternity leave (days paid)	..		84	
Maternity leave benefits (% of wages paid)	..		100	
Employment to population ratio (% ages 15+)	35	70	23	49
Employment to population ratio (% ages 15–24)	26	42	9	16
Firms with female participation in ownership (%)	..		..	
Firms with a female top manager (%)	..		..	
Children in employment (% of children ages 7–14)	8	7	..	..
Unemployment rate (% of labor force ages 15+)	9	6	6	4
Unemployment rate (% of labor force ages 15–24)	20	13	19	10
Internet users (%)	..	..	..	..
Account at a financial institution (% age 15+)	..	..	..	..
Mobile account (% age 15+)	..	..	..	..
Saved any money last year (% age 15+)	..	..	..	..
Public life and decision making				
Seats held by women in national parliament (%)	..		38	
Female legislators, senior officials and managers (% of total)	..		10	
Proportion of women in ministerial level positions (%)	..		13	
Agency				
Total fertility rate (births per woman)	7.1		5.2	
Adolescent fertility rate (births per 1,000 women ages 15–19)	71		48	
Women first married by age 18 (% of women ages 20–24)	..		19	

Togo

Sub-Saharan Africa			Low income	
Population (millions)				7
GNI, Atlas ($ billions)				4
GNI per capita, Atlas ($)				570
Population living below $1.90 a day (%)				54

	2000		2013	
	Female	Male	Female	Male
Education				
Net primary enrollment rate (%)	77	94	..	..
Net secondary enrollment rate (%)	15	32	..	..
Gross tertiary enrollment ratio (% of relevant age group)	1	6	6	14
Primary completion rate (% of relevant age group)	48	82	74	88
Progression to secondary school (%)	79	84	82	86
Lower secondary completion rate (% of relevant age group)	13	32	30	49
Gross tertiary graduation ratio (%)	..	..	..	..
Female share of graduates in eng., manf. and constr. (%, tertiary)	..		..	
Youth literacy rate (% of population ages 15–24)	64	84	73	87
Health and related services				
Sex ratio at birth (male births per female births)	1.02		1.02	
Under-five mortality rate (per 1,000 live births)	112	130	72	84
Life expectancy at birth (years)	54	53	57	56
Pregnant women receiving prenatal care (%)	73		72	
Births attended by skilled health staff (% of total)	49		59	
Maternal mortality ratio (per 100,000 live births)	580		450	
Women's share of population ages 15+ living with HIV (%)	58		59	
Prevalence of HIV (% ages 15–24)	2.0	1.1	0.8	0.5
Economic structure, participation, and access to resources				
Labor force participation rate (% of population ages 15+)	76	82	81	81
Labor force participation rate (% of ages 15–24)	65	66	68	64
Wage and salaried workers (% of employed ages 15+)	..	..	..	..
Self-employed workers (% of employed ages 15+)	..	..	..	..
Unpaid family workers (% of employed ages 15+)	..	..	..	..
Employment in agriculture (% of employed ages 15+)	..	..	..	..
Employment in industry (% of employed ages 15+)	..	..	..	..
Employment in services (% of employed ages 15+)	..	..	..	..
Women in wage employment in the nonagricultural sector (%)	..		..	
Women's share of part-time employment (% of total)	..			
Maternity leave (days paid)	..		98	
Maternity leave benefits (% of wages paid)	..		100	
Employment to population ratio (% ages 15+)	70	76	75	76
Employment to population ratio (% ages 15–24)	58	59	60	58
Firms with female participation in ownership (%)	..			
Firms with a female top manager (%)	..		..	
Children in employment (% of children ages 7–14)	..	..	47	50
Unemployment rate (% of labor force ages 15+)	8	7	7	7
Unemployment rate (% of labor force ages 15–24)	12	7	11	10
Internet users (%)	..	..	..	..
Account at a financial institution (% age 15+)	..	..	14	21
Mobile account (% age 15+)	..	..	1.3	1.5
Saved any money last year (% age 15+)	..	..	35	40
Public life and decision making				
Seats held by women in national parliament (%)	..		18	
Female legislators, senior officials and managers (% of total)	..		..	
Proportion of women in ministerial level positions (%)	..		21	
Agency				
Total fertility rate (births per woman)	5.3		4.6	
Adolescent fertility rate (births per 1,000 women ages 15–19)	95		92	
Women first married by age 18 (% of women ages 20–24)	31		25	

Tonga

Upper middle income

Population (thousands)	106
GNI, Atlas ($ millions)	453
GNI per capita, Atlas ($)	4,290
Population living below $1.90 a day (%)	..

	2000		2013	
	Female	**Male**	**Female**	**Male**
Education				
Net primary enrollment rate (%)	88	94	86	83
Net secondary enrollment rate (%)	80	73	71	67
Gross tertiary enrollment ratio (% of relevant age group)	4	3	..	..
Primary completion rate (% of relevant age group)	105	108	104	113
Progression to secondary school (%)	..	..	..	..
Lower secondary completion rate (% of relevant age group)	116	83	..	..
Gross tertiary graduation ratio (%)	..	..	..	..
Female share of graduates in eng., manf. and constr. (%, tertiary)	..		..	
Youth literacy rate (% of population ages 15–24)	..	..	100	99
Health and related services				
Sex ratio at birth (male births per female births)	1.05		1.05	
Under-five mortality rate (per 1,000 live births)	19	16	18	15
Life expectancy at birth (years)	73	69	76	70
Pregnant women receiving prenatal care (%)	..		98	
Births attended by skilled health staff (% of total)	95		98	
Maternal mortality ratio (per 100,000 live births)	91		120	
Women's share of population ages 15+ living with HIV (%)	..		..	
Prevalence of HIV (% ages 15–24)	..	..	..	..
Economic structure, participation, and access to resources				
Labor force participation rate (% of population ages 15+)	49	73	54	75
Labor force participation rate (% of ages 15–24)	31	47	32	45
Wage and salaried workers (% of employed ages 15+)	..	..	..	..
Self-employed workers (% of employed ages 15+)	..	..	..	..
Unpaid family workers (% of employed ages 15+)	..	..	..	..
Employment in agriculture (% of employed ages 15+)	..	..	..	..
Employment in industry (% of employed ages 15+)	..	..	..	..
Employment in services (% of employed ages 15+)	..	..	..	..
Women in wage employment in the nonagricultural sector (%)	..		..	
Women's share of part-time employment (% of total)	..		..	
Maternity leave (days paid)	..		0	
Maternity leave benefits (% of wages paid)	..		..	
Employment to population ratio (% ages 15+)	..	..	..	..
Employment to population ratio (% ages 15–24)	..	..	..	..
Firms with female participation in ownership (%)	..		..	
Firms with a female top manager (%)	..		..	
Children in employment (% of children ages 7–14)	..	..	..	..
Unemployment rate (% of labor force ages 15+)	..	..	..	..
Unemployment rate (% of labor force ages 15–24)	..	..	..	..
Internet users (%)	..	..	..	..
Account at a financial institution (% age 15+)	..	..	..	..
Mobile account (% age 15+)	..	..	..	..
Saved any money last year (% age 15+)	..	..	..	..
Public life and decision making				
Seats held by women in national parliament (%)	..		0	
Female legislators, senior officials and managers (% of total)	..		..	
Proportion of women in ministerial level positions (%)	..		0	
Agency				
Total fertility rate (births per woman)	4.3		3.8	
Adolescent fertility rate (births per 1,000 women ages 15–19)	22		15	
Women first married by age 18 (% of women ages 20–24)	..		6	

Trinidad and Tobago

	High income
Population (millions)	1.4
GNI, Atlas ($ billions)	21
GNI per capita, Atlas ($)	15,550
Population living below $1.90 a day (%)	..

	2000		2013	
	Female	Male	Female	Male
Education				
Net primary enrollment rate (%)	94	94	95	96
Net secondary enrollment rate (%)	..	..	..	..
Gross tertiary enrollment ratio (% of relevant age group)	7	5	..	..
Primary completion rate (% of relevant age group)	95	92	95	95
Progression to secondary school (%)	98	97	..	..
Lower secondary completion rate (% of relevant age group)	77	71	86	76
Gross tertiary graduation ratio (%)	6	4	..	..
Female share of graduates in eng., manf. and constr. (%, tertiary)	19		..	
Youth literacy rate (% of population ages 15-24)	..	..	100	100
Health and related services				
Sex ratio at birth (male births per female births)	1.04		1.04	
Under-five mortality rate (per 1,000 live births)	26	31	18	22
Life expectancy at birth (years)	72	65	74	66
Pregnant women receiving prenatal care (%)	92		..	
Births attended by skilled health staff (% of total)	96		100	
Maternal mortality ratio (per 100,000 live births)	59		84	
Women's share of population ages 15+ living with HIV (%)	..		..	
Prevalence of HIV (% ages 15-24)	..	..	..	..
Economic structure, participation, and access to resources				
Labor force participation rate (% of population ages 15+)	47	76	53	76
Labor force participation rate (% of ages 15-24)	41	61	41	57
Wage and salaried workers (% of employed ages 15+)	80	75	..	..
Self-employed workers (% of employed ages 15+)	19	24	..	..
Unpaid family workers (% of employed ages 15+)	2.9	0.6	..	..
Employment in agriculture (% of employed ages 15+)	3	10	..	..
Employment in industry (% of employed ages 15+)	13	37	..	..
Employment in services (% of employed ages 15+)	84	53	..	..
Women in wage employment in the nonagricultural sector (%)	40		46	
Women's share of part-time employment (% of total)	46		..	
Maternity leave (days paid)	..		98	
Maternity leave benefits (% of wages paid)	..		61	
Employment to population ratio (% ages 15+)	39	69	49	72
Employment to population ratio (% ages 15-24)	30	49	35	51
Firms with female participation in ownership (%)	..		45	
Firms with a female top manager (%)	..		21	
Children in employment (% of children ages 7-14)	3	5	..	..
Unemployment rate (% of labor force ages 15+)	15	10	8	5
Unemployment rate (% of labor force ages 15-24)	28	20	17	11
Internet users (%)	..	..	..	..
Account at a financial institution (% age 15+)	..	..	70	82
Mobile account (% age 15+)	..	..	..	..
Saved any money last year (% age 15+)	..	..	..	..
Public life and decision making				
Seats held by women in national parliament (%)	..		29	
Female legislators, senior officials and managers (% of total)	39		..	
Proportion of women in ministerial level positions (%)	..		10	
Agency				
Total fertility rate (births per woman)	1.8		1.8	
Adolescent fertility rate (births per 1,000 women ages 15-19)	41		32	
Women first married by age 18 (% of women ages 20-24)	..		..	

Tunisia

Middle East & North Africa	Upper middle income

Population (millions)	11
GNI, Atlas ($ billions)	46
GNI per capita, Atlas ($)	4,210
Population living below $1.90 a day (%)	<2

	2000		2013	
	Female	Male	Female	Male
Education				
Net primary enrollment rate (%)	95	97	..	..
Net secondary enrollment rate (%)	..	..	..	..
Gross tertiary enrollment ratio (% of relevant age group)	19	18	42	26
Primary completion rate (% of relevant age group)	90	91	98	97
Progression to secondary school (%)	93	91	95	91
Lower secondary completion rate (% of relevant age group)	..	..	80	64
Gross tertiary graduation ratio (%)	..	..	33	15
Female share of graduates in eng., manf. and constr. (%, tertiary)	..		41	
Youth literacy rate (% of population ages 15–24)	..	..	96	98
Health and related services				
Sex ratio at birth (male births per female births)	1.05		1.05	
Under-five mortality rate (per 1,000 live births)	29	35	13	15
Life expectancy at birth (years)	75	71	76	72
Pregnant women receiving prenatal care (%)	92		98	
Births attended by skilled health staff (% of total)	90		99	
Maternal mortality ratio (per 100,000 live births)	65		46	
Women's share of population ages 15+ living with HIV (%)	25		27	
Prevalence of HIV (% ages 15–24)	0.1	0.1	0.1	0.1
Economic structure, participation, and access to resources				
Labor force participation rate (% of population ages 15+)	24	72	25	71
Labor force participation rate (% of ages 15–24)	25	48	20	42
Wage and salaried workers (% of employed ages 15+)	..	..	79	69
Self-employed workers (% of employed ages 15+)	..	..	21	31
Unpaid family workers (% of employed ages 15+)	..	..	8.0	3.2
Employment in agriculture (% of employed ages 15+)	..	..	..	..
Employment in industry (% of employed ages 15+)	..	..	..	..
Employment in services (% of employed ages 15+)	..	..	..	..
Women in wage employment in the nonagricultural sector (%)	24		28	
Women's share of part-time employment (% of total)	..		..	
Maternity leave (days paid)			30	
Maternity leave benefits (% of wages paid)	..		67	
Employment to population ratio (% ages 15+)	19	61	21	62
Employment to population ratio (% ages 15–24)	17	31	14	29
Firms with female participation in ownership (%)	..		50	
Firms with a female top manager (%)	..		9	
Children in employment (% of children ages 7–14)	..	..	3	4
Unemployment rate (% of labor force ages 15+)	19	15	16	12
Unemployment rate (% of labor force ages 15–24)	31	34	29	32
Internet users (%)	..	..	..	..
Account at a financial institution (% age 15+)	..	..	21	34
Mobile account (% age 15+)	..	..	0.4	0.9
Saved any money last year (% age 15+)	..	..	37	39
Public life and decision making				
Seats held by women in national parliament (%)	..		31	
Female legislators, senior officials and managers (% of total)	..		..	
Proportion of women in ministerial level positions (%)	..		11	
Agency				
Total fertility rate (births per woman)	2.1		2.3	
Adolescent fertility rate (births per 1,000 women ages 15–19)	8		7	
Women first married by age 18 (% of women ages 20–24)	..		2	

Turkey

Europe & Central Asia	Upper middle income
Population (millions)	76
GNI, Atlas ($ billions)	823
GNI per capita, Atlas ($)	10,840
Population living below $1.90 a day (%)	<2

	2000		2013	
	Female	Male	Female	Male
Education				
Net primary enrollment rate (%)	90	98	94	95
Net secondary enrollment rate (%)	56	71	87	90
Gross tertiary enrollment ratio (% of relevant age group)	21	30	73	85
Primary completion rate (% of relevant age group)	..	..	100	102
Progression to secondary school (%)	..	..	90	92
Lower secondary completion rate (% of relevant age group)	..	..	95	99
Gross tertiary graduation ratio (%)	8	11	27	28
Female share of graduates in eng., manf. and constr. (%, tertiary)	25		25	
Youth literacy rate (% of population ages 15–24)	..	..	99	100
Health and related services				
Sex ratio at birth (male births per female births)	1.05		1.05	
Under-five mortality rate (per 1,000 live births)	37	42	12	15
Life expectancy at birth (years)	74	66	79	72
Pregnant women receiving prenatal care (%)	68		..	
Births attended by skilled health staff (% of total)	81		..	
Maternal mortality ratio (per 100,000 live births)	33		20	
Women's share of population ages 15+ living with HIV (%)	..		..	
Prevalence of HIV (% ages 15–24)	..	..	..	..
Economic structure, participation, and access to resources				
Labor force participation rate (% of population ages 15+)	26	73	29	71
Labor force participation rate (% of ages 15–24)	28	58	26	53
Wage and salaried workers (% of employed ages 15+)	35	54	57	67
Self-employed workers (% of employed ages 15+)	65	47	43	33
Unpaid family workers (% of employed ages 15+)	52.1	10.4	31.4	4.5
Employment in agriculture (% of employed ages 15+)	61	27	37	18
Employment in industry (% of employed ages 15+)	13	28	15	31
Employment in services (% of employed ages 15+)	26	45	48	52
Women in wage employment in the nonagricultural sector (%)	20		26	
Women's share of part-time employment (% of total)	55		60	
Maternity leave (days paid)	..		112	
Maternity leave benefits (% of wages paid)	..		67	
Employment to population ratio (% ages 15+)	25	68	26	64
Employment to population ratio (% ages 15–24)	25	51	20	43
Firms with female participation in ownership (%)	..		25	
Firms with a female top manager (%)	..		5	
Children in employment (% of children ages 7–14)	4	5	..	..
Unemployment rate (% of labor force ages 15+)	6	7	12	9
Unemployment rate (% of labor force ages 15–24)	12	13	24	19
Internet users (%)	..	..	..	..
Account at a financial institution (% age 15+)	..	..	44	69
Mobile account (% age 15+)	..	..	0.7	1.0
Saved any money last year (% age 15+)	..	..	37	45
Public life and decision making				
Seats held by women in national parliament (%)	..		14	
Female legislators, senior officials and managers (% of total)	8		10	
Proportion of women in ministerial level positions (%)	..		4	
Agency				
Total fertility rate (births per woman)	2.5		2.0	
Adolescent fertility rate (births per 1,000 women ages 15–19)	48		28	
Women first married by age 18 (% of women ages 20–24)	23		..	

Turkmenistan

Europe & Central Asia	Upper middle income
Population (millions)	5
GNI, Atlas ($ billions)	43
GNI per capita, Atlas ($)	8,020
Population living below $1.90 a day (%)	..

	2000		2013	
	Female	Male	Female	Male
Education				
Net primary enrollment rate (%)	..	..	..	..
Net secondary enrollment rate (%)	..	..	..	..
Gross tertiary enrollment ratio (% of relevant age group)	..	..	6[a]	10[a]
Primary completion rate (% of relevant age group)	..	..	..	..
Progression to secondary school (%)	..	..	..	..
Lower secondary completion rate (% of relevant age group)	..	..	..	..
Gross tertiary graduation ratio (%)	..	..	..	..
Female share of graduates in eng., manf. and constr. (%, tertiary)	..		..	
Youth literacy rate (% of population ages 15–24)	..	..	100	100
Health and related services				
Sex ratio at birth (male births per female births)	1.05		1.05	
Under-five mortality rate (per 1,000 live births)	71	92	44	59
Life expectancy at birth (years)	68	60	70	61
Pregnant women receiving prenatal care (%)	98		..	
Births attended by skilled health staff (% of total)	97		..	
Maternal mortality ratio (per 100,000 live births)	81		61	
Women's share of population ages 15+ living with HIV (%)	..		..	
Prevalence of HIV (% ages 15–24)	..	..	..	..
Economic structure, participation, and access to resources				
Labor force participation rate (% of population ages 15+)	48	74	47	77
Labor force participation rate (% of ages 15–24)	33	54	33	58
Wage and salaried workers (% of employed ages 15+)	..	..	..	..
Self-employed workers (% of employed ages 15+)	..	..	..	..
Unpaid family workers (% of employed ages 15+)	..	..	..	..
Employment in agriculture (% of employed ages 15+)	..	..	..	..
Employment in industry (% of employed ages 15+)	..	..	..	..
Employment in services (% of employed ages 15+)	..	..	..	..
Women in wage employment in the nonagricultural sector (%)	42		..	
Women's share of part-time employment (% of total)	..		..	
Maternity leave (days paid)	..		..	
Maternity leave benefits (% of wages paid)	..		..	
Employment to population ratio (% ages 15+)	42	66	42	69
Employment to population ratio (% ages 15–24)	26	44	26	46
Firms with female participation in ownership (%)	..		..	
Firms with a female top manager (%)	..		..	
Children in employment (% of children ages 7–14)	..	..	..	..
Unemployment rate (% of labor force ages 15+)	11	11	11	11
Unemployment rate (% of labor force ages 15–24)	23	20	22	19
Internet users (%)	..	..	..	..
Account at a financial institution (% age 15+)	..	..	2	2
Mobile account (% age 15+)	..	..	..	..
Saved any money last year (% age 15+)	..	..	54	61
Public life and decision making				
Seats held by women in national parliament (%)	..		26	
Female legislators, senior officials and managers (% of total)	..		..	
Proportion of women in ministerial level positions (%)	..		6	
Agency				
Total fertility rate (births per woman)	2.8		2.3	
Adolescent fertility rate (births per 1,000 women ages 15–19)	25		17	
Women first married by age 18 (% of women ages 20–24)	9		..	

Turks and Caicos Islands

	High income
Population (thousands)	34
GNI, Atlas ($ millions)	..
GNI per capita, Atlas ($)	..
Population living below $1.90 a day (%)	..

	2000		2013	
	Female	Male	Female	Male
Education				
Net primary enrollment rate (%)	..	..	..	..
Net secondary enrollment rate (%)	..	..	..	..
Gross tertiary enrollment ratio (% of relevant age group)	..	..	..	..
Primary completion rate (% of relevant age group)	..	..	..	..
Progression to secondary school (%)	82	82	..	..
Lower secondary completion rate (% of relevant age group)	..	..	..	..
Gross tertiary graduation ratio (%)	..	..	..	..
Female share of graduates in eng., manf. and constr. (%, tertiary)	..		..	
Youth literacy rate (% of population ages 15–24)	..	..	..	..
Health and related services				
Sex ratio at birth (male births per female births)		..		..
Under-five mortality rate (per 1,000 live births)	..	..	..	..
Life expectancy at birth (years)	..	..	..	..
Pregnant women receiving prenatal care (%)	100		..	
Births attended by skilled health staff (% of total)	88		..	
Maternal mortality ratio (per 100,000 live births)	..		..	
Women's share of population ages 15+ living with HIV (%)	..		..	
Prevalence of HIV (% ages 15–24)	..	..	..	..
Economic structure, participation, and access to resources				
Labor force participation rate (% of population ages 15+)	..	..	..	..
Labor force participation rate (% of ages 15–24)	..	..	..	..
Wage and salaried workers (% of employed ages 15+)	..	..	..	..
Self-employed workers (% of employed ages 15+)	..	..	..	..
Unpaid family workers (% of employed ages 15+)	..	..	..	..
Employment in agriculture (% of employed ages 15+)	..	..	..	..
Employment in industry (% of employed ages 15+)	..	..	..	..
Employment in services (% of employed ages 15+)	..	..	..	..
Women in wage employment in the nonagricultural sector (%)	..		..	
Women's share of part-time employment (% of total)	..		..	
Maternity leave (days paid)	..		..	
Maternity leave benefits (% of wages paid)	..		..	
Employment to population ratio (% ages 15+)	..	..	..	..
Employment to population ratio (% ages 15–24)	..	..	..	..
Firms with female participation in ownership (%)	..		..	
Firms with a female top manager (%)	..		..	
Children in employment (% of children ages 7–14)	..	..	..	..
Unemployment rate (% of labor force ages 15+)	..	..	..	..
Unemployment rate (% of labor force ages 15–24)	..	..	..	..
Internet users (%)	..	..	..	..
Account at a financial institution (% age 15+)	..	..	..	..
Mobile account (% age 15+)	..	..	..	..
Saved any money last year (% age 15+)	..	..	..	..
Public life and decision making				
Seats held by women in national parliament (%)	..		..	
Female legislators, senior officials and managers (% of total)	..		..	
Proportion of women in ministerial level positions (%)	..		..	
Agency				
Total fertility rate (births per woman)	..		..	
Adolescent fertility rate (births per 1,000 women ages 15–19)	..		..	
Women first married by age 18 (% of women ages 20–24)	..		..	

Tuvalu

East Asia & Pacific	Upper middle income
Population (thousands)	10
GNI, Atlas ($ millions)	58
GNI per capita, Atlas ($)	5,840
Population living below $1.90 a day (%)	..

	2000		2013	
	Female	Male	Female	Male
Education				
Net primary enrollment rate (%)	..	..	75	76
Net secondary enrollment rate (%)	..	..	89	70
Gross tertiary enrollment ratio (% of relevant age group)	..	..	..	..
Primary completion rate (% of relevant age group)	108	96	91	82
Progression to secondary school (%)	53	85	..	..
Lower secondary completion rate (% of relevant age group)	..	..	..	..
Gross tertiary graduation ratio (%)	..	..	..	..
Female share of graduates in eng., manf. and constr. (%, tertiary)	..		..	
Youth literacy rate (% of population ages 15–24)	..	..	..	..
Health and related services				
Sex ratio at birth (male births per female births)	..		..	
Under-five mortality rate (per 1,000 live births)	39	46	25	30
Life expectancy at birth (years)	..		..	
Pregnant women receiving prenatal care (%)	..		..	
Births attended by skilled health staff (% of total)	100		..	
Maternal mortality ratio (per 100,000 live births)	..		..	
Women's share of population ages 15+ living with HIV (%)	..		..	
Prevalence of HIV (% ages 15–24)	..	..	..	..
Economic structure, participation, and access to resources				
Labor force participation rate (% of population ages 15+)	..	..	..	..
Labor force participation rate (% of ages 15–24)	..	..	..	..
Wage and salaried workers (% of employed ages 15+)	98	96	..	..
Self-employed workers (% of employed ages 15+)	3	4	..	..
Unpaid family workers (% of employed ages 15+)	0.1	0.2	..	..
Employment in agriculture (% of employed ages 15+)	..	..	..	..
Employment in industry (% of employed ages 15+)	..	..	..	..
Employment in services (% of employed ages 15+)	..	..	..	..
Women in wage employment in the nonagricultural sector (%)	34		..	
Women's share of part-time employment (% of total)	..		..	
Maternity leave (days paid)	..		..	
Maternity leave benefits (% of wages paid)	..		..	
Employment to population ratio (% ages 15+)	..	..	..	..
Employment to population ratio (% ages 15–24)	..	..	..	..
Firms with female participation in ownership (%)	..		..	
Firms with a female top manager (%)	..		..	
Children in employment (% of children ages 7–14)	..	..	..	..
Unemployment rate (% of labor force ages 15+)	..	..	..	..
Unemployment rate (% of labor force ages 15–24)	..	..	..	..
Internet users (%)	..	..	..	..
Account at a financial institution (% age 15+)	..	..	..	..
Mobile account (% age 15+)	..	..	..	..
Saved any money last year (% age 15+)	..	..	..	..
Public life and decision making				
Seats held by women in national parliament (%)	..		7	
Female legislators, senior officials and managers (% of total)	25		..	
Proportion of women in ministerial level positions (%)	..		14	
Agency				
Total fertility rate (births per woman)	..		..	
Adolescent fertility rate (births per 1,000 women ages 15–19)	..		..	
Women first married by age 18 (% of women ages 20–24)	..		..	

Uganda

Sub-Saharan Africa				Low income

Population (millions)				38
GNI, Atlas ($ billions)				26
GNI per capita, Atlas ($)				680
Population living below $1.90 a day (%)				33

	2000		2013	
	Female	Male	Female	Male
Education				
Net primary enrollment rate (%)	..	..	93	90
Net secondary enrollment rate (%)	12	15	22	23
Gross tertiary enrollment ratio (% of relevant age group)	2	3	4	5
Primary completion rate (% of relevant age group)	53	66	54	55
Progression to secondary school (%)	47	42	61	64
Lower secondary completion rate (% of relevant age group)	13	17	27	30
Gross tertiary graduation ratio (%)	1	2	..	..
Female share of graduates in eng., manf. and constr. (%, tertiary)	10		..	
Youth literacy rate (% of population ages 15–24)	76	86	82	86
Health and related services				
Sex ratio at birth (male births per female births)	1.03		1.03	
Under-five mortality rate (per 1,000 live births)	137	160	49	60
Life expectancy at birth (years)	48	48	60	58
Pregnant women receiving prenatal care (%)	92		93	
Births attended by skilled health staff (% of total)	39		57	
Maternal mortality ratio (per 100,000 live births)	650		360	
Women's share of population ages 15+ living with HIV (%)	54		58	
Prevalence of HIV (% ages 15–24)	2.4	1.4	3.7	2.3
Economic structure, participation, and access to resources				
Labor force participation rate (% of population ages 15+)	81	83	76	79
Labor force participation rate (% of ages 15–24)	67	63	59	60
Wage and salaried workers (% of employed ages 15+)	8	20	..	..
Self-employed workers (% of employed ages 15+)	92	80	..	..
Unpaid family workers (% of employed ages 15+)	43.3	19.9	..	..
Employment in agriculture (% of employed ages 15+)	..	..	..	..
Employment in industry (% of employed ages 15+)	..	..	..	..
Employment in services (% of employed ages 15+)	..	..	..	..
Women in wage employment in the nonagricultural sector (%)	..		35	
Women's share of part-time employment (% of total)	..		..	
Maternity leave (days paid)	..		84	
Maternity leave benefits (% of wages paid)	..		100	
Employment to population ratio (% ages 15+)	78	81	72	77
Employment to population ratio (% ages 15–24)	64	61	55	56
Firms with female participation in ownership (%)	..		27	
Firms with a female top manager (%)	..		15	
Children in employment (% of children ages 7–14)	..	..	36	37
Unemployment rate (% of labor force ages 15+)	3	2	5	3
Unemployment rate (% of labor force ages 15–24)	5	5	7	6
Internet users (%)	..	..	..	..
Account at a financial institution (% age 15+)	..	..	23	32
Mobile account (% age 15+)	..	..	29.0	41.2
Saved any money last year (% age 15+)	..	..	72	78
Public life and decision making				
Seats held by women in national parliament (%)	..		35	
Female legislators, senior officials and managers (% of total)	..		..	
Proportion of women in ministerial level positions (%)	..		30	
Agency				
Total fertility rate (births per woman)	6.9		5.9	
Adolescent fertility rate (births per 1,000 women ages 15–19)	180		115	
Women first married by age 18 (% of women ages 20–24)	54		40	

Ukraine

Europe & Central Asia				Lower middle income

Population (millions)				45
GNI, Atlas ($ billions)				152
GNI per capita, Atlas ($)				3,560
Population living below $1.90 a day (%)				<2

	2000		2013	
	Female	Male	Female	Male
Education				
Net primary enrollment rate (%)	92	92	98	97
Net secondary enrollment rate (%)	93	89	87	87
Gross tertiary enrollment ratio (% of relevant age group)	52	46	86	72
Primary completion rate (% of relevant age group)	91	91	111	109
Progression to secondary school (%)	100	99	100	100
Lower secondary completion rate (% of relevant age group)	97	94	99	99
Gross tertiary graduation ratio (%)	..	..	..	..
Female share of graduates in eng., manf. and constr. (%, tertiary)	..		26	
Youth literacy rate (% of population ages 15–24)	100	100	100	100
Health and related services				
Sex ratio at birth (male births per female births)	1.06		1.06	
Under-five mortality rate (per 1,000 live births)	16	20	8	10
Life expectancy at birth (years)	74	62	76	66
Pregnant women receiving prenatal care (%)	..		99	
Births attended by skilled health staff (% of total)	100		99	
Maternal mortality ratio (per 100,000 live births)	35		23	
Women's share of population ages 15+ living with HIV (%)	..		..	
Prevalence of HIV (% ages 15–24)	0.5	0.7	0.6	0.2
Economic structure, participation, and access to resources				
Labor force participation rate (% of population ages 15+)	52	65	53	67
Labor force participation rate (% of ages 15–24)	38	43	36	47
Wage and salaried workers (% of employed ages 15+)	89	91	80	81
Self-employed workers (% of employed ages 15+)	11	9	20	19
Unpaid family workers (% of employed ages 15+)	1.5	0.8	0.3	0.4
Employment in agriculture (% of employed ages 15+)	..	..	..	..
Employment in industry (% of employed ages 15+)	..	..	..	..
Employment in services (% of employed ages 15+)	..	..	..	..
Women in wage employment in the nonagricultural sector (%)	50		49	
Women's share of part-time employment (% of total)	..		..	
Maternity leave (days paid)	..		126	
Maternity leave benefits (% of wages paid)	..		100	
Employment to population ratio (% ages 15+)	47	57	50	61
Employment to population ratio (% ages 15–24)	29	32	30	38
Firms with female participation in ownership (%)	..		32	
Firms with a female top manager (%)	..		19	
Children in employment (% of children ages 7–14)	..	..	5	5
Unemployment rate (% of labor force ages 15+)	10	13	7	9
Unemployment rate (% of labor force ages 15–24)	24	26	16	19
Internet users (%)	..	..	39	44
Account at a financial institution (% age 15+)	..	..	52	54
Mobile account (% age 15+)	..	..	..	..
Saved any money last year (% age 15+)	..	..	39	42
Public life and decision making				
Seats held by women in national parliament (%)	..		12	
Female legislators, senior officials and managers (% of total)	37		38	
Proportion of women in ministerial level positions (%)	..		11	
Agency				
Total fertility rate (births per woman)	1.1		1.5	
Adolescent fertility rate (births per 1,000 women ages 15–19)	35		25	
Women first married by age 18 (% of women ages 20–24)	14		9	

United Arab Emirates

High income

Population (millions)	9
GNI, Atlas ($ billions)	411
GNI per capita, Atlas ($)	45,200
Population living below $1.90 a day (%)	..

	2000		2013	
	Female	**Male**	**Female**	**Male**
Education				
Net primary enrollment rate (%)	83	83	90	92
Net secondary enrollment rate (%)	79	73	..	..
Gross tertiary enrollment ratio (% of relevant age group)	..	..	..	..
Primary completion rate (% of relevant age group)	90	88	106	116
Progression to secondary school (%)	100	100	99	98
Lower secondary completion rate (% of relevant age group)	..	..	..	..
Gross tertiary graduation ratio (%)	..	..	..	..
Female share of graduates in eng., manf. and constr. (%, tertiary)	..		31	
Youth literacy rate (% of population ages 15–24)	..	..	..	..
Health and related services				
Sex ratio at birth (male births per female births)	1.04		1.05	
Under-five mortality rate (per 1,000 live births)	10	12	6	8
Life expectancy at birth (years)	75	73	78	76
Pregnant women receiving prenatal care (%)	..		..	
Births attended by skilled health staff (% of total)	..		..	
Maternal mortality ratio (per 100,000 live births)	11		8	
Women's share of population ages 15+ living with HIV (%)	..		..	
Prevalence of HIV (% ages 15–24)	..	..	..	..
Economic structure, participation, and access to resources				
Labor force participation rate (% of population ages 15+)	34	92	47	92
Labor force participation rate (% of ages 15–24)	24	64	34	64
Wage and salaried workers (% of employed ages 15+)	..	..	..	..
Self-employed workers (% of employed ages 15+)	..	..	..	..
Unpaid family workers (% of employed ages 15+)	..	..	..	..
Employment in agriculture (% of employed ages 15+)	0	9	..	..
Employment in industry (% of employed ages 15+)	14	36	..	..
Employment in services (% of employed ages 15+)	86	55	..	..
Women in wage employment in the nonagricultural sector (%)	..		..	
Women's share of part-time employment (% of total)	..		..	
Maternity leave (days paid)	..		45	
Maternity leave benefits (% of wages paid)	..		100	
Employment to population ratio (% ages 15+)	32	90	43	89
Employment to population ratio (% ages 15–24)	21	61	28	58
Firms with female participation in ownership (%)	..		..	
Firms with a female top manager (%)	..		..	
Children in employment (% of children ages 7–14)	..	..	..	..
Unemployment rate (% of labor force ages 15+)	6	2	9	3
Unemployment rate (% of labor force ages 15–24)	11	5	17	8
Internet users (%)	..	..	83	86
Account at a financial institution (% age 15+)	..	..	66	90
Mobile account (% age 15+)	..	..	9.7	12.2
Saved any money last year (% age 15+)	..	..	58	70
Public life and decision making				
Seats held by women in national parliament (%)	..		18	
Female legislators, senior officials and managers (% of total)	8		..	
Proportion of women in ministerial level positions (%)	..		17	
Agency				
Total fertility rate (births per woman)	2.6		1.8	
Adolescent fertility rate (births per 1,000 women ages 15–19)	26		29	
Women first married by age 18 (% of women ages 20–24)	..		..	

United Kingdom

Population (millions)	65
GNI, Atlas ($ billions)	2,754
GNI per capita, Atlas ($)	42,690
Population living below $1.90 a day (%)	..

	2000 Female	2000 Male	2013 Female	2013 Male
Education				
Net primary enrollment rate (%)	100	100	*100*	*100*
Net secondary enrollment rate (%)	95	94	98	98
Gross tertiary enrollment ratio (% of relevant age group)	63	53	69	51
Primary completion rate (% of relevant age group)	..	..	..	..
Progression to secondary school (%)	..	..	..	..
Lower secondary completion rate (% of relevant age group)	..	..	..	..
Gross tertiary graduation ratio (%)	42	35	*56*	*40*
Female share of graduates in eng., manf. and constr. (%, tertiary)	18		22	
Youth literacy rate (% of population ages 15–24)	..	..	..	..
Health and related services				
Sex ratio at birth (male births per female births)	*1.05*		1.05	
Under-five mortality rate (per 1,000 live births)	6	7	4	5
Life expectancy at birth (years)	80	75	83	79
Pregnant women receiving prenatal care (%)	..		..	
Births attended by skilled health staff (% of total)	99		..	
Maternal mortality ratio (per 100,000 live births)	11		8	
Women's share of population ages 15+ living with HIV (%)	..		..	
Prevalence of HIV (% ages 15–24)	..	..	..	..
Economic structure, participation, and access to resources				
Labor force participation rate (% of population ages 15+)	54	70	56	69
Labor force participation rate (% of ages 15–24)	63	70	57	61
Wage and salaried workers (% of employed ages 15+)	92	84	90	81
Self-employed workers (% of employed ages 15+)	8	16	10	19
Unpaid family workers (% of employed ages 15+)	0.6	0.2	0.5	0.3
Employment in agriculture (% of employed ages 15+)	1	2	*1*	*2*
Employment in industry (% of employed ages 15+)	12	36	8	29
Employment in services (% of employed ages 15+)	87	61	*91*	*69*
Women in wage employment in the nonagricultural sector (%)	48		49	
Women's share of part-time employment (% of total)	79		74	
Maternity leave (days paid)	..		14	
Maternity leave benefits (% of wages paid)	..		90	
Employment to population ratio (% ages 15+)	51	66	52	63
Employment to population ratio (% ages 15–24)	56	60	46	48
Firms with female participation in ownership (%)	..		..	
Firms with a female top manager (%)	..		..	
Children in employment (% of children ages 7–14)	..	..	..	..
Unemployment rate (% of labor force ages 15+)	5	6	7	8
Unemployment rate (% of labor force ages 15–24)	10	14	18	23
Internet users (%)	..	..	89	91
Account at a financial institution (% age 15+)	..	..	99	99
Mobile account (% age 15+)	..	..	..	..
Saved any money last year (% age 15+)	..	..	70	73
Public life and decision making				
Seats held by women in national parliament (%)	..		29	
Female legislators, senior officials and managers (% of total)	35		*34*	
Proportion of women in ministerial level positions (%)	..		23	
Agency				
Total fertility rate (births per woman)	1.6		1.9	
Adolescent fertility rate (births per 1,000 women ages 15–19)	28		15	
Women first married by age 18 (% of women ages 20–24)	..		..	

United States

	High income
Population (millions)	319
GNI, Atlas ($ billions)	17,601
GNI per capita, Atlas ($)	55,200
Population living below $1.90 a day (%)	..

	2000 Female	2000 Male	2013 Female	2013 Male
Education				
Net primary enrollment rate (%)	96	96	91	92
Net secondary enrollment rate (%)	87	84	88	86
Gross tertiary enrollment ratio (% of relevant age group)	78	59	103	76
Primary completion rate (% of relevant age group)	..	..	..	..
Progression to secondary school (%)	..	..	..	..
Lower secondary completion rate (% of relevant age group)	..	..	..	..
Gross tertiary graduation ratio (%)	37	27	47	34
Female share of graduates in eng., manf. and constr. (%, tertiary)	19		18	
Youth literacy rate (% of population ages 15–24)	..	..	..	..
Health and related services				
Sex ratio at birth (male births per female births)	1.05		1.05	
Under-five mortality rate (per 1,000 live births)	8	9	6	7
Life expectancy at birth (years)	79	74	81	77
Pregnant women receiving prenatal care (%)	..		..	
Births attended by skilled health staff (% of total)	..		..	
Maternal mortality ratio (per 100,000 live births)	13		28	
Women's share of population ages 15+ living with HIV (%)	..		..	
Prevalence of HIV (% ages 15–24)	..	..	..	..
Economic structure, participation, and access to resources				
Labor force participation rate (% of population ages 15+)	59	74	56	69
Labor force participation rate (% of ages 15–24)	60	65	49	52
Wage and salaried workers (% of employed ages 15+)	94	91	95	99
Self-employed workers (% of employed ages 15+)	6	9	6	8
Unpaid family workers (% of employed ages 15+)	0.1	0.1	0.1	0.1
Employment in agriculture (% of employed ages 15+)	1	4	1	2
Employment in industry (% of employed ages 15+)	12	33	7	25
Employment in services (% of employed ages 15+)	86	64	92	72
Women in wage employment in the nonagricultural sector (%)	47		48	
Women's share of part-time employment (% of total)	68		66	
Maternity leave (days paid)[d]	..		..	
Maternity leave benefits (% of wages paid)	..		..	
Employment to population ratio (% ages 15+)	57	71	52	64
Employment to population ratio (% ages 15–24)	54	58	42	43
Firms with female participation in ownership (%)	..		..	
Firms with a female top manager (%)	..		..	
Children in employment (% of children ages 7–14)	..	..	..	..
Unemployment rate (% of labor force ages 15+)	4	4	7	8
Unemployment rate (% of labor force ages 15–24)	9	10	14	17
Internet users (%)	..	..	70	69
Account at a financial institution (% age 15+)	..	..	95	92
Mobile account (% age 15+)	..	..	..	..
Saved any money last year (% age 15+)	..	..	73	78
Public life and decision making				
Seats held by women in national parliament (%)	..		19	
Female legislators, senior officials and managers (% of total)	..		..	
Proportion of women in ministerial level positions (%)	..		26	
Agency				
Total fertility rate (births per woman)	2.1		1.9	
Adolescent fertility rate (births per 1,000 women ages 15–19)	46		24	
Women first married by age 18 (% of women ages 20–24)	..		..	

Uruguay

High income

Population (millions)	3
GNI, Atlas ($ billions)	56
GNI per capita, Atlas ($)	16,350
Population living below $1.90 a day (%)	<2

	2000		2013	
	Female	**Male**	**Female**	**Male**
Education				
Net primary enrollment rate (%)	..	..	..	..
Net secondary enrollment rate (%)	..	..	76	68
Gross tertiary enrollment ratio (% of relevant age group)	44	25	80	47
Primary completion rate (% of relevant age group)	100	95	104	105
Progression to secondary school (%)	88	75	..	..
Lower secondary completion rate (% of relevant age group)	79	61	84	65
Gross tertiary graduation ratio (%)	8	6	..	..
Female share of graduates in eng., manf. and constr. (%, tertiary)	..		43	
Youth literacy rate (% of population ages 15–24)	..	..	99	99
Health and related services				
Sex ratio at birth (male births per female births)	1.05		1.05	
Under-five mortality rate (per 1,000 live births)	15	19	9	11
Life expectancy at birth (years)	78	71	81	74
Pregnant women receiving prenatal care (%)	..		..	
Births attended by skilled health staff (% of total)	100		100	
Maternal mortality ratio (per 100,000 live births)	35		14	
Women's share of population ages 15+ living with HIV (%)	16		17	
Prevalence of HIV (% ages 15–24)	0.1	0.6	0.1	0.4
Economic structure, participation, and access to resources				
Labor force participation rate (% of population ages 15+)	52	76	56	77
Labor force participation rate (% of ages 15–24)	51	68	47	64
Wage and salaried workers (% of employed ages 15+)	77	70	76	71
Self-employed workers (% of employed ages 15+)	22	30	24	29
Unpaid family workers (% of employed ages 15+)	2.3	0.8	1.6	0.6
Employment in agriculture (% of employed ages 15+)	1	6	..	..
Employment in industry (% of employed ages 15+)	13	33	..	..
Employment in services (% of employed ages 15+)	85	61	..	..
Women in wage employment in the nonagricultural sector (%)	46		49	
Women's share of part-time employment (% of total)	63		65	
Maternity leave (days paid)	..		98	
Maternity leave benefits (% of wages paid)	..		100	
Employment to population ratio (% ages 15+)	45	70	51	73
Employment to population ratio (% ages 15–24)	35	53	36	54
Firms with female participation in ownership (%)	..		23	
Firms with a female top manager (%)	..		19	
Children in employment (% of children ages 7–14)	..	..	..	..
Unemployment rate (% of labor force ages 15+)	14	8	8	5
Unemployment rate (% of labor force ages 15–24)	32	21	22	16
Internet users (%)	..	..	54	55
Account at a financial institution (% age 15+)	..	..	41	50
Mobile account (% age 15+)	..	..	0.4	2.2
Saved any money last year (% age 15+)	..	..	35	42
Public life and decision making				
Seats held by women in national parliament (%)	..		16	
Female legislators, senior officials and managers (% of total)	36		44	
Proportion of women in ministerial level positions (%)	..		14	
Agency				
Total fertility rate (births per woman)	2.2		2.0	
Adolescent fertility rate (births per 1,000 women ages 15–19)	65		57	
Women first married by age 18 (% of women ages 20–24)	..		..	

Uzbekistan

Europe & Central Asia	Lower middle income
Population (millions)	31
GNI, Atlas ($ billions)	64
GNI per capita, Atlas ($)	2,090
Population living below $1.90 a day (%)	..

	2000		2013	
	Female	Male	Female	Male
Education				
Net primary enrollment rate (%)	..	..	87	90
Net secondary enrollment rate (%)	..	..	..	..
Gross tertiary enrollment ratio (% of relevant age group)	12	14	7	11
Primary completion rate (% of relevant age group)	100	101	91	93
Progression to secondary school (%)	97	100	98	100
Lower secondary completion rate (% of relevant age group)	96	97	97	97
Gross tertiary graduation ratio (%)	..	..	10	13
Female share of graduates in eng., manf. and constr. (%, tertiary)	..		11	
Youth literacy rate (% of population ages 15–24)	100	100	100	100
Health and related services				
Sex ratio at birth (male births per female births)	1.05		1.05	
Under-five mortality rate (per 1,000 live births)	56	71	34	44
Life expectancy at birth (years)	70	64	72	65
Pregnant women receiving prenatal care (%)	97		..	
Births attended by skilled health staff (% of total)	96		..	
Maternal mortality ratio (per 100,000 live births)	48		36	
Women's share of population ages 15+ living with HIV (%)	34		43	
Prevalence of HIV (% ages 15–24)	0.1	0.1	0.1	0.1
Economic structure, participation, and access to resources				
Labor force participation rate (% of population ages 15+)	47	72	48	76
Labor force participation rate (% of ages 15–24)	33	54	34	57
Wage and salaried workers (% of employed ages 15+)	..	..	..	..
Self-employed workers (% of employed ages 15+)	..	..	..	..
Unpaid family workers (% of employed ages 15+)	..	..	..	..
Employment in agriculture (% of employed ages 15+)	..	..	..	..
Employment in industry (% of employed ages 15+)	..	..	..	..
Employment in services (% of employed ages 15+)	..	..	..	..
Women in wage employment in the nonagricultural sector (%)	37		..	
Women's share of part-time employment (% of total)	..		..	
Maternity leave (days paid)		126		
Maternity leave benefits (% of wages paid)		100		
Employment to population ratio (% ages 15+)	42	64	43	68
Employment to population ratio (% ages 15–24)	26	43	26	46
Firms with female participation in ownership (%)	..		29	
Firms with a female top manager (%)	..		13	
Children in employment (% of children ages 7–14)	14	22	..	..
Unemployment rate (% of labor force ages 15+)	11	11	11	11
Unemployment rate (% of labor force ages 15–24)	22	20	22	19
Internet users (%)	..	..	..	..
Account at a financial institution (% age 15+)	..	..	39	42
Mobile account (% age 15+)	..	..	..	..
Saved any money last year (% age 15+)	..	..	43	44
Public life and decision making				
Seats held by women in national parliament (%)	..		16	
Female legislators, senior officials and managers (% of total)	..		..	
Proportion of women in ministerial level positions (%)	..		11	
Agency				
Total fertility rate (births per woman)	2.6		2.2	
Adolescent fertility rate (births per 1,000 women ages 15–19)	27		18	
Women first married by age 18 (% of women ages 20–24)	13		..	

Vanuatu

Population (thousands)	259
GNI, Atlas ($ millions)	782
GNI per capita, Atlas ($)	3,090
Population living below $1.90 a day (%)	15

	2000		2013	
	Female	Male	Female	Male
Education				
Net primary enrollment rate (%)	97	98	..	..
Net secondary enrollment rate (%)	36	31	53	51
Gross tertiary enrollment ratio (% of relevant age group)	3	6	..	..
Primary completion rate (% of relevant age group)	94	90	96	90
Progression to secondary school (%)	46	44	..	..
Lower secondary completion rate (% of relevant age group)	34	33	54	48
Gross tertiary graduation ratio (%)	..	..	..	..
Female share of graduates in eng., manf. and constr. (%, tertiary)	..		..	
Youth literacy rate (% of population ages 15–24)	..	..	95	95
Health and related services				
Sex ratio at birth (male births per female births)	1.07		1.07	
Under-five mortality rate (per 1,000 live births)	26	31	25	30
Life expectancy at birth (years)	69	66	74	70
Pregnant women receiving prenatal care (%)	..		76	
Births attended by skilled health staff (% of total)	88		89	
Maternal mortality ratio (per 100,000 live births)	120		86	
Women's share of population ages 15+ living with HIV (%)	..		..	
Prevalence of HIV (% ages 15–24)	..	..	..	..
Economic structure, participation, and access to resources				
Labor force participation rate (% of population ages 15+)	70	84	62	80
Labor force participation rate (% of ages 15–24)	62	72	51	62
Wage and salaried workers (% of employed ages 15+)	..	..	..	..
Self-employed workers (% of employed ages 15+)	..	..	..	..
Unpaid family workers (% of employed ages 15+)	..	..	..	..
Employment in agriculture (% of employed ages 15+)	..	..	..	..
Employment in industry (% of employed ages 15+)	..	..	..	..
Employment in services (% of employed ages 15+)	..	..	..	..
Women in wage employment in the nonagricultural sector (%)	..		..	
Women's share of part-time employment (% of total)	..		..	
Maternity leave (days paid)	..		..	
Maternity leave benefits (% of wages paid)	..		..	
Employment to population ratio (% ages 15+)	..	..	..	..
Employment to population ratio (% ages 15–24)	..	..	..	..
Firms with female participation in ownership (%)	..		..	
Firms with a female top manager (%)	..		..	
Children in employment (% of children ages 7–14)	..	..	..	..
Unemployment rate (% of labor force ages 15+)	..	..	..	..
Unemployment rate (% of labor force ages 15–24)	..	..	..	..
Internet users (%)	..	..	..	..
Account at a financial institution (% age 15+)	..	..	..	..
Mobile account (% age 15+)	..	..	..	..
Saved any money last year (% age 15+)	..	..	..	..
Public life and decision making				
Seats held by women in national parliament (%)	..		0	
Female legislators, senior officials and managers (% of total)	..		..	
Proportion of women in ministerial level positions (%)	..		0	
Agency				
Total fertility rate (births per woman)	4.4		3.4	
Adolescent fertility rate (births per 1,000 women ages 15–19)	58		43	
Women first married by age 18 (% of women ages 20–24)	..		21	

Venezuela, RB

	High income
Population (millions)	31
GNI, Atlas ($ billions)	396
GNI per capita, Atlas ($)	12,890
Population living below $1.90 a day (%)	..

	2000		2013	
	Female	Male	Female	Male
Education				
Net primary enrollment rate (%)	88	87	90	92
Net secondary enrollment rate (%)	56	46	78	72
Gross tertiary enrollment ratio (% of relevant age group)	34	23	..	..
Primary completion rate (% of relevant age group)	86	80	97	95
Progression to secondary school (%)	97	100	99	100
Lower secondary completion rate (% of relevant age group)	58	43	85	75
Gross tertiary graduation ratio (%)	9	5	..	..
Female share of graduates in eng., manf. and constr. (%, tertiary)	39		..	
Youth literacy rate (% of population ages 15–24)	98	96	98	97
Health and related services				
Sex ratio at birth (male births per female births)	1.05		1.05	
Under-five mortality rate (per 1,000 live births)	19	24	13	17
Life expectancy at birth (years)	75	70	78	72
Pregnant women receiving prenatal care (%)	94		..	
Births attended by skilled health staff (% of total)	94		96	
Maternal mortality ratio (per 100,000 live births)	91		110	
Women's share of population ages 15+ living with HIV (%)	31		35	
Prevalence of HIV (% ages 15–24)	0.2	0.3	0.2	0.2
Economic structure, participation, and access to resources				
Labor force participation rate (% of population ages 15+)	49	82	51	79
Labor force participation rate (% of ages 15–24)	34	64	30	55
Wage and salaried workers (% of employed ages 15+)	58	58	64	56
Self-employed workers (% of employed ages 15+)	42	42	33	37
Unpaid family workers (% of employed ages 15+)	2.3	1.4	0.9	0.4
Employment in agriculture (% of employed ages 15+)	2	16	2	13
Employment in industry (% of employed ages 15+)	13	29	11	29
Employment in services (% of employed ages 15+)	86	56	87	58
Women in wage employment in the nonagricultural sector (%)	40		44	
Women's share of part-time employment (% of total)	60		60	
Maternity leave (days paid)	..		182	
Maternity leave benefits (% of wages paid)	..		100	
Employment to population ratio (% ages 15+)	42	72	47	74
Employment to population ratio (% ages 15–24)	24	50	24	48
Firms with female participation in ownership (%)	..		31	
Firms with a female top manager (%)	..		31	
Children in employment (% of children ages 7–14)	..	..	..	..
Unemployment rate (% of labor force ages 15+)	14	13	8	7
Unemployment rate (% of labor force ages 15–24)	28	22	20	14
Internet users (%)	..	..	51	48
Account at a financial institution (% age 15+)	..	..	53	61
Mobile account (% age 15+)	..	..	2.7	3.3
Saved any money last year (% age 15+)	..	..	46	49
Public life and decision making				
Seats held by women in national parliament (%)	..		17	
Female legislators, senior officials and managers (% of total)	..		..	
Proportion of women in ministerial level positions (%)	..		23	
Agency				
Total fertility rate (births per woman)	2.8		2.4	
Adolescent fertility rate (births per 1,000 women ages 15–19)	89		80	
Women first married by age 18 (% of women ages 20–24)	..		..	

Vietnam

East Asia & Pacific	Lower middle income
Population (millions)	91
GNI, Atlas ($ billions)	172
GNI per capita, Atlas ($)	1,890
Population living below $1.90 a day (%)	3

	2000		2013	
	Female	Male	Female	Male
Education				
Net primary enrollment rate (%)	..		..	
Net secondary enrollment rate (%)	..	..	..	..
Gross tertiary enrollment ratio (% of relevant age group)	8	11	23	26
Primary completion rate (% of relevant age group)	95	100	98	97
Progression to secondary school (%)	92	94	87	100
Lower secondary completion rate (% of relevant age group)	63	69	81	78
Gross tertiary graduation ratio (%)	..	..	12	15
Female share of graduates in eng., manf. and constr. (%, tertiary)	..		31	
Youth literacy rate (% of population ages 15–24)	94	96	..	..
Health and related services				
Sex ratio at birth (male births per female births)	1.07		1.10	
Under-five mortality rate (per 1,000 live births)	29	38	19	25
Life expectancy at birth (years)	78	69	80	71
Pregnant women receiving prenatal care (%)	68		94	
Births attended by skilled health staff (% of total)	70		93	
Maternal mortality ratio (per 100,000 live births)	82		49	
Women's share of population ages 15+ living with HIV (%)	15		31	
Prevalence of HIV (% ages 15–24)	0.1	0.4	0.2	0.3
Economic structure, participation, and access to resources				
Labor force participation rate (% of population ages 15+)	73	83	73	82
Labor force participation rate (% of ages 15–24)	67	71	61	65
Wage and salaried workers (% of employed ages 15+)	15	22	29	40
Self-employed workers (% of employed ages 15+)	83	77	71	60
Unpaid family workers (% of employed ages 15+)	53.1	21.2	22.6	12.0
Employment in agriculture (% of employed ages 15+)	66	64	50	45
Employment in industry (% of employed ages 15+)	10	15	17	25
Employment in services (% of employed ages 15+)	24	21	34	29
Women in wage employment in the nonagricultural sector (%)	41		41	
Women's share of part-time employment (% of total)	..		..	
Maternity leave (days paid)			180	
Maternity leave benefits (% of wages paid)	..		100	
Employment to population ratio (% ages 15+)	72	81	71	81
Employment to population ratio (% ages 15–24)	64	68	57	62
Firms with female participation in ownership (%)	..		..	
Firms with a female top manager (%)	..		..	
Children in employment (% of children ages 7–14)	..	..	10	12
Unemployment rate (% of labor force ages 15+)	2	2	2	2
Unemployment rate (% of labor force ages 15–24)	4	5	6	5
Internet users (%)	..	..		
Account at a financial institution (% age 15+)	..	..	32	30
Mobile account (% age 15+)	..	..	0.5	0.5
Saved any money last year (% age 15+)	..	..	63	64
Public life and decision making				
Seats held by women in national parliament (%)	..		24	
Female legislators, senior officials and managers (% of total)	17		..	
Proportion of women in ministerial level positions (%)	..		9	
Agency				
Total fertility rate (births per woman)	2.0		1.7	
Adolescent fertility rate (births per 1,000 women ages 15–19)	29		38	
Women first married by age 18 (% of women ages 20–24)	11		9	

Virgin Islands (U.S.)

	High income
Population (thousands)	104
GNI, Atlas ($ millions)	..
GNI per capita, Atlas ($)	..
Population living below $1.90 a day (%)	..

	2000 Female	2000 Male	2013 Female	2013 Male
Education				
Net primary enrollment rate (%)	..	..	..	..
Net secondary enrollment rate (%)	..	..	..	..
Gross tertiary enrollment ratio (% of relevant age group)	..	..	..	..
Primary completion rate (% of relevant age group)	..	..	..	..
Progression to secondary school (%)	..	..	..	..
Lower secondary completion rate (% of relevant age group)	..	..	..	..
Gross tertiary graduation ratio (%)	..	..	..	..
Female share of graduates in eng., manf. and constr. (%, tertiary)	..		..	
Youth literacy rate (% of population ages 15–24)	..	..	..	..
Health and related services				
Sex ratio at birth (male births per female births)	1.06		1.06	
Under-five mortality rate (per 1,000 live births)	..	..	..	..
Life expectancy at birth (years)	80	73	83	77
Pregnant women receiving prenatal care (%)	..			
Births attended by skilled health staff (% of total)	98		..	
Maternal mortality ratio (per 100,000 live births)	..		..	
Women's share of population ages 15+ living with HIV (%)	..		..	
Prevalence of HIV (% ages 15–24)	..	..	..	..
Economic structure, participation, and access to resources				
Labor force participation rate (% of population ages 15+)	53	77	54	72
Labor force participation rate (% of ages 15–24)	39	55	45	56
Wage and salaried workers (% of employed ages 15+)	..	..	..	..
Self-employed workers (% of employed ages 15+)	..	..	..	..
Unpaid family workers (% of employed ages 15+)	..	..	..	..
Employment in agriculture (% of employed ages 15+)	..	..	..	..
Employment in industry (% of employed ages 15+)	..	..	..	..
Employment in services (% of employed ages 15+)	..	..	..	..
Women in wage employment in the nonagricultural sector (%)	..		..	
Women's share of part-time employment (% of total)	..		..	
Maternity leave (days paid)	..		..	
Maternity leave benefits (% of wages paid)	..		..	
Employment to population ratio (% ages 15+)	..	..	..	..
Employment to population ratio (% ages 15–24)	..	..	..	..
Firms with female participation in ownership (%)	..		..	
Firms with a female top manager (%)	..		..	
Children in employment (% of children ages 7–14)	..	..	..	..
Unemployment rate (% of labor force ages 15+)	..	..	..	..
Unemployment rate (% of labor force ages 15–24)	..	..	..	..
Internet users (%)	..	..	..	..
Account at a financial institution (% age 15+)	..	..	..	..
Mobile account (% age 15+)	..	..	..	..
Saved any money last year (% age 15+)	..	..	..	..
Public life and decision making				
Seats held by women in national parliament (%)	..		..	
Female legislators, senior officials and managers (% of total)	..		..	
Proportion of women in ministerial level positions (%)	..		..	
Agency				
Total fertility rate (births per woman)	2.1		1.8	
Adolescent fertility rate (births per 1,000 women ages 15–19)	55		44	
Women first married by age 18 (% of women ages 20–24)	..		..	

West Bank and Gaza

Middle East & North Africa	Lower middle income
Population (millions)	4
GNI, Atlas ($ billions)	13
GNI per capita, Atlas ($)	3,060
Population living below $1.90 a day (%)	..

	2000 Female	2000 Male	2013 Female	2013 Male
Education				
Net primary enrollment rate (%)	89	90	92	91
Net secondary enrollment rate (%)	79	75	84	77
Gross tertiary enrollment ratio (% of relevant age group)	23	25	55	37
Primary completion rate (% of relevant age group)	98	97	93	93
Progression to secondary school (%)	100	99	99	97
Lower secondary completion rate (% of relevant age group)	70	61	84	69
Gross tertiary graduation ratio (%)	13	13	37	23
Female share of graduates in eng., manf. and constr. (%, tertiary)	22		31	
Youth literacy rate (% of population ages 15–24)	..	..	99[a]	99[a]
Health and related services				
Sex ratio at birth (male births per female births)	1.05		1.05	
Under-five mortality rate (per 1,000 live births)	27	32	19	23
Life expectancy at birth (years)	72	69	75	72
Pregnant women receiving prenatal care (%)	96		98	
Births attended by skilled health staff (% of total)	97		99	
Maternal mortality ratio (per 100,000 live births)	59		47	
Women's share of population ages 15+ living with HIV (%)	..		..	
Prevalence of HIV (% ages 15–24)	..	..	..	..
Economic structure, participation, and access to resources				
Labor force participation rate (% of population ages 15+)	11	65	15	66
Labor force participation rate (% of ages 15–24)	6	45	9	42
Wage and salaried workers (% of employed ages 15+)	56	68	65	69
Self-employed workers (% of employed ages 15+)	44	32	35	31
Unpaid family workers (% of employed ages 15+)	33.4	5.2	20.9	4.8
Employment in agriculture (% of employed ages 15+)	35	10	24	9
Employment in industry (% of employed ages 15+)	11	39	9	30
Employment in services (% of employed ages 15+)	54	52	68	61
Women in wage employment in the nonagricultural sector (%)	14		16	
Women's share of part-time employment (% of total)	..		..	
Maternity leave (days paid)			70	
Maternity leave benefits (% of wages paid)	..		100	
Employment to population ratio (% ages 15+)	10	56	12	51
Employment to population ratio (% ages 15–24)	5	36	4	28
Firms with female participation in ownership (%)	..		13	
Firms with a female top manager (%)	..		1	
Children in employment (% of children ages 7–14)	..	..	..	..
Unemployment rate (% of labor force ages 15+)	11	15	21	24
Unemployment rate (% of labor force ages 15–24)	25	20	56	35
Internet users (%)	..	..	34	45
Account at a financial institution (% age 15+)	..	..	21	27
Mobile account (% age 15+)	..	..	..	..
Saved any money last year (% age 15+)	..	..	25	21
Public life and decision making				
Seats held by women in national parliament (%)	..		..	
Female legislators, senior officials and managers (% of total)	13		..	
Proportion of women in ministerial level positions (%)	..		..	
Agency				
Total fertility rate (births per woman)	5.4		4.0	
Adolescent fertility rate (births per 1,000 women ages 15–19)	82		59	
Women first married by age 18 (% of women ages 20–24)	..		21	

Yemen, Rep.

Middle East & North Africa	Lower middle income
Population (millions)	26
GNI, Atlas ($ billions)	33
GNI per capita, Atlas ($)	1,300
Population living below $1.90 a day (%)	..

	2000 Female	2000 Male	2013 Female	2013 Male
Education				
Net primary enrollment rate (%)	42	72	81	95
Net secondary enrollment rate (%)	18	46	34	51
Gross tertiary enrollment ratio (% of relevant age group)	5	16	6	14
Primary completion rate (% of relevant age group)	39	79	62	78
Progression to secondary school (%)	..	..	89	91
Lower secondary completion rate (% of relevant age group)	27	65	40	57
Gross tertiary graduation ratio (%)	..	..	..	..
Female share of graduates in eng., manf. and constr. (%, tertiary)	..		..	
Youth literacy rate (% of population ages 15–24)	..	..	80	97
Health and related services				
Sex ratio at birth (male births per female births)	1.05		1.05	
Under-five mortality rate (per 1,000 live births)	91	100	38	46
Life expectancy at birth (years)	62	59	64	62
Pregnant women receiving prenatal care (%)	..		..	
Births attended by skilled health staff (% of total)	..		..	
Maternal mortality ratio (per 100,000 live births)	370		270	
Women's share of population ages 15+ living with HIV (%)	27		36	
Prevalence of HIV (% ages 15–24)	0.1	0.1	0.1	0.1
Economic structure, participation, and access to resources				
Labor force participation rate (% of population ages 15+)	22	71	25	72
Labor force participation rate (% ages 15–24)	20	53	22	53
Wage and salaried workers (% of employed ages 15+)	14	51	58	67
Self-employed workers (% of employed ages 15+)	86	49	42	33
Unpaid family workers (% of employed ages 15+)	61.9	12.8	..	..
Employment in agriculture (% of employed ages 15+)	88	43	28	25
Employment in industry (% of employed ages 15+)	3	14	15	19
Employment in services (% of employed ages 15+)	9	43	57	56
Women in wage employment in the nonagricultural sector (%)	7		12	
Women's share of part-time employment (% of total)	..		..	
Maternity leave (days paid)			70	
Maternity leave benefits (% of wages paid)	..		100	
Employment to population ratio (% ages 15+)	14	65	16	65
Employment to population ratio (% ages 15–24)	10	43	10	42
Firms with female participation in ownership (%)	..		7	
Firms with a female top manager (%)	..		2	
Children in employment (% of children ages 7–14)	14	12	15	17
Unemployment rate (% of labor force ages 15+)	39	9	39	10
Unemployment rate (% of labor force ages 15–24)	53	19	54	20
Internet users (%)	..	..	..	..
Account at a financial institution (% age 15+)	..	..	2	11
Mobile account (% age 15+)	..	..	..	..
Saved any money last year (% age 15+)	..	..	25	16
Public life and decision making				
Seats held by women in national parliament (%)	..		0	
Female legislators, senior officials and managers (% of total)	4		5	
Proportion of women in ministerial level positions (%)	..		10	
Agency				
Total fertility rate (births per woman)	6.4		4.1	
Adolescent fertility rate (births per 1,000 women ages 15–19)	96		62	
Women first married by age 18 (% of women ages 20–24)	..		32	

Zambia

Sub-Saharan Africa			Lower middle income	
Population (millions)				16
GNI, Atlas ($ billions)				26
GNI per capita, Atlas ($)				1,680
Population living below $1.90 a day (%)				64

	2000		2013	
	Female	Male	Female	Male
Education				
Net primary enrollment rate (%)	69	72	92	91
Net secondary enrollment rate (%)	..	..	..	..
Gross tertiary enrollment ratio (% of relevant age group)	2	3	..	..
Primary completion rate (% of relevant age group)	58	69	82	85
Progression to secondary school (%)	69	62	62	66
Lower secondary completion rate (% of relevant age group)	23	29	53	61
Gross tertiary graduation ratio (%)	..	..	..	..
Female share of graduates in eng., manf. and constr. (%, tertiary)	..		..	
Youth literacy rate (% of population ages 15–24)	66	73	..	..
Health and related services				
Sex ratio at birth (male births per female births)	1.02		1.02	
Under-five mortality rate (per 1,000 live births)	154	172	59	69
Life expectancy at birth (years)	42	42	60	56
Pregnant women receiving prenatal care (%)	83		..	
Births attended by skilled health staff (% of total)	47		..	
Maternal mortality ratio (per 100,000 live births)	610		280	
Women's share of population ages 15+ living with HIV (%)	50		52	
Prevalence of HIV (% ages 15–24)	6.4	4.7	4.2	3.3
Economic structure, participation, and access to resources				
Labor force participation rate (% of population ages 15+)	75	85	73	86
Labor force participation rate (% of ages 15–24)	66	71	64	70
Wage and salaried workers (% of employed ages 15+)	9	26	..	..
Self-employed workers (% of employed ages 15+)	91	74	..	..
Unpaid family workers (% of employed ages 15+)	61.8	25.4	..	..
Employment in agriculture (% of employed ages 15+)	80	65	..	..
Employment in industry (% of employed ages 15+)	2	9	..	..
Employment in services (% of employed ages 15+)	18	26	..	..
Women in wage employment in the nonagricultural sector (%)	22		..	
Women's share of part-time employment (% of total)	..		..	
Maternity leave (days paid)			84	
Maternity leave benefits (% of wages paid)	..		100	
Employment to population ratio (% ages 15+)	67	73	65	73
Employment to population ratio (% ages 15–24)	53	54	50	51
Firms with female participation in ownership (%)			50	
Firms with a female top manager (%)	..		24	
Children in employment (% of children ages 7–14)	..	..	..	..
Unemployment rate (% of labor force ages 15+)	11	15	11	15
Unemployment rate (% of labor force ages 15–24)	20	24	23	27
Internet users (%)	..	..	..	..
Account at a financial institution (% age 15+)	..	..	30	33
Mobile account (% age 15+)	..	..	9.5	14.9
Saved any money last year (% age 15+)	..	..	69	72
Public life and decision making				
Seats held by women in national parliament (%)	..		13	
Female legislators, senior officials and managers (% of total)	..		..	
Proportion of women in ministerial level positions (%)	..		20	
Agency				
Total fertility rate (births per woman)	6.1		5.7	
Adolescent fertility rate (births per 1,000 women ages 15–19)	143		93	
Women first married by age 18 (% of women ages 20–24)	42		..	

Zimbabwe

Sub-Saharan Africa				Low income

Population (millions)				15
GNI, Atlas ($ billions)				13
GNI per capita, Atlas ($)				830
Population living below $1.90 a day (%)				..

	2000		2013	
	Female	Male	Female	Male
Education				
Net primary enrollment rate (%)	85	85	95	93
Net secondary enrollment rate (%)	38	42	44	44
Gross tertiary enrollment ratio (% of relevant age group)	..	..	5	6
Primary completion rate (% of relevant age group)	88	93	93	91
Progression to secondary school (%)	73	76	..	..
Lower secondary completion rate (% of relevant age group)	..	..	..	..
Gross tertiary graduation ratio (%)	..	..	..	..
Female share of graduates in eng., manf. and constr. (%, tertiary)	..		21	
Youth literacy rate (% of population ages 15–24)	..	..	92	90
Health and related services				
Sex ratio at birth (male births per female births)	1.02		1.02	
Under-five mortality rate (per 1,000 live births)	98	113	65	76
Life expectancy at birth (years)	44	44	61	59
Pregnant women receiving prenatal care (%)	93		90	
Births attended by skilled health staff (% of total)	73		66	
Maternal mortality ratio (per 100,000 live births)	680		470	
Women's share of population ages 15+ living with HIV (%)	57		59	
Prevalence of HIV (% ages 15–24)	14.9	7.9	7.0	4.8
Economic structure, participation, and access to resources				
Labor force participation rate (% of population ages 15+)	69	81	83	90
Labor force participation rate (% of ages 15–24)	55	65	77	82
Wage and salaried workers (% of employed ages 15+)	23	55	..	..
Self-employed workers (% of employed ages 15+)	77	45	..	..
Unpaid family workers (% of employed ages 15+)	16.1	13.7	..	..
Employment in agriculture (% of employed ages 15+)	70	51	..	..
Employment in industry (% of employed ages 15+)	5	19	..	..
Employment in services (% of employed ages 15+)	26	30	..	..
Women in wage employment in the nonagricultural sector (%)	20		34	
Women's share of part-time employment (% of total)	66		..	
Maternity leave (days paid)	..		98	
Maternity leave benefits (% of wages paid)	..		100	
Employment to population ratio (% ages 15+)	65	75	79	85
Employment to population ratio (% ages 15–24)	49	54	70	74
Firms with female participation in ownership (%)	..		56	
Firms with a female top manager (%)	..		17	
Children in employment (% of children ages 7–14)	13	15	..	..
Unemployment rate (% of labor force ages 15+)	5	8	5	5
Unemployment rate (% of labor force ages 15–24)	11	16	9	9
Internet users (%)	..	..	..	..
Account at a financial institution (% age 15+)	..	..	15	19
Mobile account (% age 15+)	..	..	19.1	24.2
Saved any money last year (% age 15+)	..	..	53	51
Public life and decision making				
Seats held by women in national parliament (%)	..		31	
Female legislators, senior officials and managers (% of total)	..		..	
Proportion of women in ministerial level positions (%)	..		12	
Agency				
Total fertility rate (births per woman)	4.1		3.5	
Adolescent fertility rate (births per 1,000 women ages 15–19)	108		110	
Women first married by age 18 (% of women ages 20–24)	29		31	

Notes

a. Data are for 2014.

b. Excludes South Sudan.

c. Paid parental leave is available.

d. Unpaid parental leave is available.

Glossary

Account at a financial institution is the percentage of respondents ages 15 and older who report having an account (by themselves or together with someone else) at a bank or another type of financial institution. Data listed for 2013 are for 2014. (World Bank, the Global Findex database)

Adolescent fertility rate is the number of births per 1,000 women ages 15–19. Data listed for 2013 are for 2014. (United Nations Population Division)

Agency is the capacity to make decisions about one's own life and act on them to achieve a desired outcome, free of violence, retribution, or fear. (Klugman, J., L. Hanmer, S. Twigg, T. Hasan, J. McCleary-Sills, and J. Santamaria. 2014. *Voice and Agency: Empowering Women and Girls for Shared Prosperity*. Washington, DC: World Bank.)

Births attended by skilled health staff are the percentage of deliveries attended by personnel trained to give the necessary supervision, care, and advice to women during pregnancy, labor, and postpartum period; to conduct deliveries on their own; and to care for newborns. (United Nations Children's Fund, and ICF International)

Children in employment are children ages 7–14 who are involved in any economic activity for at least one hour in the reference week of the survey. (Understanding Children's Work)

Employment in agriculture is the proportion of employment in agriculture—division 1 (ISIC revision 2) or tabulation categories A and B (ISIC revision 3) and includes hunting, forestry, and fishing—in total employment. (International Labour Organization Key Indicators of the Labour Market database)

Employment in industry is the proportion of employment in industry—divisions 2–5 (ISIC revision 2) or tabulation categories C–F (ISIC revision 3) and includes mining and quarrying (including oil production), manufacturing, construction, and public utilities (electricity, gas, and water)—in total employment. (International Labour Organization Key Indicators of the Labour Market database)

Employment in services is the proportion of employment in service—divisions 6–9 (ISIC revision 2) or tabulation categories G–P (ISIC revision 3) and includes wholesale and retail trade and restaurants and hotels; transport, storage, and communications; financing, insurance, real estate, and business services; and community, social, and personal service in total employment. (International Labour Organization Key Indicators of the Labour Market database)

Employment to population ratio is the proportion of a country's population that is employed. Ages 15 and older are generally considered the working-age population and ages 15–24 are generally considered the youth population. Data in the tables are modeled estimates. (International Labour Organization Key Indicators of the Labour Market database)

Glossary

Female legislators, senior officials and managers refer to the share of legislators, senior officials and managers who are female. (International Labour Organization Key Indicators of the Labour Market database)

Female share of graduates in engineering, manufacturing, and construction is the number of female graduates expressed as a percentage of the total number of graduates in engineering, manufacturing, and construction from tertiary education. (United Nations Educational, Scientific, and Cultural Organization Institute for Statistics)

Firms with a female top manager refer to the percentage of firms have a woman as the top manager. The top manager refers to the highest ranking manager or CEO of the firm, the person who makes the key decisions on a day-to-day basis. This person may be the firm's owner if she (the owner) also works as the manager of the firm. (World Bank, Enterprise Surveys)

Firms with female participation in ownership refers to the percentage of firms that have at least one woman among the firm's owners. (World Bank, Enterprise Surveys)

GNI is the sum of value added by all resident producers plus any product taxes (less subsidies) not included in the valuation of output plus net receipts of primary income (compensation of employees and property income) from abroad. Data are in current U.S. dollars. GNI, calculated in national currency, is usually converted to U.S. dollars at official exchange rates for comparisons across economies, although an alternative rate is used when the official exchange rate is judged to diverge by an exceptionally large margin from the rate actually applied in international transactions. To smooth fluctuations in prices and exchange rates, a special Atlas method of conversion is used by the World Bank. This applies a conversion factor that averages the exchange rate for a given year and the two preceding years, adjusted for differences in rates of inflation between the country, and through 2000, the G-5 countries (France, Germany, Japan, the United Kingdom, and the United States). From 2001, these countries include the Euro area, Japan, the United Kingdom, and the United States. Data are for 2014. (World Bank)

GNI per capita is the gross national income (GNI), converted to U.S. dollars using the World Bank Atlas method, divided by the midyear population. Data are for 2014. (World Bank)

Gross tertiary enrollment ratio is the total enrollment in tertiary level, regardless of age, to the population of the age group that officially corresponds to the tertiary education. (United Nations Educational, Scientific, and Cultural Organization Institute for Statistics)

Gross tertiary graduation ratio is the number of graduates from first degree programs (at ISCED 6 and 7) expressed as a percentage of the population of the theoretical graduation age of the most common first degree program. (United Nations Educational, Scientific, and Cultural Organization Institute for Statistics)

Glossary

Internet users are the proportion of individuals who have used the Internet (from any location) in the last 12 months. Internet can be used via a computer, mobile phone, personal digital assistant, games machine, digital TV, etc. Age groups may differ by country. (International Telecommunication Union)

Labor force participation rate is the proportion of the population that is economically active: all people who supply labor for the production of goods and services during a specified period. Ages 15 and older are generally considered the working-age population and ages 15–24 are generally considered the youth population. Data in the tables are modeled estimates. (International Labour Organization Key Indicators of the Labour Market database)

Life expectancy at birth is the number of years a newborn infant would live if prevailing patterns of mortality at the time of its birth were to stay the same throughout its life. (United Nations Population Division, United Nations Statistics Division, national statistical offices, Eurostat, Secretariat of the Pacific Community, United States Census Bureau, and World Bank).

Lower secondary completion rate is measured as the gross intake ratio to the last grade of lower secondary education (general and prevocational). It is calculated as the number of new entrants in the last grade of lower secondary education, regardless of age, divided by the population at the entrance age for the last grade of lower secondary education. (United Nations Educational, Scientific, and Cultural Organization Institute for Statistics)

Maternal mortality ratio is the number of women who die from pregnancy-related causes while pregnant or within 42 days of pregnancy termination per 100,000 live births. The data are estimated with a regression model using information on the proportion of maternal deaths among non-AIDS deaths in women ages 15–49, fertility, birth attendants, and GDP. (United Nations Maternal Mortality Estimation Inter-agency Group, World Health Organization, United Nations Children's Fund, United Nations Population Fund, the World Bank, and United Nations Population Division)

Maternity leave refers to leave related to the birth of a child that is only available to the mother; it does not cover parental leave that is available to both parents. Paid maternity leave is the mandatory minimum number of calendar days that legally must be paid by the government, the employer, or both. Data listed for 2013 are for 2015. (World Bank Group, Women, Business and the Law database)

Maternity leave benefits refers to the total percentage of wages covered by all sources during paid maternity leave. Data listed for 2013 are for 2015. (World Bank Group, Women, Business and the Law database)

Mobile account is the percentage of respondents ages 15 and older who report personally using a mobile phone to pay bills or to send or receive money through a GSM Association (GSMA) Mobile Money for the Unbanked (MMU) service in the past 12 months; or receiving wages, government transfers, or payments for agricultural products through a mobile phone in the past 12 months. Data listed for 2013 are for 2014. (World Bank, the Global Findex database)

Glossary

Net primary enrollment rate is the ratio of children of official school age who are enrolled in primary school to the population of the age group that officially corresponds to the primary education. (United Nations Educational, Scientific, and Cultural Organization Institute for Statistics)

Net secondary enrollment rate is the ratio of children of official school age who are enrolled in secondary school to the population of the age group that officially corresponds to the secondary education. (United Nations Educational, Scientific, and Cultural Organization Institute for Statistics)

Population is the de facto definition of population, which counts all residents regardless of legal status or citizenship—except for refugees not permanently settled in the country of asylum, who are generally considered part of the population of their country of origin. The values shown are midyear estimates. Data are for 2014. (United Nations Population Division, United Nations Statistics Division, national statistical offices, Eurostat, Secretariat of the Pacific Community, United States Census Bureau, and World Bank).

Population living below $1.90 a day is the percentages of the population living on less than $1.90 a day at 2011 international prices. As a result of revisions in PPP exchange rates, poverty rates for individual countries cannot be compared with poverty rates reported in earlier editions. Note that five countries—Bangladesh, Cabo Verde, Cambodia, Jordan, and Lao PDR—use the 2005 PPP exchange rates and poverty lines. (World Bank, Development Research Group)

Pregnant women receiving prenatal care are the percentage of women attended at least once during pregnancy by skilled health personnel for reasons related to pregnancy. (United Nations Children's Fund and ICF International)

Prevalence of HIV is the percentage of people ages 15–24 who are infected with HIV. Data listed for 2013 are for 2014. (Joint United Nations Programme on HIV/AIDS).

Primary completion rate is measured as the gross intake ratio to the last grade of primary education. It is calculated as the number of new entrants in the last grade of primary education, regardless of age, divided by the population at the entrance age for the last grade of primary education. (United Nations Educational, Scientific, and Cultural Organization Institute for Statistics)

Progression to secondary school refers to the number of new entrants to the first grade of secondary school in a given year as a percentage of the number of students enrolled in the final grade of primary school in the previous year (minus the number of repeaters from the last grade of primary education in the given year). (United Nations Educational, Scientific, and Cultural Organization Institute for Statistics)

Proportion of women in ministerial level positions is the proportion of women in ministerial or equivalent positions (including deputy prime ministers) in the government. Prime Ministers/Heads of Government are included when they hold ministerial portfolios. Vice Presidents and heads of governmental or public agencies are excluded. Data listed for 2013 are for 2015. (Inter-Parliamentary Union)

Saved any money last year is the percentage of respondents ages 15 and older who report personally saving or setting aside any money for any reason and using any mode of saving in the past 12 months. Data listed for 2013 are for 2014. (World Bank, the Global Findex database)

Seats held by women in national parliament is the percentage of parliamentary seats in a single or lower chamber occupied by women. Data listed for 2013 are for 2015. (Inter-Parliamentary Union)

Self-employed workers are those workers who, working on their own account or with one or a few partners or in cooperative, hold the type of jobs defined as a "self-employment jobs." (International Labour Organization Key Indicators of the Labour Market database)

Sex ratio at birth refers to male births per female births. (United Nations Population Division, World Population Prospects)

Total fertility rate is the number of children that would be born to a woman if she were to live to the end of her childbearing years and bear children in accordance with current age-specific fertility rates of the specified year. (United Nations Population Division, United Nations Statistics Division, national statistical offices, Eurostat, Secretariat of the Pacific Community, United States Census Bureau, and World Bank)

Under-five mortality rate is the probability per 1,000 live births that a newborn baby will die before reaching age five, if subject to age-specific mortality rates of the specified year. Data listed for 2013 are for 2015. (United Nations Inter-agency Group for Child Mortality Estimation, United Nations Children's Fund, World Health Organization, World Bank, and United Nations Population Division)

Unemployment rate is the share of labor force without work but available for and seeking employment. Definitions of labor force and unemployment may differ by country. Ages 15 and older are generally considered the working-age population and ages 15–24 are generally considered the youth population. Data in the tables are modeled estimates. (International Labour Organization Key Indicators of the Labour Market database)

Unpaid family workers or contributing family workers are those who hold "self-employment jobs" as own-account workers in a market-oriented establishment operated by a related person living in the same household. (International Labour Organization Key Indicators of the Labour Market database)

Glossary

Wage and salaried workers are those workers who hold the type of jobs defined as "paid employment jobs," where the incumbents hold explicit (written or oral) or implicit employment contracts that give them a basic remuneration that is not directly dependent upon the revenue of the unit for which they work. (International Labour Organization Key Indicators of the Labour Market database)

Women first married by age 18 is the percentage of women ages 20–24 who were first married by age 18. (United Nations Children's Fund and ICF International)

Women in wage employment in the nonagricultural sector is the share of female workers in wage employment in the nonagricultural sector (industry and services), expressed as a percentage of total employment in the nonagricultural sector. Industry includes mining and quarrying (including oil production), manufacturing, construction, electricity, gas, and water, corresponding to divisions 2–5 (ISIC revision 2) or tabulation categories C–F (ISIC revision 3). Services include wholesale and retail trade and restaurants and hotels; transport, storage, and communications; financing, insurance, real estate, and business services; and community, social, and personal services, corresponding to divisions 6–9 (ISIC revision 2) or tabulation categories G–P (ISIC revision 3). (International Labour Organization)

Women's share of part-time employment is the female share of total part-time workers. Part-time worker is an employed person whose normal hours of work are less than those of comparable full-time workers. Definition of part-time varies across countries. (International Labour Organization Key Indicators of the Labour Market database)

Women's share of population ages 15+ living with HIV is the proportion of women in total population ages 15+ who are living with HIV. Data listed for 2013 are for 2014. (Joint United Nations Programme on HIV/AIDS)

Youth literacy rate is the percentage of people ages 15 to 24 who can both read and write with understanding a short simple statement about their everyday life. (United Nations Educational, Scientific, and Cultural Organization Institute for Statistics)